ON FIRST PRINCIPLES

harper ✦ torchbooks

*A reference-list of Harper Torchbooks, classified
by subjects, is printed at the end of this volume.*

ORIGEN
ON FIRST PRINCIPLES

Being Koetschau's Text of the *De Principiis*
Translated into English, Together with an
Introduction and Notes

BY

G. W. BUTTERWORTH

Introduction to the Torchbook edition

BY

HENRI DE LUBAC

HARPER TORCHBOOKS ❦ *The Cathedral Library*
Harper & Row, Publishers
NEW YORK

ON FIRST PRINCIPLES

Introduction to the Torchbook edition copyright ©
1966 by Harper & Row, Publishers

Printed in the United States of America.

This book was originally published in 1936 by the Society for Promoting Christian Knowledge, London, and is here reprinted by arrangement.

This book has been endorsed by the Committee on Reprinting of The American Theological Library Association.

First HARPER TORCHBOOK edition published 1966 by Harper & Row, Publishers, Incorporated
49 East 33rd Street
New York, N.Y. 10016.

CONTENTS

CONTENTS

INTRODUCTION TO THE TORCHBOOK EDITION

BY

HENRI DE LUBAC*

Origen's Works

When Origen died he left behind a massive body of writings numbering close to a thousand titles. This vast treasure, consisting chiefly of explications of holy Scripture, was widely used for more than a century without serious obstacles to its diffusion. There was of course no lack of criticism. It had appeared even during Origen's Alexandrian period, and it redoubled immediately after his death. In subsequent generations men like Methodius of Olympus, Peter of Alexandria, Eustathius of Antioch and Pacomius proved resolute and sometimes violent opponents. In any event it was inevitable that, as the labor of theological reflection proceeded and orthodoxy was progressively defined, the imprecisions and inadequacies in the exposition of the faith given by this greatest of ante-Nicene fathers should grow increasingly more noticeable. His very genius, which had made him play such an important part in the elaboration of the dogma, made him correspondingly more vulnerable afterwards. Nor, however, did Origen lack defenders from the very start. Apologies for him multiplied apace with the attacks against him. The admiration expressed by men as significant and as different as Athanasius and Eusebius of Caesarea could be taken for a definitive guarantee of his position. His works spread rapidly in the West as well as in the East, emerged unscathed from every skirmish and went on spreading. But from about 375 on everything changed. The massive offensive launched by Saint Epiphanius' *Panarion* unleashed the first of the storms in which Origen's writings were to founder. In the sixth century, the onslaught was still worse. The doctrinal excesses of the Syrian monk Stephen Bar Sudaili, who had concocted a strange system by mixing various traits borrowed from Gnosticism and the Cabbala with certain ideas taken from the *Periarchon,* provoked Justinian's thunderbolts. The list of fifteen anathemata, drawn up by

* From *Histoire et Esprit, l'intelligence de l'Écriture d'après Origène* by Henri de Lubac, Paris, 1950, Chapters I and II. Selected and translated by William Babcock, and here reproduced by permission of the author and his publishers, Aubier.

the Council Fathers of 553 outside their official sessions, was not the worst by far; for their sources are in fact not Origen's works at all. There followed the physical destruction of his writings. It had begun at the end of the fourth century; but this time it was carried out systematically. The emperor-theologian was in earnest and so was the zealous faction which had alerted him. Nearly all of Origen's work perished. Only two letters and a few fragments remain of his vast correspondence which originally had had four or five sections. Of the exegetical works—although the principles of exegesis had not been involved in the controversy—barely twenty have come down to us in the original. Searches through the libraries of the Middle East could produce no more than "a few insignificant scraps." There is no way to measure such a loss. Epiphanius and Justinian have served the enemies of Christian civilization well.

Luckily there was a number of Latin translations. Some were made by Saint Hilary, Saint Jerome, and several others. The greater part came from the pen of Rufinus of Aquileia. Rufinus' translations have been unjustly maligned. Recent historians who studied them have rightly reacted against an unduly severe evaluation of their worth: the translations served their purpose well. They are fluent, clear and pleasant to read, which in itself is an advantage. Though their author claims to be "incapable of rendering the movement of Origen's sentences with the eloquence" of Jerome, he does in fact often seem to render the original with a genuine felicity. Of course, we would want them to be more faithful, more literal. Still, there is hardly a translation except that of the *Periarchon* which poses any really serious problems for the historian of dogma. The translation of the commentary on the Epistle to the Romans is an abridgment, and openly admits it. What is more, it was done from a corrupt text and Rufinus himself tells us that it caused him exceedingly painstaking labor. In other cases, the translator does not hesitate to make slight adaptations. Sometimes he paraphrases; less frequently he gives extracts. He does not hesitate to add to a passage what explanations he considers necessary for Latin readers. But since he honestly informs the reader of the kind of liberty he is taking, we may trust him when he writes on occasion *"Simpliciter ut invenimus transtulimus."* These words refer to the homilies on Joshua, on Judges, and on Psalms 36-38. With respect to the homilies on Genesis, Exodus, and Leviticus the translation admits to some expansion of the original, but without giving us any reason to doubt its faithfulness to the substance. Together, the translations are of incalculable value to us. When Rufinus set to work at the urgent request of his friend Macarius, convinced though he was that his work could be of real value, he had no inkling of the unrivaled importance of his task. It is fortunate indeed that he did not let himself be discouraged by the quarrel that Jerome was trying to pick with him. He saved from final ruin some of the most precious monuments of Christian antiquity, works destined to mould Latin minds for a long time to come.

Even so, more than one historian has refused to make use of these translations. Such purism would be excessive even if the translations were ten times more suspect than they are: it is too much of an invitation to laziness and simple lack of inquiry. All kinds of precautions are necessary of course. One must not press a particular expression too far. One cannot rely upon a specific detail for fear that it may be a gloss. But when it is a question, not of a precise statement made in passing or of a specific point of doctrine, but of what constitutes so to speak the texture of thought and discourse, one stands on firmer ground. In this case more than elsewhere, the real cure does not lie in abstinence but on the contrary in massive utilization. In order to have a chance to reach the authentic Origen, one must pile citations on citations. In that way the parallel passages control, define, and comment on one another, especially when one examines, for example, a phrase in Rufinus' Latin, another in the Latin of Jerome, and finally a third preserved in the original Greek. Indeed such confrontations are not rare; and from them there emerges an impression of unity. Through all the variety of his works and through all the diversity of the versions in which they come to us, Origen looks most of the time surprisingly like himself.

By the same token, this consideration rules out another sort of suppression. Scholars at times have depreciated and even systematically brushed aside not only the homilies which we have only in translation but even those of which the Greek text still exists, and also such writings as the *Exhortation to Martyrdom*. These were considered simply as signs of a "popular Origenism"; they were "popularizations," written for public consumption, and unworthy to have a share in the reconstruction of the true Origen synthesis. Only the *Periarchon*, the *Contra Celsum* and up to a point the major commentaries could supply tried and true material. . . . Discrimination of this sort is wilful. It stems from a mistaken idea of Origen's personality and of the very nature of his thought. It is as evident as can be that not everything which came from the lips or the pen of this great man bears the same features, and that we cannot attach equal importance to it all. But nothing entitles us to think that all does not have the same sincerity, the same conviction. One must not forget that the books on Saint John's gospel and the *Exhortation to Martyrdom* are both

dedicated to the same Ambrose. Origen was not one of those curious and detached minds who "enter into sacred science like a
tourist goes into a city to look up its monuments." His Christianity was not a speculation removed from life, nor a dream in the
margins of the concerns of the great Church. In his highest medita-
tions as in his most practical exhortations, his Christianity was
"committed," to use the language of our day. We shall see the
proof below. Historians who have failed to recognize this fact
imagine him an intellectual who put on a mask to speak to the
common people, a man whose interior life had its place outside
the Christian community; these historians have gone astray in
both their method and their interpretation. In trying to pick the
trump cards out of Origen's work, they have not merely deprived
themselves of sources of the first order; they have also distorted
the meaning of the very sources they retained.

His Piety and Orthodoxy

We must rid ourselves of the view, still far too common, which
presents Origen as almost entirely an intellectual, esoteric and
rationalizing, and see him as the man of the spirit, the apostle,
the man of the Church which he was above all else. The daring
of his genius must not blind us to the drives of his piety. The
shortcomings of his doctrine—inevitable in a thinker of the third
century who was the very first to build a theology—must not
make us mistake the pure quality of his faith.

His intellectual formation, we must not forget, was entirely
Christian; we might even say entirely ecclesiastic. Many features
of his homilies remind us of it, if need be. "We of the Church,"
he says; "I, a man of the Church, living in the faith of Christ and
set in the midst of the Church. . . ." Justin, Tatian, Clement and
others like them were converts; because of a turn of mind due to
their early formation they remained philosophers. But when
Origen affectionately proclaims himself "a man of the Church,"
he underlines something like an inborn quality that is the mark
of his whole genius. When he speaks of the "world," the word is
often used in the sense it has in the gospels—the world that passes
away, especially the evil world from which Jesus Christ comes to
set us free. Despite the testimony of Eusebius, one may well ask
whether he ever figured among Clement's disciples—we are far
too much accustomed to see him in Clement's tow. Clement after
his conversion kept the vocabulary of the Greeks that had already
imposed itself on Philo, and then on Tatian; he still called the
doctrine of Moses and of Christianity itself by the name of "bar-

barian philosophy." But Origen contrasts the "barbarians" who were the Egyptians, with the "saints" who were the great men of Israel. He had been introduced to the Bible on his father's knees, and he always maintained that outside the Bible "there is nothing holy." Except in *Contra Celsum* he almost never quotes from profane authors. He is not a man who professes in private, a lecturer, but above all a catechist and preacher. He is one of those who *ecclesiastice docent verbum*. He is quite willing to include idolaters, heretics and "philosophers" in a single sweeping condemnation. He knows that "the knowledge which converts men to lead a holy life comes only from . . . Christ" and that Christ is found only "in the Church" which is filled with his splendor—the Church, pillar and firm support of the truth, where the Son of Man dwells in fulness. From the moment when he becomes a priest, he is aware that he "exercises the teaching office of the Church, of which he bears the authentic character"; he wishes to be "the faithful steward of the divine mysteries." He compares the writings of the apostles to the trumpets of Israel's army which reduced to rubble the walls of Jericho, the whole machinery of paganism, and the systems of its thinkers. These, to him, are real idolaters because "they worship the inventions of their own mind." He sees these Doctors of the world in league with the heretics against the Christian faith, an insult to its simplicity. This "simplicity of faith" is, in his view, altogether different from a simple adherence to "the bare letter"; it is a positive virtue, a form of perfection. It is this simplicity which renders the bride of Christ so glorious, which causes her to be without spot or wrinkle. Origen professes for it a real worship; it is, he says, "the virginity of the soul." A childlike and humble spirit follows in its wake.

In Origen's devotion to the Person of the Savior one discerns a note of tenderness that is all his own. It is not just that in his apology against Celsus he spoke of Christ with a nobility mindful of Pascal. It is not just that in the *Periarchon* he exalted in particularly solemn terms the mystery of the Incarnation, that mystery more wonderful and more disturbing than all the others, which "we must contemplate with fear and trembling." It is not only that in his commentary on the Song of Songs he adopted the voice of the Church which comes from the Gentiles, to cry out: "For because of thy word, O Christ, which I recognized as the true word, I came to thee. For all the words which were said to me, and which I heard while I was in my own country, from worldly teachers and philosophers, were not true words. That only is the true word, which is in thee." He speaks in more intimate tones as well. He greets with deep emotion the first appearance of Jesus' name in the Bible, and observes that nowhere in the

Bible is the name ever borne by a sinner. We ought to imitate
no one, he says, save only Jesus. Apart from Jesus, nothing to him
is worthy of being loved. He would have us love Jesus with the
same love that we owe to God; more, he would have us love God
in him. He prays to him and would have us pray to him even as
to the Father. The absence of Christ is for Origen a desert barren
of righteousness. In his homilies vibrate some of the first notes of
that human piety toward Jesus which to us seems to have become
inseparable from our religion. Without cutting it off from its dogmatic roots he here brings to perfection an aspect of devotion
which had not yet won its place in the great tradition and which
was not to unfold fully until much later. A distant precursor of
Saint Bernard, Origen celebrates the power and the sweetness of
Jesus' name. He knows that Jesus can be "found" only in the
solitude and silence of the heart. He wants us to seek him with
zeal, with perseverance, if need be in anguish and sorrow; to live
with him ever present; to ask him questions and to listen to his
replies: this, to Origen, is what the search for the meaning of
Scripture really means; he wants us to humble ourselves deeply
so that we may deserve to hear the sweetness of his voice. He declares that all the good things which man can expect and which
God can give are summed up in Jesus. He praises those who contemplate Christ and who remain bound to him "by a bond of
tender affection"—and those who prefer to put their trust in his
words rather than in their own conscience. Even as Origen smiles
at Jesus' childhood, so he suffers with him the suffering and humiliation of his Passion which he at times evokes with startling
realism. He admires the majesty of his silence. He also meditates
on the first pages of the gospel; and from Jesus' submission to
Joseph he learns that, no matter how great one may be, there is
no better thing than to live in humble submission. He announces
that there is no true Christian life in separation from the man who
was the Christ and from Mary his mother. He often speaks of
"my Jesus," "my Lord," "my Savior." This personal touch had
become so much a habit with him that he at times slipped into
introducing it even into his quotations from Scripture. It is a
Pauline trait; but Origen's insistent usage makes something new
of it, a sort of conquest of Christian piety. No doubt Tertullian
had already spoken of "my Christ," but this expression simply
meant: Christ as I see him, as my faith shows him to me and as
I claim him to be, in contrast to the Christ whom Marcion imag-
ines, "Marcion's Christ." In an analogous way, he could say that
the true Christ is the "Christ of the Creator," the "Christ of
Isaiah," the "Christ of the Prophets," and so on; or again, in a
discussion of Moses or of Paul, he said just as easily: "my Moses,"

"my Apostle." . . . In these polemical chapters from the *Adversus Marcionem*, the point at issue was "two Christs," that is, two conceptions of Christ opposing one another. If Tertullian made use of the first person singular—*meus, mihi*—it was because of the personal character which he gave to the battle with his adversary. It was two men who fought a duel: "your Christ," says Tertullian in addressing Marcion. Two men, but in the name of two Churches: the heretical Church of Marcion and the great Church Catholic. Tertullian's "my Christ" was thus simply the equivalent of "the Christ of the Church, of the Catholic tradition, of the orthodox faith"; and the possessive pronoun simply expresses the personal attachment that this forceful fighter felt for that faith. But Origen is a man of another cast. Like John the Evangelist, he "reclined at the breast of Jesus." The one for whom he as a boy would have wished to meet martyrdom had forever enraptured the depths of his soul.

His piety was redoubled by a very strong concern with orthodoxy. For example, in one of his homilies on Saint Luke he says: "As for myself, my wish is to be truly a man of the Church, to be called by the name of Christ and not that of any heresiarch, to have this name which is blessed all over the earth; I desire to be, and to be called, a Christian, in my works as in my thoughts." Love and faith are fused in this outcry; it is the force of love which exacts rightness of faith. He often alerts us to the danger of false doctrines from which, he observes, "human nature finds it difficult to purify itself." Such doctrines are for him in the true sense, so to speak, "the abomination of desolation." He insists that one must protect oneself against them by vigilance and by prayer. Not content to invoke "the rule of the Scriptures" or "the evangelical and apostolic rule," he constantly appeals to "the rule of the Church," "the faith of the Church," "the word of the Church," "the preaching of the Church," "the tradition of the Church," "the doctrine of the Church," "the thought and teaching of the Church." In the bones of the paschal Lamb he sees a symbol of the "holy dogmas of the Church" of which not one shall be broken. He does not want "that there be any disagreement on doctrine among Churches." He is Adamantius, "the man of iron"; "doctrinal firmness" is one of the virtues closest to his heart. He exalts constancy in the faith and stability of dogma. Even before Saint Augustine, he speaks of "chastity of the heart," that is, of the understanding, and doctrines that stray from the rule of faith seem to him worse than evil ways of life. Again, he says that "one must guard oneself against committing an offense of the head" and against eating the sacred foods outside the temple, that is, "against harboring thoughts different from the faith of the Church on divine dogmas." One must receive the faith of God in the spirit which the Church teaches us, and must not do like the heretics who search the Scriptures only in order to find some confirmation of their own doctrines. Their pride raises them "higher than the cedars of Lebanon" and their sophistries are full of deceit. But it is no use for them to pretend that they have a tradition which comes down from the apostles; they are professors of error. While the faithful Christian in no way strays from the great tradition, they appeal to secret Scriptures or to secret traditions in order to confirm their lies. Thus they want to make us worship a Christ whom they have invented "in solitude," while the only authentic Christ reveals himself "within the house." They disfigure those vessels of gold and silver which are the sacred texts, in order to fashion them into objects according to their own fancy. They are thieves and adulterers who seize the divine words only to deform them by their perverse interpretations. They are counterfeiters for they have coined their doctrine outside the Church. False teachers, false prophets, spinning out of their own minds what they propound, they are the liars of whom Ezekiel speaks. By a perverse trickery they often cover their idols, that is, their empty dogmas, with sweetness and chastity so that their propositions may be smuggled more easily into the ears of their listeners and lead them astray more surely. They all call Jesus their master and embrace him; but their kiss is the kiss of Judas.

Is this truly the same man as the "allegorist" of whom we have been told? And if the two representations are incompatible, which are we to choose? Tillemont was clear-eyed when he wrote that Origen "seems to have had a very humble spirit, very submissive to the Church, very respectful of her doctrines and decisions, very devoted to her unity." His feeling for the Church did in fact run as deep as his feeling for Christ. He was in the habit of calling her "Mother," and saw the Christians as her "children." The voice of her teaching was pleasing to him, and he was convinced that the more spiritual one grows, the more one recognizes the beauty of her face. He thought that the greatest misfortune is to be "cut off from the Mystery of the Church" like that plant from Jerusalem which, when transplanted into Canaan, withered at once because it was no longer cared for by the hand of God. All this surely is out of keeping with the sort of allegorism that many have attributed to Origen. But in turn it all is very much in keeping with the allegorism he actually practiced. And we must go further. Concern for orthodoxy and devotion to the faith, love for the "dogmas of the truth" are precisely among the reasons for Origen's allegorism. One of his goals is "to shut Pharaoh's mouth" with an explication of Scripture that "conforms to sound doctrine." For example, when he runs up against anthropomorphic passages in the Bible, he feels the need to interpret them, not primarily in the name of reason, but in the name of the faith of the Church: *Alienum hoc est ab Ecclesiae fide*. Similarly, he supposes, "who will dare say that the Word of God is of no use and contributes in no way to salvation, but does no more than tell of events that happened in the past and have no relation to us? *Impia haec, et aliena a catholica fide sententia est*." To maintain such an opinion, one must deny the unity of the Law and the gospel, the unity of the God of Moses and God the Father of our Lord Jesus Christ. On the contrary, to seek the "spiritual meaning" of Scripture in order to draw nourishment from it is to use Scripture in catholic fashion, *verbum Dei catholice tractari*. It is to receive the Word from Jesus' hands and to have him read it to you. It is to act as "a son of the Church." If there is one fundamental obligation for the Christian, it is that of keeping "to the rule of the heavenly Church of Jesus Christ, through the succession from the apostles." In concrete terms then, what is this rule? Saint Irenaeus had already given the answer: it is the interpretation of Scripture by the spirit.

Wisdom and the Cross

How colorless the human wisdom of the philosophers looks to Origen beside these treasures of divine knowledge in which he thus steeps himself! His writings yield nothing comparable to those elaborations which Clement, in the first book of his *Stromateis*, devoted to the praise of philosophy. Not that Origen allows no place for the profane disciplines within ecclesiastical doctrine: for him, the spoils of Egypt are fair game! Origen did not invent this metaphor which was destined to become famous, but he did make it his own. When one thinks that it was to reappear from the pen not only of such men as Alcuin or John Duns Scotus, but also of Peter Damian and even Gregory IX, one is less inclined to view it as evidence of unbounded intellectualism. We note, besides, that these "spoils" are of value only if they are brought back to the holy land for the building of the Temple. By contrast, he who goes down into Egypt to devote himself there to the profane sciences runs great risks. If he lingers there as did Ader the Idumean, if he lets himself be seduced by philosophy, he will return only to corrupt the faith and to break up the unity of his brothers. Those who escape this ruin are rare indeed.

Yet these disciplines also have a propaedeutic role. For a person capable of acquiring genuine education it is desirable that he

"draw from Greek philosophy the system of knowledge that is
fit to serve as an introduction to Christianity." Certain ideas of
geometry and astronomy," for example, will be useful to him also
"to explain the sacred writings." By the same token, the apologist
will imitate the patriarchs who did not hesitate to enter into un-
ions with concubines or an alien woman, even in old age, with a
mind to having descendants conceived in chastity. Thus he will
bring together for his instruction "literature, grammar, geometry,
arithmetic, dialectic"; "and if such marriages enable us to present
our ideas, to discuss them, and to refute those who oppose them,
and if in this way we should be able to convert a few men to the
faith; if, by using their own methods more skilfully than they do
themselves, we persuade them to accept the true philosophy of
Christ and the true piety of God, then we can say that we have
had children by dialectic or rhetoric, as by an alien woman or a
concubine." And again, just as Moses accepted the counsel of his
father-in-law Jethro, priest of an alien God, just so "if we happen
to find a word of wisdom on the lips of a pagan, we should not
immediately disdain the word itself because of the speaker; because it is not right for us to swell with pride and scorn the words
of wise men on the pretext that we possess a law given to us by
God. Rather, as the Apostle says, we must test everything and
retain what is good." In any case, one must never make use of
secular doctrines without first cleansing them and cutting out
whatever in them is barren or dead. For, while every science comes
from above, that is from God, there is not one that has not been
more or less corrupted by the malice of men or of demons. No
doubt, side by side with its falsehoods, "hellenic philosophy" contains elements of truth which are not to be despised; Saint Paul
"saw a manifest greatness in the words of worldly wisdom"—only
to judge them in the end all the more captious and vain. If one
reviews everything that philosophy, Greek or barbarian, teaches,
one will recognize that every time it fails to agree with Christ's
teaching it is sheer folly. These "alien doctrines" must always be
"controlled and held in subjection." Origen knows that this is not
easy: "I, too, may tell what I have learned from experience, that
rare is the man who succeeded in taking from Egypt only its useful things, and then going away to employ them for the service
of God." Lest one be taken by surprise, one will always recall that
philosophy and the faith, like Isaac and Abimelech, are now at
peace and now at war, and that nothing must be accepted from the
first until we have verified its agreement with the second.

Still more often Origen warns us against the dangers of philosophy. He condemns the "wisdom of the rulers of this world" without
making distinctions. It is not just false knowledge, it is perverse

to the core. It consists above all of magic and divination, "the secrets of the Egyptians, occult philosophy, the astrology of the Chaldeans and Indians, the countless opinions of the Greeks concerning divinity." With this wisdom no compromise is possible. It is the wisdom of those who conspired against the Lord and crucified him. As for the "wisdom of this world," which consists of the profane arts and sciences, "poetry, grammar, geometry, rhetoric, music, and perhaps medicine," it too is dangerous in the form in which it is offered. Without being radically evil, it has become a tool of the demons; and its spirit is now contrary to Jesus Christ. It is an alien wisdom which God scatters to the winds, "the wealth of sinners." It is opposed to divine wisdom as the spirit of the world is opposed to the spirit of God. Its adepts seek to overthrow the gospel with the deceits of their dialectic. Origen compares it to the food consecrated to idols which the Apostle condemned, to "the leaven of the Pharisees" which Jesus denounced before his disciples, to the bar of gold that Achan stole at Jericho in spite of Joshua's order: a cursed object which seduces us with its brilliant beauty and contaminates the whole people. He accuses it of corrupting the faith with its sophistries as Eve was seduced by the guile of the serpent, of deceiving the wise man with the variety of its theses as Solomon was deceived by his wives. He points out that it invariably leaves those who follow it in uncertainty and doubt; like Abimelech's wife and maidservants, it remains barren so long as God has not come to heal it. "Do not touch," he says, "the furtive loaves of perverse doctrine. Do not long for the deceitful foods of philosophy which entice you away from the truth. This is the fast which is pleasing to God." True, Origen does not refuse the use of such nourishment "to those who have received full knowledge of the truth"; his language and method with a small group of fervent and cultivated disciples will be different from those he uses with the mass of the Christian people. But this is only normal, as any experienced educator will agree. The risks and the needs are not in fact the same in both cases; what is profitable in one could become fatal in the other. Thus one must always be alert "not to wound those who still have little training in Christ" and who might get caught in the trap.

In the last analysis, then, it is hardly an exaggeration to speak, with one of Origen's recent interpreters, of "the surprising aversion" that he feels toward this philosophy "which he knows very well nonetheless." No doubt one must make allowances for Origen's rhetoric. But there is in his faith in Christ a seriousness and sincerity, a power of conviction at once firm and measured and, all in all, a strength of faith that bears the signs of the Christian victory beforehand. Who could believe henceforth that for the use of those whom he called the "perfect" Origen transformed Christianity into a sort of philosophical wisdom, that he made it into a "platonic gnosis" and abandoned the cross of Christ to the "beginners"? This manner of presenting his thought is unfaithful. And it is even more of a grievous mistake to propose that according to him salvation consists only in the work of the cross "for the ordinary Christian," while "for the Christian gnostic" it will be no more than "a higher teaching"; and that to the former, the redeemer and healer is present in the Christ of history, to the latter, the eternal Logos simply as a teacher. At the root of such interpretations we find the same misunderstanding which we have already noted in several of its forms. It is quite true that Origen throws into relief the role of the incarnate Logos as educator and illuminator of souls; but this trait, far from making him akin to the "gnostic" theologians, puts him in opposition to them. It is quite true also that he, once again following Saint Paul, means to preach a wisdom that surpasses "the simple faith" and that his "perfect believer" must go beyond the letter which the narrative of the Savior's Passion and death traces for him. But let us not forget that for him this wisdom is a grace of God, altogether different from that prideful and miserable knowledge which "the simplest of the Christians put to shame." It is this "true wisdom" which was given of old to such men as Isaiah and Jeremiah and which today is shared by those who are born in the Spirit. "When we understand, we understand by faith"; and to be "set free by the truth" we must "abide in the faith." Let us not ascribe to Origen's views some sort of disdainful arrogance. "Simple faith" or faith in the "simple letter" do not mean to him the faith of the simple or the lowly, of "those who are inferior according to human judgment." One of the characteristics of Jesus' preaching, Origen notes repeatedly, is that it is addressed to all, to the barbarians as to the Greeks, to the uneducated as to the learned. By the same token, he thinks, a true apostle of Jesus is recognizable by the fact that he "does not despise simple people." He who counts himself a believer and wise is, on the contrary, quite close to being an unbeliever if he disdains what the world takes for folly but what God has chosen: such are the Pharisees who, thinking themselves superior, keep themselves apart from the multitude.

Nor does Origen confuse wisdom with wisdom. We cite once again his clear declaration against Celsus' haughty reflections: "Human wisdom is what we call 'the wisdom of the world,' which is 'foolishness with God.' But the divine wisdom, which is different from the human if it really is divine, comes by the grace of God who gives it to those who prove themselves to be suitable persons

to receive it. . . . Celsus describes as *very uneducated* and as
slaves and as *quite ignorant* those who . . . have not been educated in the learning of the Greeks. But the people whom we call
very uneducated are those who are not ashamed to address lifeless
objects. . . ." However, there is some excuse here for the error.
It stems above all from the exegesis which Origen habitually gives
to a text from the first Epistle to the Corinthians: "For I decided
to know nothing among you except Jesus Christ and him crucified." In the knowledge of which the Apostle here speaks, Origen
sees no more than a knowledge that is still inferior, in other words
a knowledge that is ignorant of Christ's person and work. Where
Paul intended to speak of the "mystery of the cross" which he had
"preached in all its starkness," Origin believes that it is simply a
question of preaching the external fact of the crucifixion without
revealing its mystery. Those who know only Jesus crucified, he
thinks, are those who "suppose that the Word made flesh is the
whole Word," who know nothing of his "glory" or his divinity. For
this reason they are incapable of comprehending the meaning of
the cross, which is to say that they do not know the mystery of
our redemption. They have not as yet crossed the Jordan with the
armies of the true Jesus and pushed on to the interior of the
promised land to wage the final battles there. Origen sees in
Paul's text an intention more restrictive than it really is. To him,
the Christians who keep to this first sermon do not actually have
"an elementary catechism"; they are at most still in the stage of
a preparatory catechism. Such people are not necessarily weak
in spirit; they may be wise according to the world. But they are
still carnal men. As yet they know Christ only "according to the
flesh," and if they wish to remain so, they would deserve the
Apostle's blame. The Apostle decided at first to know nothing
else while he was among them because they could then bear no
more. Their soul had not been made ready. But when he wrote to
them later, he made it clear that he possessed a wisdom nonetheless: a wisdom not of this world but of God, "a secret and hidden
wisdom" which he "proclaims among the perfect." This wisdom
does not annul the first knowledge but completes and transforms
it. It is a more profound teaching which constitutes the understanding of the initial datum. It is the solid food which takes the
place of the milk of infants, that is, once again, the milk not of
the "weak," of those who are simple according to the world, but
of the νήπιοι in the Pauline sense, of those who "had not yet been
purified in their habits." There are not, then, two categories of
Christians separated by the power of their intelligence. There is
not a popular preaching and a different, more refined, teaching for
the intellectuals. Our religion "is at once spiritual and corporeal."

And if in certain cases it is necessary to begin by preaching "the corporeal gospel," this must always be with the desire to come to the point of showing forth the "glory of the only-begotten Son" underneath "the form of a servant." Once one has aroused in the souls the taste for "the heavenly wisdom," one will be able "to communicate to it the knowledge which will lead it from the Incarnation even to the one who was with God in the beginning."

But the proclamation of Jesus crucified remains no less essential. For "the economy of the Passion" is central. It is "the Economy" *par excellence*. Origen knows that without the wood of the cross the leprosy of sin cannot be healed. He knows that it is the whole Church, without any distinction of categories, that was saved by the blood of Christ. He knows that the death of Christ is the Tree of Life for all of us, that all fruitfulness comes from this death as from the grain of wheat which must fall into the earth and seem to perish. He declares that all the glory and all the riches of the Church lie in Christ's Passion. For him, to be converted is "to come to the cross of Christ"; and the wisdom of the perfect consists not in some other knowledge, but in the contemplation of "the profound mysteries which Paul uncovers there for us" and then in rejecting all the more strongly the wisdom of the world. It is to be crucified to this world's wisdom. For there is total opposition between the narrow way of salvation shown to us in the cross of Christ, and the wide and easy way on which the philosophy of the wise men of the world seeks to engage us. The "vision of the Logos" can be attained only at the price of death to the world and at the cost of great tribulation; and no matter how sublime this vision may be, it will never make us lose sight of the crucified Jesus, at once priest and victim. There is no wisdom that excuses from taking up his cross and following him. Even supposing that, like Paul, one has been caught up to the third heaven, there is only one way not to fall back; and it is precisely this, to "take up the cross and follow Jesus in whom 'we have a great high priest who has passed through the heavens.'"

Origen delights in commenting on the Prophet's oracles concerning the suffering Servant of Yahweh. He admires the profound "philosophy" which the Apostle discerns in the Passion. He binds himself to Paul's statement: Jesus "humbled himself even unto death and became obedient even to the cross." Sadly he confirms the fact that many do not understand this text and "imagine a Jesus inaccessible to suffering" and altogether superior, so they think, to all such abasement. "Under the guise of religious respect for Jesus," when they come to the rending cry *Quare me dereliquisti?* they wish to see no more than a token of humility. Origen himself, on the other hand, most certainly had a vivid sense of the scandal of the *mysterium crucis*. To say that the Lord of Majesty was crucified, he who had come down from heaven, how "tortuous" such an affirmation appears; how hard to believe! Nonetheless, he will not blush at his Savior's cross. It is just this supreme humiliation of the Son of Man, which is ridiculed by the philosophers, from which the believer draws the power to scorn their laughter and their sarcasm. "The Christian faith has no fear of scandal." This scandal becomes a triumph of faith, and that which seemed "folly" is transformed into wisdom, "into a wisdom so great that it swallows all the wisdom of the Egyptians, that is, of this world." When the light of the cross penetrates the Christian's intelligence, it dispels all the dark shadows which the mistakes of the philosophers had accumulated there. It is this light of the cross which illumines the lives of the saints and makes them all martyrs, that is, witnesses of the Savior. It is the power of the cross that annihilates all evil desires; by it, "the whole army of sin and the flesh is put to rout." So great is this power that it procures healing and salvation not only for present and future generations, but even for those of past centuries. Even more, it is sufficient to save not only all mankind but also the celestial orders and powers. It is through union with the cross that our mutual union in the Father and the Son is realized. And no man was ever better placed to hear such a promise than he who hung with Jesus on the cross: "For he was a plant worthy of paradise, who was joined to the Tree of Life in this way." "The death of Christ reduced to impotence those powers which war against the human race. . . ." If the demons fear and tremble, the cause is again nothing else but the cross: the blood that flows down from it does not appease their thirst but destroys their power. It is the cross which has vanquished them and by which we shall vanquish them in our turn. "The power of the cross" is irresistible. And so we must faithfully bear its sign, take up "the standard of the cross" to meet its struggles and persecutions, so that we too may be able to say with Paul: "Far be it from me to glory except in the cross of our Lord Jesus Christ."

In summing up, we may say that there is, as it were, a twofold advent of the Logos in the soul. At the first advent, Christ barely begins to be known; the soul, still "untaught" [*rudis*] does not see his beauty; it discerns only the birth and the crucifixion in the flesh. But the second advent corresponds in some way, within the soul, to that advent which will be the consummation of the world; to him who reaches perfection, or simply Christian maturity, Christ appears transfigured in his beauty and his glory. Then, far from rejecting the mystery of the Incarnation or of the cross, the soul understands at last. Its faith becomes luminous. It finds its own glory in this mystery "by which the world has been crucified to me and I to the world." It sees in all clarity that this death to the world in Christ is a "blessed death." Such is, not the public and provisional teaching adapted to those who are "weak" or to the first stage of the beginners, but rather the final state of the perfect, itself a sign and anticipation within the soul of the final consummation. For to him for whom the world has been crucified and who no longer glories except in the cross, the end of the world has come, so to speak. With Romano Guardini, Origen could have said: "The cross is the absolute symbol."

INTRODUCTION

BY

G. W. Butterworth

I

LIFE AND WRITINGS OF ORIGEN

'THE greatest teacher of the Church after the apostles'—
such was the description of Origen which Jerome adopted
from Didymus, the blind theologian of Alexandria, and
inserted in the preface to his translation of the great master's
Homilies on Ezekiel.[1] In the preface to his own work, *On
the Meaning of Hebrew Names,* Jerome repeated the tribute,
remarking that 'all but the ignorant' recognised it to be
true.[2] Later on, when his enthusiasm for Origen had cooled,
Jerome found it embarrassing to be reminded of these early
laudations. Yet his first judgment was certainly sound, and
few who study the works of Origen to-day will be disposed
to contest it.

The story of Origen's life is easily accessible to the
student,[3] and need not be retold here except in outline. He
was born A.D. 185-186, probably at Alexandria, of Christian
parents. At the age of seventeen he narrowly escaped death
in the persecution of Severus, when his father Leonides was
martyred and Origen was with great difficulty prevented
from voluntarily sharing his fate. Owing to the departure
of Clement from Alexandria in the same persecution the
headship of the Catechetical School became vacant, and
such was the ability and industry of Origen that he was
appointed to fill this post at the age of eighteen. He
laboured with increasing success as a teacher, working
almost day and night with the crowds, including heretics
and non-Christians as well as members of the Church, who
attended his lectures or came to consult him privately.
About A.D. 215 he visited Cæsarea in Palestine, where his
friends Alexander bishop of Jerusalem and Theoctistus
bishop of Cæsarea asked him to lecture in church on the
Scriptures. Demetrius, patriarch of Alexandria, objected to
this, for Origen had not been ordained. In spite of the

[1] See Jerome, *Praef. in Hom. Orig. in Ezech.* (Lommatzsch XIV 4).
Rufinus, *Apol.* II. 13 (Migne P.L. XXI. 596).
[2] Rufinus, *Apol.* II. 16 (Migne P.L. XXI. 597).
[3] See Bibliography, p. xxvii. Most of our information comes from
Eusebius, *His. Eccl.* Bk. VI.

protests of Origen's friends Demetrius demanded his return to Alexandria, and he obeyed.

During the next period of his life, lasting from twelve to fifteen years, Origen began the literary work which established his fame throughout the whole Church. A wealthy layman named Ambrose, whom he had restored from heresy to the orthodox faith, became his life-long friend, and supplied him with the means to write and publish his books. The first parts of the *Commentary on St. John* were composed then, and following them came the treatise on *First Principles,* a comprehensive investigation of Christian doctrine on a scale never before attempted. It is probable that this work aroused opposition. Origen's mind was such that he could leave no question unprobed; and in the effort to reduce the Church's faith to a single, logical system, based on the Scriptures as they were then understood, he was led into speculations which to simpler folk appeared fantastic and dangerous. Owing either to this, or else to jealousy on the part of Demetrius, or perhaps to a combination of both, the relations between Origen and his bishop became strained and he took advantage of an invitation to visit Greece. Calling at Cæsarea on the way, he was there ordained presbyter by Theoctistus and Alexander. This act caused a final break with Demetrius, who strongly disapproved of it; and when Origen returned to Alexandria at the conclusion of his visit to Greece it became evident that he must seek another home.

Demetrius called a synod of Egyptian bishops, who decided that Origen should no longer be allowed to teach at Alexandria. Soon afterwards he was excommunicated, on what grounds we do not know, except that Jerome tells us they were not doctrinal.[1] But the sentence, though accepted at Rome and throughout a considerable part of the Christian world, had little practical effect outside Egypt; and Origen was gladly received by Theoctistus at Cæsarea, where he became at once an honoured teacher of the Church. Here he worked from A.D. 231 for the rest of his life. In addition to his writing, he expounded the Scriptures to the ordinary church congregations and lectured on deeper theological subjects to educated students. One of these, Gregory, afterwards called Thaumaturgus, or the Wonderworker, has

---

[1] Jerome *Ep. XXXIII. ad Paulam.* The passage is rhetorical, but it suggests clearly enough that jealousy was the motive for Origen's condemnation, and ecclesiastical irregularities the excuse.

left us, in his *Panegyric*,[1] a striking description of Origen. No higher tribute has ever been paid by a pupil to a revered master. Gregory was a young man, on his way to study law at Berytus, when he met with Origen. At the time it seemed a chance meeting, but afterwards Gregory could only attribute it to divine providence. Origen's charm of manner, his generous friendship, his wide sympathy and consummate wisdom captivated him. For five years he remained at Cæsarea, and when at last he left to return to his native land he felt, to use his own simile, like the prodigal son going from his father's house into the far country. A letter of Origen's reached him shortly after, urging him to dedicate his great gifts to God's service in the ministry of the Church; and in spite of much genuine hesitation Gregory became bishop of Neo-Cæsarea, where he achieved marvellous success.[2]

The literary work of Origen was enormous in extent. Before he left Alexandria he had already written, besides the *First Principles* and five books of the *Commentary on St. John*, two volumes on *The Resurrection*, ten volumes of *Stromata* or *Miscellanies*, a *Commentary on Psalms* i—xxv, eight volumes on *Genesis* and five on *Lamentations*. This activity was continued at Cæsarea. He produced *Commentaries* on almost every book of the Bible, both Old and New Testaments. A treatise on *Prayer* was addressed to Ambrose and Tatiana; and when, during the persecution of Maximin (235-237) Ambrose and Protoctetus, a presbyter of Cæsarea, were imprisoned, Origen wrote the *Exhortation to Martyrdom* for their encouragement. Of a different character are the eight books *Against Celsus*, which contain a detailed answer to a clever attack on Christianity made by an educated Greek about half a century before. Until he was sixty Origen would not allow his homilies delivered extemporaneously in church to be taken down and published. But he then withdrew his prohibition, and more than two hundred have been preserved, for the most part in Latin translations by Rufinus.

A further proof of his untiring industry, and also of his deep reverence for the Scriptures, can be found in the

---

[1] For the text see Koetschau, *Das Gregorios Thaumaturgos Dankrede an Origenes*, Leipzig 1894. Eng. trans. by W. Metcalfe, S.P.C.K. 1920, and *Ante-Nicene Christian Library*, Vol. XX., p. 36.
[2] For Origen's letter to Gregory see Koetschau's edition of the *Panegyric* already referred to; also Robinson, *Philocalia*, Ch. XIII. (p. 64). Eng. Trans. in Metcalfe *op. cit.* and *Ante-Nicene Christian Library*, Vol. X., p. 388.

Hexapla. This was a text of the Old Testament, in which six, and sometimes even more, different versions were placed side by side in columns for purposes of comparison. The six versions were the Hebrew, a transliteration of it in Greek characters, and the Greek versions of Aquila, of Symmachus, of the Septuagint and of Theodotion. It took Origen twenty-eight years to accomplish this task, the object of which was to ascertain the true text of the Septuagint. The work extended to fifty volumes, and being too large to be copied it did not survive for long. To-day nothing remains of it but some fragments, not inconsiderable in their total bulk, of the Septuagint.

Origen wrote many letters, and Eusebius was able to collect a hundred of them. Unfortunately all but three have perished. No loss of his writings is so regrettable as the loss of these letters. They would have given us a picture of the man, in his extraordinary attractiveness as a teacher and friend, which his theological compositions cannot be expected to supply. Those that remain are the letter to Gregory Thaumaturgus already referred to,[1] one to Africanus,[2] and portions of a third quoted in Latin by Jerome and Rufinus. The authenticity of this latter is not, however, absolutely beyond doubt. The letter to Africanus was in answer to one which Africanus had written on the subject of the History of Susanna, attached to the book of Daniel in the Septuagint. Africanus urged that it was a late addition and not part of the original Daniel. In quite modern critical fashion he argued that the story was not contained in the Hebrew; that it was different in style from the rest of Daniel; and above all that it contained plays on Greek words which in Hebrew would have been pointless. Origen's reply was to defend the passage. He was unwilling to reject a story which had great value for purposes of instruction and which had always been accepted in the Church. He had consulted Jewish scholars about the puns, but found that they would not commit themselves; there might possibly be Hebrew equivalents or analogies, although they could not produce them. This was Origen's own conclusion. In regard to the alleged difference in style, he replies simply that he cannot see it. Origen was no higher critic. This letter is of prime importance for all who would understand Origen's character, for it shows that he was

---

[1] See above p. iii.
[2] For the text see Migne P. G. XI. p. 47 ff. Eng. trans. *Ante-Nicene Christian Library*, Vol. X., pp. 369 ff.

essentially and before all else a Christian pastor, whose main concern was for the spiritual needs of Christians and the traditional faith of the Church. This remains true in spite of the undoubted fact that he was chiefly a teacher of the educated, and that he felt the *simpliciores* needed correction on many points.

Origen's later life at Cæsarea was varied by visits to different parts of Palestine, to Athens and to Arabia. The first Arabian visit was made in order to convince Beryllus, bishop of Bostra, of the falsity of his views on the subject of the Incarnation, and the second to deal with errors concerning the Resurrection. In both cases he was successful. All through his life Origen appears as a defender of orthodox doctrine against heresy; and what is more, as one who could win men to his own viewpoint by persuasion and sympathy. Finally, in A.D. 250, when the persecution of Decius broke out, Origen was imprisoned, probably at Tyre. His friend Alexander of Jerusalem died in prison. Origen himself was cruelly tortured, but bore his suffering with the same undaunted spirit that he had displayed since boyhood. The death of Decius in 251 gave him release from prison. But his health was broken by all that he had undergone, and he died at Tyre in 253, in the seventieth year of his age. His tomb was still to be seen there at the close of the twelfth century.

Origen is one of those figures, none too common even in Church history, of whose character we can say that we know nothing but what is good. He was humble and free from envy, caring neither for power nor wealth. He bore unmerited suffering, from friends and foes alike, without complaint. His life, from beginning to end, was hard and strenuous. His courage never failed, and he died in reality a martyr's death. He loved truth with a sincerity and devotion rarely equalled, and never excelled. Intellectually he stands pre-eminent and alone, towering above the Greek fathers as Augustine towers above the Latins. The wide sweep of his thought is amazing. He contemplates a universe, not small and narrow as was that of many of his contemporaries, but of immense magnitude, world following world in almost infinite sequence, from the dim primeval epoch when God created all souls equal and free, to the far-off event when after countless vicissitudes of degradation and suffering they shall return to their original unity and perfection, and 'God shall be all in all'. It may be that the Church of those days was right in warning her children off these speculations, and keeping them to the path of a simpler and more definite faith; lest perhaps, through over-much thinking on problems insoluble to man, weaker souls should find themselves, like Milton's angels, 'in wandering mazes lost'. We of these days, however, cannot help regretting, not without a sense of shame, that this salutary warning should have been accompanied, as it was, by fierce denunciations which are neither Christian nor rational. And yet the fact that Origen stands outside the formal calendar of Christian saints gives him a certain solitariness which is not altogether inappropriate. For it can be said with truth that there is no father of the Church whose works are more profitable for study and whose temper and character are more worthy of our imitation.

II

THE FIRST PRINCIPLES. DATE AND CIRCUMSTANCES OF ITS COMPOSITION

THE treatise on *First Principles* was written before Origen left Alexandria for good in A.D. 231, that is, before he was forty-six years of age. When we seek for a more precise date we encounter difficulties. Our sources of information are the treatise itself and Eusebius, *Hist. Eccl.* VI. 14-24. From the first we obtain the following facts.

In Bk. II., Ch. iii. 6 (see p. 91 below) Origen refers to his *Commentary on Genesis* I. 1, as a work already written. On the contrary, in Bk. I., Ch. ii. 6 (see p. 18 below), when mentioning Genesis I. 26, he promises to explain the verse more carefully when he reaches it in his Commentary. The verse was in fact expounded in the fourth book of the Commentary and Genesis I. 16-18 in the third. As there were eight books of this Commentary written before the year 231, it seems probable that the work was begun quite early, especially when we remember that Origen was engaged in several different compositions at the same time.

In Bk. II., Ch. iv. 4 (see p. 100 below) Origen refers the reader to his *Commentary on the Second Psalm*. Evidently this work also was being written contemporaneously with the *First Principles*.

In Bk. II., Ch. x. 1 (see p. 138 below) mention is made of the books on the *Resurrection* which were an early work, being themselves quoted, according to Eusebius, in the *Commentary on Lamentations*.

From these passages all the knowledge we obtain is that the books on *First Principles* were written at a time when Origen was also at work on the Commentaries on *Genesis,* the *Psalms* and *Lamentations.* These were not, however, his earliest compositions, for the books on the *Resurrection* preceded them, as did also the beginning of the *Commentary on St. John,* which he calls 'the firstfruits of my labours in Alexandria.'[1]

The question is, therefore, when were the Commentaries begun? This turns on our view of the chronology of Eusebius in the Sixth Book of his *Ecclesiastical History.* In Ch. 23 of this Book Eusebius implies that Origen began his Commentaries immediately after his return from the interview with Mammæa, the aunt of the Emperor Elagabalus (218-222), and the mother of his successor, Alexander Severus (222-235). Mammæa would have been at Antioch in the year 218, when her nephew visited the city after his victory over Macrinas. But the text of Eusebius appears to date this visit in the time of Alexander. If this were so, it would either be a visit at the beginning of Alexander's reign, of which otherwise we know nothing, or else one that occurred after 231. The latter is very improbable, since Eusebius does not mention Origen's departure from Alexandria until Ch. 26, after giving a long account of his exegetical work in that city in Chs. 24 and 25. While we need not suppose that every detail of Eusebius' chronology is correct, it is evident that he is taking pains to place events in what he regards as their proper order. We may therefore conclude that, although the mention of Alexander in Ch. 21 brings to his mind the invitation sent by this Emperor's mother to Origen, the incident belongs in reality to the reign of Elagabalus, whom Eusebius has mentioned under his true name Antoninus only a few lines previously. It was after 218, then, that Origen began his Commentaries, 'at the urgent desire of Ambrose, who not only employed innumerable incentives in the form of requests and exhortations, but also furnished abundant means for the work'.[2]

The *First Principles* may have been written, therefore, at any date between, let us say, 219 and 230. But in view of the fact that the references contained in it to the commentaries on *Genesis* and the *Psalms* are to quite early parts of these works, we can with reasonable certainty fix the date

---

[1] *Comm. in Ioh.* I. 2.
[2] Eusebius, *Hist. Eccl.* VI. 23.

not later than A.D. 225. Origen would then have been between thirty-five and forty years old when the work was complete.

It is true that some scholars favour an earlier date than this. Schnitzer gives 213 and Preuschen 212-215. These dates can only be maintained on the assumption that the chronology of Eusebius is altogether unreliable. But there is good reason on general grounds for holding to 218 as the time when Origen began his work of writing Commentaries. The first years of his adult life, after the departure of Clement in 202, were so fully occupied with teaching at Alexandria that, as we are distinctly told, he had no time to study the Scriptures properly. Then he called Heracles to take a share in the work of the school, and immediately began his researches on the Biblical text which culminated in the *Hexapla*. This was doubtless a preliminary to the production of the Commentaries. The need for these was only slowly becoming apparent in the Church; although Heracleon the Gnostic had written a Commentary on St. John some forty or fifty years previously, and it was this which in all probability inspired Origen to attempt his own work on the same Gospel. Then, after the first visit to Cæsarea, came the definite request of Ambrose that he should produce Commentaries systematically and on a large scale. With the request was joined, as we have seen, the offer of ample financial help which enabled Origen to accede to it.

The *First Principles* was a work of an entirely different character from the Commentaries. For if these latter were, at least in the form and scope which Origen gave them, new to the Church, the *First Principles* was a fresh departure altogether. Not that it was without precursors. Its originality consisted in its vastness of plan, in the unity of its purpose, and in the genius with which it was executed. Origen would certainly not have regarded himself as a pioneer, still less as a teacher of doubtful orthodoxy. He was the exponent of the Christian tradition to thoughtful and cultivated men; but he would subject that tradition to a far keener examination than his predecessors had ventured upon. De Faye, in his recent work on Origen,[1] has suggested that the *First Principles* was designed to take the place of the *Didaskalos*, or Teacher, which Clement had planned to follow on his *Protreptikos* and *Paidagogos*, but which he was never able

---

[1] Eugène de Faye, *Origène, sa vie, son oeuvre, sa pensée*. Paris, 1923.

to write.[1] It is more natural to suppose that the *Stromata* and the *Hypotyposes* were intended to be the continuation of the two works just mentioned. But it would appear that Clement himself composed a work on *First Principles and Theology*.[2] It is no longer extant; in fact we have no certain mention of it except in his own works. Perhaps it was never published at all in the strict sense of the word, but used solely for the students to whom Clement lectured in the Catechetical School. This treatise probably dealt with the origin of the world, among other subjects, and it is not unreasonable to regard it as having laid down the lines which Origen afterwards followed. In both works the substance was simply the lectures delivered to students in the School. Zahn has conjectured that a fragment found in John Malalas may refer to this lost work of Clement's. It runs as follows: 'The Syrian, the son of Agenor, was a man of wisdom, who composed his Arithmetical Philosophy in the Phœnician language. He suggested that first principles were incorporeal, that bodies underwent changes, and that souls entered into different kinds of animals. He first expounded these doctrines, as the most wise Clement wrote of them.'[3] The likeness between this and some of the contents of Origen's *First Principles* is at once evident. Even if Zahn's identification is not correct, we can yet see that Origen was dealing with questions which had been raised and discussed in the School before his time, and which were then admitted to be legitimate subjects for inquiry.

III

THE TRANSLATION OF RUFINUS. CIRCUMSTANCES OF ITS COMPOSITION

As I have already remarked, the grounds on which Origen was condemned by the Synod of bishops called by Demetrius in Alexandria were not doctrinal.[4] That is to say, the *First Principles* was not then and there held to be heretical; if it had been, the fact would certainly have come into prominence. None the less, the work could scarcely fail to cause offence, in so far as it came to the knowledge of the

---

[1] De Faye, *op. cit.* I. 28.
[2] Clem. Alex. *III Storm.* 13, 1 and 21, 2, and *Quis Dives Salvetur* 26, 8 (Stählin II 201, 12 and 205, 11 and III 177, 25, 26).
[3] Zahn, *Supplementum Clementinum*, p. 59.
[4] See above, p. ii.

simpliciores, who even in Clement's day were disposed to fear all thinking and to raise the cry, 'Only believe'.[1] As time went on the offence would be likely to increase. For Origen was not a lonely figure in the Church. He had many followers, who admired him not only for his interpretations of the Scriptures but also for his theological doctrines.

The first serious attack was made by Methodius, bishop of Patara in Lycia, in the early years of the fourth century. He wrote vigorously against Origen and his followers in regard to doctrines characteristic of the *First Principles,* viz : the eternity of creation, the pre-existence of souls and the spiritual nature of the resurrection body. At the Council of Nicæa Origen's name and authority do not appear to have been invoked by either side, but in the controversies which followed it was not long before the Arians discovered that some support for their distinctive teaching might be drawn from the considerable degree of subordination which he had predicated of the Son. Others, however, including such great names as Athanasius and the Cappadocian fathers, Basil and the two Gregories, while admitting that his works were not wholly free from error, yet regarded him as orthodox in the main and defended him.

Towards the end of the fourth century Epiphanius, bishop of Salamis in Cyprus, renewed the attack. In two works, the *Anchoratus* and the *Adv. Hæreses,* he includes Origen among the heretics, on the grounds previously set forth by Methodius and on others dealing with the nature of the Son and his relation to the Father. Origen was charged with teaching that the Son, though generated from the essence of the Father, was nevertheless a creature, bearing the title Son by courtesy and not by right; that the Holy Spirit was also a creature; and that one day the Kingdom of Christ would come to an end and all beings, including the devil himself, would be reconciled and restored to God.

Epiphanius felt it to be not enough to write against Origen; in his old age he travelled to Palestine in order to extirpate, if possible, from the minds of all who were well-disposed towards the great theologian every trace of what he considered to be pestilent heresies. Origen had now been dead nearly one hundred and forty years, and the Church had changed from being a body of persecuted believers into a victorious institution, honoured and privileged by the

[1] Clem. Alex. *Strom.* I. 43 i; (Stählin II. 28, 20).

State. The zeal for repression of which she had once been the victim was now directed against all who would not conform to the type of thought now in favour, a type more rigid than that which was held to be permissible for educated men in the days of Origen. Epiphanius was a true representative of his age in this respect. There were living near Jerusalem at this time Rufinus, who had established a monastery on the Mount of Olives in A.D. 377, and Jerome, who had dwelt similarly at Bethlehem since 386. Both were admirers of Origen; and so, too, was John, bishop of Jerusalem. Not one of these would have consented to be bound by every fragment of Origen's teaching, but they respected his genius and revered his memory. Jerome, in particular, had begun to translate Origen's *Homilies* even before he left Rome. He used Origen's Commentary on *Ephesians* freely in writing his own Commentary on that epistle, borrowing then without question much of Origen's speculation on the angelic beings which he afterwards repudiated. His prefaces, too, as we have seen, speak of Origen in the highest possible terms.

The first act of Epiphanius was to preach, at the invitation of the bishop, in the Church of the Resurrection at Jerusalem. The sermon was a fierce attack upon Origenism directed, as it seemed to those who heard it, against the bishop himself. He followed this up by urging the monks to dissociate themselves from their bishop until he had cleared himself from the suspicion of heresy. Jerome took alarm at this, for he was sensitive to the least imputation of heresy, and adopted the attitude recommended by Epiphanius. Rufinus, however, was the leading member of a group of clergy who supported the bishop. This caused the first breach between Jerome and Rufinus; but it did not last long, for after Epiphanius had returned to Cyprus the two friends were reconciled, and Jerome returned to communion with his bishop.

It is clear, however, that there still remained a diversity of feeling and outlook upon the subject of Origen which was likely to cause trouble if ever the dispute should arise again. To us Jerome appears to have shown extreme timidity in the face of an accusation which was not directed against him personally and which he could easily have rebutted. We must remember, on the other hand, that a charge of heresy, if substantiated, was then becoming a serious matter for any man of prominence in the Church, involving perhaps loss of liberty, or even of life itself.

Jerome, too, was a Latin, and had little sympathy with the Greek habit of thinking out problems. Anyway it is certain that, in spite of all he had previously written in Origen's praise, he determined that for the future he would say or do nothing to compromise himself.

There the matter might have ended, had not Rufinus returned to Italy in 397. He had read and lectured in Greek for many years, and was familiar with the writings of the early Greek fathers, including Origen. He brought back with him many manuscripts of these works. They were then unknown in Italy. Even Pope Anastasius, when asked a little later on to condemn Origen, while readily agreeing to do so on the basis of a few extracts from the *First Principles,* yet admitted that he did not know either the author or his writings. But there was a certain friend of Rufinus, named Macarius, who had heard of the *First Principles* and was anxious to read it, hoping to find in it some arguments to help him in a controversy in which he was then engaged with the *mathematici,* or pagan astrologers. He had dreamed of a ship coming to Italy laden with the spoils of the East; and when Rufinus appeared he interpreted the dream as an indication of his return and begged him to translate the work, for he was unable himself to read it in Greek. Rufinus hesitated, knowing well the odium which would gather round any man who seemed to be friendly towards Origen. Finally, however, he consented, and produced the version which is now before us.

Rufinus did not believe that the Greek text which had come down to him was in every detail authentic. He could not imagine a time when Christian thought had been more fluid than it was in his own day; and although he was well aware that Origen was a bold thinker, he felt it to be quite impossible that he should have differed on any material point from the theology of the fourth century. That the text of the *First Principles* did so differ was plain. It was daily being quoted as evidence of its author's heresy. Rufinus maintained, without any doubt in all honesty, that the text had been tampered with by heretics. To prove this he translated and published with his version of the *First Principles* the first book of the *Defence of Origen,* a work composed by Pamphilus the martyr in collaboration with Eusebius of Cæsarea, the Church historian.[1] The object

---

[1] S. Pamphili Martyris *Apologia pro Origene,* Migne P. G. XVII. 539.

of this work was to refute the attacks made on Origen by
Methodius and others.

Jerome asserted afterwards that this book was written by
Eusebius and not by Pamphilus; but this is contradicted by
the statement of Eusebius himself and by the later testimony
of Photius, who tells us that Eusebius and Pamphilus wrote
the first five books together and that the sixth was composed
by Eusebius alone after the martyr's death.[1]   Rufinus attributes the first book to Pamphilus alone; and in this he was
probably correct, since in it the name of Pamphilus is pre-
fixed, in dialogue fashion, to all the paragraphs which state
the objections made to Origen's teaching or introduce his
replies, the latter being presented largely in Origen's own
words.   Moreover at the beginning of the book the first
person singular is used.   The authority of Pamphilus the
martyr was very great, and it was a natural method of
protection for Rufinus to make the *Defence of Origen* known
to the Latin world as a preliminary to the publication of
the *First Principles*.

The *Defence,* so far as we have it in Rufinus' translation,
opens with five chapters wherein Origen's faith in regard
to the Church tradition, the nature of heresy, and the
doctrines of the Father, Son and Holy Spirit, together with
the Incarnation is defined by quotations made from his own
writings.   These chapters are wholly orthodox; for, as we
have already said, Origen counted it his business to defend
the Church tradition and to explain its meaning to intelligent
men.   Pamphilus sums up this section by exclaiming:
'What can be so correct as this, what so true, what so
catholic, what more useful for general instruction even among
those who rage against him with bitter enmity, what so
entirely free from blame?'

We are, however, almost completely dependent upon
Rufinus for our knowledge of what actually it was that
Origen said and Pamphilus praised.   Only in a few cases
do we possess the Greek which enables us to check him, and
when we can do this the result is not satisfactory.   For
instance, in Ch. IV., on the Holy Spirit, Rufinus writes as
follows: 'But for us there is one God the Father, from
whom are all things.   There is therefore one true God who,
as I said, is the fount of deity, and one Christ the maker of
christs, and one Holy Spirit who makes the Holy Spirit in
the soul of every saint.'   Now Origen's own statement, as

[1] Photius, *Bibl. Cod.* 118.

Pamphilus quoted it in Greek, was to the effect that the Father's work embraces the whole universe, the work of the Son extends to rational creatures only, and the work of the Spirit is confined to the saints. The Son is therefore 'less' than the Father, and the Spirit 'still less' than the Son. It could not have been by accident or by a mere habit of loose translation that these offensive phrases were avoided; the omission was deliberate. When Pamphilus quoted this passage of Origen, clearly he did not realise that it might be called heretical. This point weakens considerably the contention of Rufinus that the text of Origen had been corrupted by heretics; if anything had changed it was the authorised theology of the Church.

The *Defence* goes on to enumerate nine charges made against Origen's teaching and to give answers to them in his own words supplemented by the explanations of Pamphilus. Most of the charges are easily disposed of; for they relate to questions which are satisfactorily dealt with in the *First Principles,* even though Origen's statements may sometimes lend themselves to perversion by hostile critics. For instance, some affirmed that he denied the literal truth of Scripture and the events of our Lord's earthly life. But Origen's teaching is quite clear : he only denied the literal truth in such stories as the Garden of Eden and the Fall, or others containing similar anthropomorphisms, where it seemed to him to be incredible. Ordinary historical facts he accepted readily enough, although often he did not consider them important or even edifying. The charge, therefore, while not wholly unintelligible, admits of a reasonable answer.

A more serious charge is that Origen denied the reality of punishment in the next life, because men would then have no bodies. Again, Origen's doctrine on these questions, though it ran counter to the gross materialism of many in his time, is both rational and scriptural. He found the term 'spiritual body' in the Scriptures and held fast to it. The body, he contended, must be suitable to the sphere in which it has to live, and in a spiritual world we shall need spiritual bodies. These would be the same bodies which we have now, because they would be garments of the same personality; but they would not resemble the earthly body in appearance or structure or function. Punishment, too, must be disciplinary and remedial in character and not a mere infliction of pain, which would be unworthy of God. All this is clearly and intelligently argued in the *First*

Principles; in fact, it proceeds directly from Origen's idea
of God and forms the basis of his whole system of theology.
But it lay open to attack by men whose ideas of heaven
were framed after the pattern of things on earth. Pamphilus
spends much space in answering this charge on Origen's
lines. Once again, however, we have to complain of a
serious mistranslation by Rufinus. He deliberately omits
the phrase 'spiritual bodies', found both in Origen and in
Pamphilus. He could not possibly have claimed that heretics had inserted this in the text, when its source was so
obvious. It was omitted in the hope of conciliating his
Latin readers.

A further charge is that Origen held false opinions about
the soul. Here, too, Pamphilus feels the need of defending
him at some length. The Church, he says, had not spoken
decisively on this question. If it had, then Origen might
have been deserving of blame; but in fact many different
opinions were held by Christians about the origin and
nature of the soul. Moreover, here as elsewhere, Origen
put forward his views for discussion, and not as settled
dogmas. The last charge of all, and perhaps the most difficult one to counter, is that Origen taught the doctrine of
transmigration of souls. Now any reader of the *First
Principles,* if he takes into consideration, as he must do, the
irrefutable evidence of Jerome and the Emperor Justinian,
will be forced to admit that Origen at least allowed the
possibility of transmigration. That is putting the case at its
lowest. Pamphilus does not quote the evidence of the *First
Principles.* He relies on passages from the *Commentary
on St. Matthew,* in which Origen argues against the doctrine.
We possess the Greek text of this passage, so that there can
be no doubt of its genuineness. The argument runs as
follows : if such transmigration should occur, it would
happen, by hypothesis, as a punishment for sin. What
then could prevent the process from going on infinitely, and
destroying the possibility of a time when 'heaven and earth
shall pass away'? If, on the other hand, men should at
last, one by one and through infinite ages, become purified
so as no longer to need bodies, what then becomes of the
statement of Scripture, 'When the Son of Man cometh,
shall He find faith on the earth?' This reasoning is very
different from that in the *First Principles.* It is possible
that Origen's opinion had changed in the intervening years.
Or he may have felt that more caution was needed in a
commentary which would circulate widely among all classes

of Christians, than in a treatise which reflected for the most part the discussions between himself and his students in the Catechetical School.

One result of this examination of Pamphilus' *Defence* is to put us on our guard when reading Rufinus. Pamphilus, enthusiastic though he was, had felt it needful to exercise caution and to make certain admissions when defending Origen. Rufinus did not dare to let even Pamphilus speak for himself. What then would he do with Origen? He is perfectly candid with his readers, at least in a general way. He would alter Origen where he thought him wrong; not arbitrarily, of course, but in accordance with statements of an orthodox character to be found elsewhere in his writings. But to justify himself still further, Rufinus wrote a small pamphlet on 'The Corruption of the Works of Origen' and attached it to the translation of the *First Principles*.[1] Here he gives more fully his reasons for altering the text. They are as follows:

(i) *It was impossible to suppose that so intelligent and learned a man as Origen should have contradicted himself. A difference between works written in youth and old age might be natural, due either to forgetfulness or to change of opinion in the interval. But Origen exhibits contradictions in the same passage, almost in successive sentences.*

This argument is answered by Jerome in his Apology, Bk. II., Ch. 16. Rufinus brings forward but one instance, namely, that in the same passage Origen says that the Holy Spirit is of the divine essence and also numbers him among created beings. This is from the *First Principles*. Jerome points out that Eusebius and Didymus had both accepted the offensive passage as orthodox. Neither Didymus, who was himself a commentator on the *First Principles*, nor Eusebius, had ever complained that the text had been interpolated by heretics. What Didymus said was that, to use Jerome's words, 'simple men like us' did not understand Origen's real meaning, which was quite orthodox. Of course it was, we must agree. For Origen accepted the Church tradition that Father, Son and Holy Spirit were consubstantial. What he had to account for was the order of the Persons, and in particular the priority of the Father. If Origen's solution of the problem was wrong, the proper course was to propose a better one.

[1] *Liber de adulteratione librorum Origenis*, Migne P. G. XVII. 615.

Jerome and Rufinus both preferred to leave this problem
unsolved and to be content with the acceptance of a formula.
But they dealt with Origen in different ways, the one calling him a heretic, the other defending him by imputing his
reasonings to heretics.

(ii) *Other writers of unquestioned orthodoxy had had
their works corrupted by heretics; as for instance
Clement of Rome, Clement of Alexandria and
Dionysius of Alexandria.*

In regard to Clement of Rome Rufinus was misled by
the universal opinion of his day that the *Recognitions* were
his work. As for the others, the natural inference is, as
Jerome clearly sees, that (supposing the incriminated
passages to be heretical) the authors may have made mistakes;
or that incautious statements may have been allowed before
the time of Arius but carefully scrutinized after; or that
unskilful copyists may have changed the text inadvertently.
We need not spend longer on this.

(iii) *Origen himself had complained, in a letter still
extant, that his works had been corrupted by
heretics.*

The letter of Origen, which Rufinus here professes to
translate, is of great interest. It deals only with one specific
point, the possibility of the devil's salvation. Origen denies
that he ever asserted this; only a madman could have done
so. A discussion had taken place between himself and a
heretic, of which notes had been made and afterwards
published. Origen declares that he had never given the
matter a second thought until it was brought to his notice
that an incorrect version was being circulated. He discovered on inquiry that the notes had been revised for
publication with the object, as the author calmly admitted,
of 'improving' them. The letter, as given by Rufinus, goes
on to speak of a forged work which had been published
under Origen's name and which contained heretical statements. The author of this was discovered and his work
condemned as a forgery in his own presence by a group of
Origen's friends.

The only point we need consider here is that relating to
the devil's salvation. According to the *First Principles*
Origen did assert that the devil would at last be saved. It
is indeed an essential part of his system of thought. Again
and again he returns to his favourite text, 'that God may be
all in all'. Why then should he have denied it? We should
be tempted to suppose that the letter is not authentic, but

for the fact that it was available to Jerome also and must therefore have been one of the collection of Origen's letters known then to all the Greek world. But again Jerome gives us at any rate a partial answer to the argument of Rufinus. He proves that the latter has not presented the letter fairly. He has omitted the first part, which explains the second. Jerome translates this first part for us.[1] It is a bold and outspoken defence of himself by Origen against Demetrius of Alexandria and others who had condemned him. The contents are quite in Origen's manner. The Scripture itself declares, he says, that leaders and princes may go wrong; this is now being fulfilled. Yet we must not hate them, but rather pity and pray for them. We must not speak evil of any man. Michael would not even rail at the devil, but left it to God to rebuke him. Now, Origen continues, not only gross sinners, such as adulterers and thieves, shall be shut out of the kingdom of God, but evil speakers too. So careful is he, therefore, in view of this warning, that he will not even rail at the devil. But as a result of this care, some have charged him with asserting the salvation of the devil, which only a madman would assert.

By suppressing the first part of the letter with its inconvenient criticism of bishops, and also the definite statement of Origen that he will not rail even at the devil, Rufinus has given a false impression of the letter, in spite of the superficial accuracy of such portions as he quotes.

Jerome goes on to relate another fact which bears upon this question. There was current a dialogue between Origen and Candidus, a Valentinian. Candidus asserted that the devil was of a wholly evil nature and could not be saved. Origen maintained that it was by his own fault and not by his evil nature that the devil fell, and that he might have been saved if he had so willed. Candidus turns this into an admission that the devil will be saved, which Origen denies.

It is clear from all this that what Origen was forced by the logic of his thought to assert was the theoretical possibility of the devil's salvation. In no way could he avoid this. When he is dealing with ultimate problems, as in the *First Principles,* he is certainly carried beyond this theoretical possibility. In the last resort, when God is 'all in all', there is no room for a devil as such. Must we then agree with Denis, that this letter, if genuine, would prove 'that

---

[1] Jerome, *Apol.* II. Chs. 18, 19.

Origen was weak enough to retract . . . not only what he had thought, but what he continued to think'?[1] We need not go so far as this. When working out a speculative theology, as in the *First Principles,* an author must be allowed freedom to indicate, not dogmatically but suggestively for discussion, where his principles appear to lead. Practical teaching to an uneducated multitude is another thing. More care would be needed then, and a bold teacher ought not to be pressed to reduce all his speculative conclusions to categorical dogmas. Origen may quite justly have claimed this protection, especially if it be the case, as he is said to have asserted in his letter to Fabian of Rome, that the *First Principles* was published in the beginning by Ambrose without his knowledge.[2]

We need not deal with the other examples given by Rufinus of the corruption of writings by heretics. They add nothing to the force of his argument. He has certainly not established any right to give the world a garbled version of Origen's work. On the contrary, he has laid himself under the suspicion that fear of heresy is with him a stronger motive than love of truth. Both when translating Pamphilus and when quoting Origen's letter he has shown himself willing to alter the text, or to omit portions of it, on no evidence whatever, and for no purpose except to conciliate the prejudices of his readers and to give greater authority to his translation. But if he uses so much freedom in framing this preliminary defence of his work, we must clearly examine the translation itself with critical eyes. For our desire is simply to discover what Origen taught. Only by adhering strictly to the truth can we rightly estimate his services to the Church and his position in the development of Christian doctrine.

IV

THE CONTROVERSY BETWEEN JEROME AND RUFINUS

BESIDES fortifying himself by the publication of the two abovementioned introductory essays Rufinus used another weapon of defence. In his own preface he referred in glowing terms to the previous translations of Origen's works made by Jerome. Now when we recall the disturbance at

---

[1] Denis, *De la Philosophie d'Origène,* p. 375.
[2] Jerome, *Ep.* lxxxiv *ad Pamm. et Ocean.* 9.

Jerusalem only a few years before, when Jerome had openly taken his stand against Origen, we can hardly acquit Rufinus of guile in making these allusions. Jerome, according to him, 'had inspired every one with a deep longing to read Origen and study him earnestly'. He had promised to continue his own translations, but the desire to be a 'father of the word' and not a mere translator had conquered him, and he was now much too busy with his own compositions. Consequently Rufinus had consented to 'take up the work which was begun and approved by him', although he confesses that he cannot bring to it an ability comparable with that of Jerome. He goes on to describe the method of his translation, and to declare that it was the same method as that followed by Jerome himself, who had so 'smoothed over and emended' any passages likely to cause offence, that ' a Latin reader would find in them nothing out of harmony with our faith'.

All this was strictly true, but seeing that Jerome had by this time changed his opinion about Origen we cannot be surprised that he took exception to Rufinus' statements when he heard of them. For their effect was at the very least to represent him as acquiescing in every doctrine of Origen which Rufinus had thought fit not to remove from his translation. In the quarrel at Jerusalem Rufinus had taken an opposite side to Jerome, as we have seen. That is to say, he was more liberal-minded than Jerome in regard to what was or was not permissible as speculation for purposes of discussion. If, knowing Jerome as he did, Rufinus really thought that he would take his eulogy as a sincere compliment, he must have been singularly dull. We must admit, however, that in his subsequent *Defence* he does protest most strongly that his praise was sincerely meant.

The translation of the *First Principles* soon came into the hands of Jerome's friends in Italy, of whom Pammachius, Oceanus and Marcella were the chief. They were horrified by some of the doctrines still remaining in it and by the implied suggestion that Jerome would raise no objection to them. They sent him, therefore, a copy of the work with a request for information. Jerome replied by making a faithful Latin translation of the whole of the *First Principles* and sending it to Pammachius with a covering letter.[1] He admits that he had once praised Origen

[1] i.e., *Ep.* lxxxiv *ad Pamm. et Ocean.*

for his good work; he would still do so if others would not praise his errors. Origen's doctrines on the nature of the Son and the Holy Spirit, on the pre-existence of souls, on the resurrection, and on the ultimate restitution of all things, when it will be 'the same for Gabriel as for the devil, for Paul as for Caiaphas, for virgins as for prostitutes', were poisonous heresies. No Latin writer had ever yet ventured to translate his works on the *Resurrection* and on *First Principles,* or the *Stromata* and the *Commentaries,* but only the *Homilies,* or popular addresses, which were harmless. The assertion that Origen's works had been corrupted by heretics Jerome denies; both Eusebius and Didymus had taken for granted that Origen held the incriminated views. Moreover, Jerome cannot believe that Pamphilus wrote the first book of the *Defence*; it must be by Eusebius. If, however, Pamphilus did write it, his martyrdom would wash away the fault.

Jerome's defence was in the main a reasonable one. He had a right to change his opinion of Origen if he so wished. But he was not candid enough to confess that in his previous writings he had adopted as his own without question some at least of the doctrines which he was now condemning, namely, the fall of souls from a heavenly state into human bodies and the subjection of Lucifer and the other opposing powers to the rule of Christ in his future kingdom. Moreover, he cannot restrain his pen from making remarks about Rufinus which are both spiteful and untrue. The letter, however, was not addressed to Rufinus and presumably need never have come to his knowledge. Jerome had enclosed with it a short letter for Rufinus, which Pammachius was asked to deliver. This was written in a different strain. It expostulated with him for the language he had used in the preface to the *First Principles,* but it also contained expressions of esteem and friendship which should have been sufficient to avert a quarrel between the two. Unfortunately Pammachius, by what we can only regard as a gross breach of faith, did not deliver this letter. Instead, he and his friends published Jerome's letter to him, and when this came to the knowledge of Rufinus, he felt it necessary to record his own case in the form of a lengthy *Defence.*

The *Defence* enumerates, as was inevitable, the instances in which Jerome in his early days had freely accepted Origen's opinions. If Jerome had frankly admitted a change of views all this would have been irrelevant; but, as we have seen, he shrank from doing this. Little exception can be taken to the tone of Rufinus' statements; he writes warmly, but in a Christian spirit. The facts were proved beyond dispute from Jerome's own writings; he had actually used many passages of Origen which he now objected to. But over and above this there emerge from the discussion three points which reveal the different tempers of the two men. A consideration of these will help us to view the controversy in a true light.

First, Rufinus comments on Jerome's lack of charity. He is aware of his opponent's literary skill, that he can so handle words as 'to make one whom he wishes to injure and to wound appear to have received neither wounds nor injuries'. 'Any idle gossip stirs him up to fault-finding and vituperation.'[1] 'I will pardon him then, though he never pardons others, but condemns them for their words without any thought of charity.'[2] As for himself, he adds at the close : 'I ask for pardon, if I have handled the matter too roughly'.[3] Jerome's great services to the Church are sadly marred by his dogmatic and overbearing manner and by the use of his brilliant gifts for attacking those whom personally he disliked.

Again, Rufinus upholds the position that Christians are free to discuss questions even though they may not be able to reach the complete truth about them. Jerome and the world to which he belonged appear to have ruled out all discussion whatever. They are aware of no difficulties; they are troubled by no problems. It is important to remember that Rufinus, whose own belief was severely orthodox, should have been ready to defend Origen on this point, as Pamphilus had done before him. When questions are raised which the Apostle does not plainly answer, then, he says, 'we either say that we do not know, or that we stand in doubt ; and that since we do not get a full understanding but only a hint of his meaning, we do not declare but suggest the explanation'.[4] It is evidence of a genuine feeling for truth that Rufinus should have left as much as he did of the inquiries of Origen, whereas Jerome regarded them as wholly illegitimate and productive of harm.

The third point is but a particular instance of the second. Origen's only motive in ascribing a pre-existence to souls was to defend the justice of God. The different surroundings into which men were born was to him a real difficulty.

---

[1] Rufinus, *Apol.* I. 3.
[2] Rufinus, *Apol.* I. 31 (a).
[3] Rufinus, *Apol.* II. 44.
[4] Rufinus, *Apol.* I. 39.

There is probably no other Christian father who has a heart so tender, so sensitive to human suffering, as Origen had. Jerome had once followed Origen in his explanation of the problem, but afterwards, terrified by the possibility of being thought a heretic, he contemptuously rejected all such speculations. They were, he said, of pagan origin. Rufinus answered him in words that are dignified and memorable : 'Neither you (i.e. Jerome) nor Origen are forthwith to be reckoned among pagans if, as you yourself have said, it was with the desire of vindicating God's justice and of answering those who assert that all things are governed by chance or fate, with the desire, I say, of showing that the providence of God which controls the universe is just, that you declared that each soul has acquired the causes of its inequality from its movements and feelings in that previous existence which it had in the heavenly places; or even if you said that it was in harmony with the good and unchangeable and simple nature of the Trinity that every creature should at the end of all things be restored to the original condition in which it was created at the first, and that this would happen after long punishments continuing through ages of time, which God inflicts on each soul not in the spirit of one who is angry but of a healer, whose admonitions are without fault, and who because his object is to restore and to heal will at last bring his punishments to an end. How far these words are true God must judge; but they seem to me to contain little impiety against God, nor any paganism, especially when they are spoken with the desire and intention of finding some argument by which the justice of God might be vindicated.'[1] The man who could write thus, at considerable risk to his reputation, deserves our respect and gratitude.

Jerome's friends in Italy sent him notes of the chief points of Rufinus' attack. His brother Paulinian saw a copy of the work and, committing some portions to memory, communicated them to Jerome in Palestine, whither he was returning after some years' absence. From these two sources Jerome obtained sufficient information to write two books of a counter *Defence*. His one anxiety is to clear himself from any suspicion of heresy. But he will not see that the only satisfactory way of doing this is to admit that, on his own principles, he had formerly made a mistake in including Origen's opinions in his works. He says that

---

[1] Rufinus, *Apol.* II. 9. (2).

these opinions were given side by side with others, for the reader to choose from, and that sometimes he had indicated his dissent from them. 'What is my fault?' he naively asks. The fault was that, if the opinions in question were poisonous heresies, he should not have inserted them in his *Commentary on Ephesians* without the slightest warning to the reader that they were such. If on the other hand they were permissible speculations he had no ground of complaint against Rufinus for translating them into Latin.

A copy of these two books was brought to Rufinus by the captain of a trading ship which was carrying goods to Aquileia. Rufinus was disposed to reply still further, but the Christian world was now becoming scandalized at this unedifying controversy, and Chromatius the bishop of Aquileia prevailed upon him to desist. Yet he sent back a letter to Jerome which was far from friendly in tone. He intimated, apparently, that he could have published if he had so desired other facts which would have destroyed his adversary's reputation for ever. Jerome answered with a third book of his *Defence*. It adds little to the others. One characteristic sentence may be quoted : 'We were once zealous in our praise of Origen ; let us be equally zealous in condemning him now that he is condemned by the whole world.'[1] With this may be compared the utterance of Gelasius, in regard to authors whose works were prohibited to Latin readers after the Roman Council of A.D. 494. 'Rufinus, a highly religious man, wrote many books on ecclesiastical matters and certain commentaries on the Scriptures ; but since the blessed Jerome controverted him on certain points concerning freewill, we must hold the same belief as the aforementioned Jerome ; and this not only in the case of Rufinus, but of all persons whatever whom that man of faith and piety has censured.'[2]

Whatever the mistakes of Rufinus may have been, he could have stood little chance of obtaining a just hearing in the face of such a spirit as this.

V

CHARACTER OF RUFINUS' TRANSLATION

THE foregoing chapters have made it clear that we must look back upon Rufinus with two minds. First, we owe

---

[1] Jerome, *Apol.* III. 9. [2] Migne, P. G. LIX. 173.

him deep gratitude that he undertook the translation of the
First Principles at all.   He saw what a magnificent work
it was, when most of his contemporaries were content to
throw it aside as worthless.   Apart from Rufinus we might
have remained almost in the dark about its contents, and a
whole world of Christian speculation characteristic of one
of the most vigorous and brilliant periods of Church history
would have been lost to us.   And we must admire his
courage; for with all his care to cut out or soften down the
worst audacities of Origen he yet left enough to bring him
into deep suspicion with the narrower minds who then
controlled the Church in the west.   On the other hand, the
fact must be faced that we cannot trust him.   We have
already seen how he will alter anything that appears to him
to need alteration, on no other evidence than his own
subjective impression.   His most recent defender, M. Gustave
Bardy, says that 'the gaps and alterations which we discover
here and there do not astonish us, for they were announced
and foreseen'.[1]   But the truth is that no one who had nothing to go upon except the innocent-looking prefaces of
Rufinus would have the least conception of the scope of the
changes which he made.   There are not only long additions
and omissions, but mistranslations, some deliberate, some
perhaps unconscious, paraphrases in which the point and
force of the original is completely lost, and countless minor
alterations which must be studied in detail before their
cumulative effect can be appreciated.   After gathering every
Greek fragment that can be found there is less than one-
sixth of the original work available by which to check
Rufinus.   Included in this proportion are the most controverted, and therefore the more seriously altered, parts of
the work.   But even in the other parts, where fewer disputed
points of doctrine occur, we can never be quite sure that we
have Origen's thought as he himself expressed it.   The
sharp edges of the Greek have been rubbed smooth by the
rhetorical prose of Rufinus, and even with a full knowledge
of such other works of Origen as have come down to us in
the Greek it is often impossible to reconstruct the original
with any certainty.

All the fragments, whether in Greek or in Latin, that
are available for checking Rufinus have been known to
scholars for long past.   But they have not been fully utilised.

[1] Gustave Bardy, *Recherches sur l'histoire du texte et des versions latines du De Principiis d'Origène*, p. 206, Paris, 1923.

The publication of Dr. Paul Koetschau's text of the *First Principles* in 1913 marked a new era. He placed in the body of the text all the material we possess which can justly claim to belong to Origen; and not only that, but he also quoted in footnotes many passages from Jerome and other writers which are indispensable for reference. This work renders all previous texts of Origen out of date, and consequently makes it imperative to read with caution all previous descriptions of his theology. 'It is not too much to say,' comments M. de Faye, 'that the confidence which has always been placed in these Latin versions renders obsolete every exposition of Origen's theology which saw the light before M. Koetschau's edition of the *De Principiis*.'[1] In the following translation I have followed Koetschau's reconstruction throughout; not simply because it is the only one we possess, but also because in the course of many years' reading of the text I have seen no reason to differ materially from his conclusions. I acknowledge with much gratitude all the help I have received from this admirable work.[2]

Koetschau's Introduction, pp. lxxxviii-cxxxvii, contains a complete examination of Rufinus' translation and a list of the passages available for correcting it. The reader who wishes to study the matter in detail will do well to turn to this. Here, however, I will make a brief summary of the material referred to.

i. The *Philocalia*,[3] a collection of extracts from Origen's works made by Basil and Gregory of Nazianzus, contains Bk. III. Ch. i and Bk. IV. Chs. i-iii of the *First Principles*. These form by far the greater part of the Greek fragments now extant.

ii. The treatise or letter sent by Justinian to Mennas, Patriarch of Constantinople, before the 2nd Council of Constantinople, A.D. 553.[4] This letter contains numerous extracts from the *First Principles*, which formed the basis on which Origen was condemned at the Council. Whether this condemnation took place at the Council itself, or pre-

---

[1] Eugène de Faye, *op. cit.* i. p. 54.
[2] *Die griechischen christlichen Schriftsteller der Ersten Drei Jahrhunderte. Origenes Werke, De Principiis, herausgegeben von Dr. Paul Koetschau.* Leipzig 1913.
[3] The *Philocalia of Origen*, by J. Armitage Robinson. Cambridge, 1893. Eng. Trans. of the *Philocalia*, by the Rev. George Lewis, T. & T. Clark, 1911.
[4] The letter is printed in Mansi, *Concilia*, Vol. IX. pp. 524-533.

viously at the local synod of A.D. 543, makes no difference
for our purpose.

iii. The fifteen Anathemas against Origen decreed at
the above-mentioned Council or synod.[1] Koetschau gives
a place in his text to Nos. 2 to 6 of these Anathemas, on
the ground that they record, though not perhaps always
word for word, the teaching of Origen in the *First
Principles*.

iv. Various fragments taken from Antipater of Bostra,
Leontius of Byzantium, Theophilus of Alexandria, Epiphanius, Gregory of Nyssa and others.

Koetschau admits in all forty-three Greek fragments,
varying in length from a few words to the extensive passages
taken from the *Philocalia*. Of these some fourteen are
entirely missing from the text of Rufinus; nine are shortened, altered or incomplete; five are inaccurately translated;
and the remaining fifteen are given with reasonable, though
not always strict, accuracy.

As I have stated above, M. Gustave Bardy disputes the
conclusions reached by Koetschau in regard to the passages
taken from Justinian's letter to Mennas and the Anathemas.
He contends that the former are divorced from their context
and that in some cases they may be deformed or interpolated.
This is not likely. The fact that there were many followers
of Origen even in the sixth century—it was their existence
and influence which made Justinian so eager to secure
Origen's condemnation—would have rendered it necessary
to be careful. There was also plenty of material for condemnation, according to Justinian's ideas, without the need
of perversion or exaggeration. Bardy does not in fact deny
that Justinian's letter gives us our best information about
Origen's true teaching, though he would use it with caution.
But he makes a strong objection to the inclusion of the
Anathemas in the text. These have in view, according to
him, not so much Origen himself as the 'so-called Origenists
who were contemporaries of Justinian'.[2] An examination
will show, however, that they differ but little from the letter
of Justinian. In regard to Bardy's further objection to
Koetschau's reconstruction of Bk. I. Ch. viii.,[3] on the
ground that it is too hazardous, we must admit that the
piecing together of the different fragments is ingeniously
done and that too much reliance must not be placed on the

---

[1] For the text see Mansi, *Concilia,* Vol. IX., pp. 396-400.
[2] Bardy, *op. cit.,* p. 205.   [3] See below, pp. 66-68.

precise order and connexion of the passages. But there
can be no doubt whatever that they belong to this chapter,
for every fragment of testimony we possess speaks with
the same voice about Origen's doctrine of the fall of the
angels and their ultimate restoration. 'Who gave you
leave', cries Jerome to Rufinus, 'to omit so much from your
translation?'[1] Unless we fill the gaps left by Rufinus
with the material which every other writer who deals with
the *First Principles* declares to have been there, we can
have no hope of ascertaining what Origen really wrote.

The Latin translation sent by Jerome to his friends in
Italy has unfortunately been lost. Jerome's usual method
of translation was no different from that of Rufinus, but on
this occasion he adhered strictly to the original. 'In my
translation of the *First Principles,*' he says, 'I expressed in
a simple way what was contained in the Greek text.'[2] And
Rufinus corroborates this when he complains of Jerome that
'he re-interpreted these very books which I had translated,
and inserted all those passages which had been omitted by
me as being of doubtful authenticity.'[3] Some years after,
this translation, though carefully kept back from publication
by Pammachius, was circulated in a garbled form by a
friend to whom he had lent it for a short time. A copy of
this came into the hands of one Avitus, who wrote to Jerome
for an explanation. In reply Jerome sent him a true copy,
accompanied by a letter containing long quotations, many
of them literal, of the alleged heretical teachings of the
work. This letter is extant and provides an authority of
first-class character for supplementing the gaps in Rufinus'
translation and correcting him elsewhere. Koetschau gives
a list of more than fifty quotations obtained from it. All
are printed in his edition, either as part of the text or in
footnotes, and all are included in the present translation.[4]

M. Bardy, however, seeks to discredit Jerome's translation. Jerome, he says, changed the delicate *nuances* of
Origen into categorical statements, presenting in an absolute
manner theories capable of a generous interpretation; he
may have translated Origen better, but he understood him
less, lacking what Rufinus possessed, the sympathy which
gives intelligence.[5] If Bardy means that Origen's theories

---

[1] Jerome, *Apol.* II. 11b.
[2] Jerome, *Apol.* I. 7.
[3] Rufinus, *Apol.* I. 21.
[4] For the letter, see Jerome, *Ep. cxxiv, ad Avitum.*
[5] Bardy, *op. cit.,* p. 206.

were always subject to revision, put forward, as he so often
reminds us, for discussion rather than as unalterable dogmas, and that while Rufinus partly understood this temper
of mind Jerome had no sympathy with it at all, then his
contention is true. It is true also that Jerome means
throughout to make the worst of Origen and Rufinus the
best, each from his own viewpoint. The modern reader can
and must allow for this. But no arguments will alter the
fact that Rufinus has left many gaps which without Jerome's
help we could not fill at all, and that time after time he
deliberately transforms, abbreviates or renders inaccurately
his original. Nor must we suppose that Origen's teaching,
though offered in humility and with a readiness to be convinced by better knowledge, lacked definiteness. It was
this definiteness which Rufinus feared, and which he endeavoured to obscure in his translation. On the other hand,
Jerome's presentation of Origen, though blunt, is full and
fair. The passages quoted in the Letter to Avitus have a
genuine Origenistic ring about them and there is no evidence
whatever of hardening or exaggeration.

Of Rufinus' ordinary method of translation we may gain
the truest idea by studying the two long passages of which
the originals are preserved in the *Philocalia*. Generally
speaking, the subject matter is here unobjectionable and
Rufinus, even when abiding by his own cautious rules, had
no need to alter, omit or interpolate. The reader of the
present translation can form his own judgment; for in it
Origen and Rufinus are set side by side and the two translations are made to agree in wording so far as is possible,
that is, wherever it seemed clear that Rufinus was endeavouring to adhere closely to his original. He does not often do
this, it is true. His method, like that of Jerome himself,
is what we should call paraphrasing rather than translating.
But he gives the general sense, for the most part, of what
Origen wrote; and where he does this we must be satisfied.

The two passages are Bk. III. Ch. i, on the subject of
Free Will, and Bk. IV. Chs. i-iii on the Inspiration and
Interpretation of the Scriptures.[1] Koetschau has examined
these carefully and obtained the following results: Rufinus
has omitted twenty-eight passages, the great majority of
which, however, are very short, consisting of only a few
words or a line or two. He has made twenty-two additions,
again mostly not more than a few words in length. And

[1] See below, pp. 157 ff. and 256 ff.

there are forty-five cases of inaccurate translation, some being due to a misunderstanding of the Greek and others to the desire of altering it for dogmatic reasons. It must be sufficient here to make a few general observations on these irregularities.

Of the additions made by Rufinus many are for the sake of clearness. He is fond, too, of rhetorical embellishment and will often put in a didactic or pietistic touch that is wanting in Origen. Sometimes, when texts are quoted, he will add an extra one that occurs to him or insert a fresh illustration. In other cases a dogmatic motive is apparent. Origen's dry, scientific statements and candid admission of difficulties are scarcely ever left as they stand. The assertion that the intelligence of some animals comes near to human reason is carefully toned down.[1] The desire of Origen to prove the goodness of God is transformed by Rufinus into a desire to keep close to the faith of the Church and to test all things by 'the rule of piety'.[2]

Some of the smaller omissions may be accidental. Others are not highly significant. But Rufinus has evidently hesitated to reproduce Origen's statement that certain of Moses' laws were irrational or impossible.[3] Similarly, he does not care to translate Origen's criticism on a literal interpretation of St. Matt. v. 28, 29—what good would it do to cut out the right eye?[4] He fears the lengths to which allegorical interpretation may go and omits the advice to discover in Scripture the 'depths of the wisdom of God'.[5] In the longest of his two omissions it has generally been supposed that the same distrust is to be observed; but I have given reasons in the notes for thinking that Rufinus did not fully understand this passage.[6]

The inaccurate renderings are often pure mistakes. Not seldom Rufinus altogether misses the point of the Greek. On the whole, however, we can gather from him fairly well the main drift of the arguments. But in the case of a keen thinker like Origen the construction of every sentence, the balance of phrases and often the very order of the words are important; and it would be folly to deny that, for all the good intentions of Rufinus, we lose much when we turn to his version from the Greek.

---

[1] See below, p. 160.
[2] See below, p. 193.
[3] See below, p. 290.
[4] See below, p. 293.
[5] See below, p. 296.
[6] See below, p. 299.

VI

THE DOCTRINE OF THE FIRST PRINCIPLES

IT is not clear what was the exact meaning attached by Origen to the title Περὶ 'Αρχῶν. The phrase may indicate that the work is an inquiry into the elementary principles of the Christian religion; or, interpreted in a wider sense, it may signify that Origen intended to present his readers with a complete philosophy of religion. This is suggested by his own assertion, made at the beginning of the book, that he was framing a 'single body of doctrine'.[1] There may be in addition some thought of the 'principalities', with whose history and destiny parts of the book are concerned, and also of the 'beginnings' of the universe, and consequently of the end which, in Origen's oft-repeated phrase, must be like the beginning. The word 'Αρχαί will cover all these meanings and probably Origen meant it to be understood in a comprehensive way. As we have seen, the title was not a new one, since Clement of Alexandria had already used it.

The thoughts to which Origen's speculations led him proved strange and disturbing to Christians of later ages. But we need not doubt that they were natural enough to the age and intellectual environment in which they arose. It never occurred to Origen that he was anything but an orthodox defender of the faith. All he tried to do was to work out its implications for the educated world of his time. Problems which do not arise in simple minds were continually being raised by his pupils and by the heretics in their rival theological schools. What is the explanation of apparently undeserved suffering? Has man free will, or is this an illusion? What happened before this world was created, and what will happen after it has come to an end? What is the origin and nature of the human soul? Are the stars alive? Are there worlds in the sky, where spirits live? Origen believed that it was right to investigate such problems. Not all of them could be solved. But some might be, and the Christian thinker must do his best.

Other problems were of even greater importance. It was universally acknowledged in the Church that Father, Son and Spirit constituted the Trinity, that each was divine, and that a vast gulf separated them from the universe of created beings. But no authority had as yet laid down precisely

---

[1] See below, p. 6.

how they were related to one another, or had attempted to answer a whole series of questions on the subject of the divine nature which present themselves at once to the mind of a thoughtful believer. This was the task which Origen, as a comparatively young man, took in hand. He was not altogether a pioneer, for Pantænus and Clement had prepared the way. Origen's achievement was to focus all previous speculation, after passing it through his own brilliant intellect, into a coherent system. Though subject to every limitation of his age, he yet had the scientific spirit and used a scientific method. He follows where reason leads him. He is sensitive to difficulties and often acknowledges ignorance. It is indeed his spirit and method rather than his conclusions which are of permanent value. For the Church, no doubt wisely in the main, set aside his chief doctrines, branding them as heretical. But she would not have reached so sure a conviction about the safe path of theological progress had it not been for the stimulus provided by this bold and clear thinker, who brought every question fearlessly into the light of day.

M. de Faye has rightly observed that Origen's system is in the same class with the Gnostic speculations of his time.[1] The Father is the fount and origin of all being, and is pure spirit. The problem is to connect him with the existent material world. The Gnostics bridged the gulf by a series of descents from spirit into matter, to be followed at last by a restoration of the spiritual seeds or sparks imprisoned in matter to their original home. On this theme they played with all manner of fantastic variations. The Christian theology, as expounded by Origen, severely avoids these extravagances; yet the process of descent and ascent runs through it all. The Son is begotten of the Father by an eternal act of will. Gnostic theories of emanation are rejected on the ground that they involve a division of the divine nature. The eternal generation of the Son is as it were an expansion rather than a division of the divine nature. But Origen, in his keen desire to represent this eternal act as proceeding from will and intelligence and not as a fatalistic process, sometimes describes the begetting as a creating, and the Son as a created being. It was this that puzzled Rufinus, how Origen could be both orthodox and unorthodox at the same time. But there is really neither any doubt about Origen's words, nor difficulty about his

[1] Eugène de Faye, *op. cit.* I., p. 100 f.

thought. He relied on such scriptural passages as 'the
first-born of all creation'[1] and he emphasises over and over
again the secondary position of the Son. The Holy Spirit
is still less in degree, but all three are consubstantial,
partaking of the fulness of the divine essence. Both Son
and Spirit are genuine Beings, not simply divine attributes,
and Origen had been taught that an indication of them was
to be seen in the two cherubim who, in Isaiah's vision,
cover the face of God.[2]

A fresh departure is made by the creation of rational
beings, called either minds or souls. These are definitely
outside the Godhead, as the Son and Spirit are definitely
within. Nevertheless they are spiritual creatures, made in
God's own image. Origen inquires whether they were made
infinite in number and decides that they were not. By a
curious limitation of the divine power, which is characteristic
of his thought, he tells us that God made exactly as many
as he could control. They were all equal, and apparently
identical. But they had free will, and this faculty caused
movements to arise within them. Some remained in their
original condition, but others fell away from God. Thus
was variety and diversity introduced into the world, not
by God's ordering, but by the free action of created souls.
The fall necessitated the use of bodies; at first bright and
transparent bodies such as stars have, and afterwards darker
and heavier ones. In this way the various orders of angelic
beings arose and below them the daemons; for all are of
one original nature and ascend or descend in accordance
with the movements of their own wills. From one class of
these spirits the human race was constituted, and the
qualities of each human soul and the environment into
which it is born are due to its merits or demerits in previous
existences. God is entirely just and has no favourites;
souls are the masters of their own destinies and each obtains
what he deserves.

The matter which was necessary to serve as bodies for
the fallen spirits was created by God and is not eternal.
Other matter had to be created to provide them with a
dwelling-place. Matter is such that it can be adapted to
an infinite variety of forms and purposes. The sojourn of
man in this present world is designed to discipline and
educate him, so that he may rise in the scale of being. He
may, however, fall; and just as the utmost heights lie open

[1] Col. i. 15.　　　[2] See below, pp. 32 and 311.

to him, so do the lowest depths. Punishment is always remedial, never purely retributive. However low a spirit may fall, he may rise again; and however high he may soar, a fresh fall is still possible. It was this condition of things which gave rise to Jerome's caustic criticism that according to Origen angels might become devils and the devil an archangel. That is indeed what Origen meant to assert; that as no limit could be placed to human wilfulness and sin, so no limit could be placed to the power of God's love, when once the human soul had responded to its healing and uplifting influence.

Logically speaking, such a process might continue indefinitely. But clear as was Origen's head, his heart insisted on having the last word here. Did not the Scriptures speak of a time when 'God shall be all in all'? Thus Origen was led to the belief that one day the love of God would prove stronger even than the freedom of man and that all created spirits would return to that unity and perfection which was theirs at the beginning. Then bodies, which had grown progressively finer as their wearers ascended, would either be discarded for ever, or would be etherealised into garments of the lightest and most tenuous nature conceivable. And this event, Origen knew well, must be far distant. He felt how intractable was the human spirit, how dull and impervious to enlightenment it could be. To meet this difficulty he assumed a succession of worlds, not identical in form, but each framed out of the materials of its predecessor and each, we may suppose, advancing a step further on the road to the ultimate perfection.

The pre-existence and the future re-incarnation of the human soul was a doctrine that met with much opposition in the Church on account of its obvious connexion with Greek and oriental speculation. But it led even Origen himself into a difficulty when he came to discuss the Incarnation. Jesus, as man, possessed a soul. Had this soul a pre-existence, like all others? Origen answered that it had. In the beginning, when other souls were declining from God, the soul of Jesus retained its innocence and continued by its own free choice in such close association with the Word of God that finally habit became changed into nature and an indissoluble union was created. It was this soul, already united with the Word of God, which took flesh of the Virgin Mary and appeared among men. And since there were multitudes of spiritual beings who had never come to earth, Origen supposed that Christ would visit them, too, in their celestial abodes, would assume their nature and would even suffer for them.

The system thus outlined was based upon a belief in man's free-will.   Origen is fully conscious of the importance of free-will and he devotes a long chapter to examining it and meeting objections.   All the Gnostic systems, and most other speculations of this period, ran in a fatalistic direction. If Origen appears to us to spend unnecessary trouble in his effort to establish the fact of human freedom, we must remember that it is largely this which gives the Christian tone and colour to all his thought.

It is obvious that, however sincerely Origen started from the simple Christian faith, he ended in speculations which were only remotely connected with it.   The real source of these speculations is to be found in the intellectual atmos-phere of the time, in which the ideas of Platonists, Stoics and orientals were mingled.   But Origen claimed to find it all in the Scriptures.   Philo the Jew had discovered, or more probably perfected, a method of using the Old Testa-ment by which its varied contents, words, phrases and stories, were made to suggest philosophical ideas.   Christian teachers at Alexandria continued to use this method, chiefly, though not solely, for the Old Testament, the diffi-culties of which, moral, theological and historical, challenged the inquiring mind to discover hidden meanings.   The Church had rested its faith too largely on the Old Testa-ment, with arguments from miracle and prophecy, to be able to look at it boldly and confess that it recorded a gradually developing revelation of God.   This never seems to enter Origen's mind as a possibility.   For him the Scriptures are everywhere perfect and complete, when rightly understood, to the minutest detail.   He feels that the marvellous success of Christianity in the face of a hostile world guarantees the New Testament story, and that this in its turn guarantees the Old which predicts it.   The Scrip-tures being thus established as divine writings may be made the basis of any thoughts which the intelligent reader can put into them or extract from them.   Origen has three chapters on the Scriptures and the true method of their interpretation.   It would be an exaggeration to say that the method is wholly arbitrary, for it has its rules.   But it despises the history, ignores the poetry, and turns all that is warm and human into frigid intellectual reasonings.   Its greatest value was that, in the hands of Origen at any rate, it kept the idea of God on a high moral and spiritual level and free from the distortions that are bound to creep in when the Old Testament is accepted in its literal sense as a perfect revelation. Beyond that, it preserved the treasure of these writings against possible rationalistic attack until the advent of happier days when the Church could with more certainty distinguish the temporary from the permanent and discern beneath superficial imperfections the abiding truth and divine inspiration.

The weakness of Origen's system, considered as a whole, lies in its assumption that the entire cosmic process is a mistake, due to the misuse of free-will. He regards it as axiomatic that the end must be like the beginning. Is there nothing, then, to be accomplished in these vast stretches of time? Can God do no more than restore things to the position they were in before the primeval fall? If we are to take Origen literally, it would appear that God cannot. History, however long drawn out, is but the mending of an original fault. We have it on good authority that in one passage he even said that perfected souls would be swallowed up in the divine essence from which they sprang.[1] Such a system of thought is at heart pessimistic, and it was perhaps some instinctive apprehension of this fact which caused the Church to turn away from it. But we must not be blind to the nobility of Origen's achievement. It is the work of a good and a brave man whose supreme desire was to know the truth. As such it is still worthy of our respectful attention, and wherever the love of truth is found, there will Origen never fail to receive his meed of gratitude and reverence.

[1] See below, pp. 254 f. note 10.

BIBLIOGRAPHY

Origenis Opera Omnia. Edited by C. and C. V. Delarue. Reprinted in Migne, *Patrologia Graeca*, Vols. XI-XVII. The *De Principiis* and the *Epistle of Africanus to Origen*, with *Origen's Reply*, are in Vol. XI. Pamphilus' *Defence of Origen* is in Vol. XVII, where it is followed by Rufinus' tract on *The Corruption of the Works of Origen*. The *Panegyric* of St. Gregory Thaumaturgus on Origen is to be found in *P. G.*, Vol. X, pp. 1049 ff.

Origenis Opera Omnia. Elited by C. H. E. Lommatzsch. Based upon Delarue, Vols. I-XXXV. Berlin, 1831-48.

Origenes Werke, in the series 'Die griechischen christlichen Schriftsteller der ersten drei Jahrhunderte, herausgegeben von der Kirchenväter Commission der königl. preussischen Akademie der Wissenschaften'. Leipsig 1891 etc. The edition of the *De Principiis*, by Dr. Paul Koetschau, is the fifth volume of this series. These texts of Origen supersede all previous ones.

P. D. Huet, *Origeniana.* Reprinted in Migne, *P. G.*, Vol. XVII, pp. 633 ff.

Realencyclopädie fur protestantische Theologie und Kirche. Herzog and Hauck. Art. *Origenes*, by E. Preuschen.

The Catholic Encyclopædia. Art. *Origen and Origenism* by F. Prat, Vol. XI, pp. 306 ff.

Smith and Wace. *Dictionary of Christian Biography.* Art. *Origenes* by B. F. Westcott.

M'Clintock and Strong. *Cyclopædia of Biblical, Theological and Ecclesiastical Literature*, Vol. VII, pp. 428 ff.

W. R. Inge. Art. *Alexandrian Theology* in *Hastings' Encyclopædia of Religion and Ethics*, Vol. I, pp. 308 ff.

A. Harnack. *History of Dogma.* English translation by Neil Buchanan and others. For Origen, see Vol. II, pp. 319-380.

Karl F. Schnitzer, *Origenes über die Grundlehren der Glaubenswissenschaft.* Stuttgart, 1835.

E. R. Redepenning. *Origenes. Eine Darstellung seines Lebens und seiner Lehre.* Bonn, 1841.

The Writings of Origen. Translated into English by the Rev. Frederick Crombie, being Vols. X and XXIII of the *Ante-Nicene Christian Library*, Edinburgh, 1869 and 1872. Vol. X contains the *De Principiis*, together with the *Letter of Africanus to Origen* and *Origen's Reply* and a *Letter of Origen to Gregory Thaumaturgus;* and also the first book of the *Contra Celsum*. Vol. XXIII contains the rest of the *Contra Celsum*.

Gregory Thaumaturgus. *Panegyric on Origen.* Translated by the Rev. S. D. F. Salmond, in Vol. XX of the *Ante-Nicene Christian Library*, Edinburgh 1871.

M. J. Denis. *De la Philosophie d'Origène*. Paris, 1884.

J. Armitage Robinson. *The Philocalia of Origen.* The Text revised with a critical Introduction and Indices. Cambridge, 1893.

A. E. Brooke. *The Commentary of Origen on S. John's Gospel.* The Text revised with a critical Introduction and Indices. Cambridge, 1896.

A. E. Brooke. *Origen* in *Lefroy's Lectures on Ecclesiastical History.* James Nisbet & Co., 1896.

G. Capitaine. *De Origenis Ethica.* Münster. 1898.

F. Diekamp. *Die Origenistischen Streitigkeiten im sechsten Jahrhundert.* Münster, 1899.

W. Fairweather. *Origen and Greek Patristic Theology.* Edinburgh, 1901.

J. Brochet, *S. Jérome et ses ennemis*, Paris, 1906.

L. B. Radford. *Three Teachers of Alexandria : Theognostus, Pierius and Peter.* A study in the early history of Origenism and Anti-Origenism. Cambridge, 1908.

The Philocalia of Origen. A compilation of selected passages from Origen's works made by St. Gregory of Nazianzus and St. Basil of Cæsarea, translated into English by the Rev. George Lewis. T. & T. Clark, 1911.

Charles Bigg. *The Christian Platonists of Alexandria.* Oxford, 1886. Reprinted, with some additions and corrections by F. E. Brightman, 1913.

Gustave Bardy. *Recherches sur l'histoire du texte et des versions latines du De Principiis d'Origène.* Paris, 1923.

Eugène de Faye. *Gnostiques et Gnosticisme.* Paris, 1925.

Eugène de Faye. *Origen and his Work.* Authorised translation by Fred Rothwell. George Allen and Unwin, 1926.

Eugène de Faye. *Origène, sa vie, son oeuvre, sa pensée.* Vol. I, Sa biographie et ses écrits. Vol. II, L'ambiance philosophique. Vol. III, La doctrine. [Vols.

37, 43 and 44 of the *Bibliothèque de l'Ecole des Hautes Etudes, Sciences Religieuses.*] Paris, 1927-8. The second volume contains, on pp. 216-239, a useful description of the works on Origen by Huet, Redepenning, Denis, Bigg and Harnack.

R. B. Tollinton. *Selections from the Commentaries and Homilies of Origen.* Translated into English. S.P.C.K., 1929.

R. B. Tollinton. *Alexandrine Teaching on the Universe.* George Allen and Unwin, 1932.

R. Cadiou. *Introduction au système d'Origène.* Paris, 1932.

PREFACE OF RUFINUS

1. I know that many of the brethren, impelled by their earnest desire to understand the scriptures, have made requests to a number of scholars well versed in Greek literature to put Origen into Roman dress and present him to Latin ears. And when, in furtherance of this object, our brother and colleague, at the entreaty of bishop Damasus, translated two of the Homilies on the Song of Songs from Greek into Latin, he composed so fine and noble a preface to that work, as to inspire everyone with a deep longing to read Origen and study him seriously. For he said that the text, 'The king hath brought me into his chamber', might well be applied to the soul of Origen; and added that while in the rest of his works Origen had surpassed all other writers, in the Song of Songs he had even surpassed himself. He promises, indeed, in that very preface, that he himself will give us not only these books on the Song of Songs but also many other works of Origen in a translation for Roman ears. I can see, however, that he derives most pleasure from the works of his own pen. He pursues a task that promises greater fame, that of being a 'father of the word'[1] and not a mere translator. For this reason I take up the work which was begun and approved by him. Nevertheless I cannot adorn the writings of this great man with a degree of eloquence comparable to his. Consequently I fear it may happen through my fault that the man whom he has deservedly praised as being the next teacher of wisdom and knowledge in the Church after the apostles may, owing to my poor style, appear far inferior to what he really is.

2. It was this oft-recurring thought which kept me silent and prevented me from yielding to the continual entreaties of the brethren to attempt this work. But so powerful is your influence, most faithful brother Macarius, that not even my want of skill could any longer provide grounds for resistance. Accordingly, not to suffer you to make too heavy a claim upon me, I gave way, even against my previous determination; but on the condition and understanding that in my translation I would follow as far as possible the rule observed by my predecessors and especially

---

[1] See Plato *Symposium* 177 D.

by the distinguished man whom I mentioned above. For
he, when translating into Latin more than seventy treatises
of Origen, called Homilies, and also a number of his commentaries on St. Paul's epistles, both of which are known
to contain in the original a good many statements likely to
cause offence, so smoothed over and emended these in his
translation, that a Latin reader would find in them nothing
out of harmony with our faith. His example, therefore, I
am following to the best of my ability; if not with an equal
degree of eloquence, yet at least observing the same rules,
and taking care not to reproduce such passages from the
books of Origen as are found to be inconsistent with and
contrary to his true teaching.

3. The cause of these variations I have explained to
you more fully in the *Apologeticus,* a work written by
Pamphilus in defence of Origen's books, to which I added
a very brief tract, showing, as I think, by clear proofs that
these have been corrupted in many places by heretics and
evilly disposed persons.[1] This is especially the case with
the books which you are now pressing me to translate,
namely those entitled *Peri Archon,* which may be rendered
either *Concerning First Principles* or *Concerning Principalities.* These books are indeed most obscure and difficult
for other reasons. For in them Origen discusses questions
on which philosophers, after spending their whole lives in
the task, have succeeded in discovering nothing. But our
author made it his aim, so far as he possibly could, to turn
into a religious direction man's belief in a Creator and his
reasonings about the created world, which philosophers have
used to advocate irreligion. Wherever, therefore, I have
found in his books anything contrary to the reverent statements made by him about the Trinity in other places, I
have either omitted it as a corrupt and interpolated passage,
or reproduced it in a form that agrees with the doctrine
which I have often found him affirming elsewhere. If,
however, speaking as he does to men of knowledge and
discernment, he has occasionally expressed himself obscurely
in the effort to be brief, I have, to make the passage clearer,
added such remarks on the same subject as I have read
in a fuller form in his other books, bearing in mind the
need of explanation. But I have said nothing of my own,
simply giving back to him his own statements found in
other places.

---

[1] See Introduction, pp. xii ff.

4. I have written thus in my preface by way of precaution, to prevent slanderers from supposing that they have once again discovered some matter for accusation against me. For you have seen what perverse and contentious men will do. The fact is, I have undertaken this heavy labour, God and your prayers helping me, not to shut the mouths of slanderers (for this is impossible, unless indeed God should do it), but to provide material for those who desire to advance towards the knowledge of things. One request, however, I solemnly make of every one who shall either transcribe or read these books, in the sight of God the Father and the Son and the Holy Spirit, by his faith in the kingdom to come, by the mystery of the resurrection from the dead, by the 'everlasting fire which is prepared for the devil and his angels',[1] that, as he would not possess for an eternal inheritance that place where there is 'weeping and gnashing of teeth',[2] and where ' their fire is not quenched and their worm dieth not',[3] he shall neither add anything to this writing, nor take anything away, nor interpolate anything, nor change anything, but shall compare his copy with the originals from which it was made, and shall emend it and make it distinct to the very letter, and shall not allow a manuscript to remain incorrect or indistinct, lest the difficulty of ascertaining the meaning, if the manuscript is not distinct, should increase the obscurities of the work for those that read it.

[1] St. Matt. XXV. 41.
[2] St. Matt. VIII. 12; St. Luke XIII. 28.
[3] Is. LXVI. 24; St. Mark IX. 48.

BOOK I

PREFACE

GREEK

1. All[1] who believe and are convinced that grace and truth came by Jesus Christ[2] and that Christ is the truth (in accordance with his own saying, 'I am the truth'[3])

LATIN

1. All who believe and are convinced that grace and truth came by Jesus Christ,[2] and who know Christ to be the truth (in accordance with his own saying, 'I am the truth'[3]),

LATIN

derive the knowledge which calls men to lead a good and blessed life from no other source but the very words and teaching of Christ. By the words of Christ we do not mean only those which formed his teaching when he was made man and dwelt in the flesh, since even before that Christ the Word of God was in Moses and the prophets. For without the Word of God how could they have prophesied about Christ? In proof of which we should not find it difficult to show from the divine scriptures how that Moses or the prophets were filled with the spirit of Christ in all their words and deeds, were we not anxious to confine the present work within the briefest possible limits. I count it sufficient, therefore, to quote this one testimony of Paul, taken from the epistle which he writes to the Hebrews, where he speaks as follows : 'By faith Moses, when he was grown up, refused to be called the son of Pharaoh's daughter, choosing rather to suffer affliction with the people of God than to enjoy the pleasures of sin for a season, accounting the reproach of Christ greater riches than the treasures of Egypt.'[4] And as for the fact that Christ spoke in his apostles after his ascension into heaven, this is shown by Paul in the following passage : 'Or do ye seek a proof of him that speaketh in me, that is, Christ?'[5]

2. Many of those, however, who profess to believe in Christ, hold conflicting opinions not only on small and trivial questions but also on some that are great and important; on the nature, for instance, of God or of the Lord Jesus Christ or of the Holy Spirit, and in addition on the natures of those created beings, the dominions and the holy powers. In view of this it seems

---

[1] Frag. 1, Koetschau, from Eusebius, *Con. Marcellum* i. 4.
[2] St. John I. 17.
[3] St. John XIV. 6.
[4] Hebr. XI. 24 ff.
[5] 2 Cor. XIII. 3.

necessary first to lay down a definite line and unmistakable rule in regard to each of these, and to postpone the inquiry into other matters until afterwards. For just as there are many among Greeks and barbarians alike who promise us the truth, and yet we gave up seeking for it from all who claimed it for false opinions after we had come to believe that Christ was the Son of God and had become convinced that we must learn the truth from him; in the same way when we find many who think they hold the doctrine of Christ, some of them differing in their beliefs from the Christians of earlier times, and yet the teaching of the church, handed down in unbroken succession from the apostles, is still preserved and continues to exist in the churches up to the present day, we maintain that that only is to be believed as the truth which in no way conflicts with the tradition of the church and the apostles.

3. But the following fact should be understood. The holy apostles, when preaching the faith of Christ, took certain doctrines, those namely which they believed to be necessary ones, and delivered them in the plainest terms to all believers, even to such as appeared to be somewhat dull in the investigation of divine knowledge. The grounds of their statements they left to be investigated by such as should merit the higher gifts of the Spirit and in particular by such as should afterwards receive through the Holy Spirit himself the graces of language, wisdom and knowledge. There were other doctrines, however, about which the apostles simply said that things were so, keeping silence as to the how or why; their intention undoubtedly being to supply the more diligent of those who came after them, such as should prove to be lovers of wisdom, with an exercise on which to display the fruit of their ability. The men I refer to are those who train themselves to become worthy and capable of receiving wisdom.

4. The kind of doctrines which are believed in plain terms through the apostolic teaching are the following:—

First, that God is one, who created and set in order all things, and who, when nothing existed, caused the universe to be.[1] He is God from the first creation and foundation of the world, the God of all righteous men, of Adam, Abel, Seth, Enos, Enoch, Noah, Shem, Abraham, Isaac, Jacob, of the twelve patriarchs, of Moses and the prophets. This God, in these last days,[2] according to the previous announcements made through his prophets, sent the Lord Jesus Christ, first for the purpose of calling Israel, and secondly, after the unbelief of the people of Israel, of calling the Gentiles also. This just and good God, the Father of our Lord Jesus Christ, himself gave the law, the prophets and the gospels, and he is God both of the apostles and also of the Old and New Testaments.

---

[1] See Hermas, *Mand.* I. 1.   [2] See Heb. I. 1.

Then again: Christ Jesus, he who came to earth, was begotten of the Father before every created thing.[1] And after he had ministered to the Father in the foundation of all things, for 'all things were made through him',[2] in these last times he emptied himself and was made man, was made flesh, although he was God;[3] and being made man, he still remained what he was, namely, God. He took to himself a body like our body, differing in this alone, that it was born of a virgin and of the Holy Spirit. And this Jesus Christ was born and suffered in truth and not merely in appearance, and truly died our common death. Moreover he truly rose from the dead, and after the resurrection companied with his disciples and was then taken up into heaven.

Then again, the apostles delivered this doctrine, that the Holy Spirit is united in honour and dignity with the Father and the Son. In regard to him it is not yet clearly known whether he is to be thought of as begotten or unbegotten,[4] or as being himself also a Son of God or not; but these are matters which we must investigate to the best of our power from holy scripture, inquiring with wisdom and diligence. It is, however, certainly taught with the utmost clearness in the Church, that

---

[1] Jerome, *Ep. ad Avitum* 2, says that in the beginning of the first book of the *De Principiis* Origen declared that 'Christ was not begotten the Son of God, but made such'. (Latin *factum* = Gr. γενητόν). Rufinus has modified this statement. It is probable, however, that γενητόν and γεννητόν were not very clearly distinguished in Origen's time. Origen certainly taught that the Son and Holy Spirit were created, but he thought that the alternative to this was to assert that they were unbegotten, which was true of the Father alone. See the quotation from this same letter below, and Int. p. xxxii.

[2] St. John I. 3.

[3] See Heb. I. 1; Phil. II. 7; St. John I. 14.

[4] Jerome (*Ep. ad Avitum* 2) says: 'As third in dignity and honour after the Father and the Son he (i.e. Origen) adds the Holy Spirit, of whom, though he professes to be ignorant whether he was created or uncreated, yet later on he has expressed his real opinion, when he insists that nothing is uncreated except God the Father alone.' Rufinus has modified Origen's 'created or uncreated' (γενητὸς ἢ ἀγένητος) to 'begotten or unbegotten' (Lat. *natus aut innatus* = Gr. γεννητὸς ἢ ἀγέννητος). Origen explains his doctrine in his *Comm. in Ioh.* II. x. 'But we must inquire whether, if it be true that "all things were created through him", the Holy Spirit also was created through him. Now I think we are forced to admit to the man who says that he was created, and who quotes the text, "All things were created through him," that the Holy Spirit was created through the Word, since the Word is older than he. But the man who is unwilling to say that the Holy Spirit is created through Christ must assert that he is unbegotten. . . . We, however, believe that there are three hypostases, the Father, the Son and the Holy Spirit, and being of opinion that no one is unbegotten except the Father, maintain the pious and true belief to be that while all things were created through the Word the Holy Spirit is of more honour than all others and first in rank of all who have been created by the Father through Christ.'

this Spirit inspired each one of the saints, both the prophets and the apostles, and that there was not one Spirit in the men of old and another in those who were inspired at the coming of Christ.

5. Next after this the apostles taught that the soul, having a substance and life of its own, will be rewarded according to its deserts after its departure from this world; for it will either obtain an inheritance of eternal life and blessedness, if its deeds shall warrant this, or it must be given over to eternal fire and torments, if the guilt of its crimes shall so determine. Further, there will be a time for the resurrection of the dead, when this body, which is now 'sown in corruption', shall 'rise in incorruption', and that which is 'sown in dishonour' shall 'rise in glory'.[1]

This also is laid down in the Church's teaching, that every rational soul is possessed of free will and choice; and also, that it is engaged in a struggle against the devil and his angels and the opposing powers; for these strive to weigh the soul down with sins, whereas we, if we lead a wise and upright life, endeavour to free ourselves from such a burden. There follows from this the conviction that we are not subject to necessity, so as to be compelled by every means, even against our will, to do either good or evil. For if we are possessed of free will, some spiritual powers may very likely be able to urge us on to sin and others to assist us to salvation; we are not, however, compelled by necessity to act either rightly or wrongly, as is thought to be the case by those who say that human events are due to the course and motion of the stars, not only those events which fall outside the sphere of our freedom of will but even those that lie within our own power.

In regard to the soul, whether it takes its rise from the transference of the seed, in such a way that the principle or substance of the soul may be regarded as inherent in the seminal particles of the body itself; or whether it has some other beginning, and whether this beginning is begotten or unbegotten, or at any rate whether it is imparted to the body from without or no; all this is not very clearly defined in the teaching.

6. Further, in regard to the devil and his angels and the opposing spiritual powers, the Church teaching lays it down that these beings exist, but what they are or how they exist it has not explained very clearly. Among most Christians, however, the following opinion is held, that this devil was formerly an angel, but became an apostate and persuaded as many angels as he could to fall away with him; and these are even now called his angels.

7. The Church teaching also includes the doctrine that this world was made and began to exist at a definite time and that

[1] 1 Cor. XV. 42 f.

by reason of its corruptible nature it must suffer dissolution. But what existed before this world, or what will exist after it, has not yet been made known openly to the many, for no clear statement on the point is set forth in the Church teaching.

8. Then there is the doctrine that the scriptures were composed through the Spirit of God and that they have not only that meaning which is obvious, but also another which is hidden from the majority of readers. For the contents of scripture are the outward forms of certain mysteries and the images of divine things. On this point the entire Church is unanimous, that while the whole law is spiritual, the inspired meaning is not recognised by all, but only by those who are gifted with the grace of the Holy Spirit in the word of wisdom and knowledge.

GREEK	LATIN
The term[1] 'incorporeal' is unknown not only to the majority of Christians but also to the Scriptures.	The term *asomaton*, that is, incorporeal, is unused and unknown, not only in many other writings but also in our

LATIN

scriptures. If, however, any one is inclined to produce it for us out of that little book called *The Teaching of Peter*, where the Saviour is represented as saying to his disciples, 'I am not an incorporeal daemon',[2] I must answer in the first place that the book itself is not included among the books of the Church and I can show that it is not a writing of Peter nor of any one else who was inspired by the Spirit of God. But even supposing this point is waived, the sense conveyed by the word 'incorporeal' in that passage is not the same as is expressed by Greek and non-Christian writers when they record a discussion by philosophers on incorporeal nature. For in the book in question the Saviour used the words 'incorporeal daemon' in order to denote that the fashion and outline, whatever it may be, of the daemonic body is not like this dense and visible body of ours. And the words must be understood in the sense intended by the author of that writing, namely, that the Saviour did not have such a body as the daemons have. Now this body is by nature a fine substance and thin like air, and on this account most people think and speak of it as incorporeal; but the Saviour had a body which was solid and capable of being handled. It is customary for

[1] Frag. 2 Koetschau, from Antipater of Bostra in John of Damascus, *Sacra Parallela* ii. 770 (Migne P. G. 96, p. 501).
[2] The extant fragments of 'The Teaching of Peter' are collected in Von Dobschütz, *Das Kerygma Petri* (*Texte und Unters.* xi. 1), and in Hilgenfeld, *N. T. extra canonem* iv. 51 ff. The above fragment is found in Greek, ὅτι οὐκ εἰμὶ δαιμόνιον ἀσώματον, in Ignatius, *ad Smyrnaeos* 3, where, however, its source is not mentioned.

everything which is not like this to be termed incorporeal by the more simple and uneducated of men, just as the air we breathe may be called incorporeal because it is not a body that can be grasped or held or that can resist pressure.

9. Nevertheless we shall inquire whether the actual thing which Greek philosophers call *asomaton* or incorporeal is found in the holy scriptures under another name. We must also seek to discover how God himself is to be conceived, whether as corporeal and fashioned in some shape, or as being of a different nature from bodies, a point which is not clearly set forth in the teaching. The same inquiry must be made in regard to Christ and the Holy Spirit, and indeed in regard to every soul and every rational nature also.

GREEK

10. It[1] has also been handed down to us in the teaching that there exist certain angels and good powers, who minister to the salvation of men; but when they were created, and what are their characteristics, no one has in any way made plain.

LATIN

10. This also is contained in the church teaching, that there exist certain angels of God and good powers, who minister to him in bringing about the salvation of men; but when these were created, and what they are like, or how they exist, is not very clearly defined. And as for

LATIN

the sun, moon and stars, the tradition does not clearly say whether they are living beings or without life.

Everyone therefore who is desirous of constructing out of the foregoing a connected body of doctrine must use points like these as elementary and foundation principles, in accordance with the commandment which says, 'Enlighten yourselves with the light of knowledge'.[2] Thus by clear and cogent arguments he will discover the truth about each particular point and so will produce, as we have said, a single body of doctrine, with the aid of such illustrations and declarations as he shall find in the holy scriptures and of such conclusions as he shall ascertain to follow logically from them when rightly understood.

---

[1] Frag. 3 Koetschau, from Antipater of Bostra in John of Damascus, *Sacra Parallela* ii. 770 (Migne P. G. 96, p. 501).
[2] Hosea X. 12 (Sept.)

CHAPTER I

<table>
<tr><td>GREEK</td><td>LATIN</td></tr>
<tr><td>THE FATHER[1]</td><td>GOD</td></tr>
</table>

LATIN

1. I am aware that there are some who will try to maintain that even according to our scriptures God is a body, since they find it written in the books of Moses, 'Our God is a consuming fire',[2] and in the Gospel according to John, 'God is spirit, and they who worship him must worship in spirit and in truth'.[3] Now these men will have it that fire and spirit are body and nothing else. But I would ask them what they have to say about this passage of scripture, 'God is light', as John says in his epistle, 'God is light, and in him is no darkness'.[4] He is that light, surely, which lightens the whole understanding of those who are capable of receiving truth, as it is written in the thirty-fifth psalm, 'In thy light shall we see light'.[5] For what other light of God can we speak of, in which a man sees light, except God's spiritual power, which when it lightens a man causes him either to see clearly the truth of all things or to know God himself who is called the truth? Such then is the meaning of the saying, 'In thy light shall we see light'; that is, in thy word and thy wisdom, which is thy Son, in him shall we see thee, the Father. For can we possibly think that, because it is termed light, it is like the light of our sun? And how can there be the slightest reason for supposing that from that material light the grounds of know-ledge could be derived and the meaning of truth discovered?

2. If then they accept this argument of ours, proved by reason itself, about the nature of light, and will admit that the use of the word light cannot possibly mean that God is to be thought of as being a body, they will allow a similar reasoning in regard to the phrase 'a consuming fire'. For what does God 'consume' by virtue of this fact of being a 'fire'? Are we to suppose that he consumes bodily matter, 'wood or hay or stubble'?[6] What is there in this statement consistent with the praises due to God, if he is a fire that consumes material substances like these? Let us rather consider that God does indeed consume and destroy, but that what he consumes are evil thoughts of the mind, shame-ful deeds and longings after sin, when these implant themselves in the minds of believers; and that he takes those souls which

---

[1] For the Greek title see Photius *Bibl. Cod.* viii. p. 4.
[2] Deut. IV. 24.
[3] St. John IV. 24.
[4] 1 John I. 5.
[5] Ps. XXXV. 10 (Sept.).
[6] See 1 Cor. III. 12.

render themselves capable of receiving his word and wisdom and dwells in them according to the saying, 'I and the Father will come and make our abode with him',[1] having first consumed all their vices and passions and made them into a temple pure and worthy of himself.

To those, however, who think that God is a body in consequence of the saying, 'God is spirit',[2] we must reply as follows. It is a custom of holy scripture, when it wishes to point to something of an opposite nature to this dense and solid body, to call it spirit, as in the saying, 'The letter killeth, but the spirit giveth life'.[3] Here undoubtedly the letter means that which is bodily, and the spirit that which is intellectual, or as we also call it, spiritual. The apostle also says, 'Even until this day, whenever Moses is read, a veil lieth upon their hearts; but when a man shall turn to the Lord, the veil shall be taken away; and where the Spirit of the Lord is, there is liberty'.[4] For so long as a man does not attend to the spiritual meaning 'a veil lies upon his heart', in consequence of which veil, in other words his duller understanding, the scripture itself is said or thought to be veiled; and this is the explanation of the veil which is said to have covered the face of Moses when he was speaking to the people,[5] that is, when the law is read in public. But if we turn to the Lord, where also the Word of God is, and where the Holy Spirit reveals spiritual knowledge, the veil will be taken away, and we shall then with unveiled face behold in the holy scriptures the glory of the Lord.

3. Further, although many saints partake of the Holy Spirit, he is not on that account to be regarded as a kind of body, which is divided into material parts and distributed to each of the saints; but rather as a sanctifying power, a share of which is said to be possessed by all who have shown themselves worthy of being sanctified through his grace. And to make this statement more easily understood let us take an illustration from things admittedly of lesser importance. There are many who share in the teaching and art of medicine; yet are we to suppose that all who share in medicine have some material substance called medicine placed before them from which they take away little particles and so obtain a share of it? Must we not rather understand that all who with ready and prepared minds gain a comprehension of the art and its teaching may be said to share in medicine? These illustrations from medicine must not be supposed to apply in every detail when compared with the Holy Spirit; they establish this point only, that a thing in which many have a share is not necessarily to be regarded as a body. The Holy Spirit is far

---

[1] See St. John XIV. 23. Origen quotes the passage in this form in two other places, *Con. Celsum* viii. 18 and *Hom. in Jerem.* viii. 1.

[2] St. John IV. 24.
[3] 2 Cor. III. 6.
[4] 2 Cor. III. 15-17.
[5] See Exod. XXXIV. 33, 35.

different from the system or science of medicine, for the Holy
Spirit is an intellectual existence, with a subsistence and being
of its own, whereas medicine is nothing of the sort.

4. We must now turn to the Gospel passage itself, where it
is written that 'God is spirit',[1] and must show that this is to
be understood in a sense agreeing with what we have just said.
Let us ask when our Saviour spoke these words, and to whom,
and in what connexion. We find undoubtedly that he uttered
them when speaking to the woman of Samaria, who thought that
men ought to worship God in Mount Gerizim according to the
belief of the Samaritans. 'God,' he told her, 'is spirit'. The
woman of Samaria, supposing him to be an ordinary Jew, was
asking him whether men ought to worship God 'in Jerusalem'
or 'in this mountain'. These were her words: 'All our fathers
worshipped in this mountain, but ye say that in Jerusalem is the
place where men ought to worship.'[2] It was this belief of the
woman, who thought that God would be worshipped rightly or
wrongly by Jews in Jerusalem or by Samaritans in Mount Gerizim
because of some special privilege attaching to the material places,
that the Saviour contradicts by saying that the man who desires
to seek for God must abandon all idea of material places. These
are his words: 'The hour cometh, when the true worshippers
shall worship the Father neither in Jerusalem nor in this
mountain. God is spirit, and they that worship him must worship in spirit and in truth.'[3] See, too, how appropriately he
associated truth with spirit, calling God spirit to distinguish him
from bodies, and truth to distinguish him from a shadow or an
image. For those who worshipped in Jerusalem, 'serving a
shadow and image of heavenly things',[4] worshipped neither in
truth nor in spirit, and the same is true of those who worshipped
in Mount Gerizim.

5. Having then refuted, to the best of our ability, every
interpretation which suggests that we should attribute to God
any material characteristics, we assert that in truth he is incomprehensible and immeasurable. For whatever may be the
knowledge which we have been able to obtain about God, whether
by perception or by reflection, we must of necessity believe that
he is far and away better than our thoughts about him. For if
we see a man who can scarcely look at a glimmer or the light
of the smallest lamp, and if we wish to teach such a one, whose
eyesight is not strong enough to receive more light than we have
said, about the brightness and splendour of the sun, shall we
not have to tell him that the splendour of the sun is unspeakably
and immeasurably better and more glorious than all this light
he can see? In the same way our mind is shut up within bars

---

[1] St. John IV. 24.
[2] St. John IV. 20.
[3] St. John IV. 21, 23, 24.
[4] Heb. VIII. 5.

of flesh and blood and rendered duller and feebler by reason of its association with such material substances; and although it is regarded as far more excellent when compared with the natural body, yet when it strains after incorporeal things and seeks to gain a sight of them it has scarcely the power of a glimmer of light or a tiny lamp. And among all intellectual, that is, incorporeal things, what is there so universally surpassing, so unspeakably and immeasurably excelling, as God, whose nature certainly the vision of the human mind, however pure or clear to the very utmost that mind may be, cannot gaze at or behold?

6. But it will not appear out of place if to make the matter clearer still we use yet another illustration. Sometimes our eyes cannot look upon the light itself, that is, the actual sun, but when we see the brightness and rays of the sun as they pour into our windows, it may be, or into any small openings for light, we are able to infer from these how great is the source and fountain of physical light. So, too, the works of divine providence and the plan of this universe are as it were rays of God's nature in contrast to his real substance and being, and because our mind is of itself unable to behold God as he is, it understands the parent of the universe from the beauty of his works and the comeliness of his creatures.

God therefore must not be thought to be any kind of body, nor to exist in a body, but to be a simple intellectual existence, admitting in himself of no addition whatever, so that he cannot be believed to have in himself a more or a less, but is Unity, or if I may so say, Oneness[1] throughout, and the mind and fount from which originates all intellectual existence or mind. Now mind does not need physical space in which to move and operate, nor does it need a magnitude discernible by the senses, nor bodily shape or colour, nor anything else whatever like these, which are suitable to bodies and matter. Accordingly that simple and wholly mental existence can admit no delay or hesitation in any of its movements or operations; for if it did so, the simplicity of its divine nature would appear to be in some degree limited and impeded by such an addition, and that which is the first principle of all things would be found to be com-

---

[1] Rufinus has kept the Greek philosophical terms *Monas* (= Unit, Unity) and *Henas* (= Oneness) probably from the difficulty of finding Latin equivalents. Some of the later Pythagoreans seem to have distinguished, as Origen does here, between the Monad, the primal Unity which gives rise to multiplicity, and the bare One, a kind of Absolute which they tried to conceive as unrelated to anything. See Zeller, *Pre-Socratic Philosophy,* trans. S. F. Alleyne, Vol. I, p. 390 ff. Clement of Alexandria, Origen's predecessor and teacher, describes the Monad thus: 'Abstract from body its physical qualities, taking away the dimension of depth, then that of breadth and then that of length. The point which remains is as it were a unit having position. Take away its position, and you get the conception of unity.' Stromata V. 71, 2 f. (Stählin ii. 374 7 ff.).

posite and diverse, and would be many and not one; since only the species of deity, if I may so call it, has the privilege of existing apart from all material intermixture.

That mind needs no space in which to move according to its own nature is certain even from the evidence of our own mind. For if this abides in its own proper sphere and nothing occurs from any cause to enfeeble it, it will never be at all retarded by reason of differences of place from acting in conformity with its own movements; nor on the other hand will it gain any increase or accession of speed from the peculiar nature of any place. And if it be objected, for example, that when men are travelling by sea and tossed by the waves, their mind is somewhat less vigorous than it is wont to be on land, we must believe this experience to be due not to the difference of place but to the movement and disturbance of the body with which the mind is joined or intermingled. For it seems almost against nature for the human body to live on the sea, and on this account the body, as if unequal to its task, appears to sustain the mind's movements in irregular and disordered manner, giving feebler assistance to its keen flashes, precisely as happens even with men on land when they are in the grip of a fever; in whose case it is certain that, if the mind fulfils its functions less effectively through the strength of the fever, the cause is to be found not in any defect of locality but in the disease of the body, which renders it disturbed and confused and altogether unable to bestow its customary services on the mind under the well-known and natural conditions. For we men are animals, formed by a union of body and soul, and thus alone did it become possible for us to live on the earth. But God, who is the beginning of all things, must not be regarded as a composite being, lest perchance we find that the elements, out of which everything that is called composite has been composed, are prior to the first principle himself.

Nor does the mind need physical magnitude in order to perform any act or movement, as an eye does when in looking at large bodies it expands and at small ones narrows and contracts for the purpose of seeing. Mind certainly needs intellectual magnitude, because it grows in an intellectual and not in a physical sense. For mind does not increase by physical additions at the same time as the body does until the twentieth or thirtieth year of its age, but by the employment of instructions and exercises a sharpening of the natural faculties is effected and the powers implanted within are roused to intelligence. Thus the capacity of the intellect is enlarged not by being increased with physical additions, but by being cultivated through exercises in learning. These it cannot receive immediately from birth or boyhood because the structure of the bodily parts which the mind uses as instruments for its own exercise is as yet weak and feeble, being neither able to endure the force of the mind's working nor sufficiently developed to display a capacity for receiving instruction.

7. But if there are any who consider the mind itself and the soul to be a body, I should like them to tell me how it can take in reasons and arguments relating to questions of great importance, full of difficulty and subtlety. Whence comes it that the power of memory, the contemplation of invisible things, yes, and the perception of incorporeal things reside in a body? How does a bodily nature investigate the teachings of the arts and the meanings and reasons of things? And divine doctrines, which are obviously incorporeal, how can it discern and understand them? One might perhaps think that, just as the bodily form and shape of the ears or eyes contributes something to hearing or to seeing, and as the various parts of our body, which have been formed by God, each possess some special capacity, due to their particular form, for doing the work for which they were by nature designed, so too, the soul or mind must be supposed to have an outward shape fitly and suitably formed, as it were, for the purpose of perceiving and understanding individual things and of being set in motion by vital movements. But what sort of appearance the mind could have, seeing that it is a mind and moves in an intellectual way, I do not know who could describe or tell us.

In further confirmation and explanation of what we have said about the mind or soul, as being superior to all bodily nature, the following remarks may be added. Each of the bodily senses is appropriately connected with a material substance towards which the particular sense is directed. For instance, sight is connected with colour, shape and size; hearing with the voice and sound; smelling with vapours pleasant and unpleasant; taste with flavours; touch with things hot or cold, hard or soft, rough or smooth. But it is clear to all that the sense of mind is far superior to the senses above mentioned. Does it not then appear absurd that these inferior senses should have substances connected with them, as objects towards which their activities are directed, whereas this faculty, the sense of mind, which is superior to them, should have no substance whatever connected with it, and that this faculty of an intellectual nature should be a mere accident arising out of bodies?[1] Those who assert this are undoubtedly speaking in disparaging terms of that substance which is the better part of their own nature; nay more, they

---

[1] Origen is hampered by an imperfect psychology, but his meaning is clear. The senses, which are regarded as bodily or material things, have their appropriate subject matter. Mind, which Origen contends is purely spiritual, must also have its appropriate 'substance' to act on. Substance (Lat. *substantia*; Gr. $\pi \acute{o}\sigma\tau\alpha\sigma\iota\varsigma$) is here to be understood in a spiritual sense; the mind's business is with God, truth and the reasons of things. Origen contradicts the view that mind is an *epiphenomenon*, or by-product of matter.

do wrong even to God himself in supposing that he can be understood through a bodily nature, since according to them that which can be understood or perceived through a body is itself a body; and they are unwilling to have it understood that there is a certain affinity between the mind and God, of whom the mind is an intellectual image, and that by reason of this fact the mind, especially if it is purified and separated from bodily matter, is able to have some perception of the divine nature.

8. But these assertions may perhaps seem to be less authoritative to those who desire to be instructed in divine things from the holy scriptures and who seek to have it proved to them from that source how God's nature surpasses the nature of bodies. See then, whether the apostle, too, does not say the same thing when he speaks as follows about Christ: 'Who is the image of the invisible God, the firstborn of all creation'.[1] It is not, as some suppose, that God's nature is visible to one and invisible to others; for the apostle did not say 'the image of God who is invisible' to men or 'invisible' to sinners, but he makes an absolutely unvarying declaration about God's very nature in these words, 'image of the invisible God'. And John, too, when he says in the gospel, 'No one hath seen God at any time',[2] plainly declares to all who are capable of understanding, that there is no existence to which God is visible; not as if he were one who is visible by nature and yet eludes and escapes the gaze of his creatures because of their frailty, but that he is in his nature impossible to be seen. :

And if you should ask me what is my belief about the Only-begotten himself, whether I would say that God's nature, which is naturally invisible, is not even visible to him, do not immediately think this question to be impious or absurd, because we shall give it a logical answer. (For as it is incongruous to say that the Son can see the Father, so it is unbefitting to believe that the Holy Spirit can see the Son).[3] It is one thing to see, another to know. To see and to be seen is a property of bodies; to know and to be known is an attribute of intellectual existence. Whatever therefore is proper to bodies must not be believed either of the Father or of the Son, the relations between whom are such as pertain to the nature of deity. And finally, Christ in the gospel did not say, 'No one seeth the Father except the

---

[1] Col. I. 15.

[2] St. John I. 18.

[3] Koetschau inserts here this sentence taken from Jerome, *Con. Ioh. Hieros. c.* 7. Origen was frequently attacked for the opinion here expressed, which Rufinus has softened down considerably. Epiphanius (*Haer.* 64, 4) adds that Origen also asserted that 'angels could not see the Spirit, nor could men see angels'. See also Justinian, *Ep. ad Mennam* (Mansi IX. 489 B) and Jerome *Ep. ad Avitum* 2. Arius used Origen's language, cp. Athanasius, *Con. Arian.* i. 6.

Son, nor the Son except the Father', but 'no one knoweth the Son except the Father, nor doth anyone know the Father except the Son'.[1] This clearly shows that what is called 'seeing' and 'being seen' in the case of bodily existences is with the Father and the Son called 'knowing' and 'being known', through the faculty of knowledge and not through our frail sense of sight. It is, therefore, because the expressions 'to see' and 'to be seen' cannot suitably be applied to incorporeal and invisible existence that in the gospel the Father is not said to be seen by the Son nor the Son by the Father, but to be known.

9. But if the question is put to us why it was said, 'Blessed are the pure in heart, for they shall see God',[2] I answer that in my opinion our argument will be much more firmly established by this passage. For what else is 'to see God in the heart' but to understand and know him with the mind, just as we have explained above? For the names of the organs of sense are often applied to the soul, so that we speak of seeing with the eyes of the heart, that is, of drawing some intellectual conclusion by means of the faculty of intelligence. So too we speak of hearing with the ears when we discern the deeper meaning of some statement. So too we speak of the soul as being able to use teeth, when it eats and consumes the bread of life who comes down from heaven. In a similar way we speak of it as using all the other bodily organs, which are transferred from their corporeal significance and applied to the faculties of the soul; as Solomon says, 'You will find a divine sense'.[3] For he knew that there were in us two kinds of senses, the one being mortal, corruptible and human, and the other immortal and intellectual, which here he calls 'divine'. By this divine sense, therefore, not of the eyes but of a pure heart, that is, the mind, God can be seen by those who are worthy. That heart is used for mind, that is for the intellectual faculty, you will certainly find over and over again in all the scriptures, both the New and the Old.

Having thus investigated the nature of God, though in a manner far from worthy by reason of the weakness of our human understanding, let us now see what meaning is to be given to the name Christ.

[1] St. Matt. XI. 27.
[2] St. Matt. V. 8.
[3] Prov. II. 5. Origen's reading, the Greek of which we have in *Con. Celsum* VII. 34, $\alpha\ddot{\iota}\sigma\theta\eta\sigma\iota\nu\ \theta\epsilon\acute{\iota}\alpha\nu\ \epsilon\dot{\upsilon}\rho\acute{\eta}\sigma\epsilon\iota\varsigma$, is different from the Septuagint, which says, 'Thou shalt find the knowledge of God'.

CHAPTER II

CHRIST

1. First we must know this, that in Christ there is one nature, his deity, because he is the only-begotten Son of the Father, and another human nature, which in very recent times he took upon him to fulfil the divine purpose. Our first task therefore is to see what the only-begotten Son of God is, seeing he is called by many different names according to the circumstances and beliefs of the different writers. He is called Wisdom, as Solomon said, speaking in the person of Wisdom: 'The Lord created me the beginning of his ways for his works. Before he made anything, before the ages he established me. In the beginning before he made the earth, before the springs of waters came forth, before the mountains were settled, before all the hills he begets me.'[1] He is also called Firstborn, as the apostle Paul says: 'who is the firstborn of all creation'.[2] The Firstborn is not, however, by nature a different being from Wisdom, but is one and the same. Finally, the apostle Paul says, 'Christ, the power of God and the wisdom of God.'[3]

2. Let no one think, however, that when we give him the name 'wisdom of God' we mean anything without hypostatic existence,[4] that is, to take an illustration, that we understand him to be not as it were some wise living being, but a certain thing which makes men wise by revealing and imparting itself to the minds of such as are able to receive its influence and intelligence. If then it is once rightly accepted that the only-begotten Son of God is God's wisdom hypostatically existing, I do not think that our mind ought to stray beyond this to the suspicion that this hypostatis or substance could possibly possess bodily characteristics, since everything that is corporeal is distinguished by shape or colour or size. And who in his sober senses ever looked for shape or colour or measurable size in wisdom, considered solely as wisdom? And can anyone who has learned to regard God with feelings of reverence suppose or believe that God the Father ever existed, even for a single moment, without begetting this wisdom? For he would either

---

[1] Prov. VIII. 22-25. Origen, in his *Hom. in Jerem.* IX. 4 *ad fin.* lays stress on the present tense (Gr. γεννᾷ : Lat. *generat*) as evidence of his doctrine of the Son's eternal generation by the Father.

[2] Col. I. 15.

[3] 1 Cor. I. 24.

[4] Lat. *aliquid insubstantivum.* It almost means 'something impersonal', but Origen wishes to make it clear that personal existence does not involve the possession of a body.

say that God could not have begotten wisdom before he did beget her, so that he brought wisdom into being when she had not existed before, or else that he could have begotten her and—what it is profanity even to say about God—that he was unwilling to do so; each of which alternatives, as everyone can see, is absurd and impious, that is, either that God should advance from being unable to being able, or that, while being able, he should act as if he were not and should delay to beget wisdom.

Wherefore we recognise that God was always the Father of his only-begotten Son, who was born indeed of him and draws his being from him, but is yet without any beginning, not only of that kind which can be distinguished by periods of time, but even of that other kind which the mind alone is wont to contemplate in itself and to perceive, if I may so say, with the bare intellect and reason. Wisdom, therefore, must be believed to have been begotten beyond the limits of any beginning that we can speak of or understand. And because in this very subsistence of wisdom there was implicit every capacity and form of the creation that was to be, both of those things that exist in a primary sense and of those which happen in consequence of them, the whole being fashioned and arranged beforehand by the power of foreknowledge, wisdom, speaking through Solomon in regard to these very created things that had been as it were outlined and prefigured in herself, says that she was created as a 'beginning of the ways' of God, which means that she contains within herself both the beginnings and causes and species of the whole creation.

3. Now just as we have learned in what sense wisdom is the 'beginning of the ways' of God and is said to have been created, in the sense, namely, that she fashions beforehand and contains within herself the species and causes of the entire creation, in the same manner also must wisdom be understood to be the Word of God. For wisdom opens to all other beings, that is, to the whole creation, the meaning of the mysteries and secrets which are contained within the wisdom of God, and so she is called the Word, because she is as it were an interpreter of the mind's secrets. Hence I consider that to be a true saying which is written in the Acts of Paul, 'He is the Word, a living being'.[1] John, however, uses yet more exalted and wonderful language in the beginning of his gospel, when by an appropriate declaration he defines the Word to be God; 'And the

---

[1] The Acts of Paul is mentioned by Eusebius (*Hist. Eccl.* III. 3, 25) as a writing used in some parts of the Church but not considered authoritative. Another quotation from it is to be found in Origen, *Comm. in Ioh.* XX. 12. In *Hom. in Jerem.* XX. 1, there is also a reference to the above passage, the Word being called ζῷον (=animal vivens). This appears to depend upon a misreading of Heb. IV. 12, ζῶν γὰρ ὁ λόγος. The Acts of Paul is not extant, and must be distinguished from the Acts of Paul and Thecla.

Word was God, and he was in the beginning with God'.[1] Let
him who assigns a beginning to the Word of God or the wisdom
of God beware lest he utters impiety against the unbegotten
Father himself, in denying that he was always a Father and that
he begat the Word and possessed wisdom in all previous times
or ages or whatever else they may be called.

4. This Son, then, is also the truth and the life[2] of all things
that exist; and rightly so. For the things that were made, how
could they live, except by the gift of life? Or the things that
exist, how could they really and truly exist, unless they were
derived from the truth? Or how could rational beings exist,
unless the Word or reason had existed before them? Or how
could they be wise, unless wisdom existed? But since it was
to happen that some should fall away from life and bring death
upon themselves by the very fact of their falling (for death is
nothing else but a departure from life), and yet it would certainly
not have been logical that beings once created by God for the
enjoyment of life should utterly perish, it was needful that before
the existence of death there should exist a power capable of
destroying the death that was to come, and that there should
exist a resurrection,[3] the figure of which was shown in our Lord
and Saviour, which resurrection should have its ground in the
very wisdom and word and life of God. Or again, since it was
to happen that some of those who were created would prove
unable, in consequence of the good being within them as an
accident and not by nature, that is, not essentially, to remain
firm and steadfast and to abide for ever in the just and temperate
use of their original blessings, but would turn and change and
fall away from their first state, the word and wisdom of God
became the way.[4] And it is called the way for this reason, that
it leads to the Father those who walk along it.

Whatever then we have said of the wisdom of God will also fitly
apply to and be understood of him in his other titles as the Son
of God, the life, the word, the truth, the way and the resurrection.
For all these titles are derived from his works and powers, and
in none of them is there the least reason to understand anything
corporeal, which might seem to denote either size or shape or
colour. But whereas the offspring of men or of the other
animals whom we see around us correspond to the seed of those
by whom they were begotten, or of the mothers in whose womb
they are formed and nourished, drawing from these parents
whatever it is that they take and bring into the light of day
when they are born, it is impious and shocking to regard God
the Father in the begetting of his only-begotten Son and in the
Son's subsistence as being similar to any human being or other
animal in the act of begetting; but there must needs be some

---

[1] St. John I. 1, 2.   [3] See St. John XI. 25.
[2] See St. John XIV. 6.   [4] See St. John XIV. 6.

exceptional process, worthy of God, to which we can find no comparison whatever, not merely in things, but even in thought and imagination, such that by its aid human thought could apprehend how the unbegotten God becomes Father of the only-begotten Son. This is an eternal and everlasting begetting, as brightness is begotten from light.[1] For he does not become Son in an external way through the adoption of the Spirit,[2] but is Son by nature.

5. Let us now see how our statements are also supported by the authority of divine scripture. The apostle Paul says that the only-begotten Son is 'the image of the invisible God', and that he is the 'firstborn of all creation';[3] and when writing to the Hebrews he says of the Son that he is the 'brightness of God's glory and the express image of his substance'.[4] But we also find, in the book of Wisdom which is said to be Solomon's, a certain description of the wisdom of God in the following terms: 'For she is a breath of the power of God, and a pure effluence (that is, emanation[5]) of the glory of the Almighty'. Therefore, 'nothing that is defiled can enter into her. For she is the brightness of the eternal light and an unspotted mirror of the working of God and an image of his goodness'.[6] Now, as we said above, the wisdom of God has her subsistence nowhere else but in him who is the beginning of all things, from whom also she took her birth. And because he himself, who alone is a Son by nature, is this wisdom, he is on this account also called the 'only-begotten'.

6. Let us now see what we ought to understand by the expression 'image of the invisible God', in order that we may learn therefrom how God can rightly be called the Father of his Son; and let us first of all consider what things are called images in ordinary human speech. Sometimes the term 'image' is applied to an object painted or carved on some material, such as wood or stone. Sometimes a child is said to be the image of its parent, when the likeness of the parent's features is in every respect faithfully reproduced in the child. Now I think that the first of these illustrations may be fitly applied to him who was made 'in the image and likeness of God',[7] that is, man. Of man, however, we shall inquire more carefully, with God's help, when we come to the exposition of this passage in Genesis.[8]

---

[1] The thought comes from Wisd. VII. 26 and Heb. I. 3.
[2] See Rom. VIII. 15.
[3] Col. I. 15.
[4] Heb. I. 3.
[5] For 'effluence' Rufinus retains the Greek ἀπόρροια, translating it afterwards by *manatio*.
[6] Wisd. VII. 25f.
[7] Gen. I. 26.
[8] Origen discusses the passage in his *Hom. in Gen.* I. 13. See Introduction, p. vi.

But in regard to the Son of God, of whom we are now speaking, the image may be compared to our second illustration; for this reason, that he is the invisible image of the invisible God, just as according to the scripture narrative we say that the image of Adam was his son Seth. It is written thus: 'And Adam begat Seth after his own image and after his own kind'.[1] This image preserves the unity of nature and substance common to a father and a son. For if 'all things that the Father doeth, these also doeth the Son likewise',[2] then in this very fact that the Son does all things just as the Father does, the Father's image is reproduced in the Son, whose birth from the Father is as it were an act of his will proceeding from the mind. And on this account my own opinion is that an act of the Father's will ought to be sufficient to ensure the existence of what he wills; for in willing he uses no other means than that which is produced by the deliberations of his will. It is in this way, then, that the existence of the Son also is begotten by him.

This point must above all be upheld by those who allow nothing to be unbegotten, that is, unborn, except God the Father only.[3] Moreover, we must take care not to fall into the absurd fables of those who imagine for themselves certain emanations, splitting the divine nature into parts and, so far as they can, dividing God the Father.[4] For it is not only the utmost impiety, but also the depth of folly, to entertain the slightest suspicion that such a thing could happen to an incorporeal being; nor is it at all consistent with our intelligence to think that a physical division of an incorporeal being is possible. Rather must we suppose that as an act of will proceeds from the mind without either cutting off any part of the mind or being separated or divided from it, in some similar fashion has the Father begotten the Son, who is indeed his image; so that as the Father is invisible by nature, he has begotten an image that is also invisible.

For the Son is the Word, and therefore we must understand that nothing in him is perceptible to the senses. He is wisdom, and in wisdom we must not suspect the presence of anything corporeal. 'He is the true light, which lighteth every man that cometh into the world',[5] but he has nothing in common with the light of our sun. Our Saviour is therefore the image of the invisible God, the Father, being the truth, when considered in

---

[1] Gen. V. 3.
[2] St. John V. 19.
[3] According to Jerome, *Ep. ad Avitum* 2, what Origen really said here was that 'nothing is *uncreated* except God the Father only'. But see above p. 3, n. 4.
[4] These were the theories of the Gnostics. See Bk. IV, ch. iv (p. 326 below).
[5] St. John I. 9.

relation to the Father himself,[1] and the image, when considered in relation to us, to whom he reveals the Father;[2]

GREEK

We, therefore,[3] having been made according to the image, have the Son, the original, as the truth of the noble qualities that are within us. And what we are to the Son, such is the Son to the Father, who is the truth.

LATIN

through which image we know the Father, whom 'no one' else 'knoweth save the Son and he to whom the Son hath willed to reveal him'.[4] And he reveals the Father by being himself understood; for whoever has understood him understands as a consequence the Father also, according to his own saying, 'He that hath seen me, hath seen the Father also.'[5] * * * * *

7. But we quoted the saying of Paul in which he speaks of Christ as being 'the brightness of God's glory, and the express image of his substance';[6] let us see, therefore, what we are to learn from this. 'God is light',[7] according to John. The only-begotten Son, therefore, is the brightness of this light, proceeding from God without separation, as brightness from light, and lightening the whole creation. For by the same method of exposition which we have used above,[8] to show how he is the

[1] Rufinus has here altered his original. See the quotation made by Jerome, *Ep. ad Avitum* 2: 'The Son, who is the image of the invisible Father, is not the truth when compared with the Father; but in relation to us, who are unable to receive the truth of God almighty, he is a shadow and semblance of the truth.' That this correctly represents what Origen wrote is shown by an anonymous defender of Origen whose book is described by Photius, *Bibl. Cod.* 117. According to this work Origen was accused of saying that 'the image of God, considered in relation to God whose image he is, and in so far as he is image, is not truth'. In Theophilus, *Ep. Synod.* 2 (the letter written after the Council at Alexandria in 400 A.D., where Origenism was condemned: see Jerome *Ep.* 92), the charge is made in the following exaggerated form; 'The Son compared with us is truth, but compared with the Father he is falsehood.' See further the Greek fragment that follows.

[2] See St. John XIV. 6.

[3] Frag. 4, Koetschau, from Justinian, *Ep. ad Mennam* (Mansi IX. 525). Rufinus has omitted this.

[4] St. Matt. XI. 27.

[5] St. John XIV. 9. Koetschau suspects an omission by Rufinus at this point, where possibly the two following passages may originally have stood. Jerome, *Ep. ad Avitum* 2, 'God the Father is light incomprehensible. In comparison with the Father, Christ is a very small brightness, though to us by reason of our weakness he seems to be a great one'. Theophilus, *Ep. Synod.* (in Jerome *Ep.* 92): 'Again, as much as Paul or Peter differ from the Saviour, so much is the Saviour less than the Father.'

[6] Heb. I. 3.

[7] 1 St. John I. 5.

[8] See Ch. II. 4 (p. 17).

way and leads to the Father, and how he is the Word who interprets and presents to the rational creation the secrets of wisdom and the mysteries of knowledge, and how he is also the truth and the life and the resurrection, must we arrive at the meaning of his being the brightness; for it is through its brightness that the nature of the light itself is known and experienced. This brightness falls softly and gently on the tender and weak eyes of mortal man and little by little trains and accustoms them, as it were, to bear the light in its clearness; and when it has removed from them all that darkens and obstructs their vision, in accordance with the Lord's saying, 'Cast out the beam out of thine eye,'[1] it renders them capable of enduring the glory of the light, becoming in this respect even a kind of mediator between men and the light.[2]

8. Christ is said, however, by the apostle to be not only 'the brightness of God's glory' but also 'the express image of his substance'[3] or subsistence. I do not think it superfluous, therefore, to turn our attention to this point, namely, how there can be said to exist, besides the actual substance or subsistence of God (whatever that substance or subsistence means), something else which is an image of his substance. See, then, whether the Son of God, who is called God's word and wisdom, and who alone knows the Father and reveals him to whom he will,[4] to those, namely, who become capable of receiving his word and wisdom, may not perhaps be said to express the image of God's substance or subsistence for this reason, that he makes God understood and known; that is, when wisdom outlines first in herself the things which she wishes to reveal to others, by means of which they are to know and understand God, then she herself may be called the express image of God's substance.[5]

In order, however, to understand still more completely how the Saviour is 'the image of God's substance' or subsistence, let us use an illustration which, although it does not fully or properly represent the subject under discussion, we may yet be allowed to employ for the sole purpose of showing that when the Son, 'who was in the form of God, emptied himself,'[6] his desire was by means of this very emptying to display to us the fulness of the godhead. Let us suppose, for example, that there existed a statue of so great a size as to fill the whole world, but which on account of its immensity was imperceptible to anyone, and that another statue was made similar to it in every detail, in shape of limbs and outline of features, in form and material, but not in its immense size, so that those who were unable to perceive and behold the immense one could yet be

---

[1] St. Matt. VII. 5, St. Luke VI. 42.
[2] See 1 Tim. II. 5.
[3] Heb. I. 3.
[4] See St. Matt. XI. 27.
[5] Heb. I. 3.
[6] Phil. II. 6, 7.

confident that they had seen it when they saw the small one, because this preserved every line of limbs and features and the very form and material with an absolutely indistinguishable similarity.[1]

It is by some such likeness as this that the Son, in emptying himself of his equality with the Father,[2] and showing to us a way by which we may know him, becomes an 'express image' of God's substance;[3] so that, through this fact of his becoming to us the brightness, we who were not able to look at the glory of pure light while it remained in the greatness of his godhead, may find a way of beholding the divine light through looking at the brightness. Needless to say, a comparison with statues, taken from the region of material things, is to be allowed for no other purpose but to show that the Son of God, though brought within the very narrow compass of a human body, yet gave indications, in the likeness of his power and works to those of God the Father, of the immense and invisible greatness that was in him; witness the words which he said to his disciples, 'He that hath seen me hath seen the Father also',[4] and, 'I and the Father are one';[5] along with which we must also interpret that similar saying of his, 'the Father in me, and I in the Father'.[6]

9. Let us now see what is the meaning of that passage which we find written in the Wisdom of Solomon, who speaks of wisdom as follows: 'She is a breath of the power of God and a pure effluence (that is, emanation) of the glory of the Almighty and the brightness of the eternal light and an unspotted mirror of the working or power of God and an image of his goodness.'[7] He gives here five definitions of God and from each of them in turn he indicates a certain characteristic belonging to God's wisdom; for he speaks of God's 'power' and 'glory' and 'eternal light' and 'working' and 'goodness'. He says, however, that wisdom is a breath not of the glory of the Almighty, nor of the eternal light, nor of the working of the Father, nor of his goodness, since it was not suitable to apply the term breath to any one of these; but in all appropriateness he says that wisdom is a breath of the 'power' of God. Now the power of God must mean that by which he is strong, that by which he both established and also preserves and controls all things visible and invisible, and that by

---

[1] Jerome refers to this passage in his *Ep. ad Avitum* 2. 'He gives an illustration of two statues, an immense one and a very small one; the former fills the world and is in a way invisible from its very size, the latter is perceptible to our sight. The former he compares to the Father, the latter to the Son.'

[2] See Phil. II. 7.
[3] See Heb. I. 3.
[4] St. John XIV. 9.
[5] St. John X. 30.
[6] St. John X. 38.
[7] Wisd. VII. 25, 26.

which he is sufficient for all things which are the objects of his providence and with all of which he is present as if they were joined in one. The breath, then, or if I may so call it, the strength of all this power, so great and so immense, comes to have a subsistence of its own; and although it proceeds from the power itself as will proceeding from mind,[1] yet nevertheless the will of God comes itself to be a power of God. There comes into existence, therefore, another power, subsisting in its own proper nature, a kind of breath, as the passage of Scripture calls it, of the first and unbegotten power of God, drawing from this source whatever existence it has; and there is no time when it did not exist.

For if anyone is inclined to describe it as being non-existent at first but coming into existence afterwards, let him tell us why the Father who caused it to exist did not do so before. And if he lays it down that there was one definite beginning when this 'breath' first proceeded from the power of God, we shall ask again why it did not so proceed before this beginning of which he has spoken. Thus by ever inquiring what happened before and going further back with our questions, we shall reach the conclusion that, since God always had both the power and the will, there was never the slightest reason or possibility that he should not always have had this good thing that he desired. This proves that there always has existed that breath of the power of God, having no beginning but God himself. Nor indeed could it have fitly had any other beginning except him from whom it takes its existence and birth, that is, God. And in regard to the apostle's saying that 'Christ is the power of God',[2] this power must be called not merely a breath of the power of God but a power proceeding from the power.

10. Let us now look into the saying that wisdom is 'an effluence', that is, an emanation, 'of the clear glory of the Almighty', and if we first consider what 'the glory of the Almighty' is, we shall then understand what its 'effluence' is. Now as one cannot be a father apart from having a son, nor a lord apart from holding a possession or a slave, so we cannot even call God almighty if there are none over whom he can exercise his power. Accordingly, to prove that God is almighty we must assume the existence of the universe. For if anyone would have it that certain ages, or periods of time, or whatever he cares to call them, elapsed during which the present creation did not exist, he would undoubtedly prove that in those ages or periods God was not almighty, but that he afterwards became almighty from the time when he began to have creatures over whom he could exercise power. Thus God will apparently have experienced a kind of progress, for there can be no doubt that it is better for him to be almighty than not to be so.

[1] See p. 19 above.   [2] 1 Cor. I. 24.

GREEK

Now[1] how is it anything but absurd that God should at first not possess something that is appropriate to him and then should come to possess it? But if there was no time when he was not almighty, there must always have existed the things in virtue of which he is almighty; and there must always have existed things under his sway, which own him as their ruler.

LATIN

Now how does it seem anything but absurd that God should at first not possess something that is appropriate to him, and afterwards by a kind of progress should come to possess it? But if there was no time when he was not almighty, then of necessity those things must always have existed, in virtue of which he is called almighty; and he must always have had creatures over which he exercised his power and which were controlled by him as king and ruler.

LATIN

Of these we shall treat more fully in the proper place, when we come to discuss the subject of God's creatures.[2] Yet even now, since we are dealing with the question how wisdom is a pure effluence, or emanation, of the glory of the Almighty, I deem it necessary to give warning, however briefly, to prevent anyone from thinking that the title of Almighty belonged to God before the birth of wisdom, through which he is called Father; for wisdom, which is the Son of God, is said to be a 'pure effluence of the glory of the Almighty'. Let him who is inclined to believe this hear what the scriptures plainly proclaim; for it says that 'thou hast made all things in wisdom',[3] and the Gospel teaches that 'all things were made by him and without him was not anything made';[4] and let him understand from this that the title of Almighty cannot be older in God than that of Father, for it is through the Son that the Father is almighty.

But the passage speaks of a glory belonging to the Almighty, of which glory wisdom is the effluence. From this we learn that wisdom, through which God is called Almighty, has a share even in the glory of omnipotence. For it is through wisdom, which is Christ, that God holds power over all things, not only by his own authority as Master, but also by the voluntary service of his subjects. And to prove to you that the omnipotence of the Father and the Son is one and the same, just as God and

---

[1] Frag. 5 Koetschau, from Justinian *Ep. ad Mennam* (Mansi IX. 528).
[2] See Ch. IV. 3-5, pp. 41-43 below.
[3] Ps. CIV. 24 (Sept. CIII. 24).
[4] St. John I. 3.

the Lord are one and the same as the Father, listen to the manner
in which John speaks in the Apocalypse: 'These things saith
the Lord God, which is and which was and which is to come,
the Almighty'.[1]   For he who 'is to come', who else is it but
Christ?   And just as no one ought to be offended because, while
the Father is God, the Saviour also is God; so too ought no
one to be offended because, while the Father is called Almighty,
the Son also is called Almighty.

Moreover we shall in this way see the truth of that saying
which Christ utters to the Father: 'All things that are mine
are thine, and thine are mine, and I am glorified in them'.[2]
Now if all things which are the Father's are Christ's, and
among all that the Father is, he is Almighty, then undoubtedly
the only-begotten Son must also be Almighty, that the Son
may have all that the Father has. 'And I am glorified,' he
says, 'in them.'   For 'in the name of Jesus every knee shall
bow, of things in heaven, and things on earth, and things under
the earth; and every tongue shall confess that Jesus is Lord in
the glory of God the Father.'[3]   He is therefore the 'effluence of
the glory of God' in this respect, that he is Almighty, God's
pure and clear wisdom itself, glorified as being the effluence of
omnipotence or glory.

We add the following, however, to make it more clearly
understood what the glory of omnipotence is.   God the Father
is almighty because he holds dominion over all things, that is,
over heaven and earth, sun, moon and stars and everything contained in them.   This dominion he exercises through his Word,
for 'in the name of Jesus every knee bows, of things in heaven,
and things on earth, and things under the earth'.   Now if every
knee bows to Jesus, then undoubtedly it is Jesus to whom all
things have been subjected, and it is he who wields dominion
over all things, and all things have been subjected to the Father
through him; for it is through wisdom, that is, by word and
reason and not by force and necessity, that they are subject.
His glory, therefore, lies in the very fact that he possesses all
things; and this is the purest and brightest glory of omnipotence,
that the universe is held in subjection by reason and wisdom, and
not by force and necessity.   It is called the 'purest and brightest'
glory of wisdom as the most suitable way of distinguishing it
from that glory which is not pure or sincere.

For every nature which is alterable and changeable, even
though it may be glorified in works of righteousness or wisdom,
cannot be said to possess a glory that is sincere and bright, by

---

[1] Rev. I. 8.
[2] St. John XVII. 10.
[3] Phil. II. 10, 11.   The Latin reads 'that the Lord Jesus is in the
glory of God the Father'.   But we have Origen's Greek in *Comm. in Ioh.*
VI. 44; *Con. Cels.* VIII. 59; *Hom. in Jerem.* XVIII. 3, and in each case
it agrees with the text of the N. T.

reason of the fact that its righteousness and wisdom are accidents, and whatever is accidental may also be separated and lost. But since the wisdom of God, which is his only-begotten Son, is in all respects unalterable and unchangeable, and since every good quality in him is essential and can never be changed or altered, his glory is on that account described as pure and sincere.

11. In the third place, wisdom is said to be the brightness of the eternal light. The force of this expression we have explained in a previous passage, where we introduced the illustration of the sun and the brightness of its rays[1] and showed to the best of our ability how the expression should be understood. We will add, however, this one point. The term everlasting or eternal properly denotes that which had no beginning of existence and can never cease to be what it is. This is the idea underlying the passage in John, where he says that 'God is light'.[2] Now God's wisdom is the brightness of that light, not only in so far as it is light, but in so far as it is everlasting light. His wisdom is therefore an everlasting brightness, enduring eternally. If this point is fully understood, it is a clear proof that the Son's existence springs from the Father himself, yet not in time, nor from any other beginning except, as we have said, from God himself.

12. Wisdom is also called an 'unspotted mirror of the *energy* or working of God'.[3] We must first understand, therefore, what the 'working' of God's power is. It is a kind of strength, so to speak, by means of which the Father works, whether in his acts of creation, or of providence, or of judgment, or in the ordering and superintendence of every detail of the universe at his own appointed time. And when wisdom is called the 'unspotted mirror' of the Father's power and working, she would have us understand her nature to be like the image reflected in a mirror, which moves and acts in correspondence with the movements and actions of him who looks into the mirror, not deviating from them in any way whatever. So too the Lord Jesus Christ, who is the wisdom of God, speaks of himself when he says, 'the works which the Father doeth, these also doeth the Son in like manner';[4] and again, 'the Son can do nothing of himself, but what he hath seen the Father doing'.[5]

As regards the power of his works, then, the Son is in no way whatever separate or different from the Father, nor is his work anything other than the Father's work, but there is one and the same movement, so to speak, in all they do; consequently the Father has called him an 'unspotted mirror', in order to make it understood that there is absolutely no dissimilarity between the Son and the Father. Some indeed have said

---

[1] See Ch. I. 6, p. 10.   [2] 1 St. John I. 5.
[3] See Wisd. VII. 25; and above ch. II. 9, p. 22. Rufinus uses the Greek word ἐνεργείας and then translates it by *inoperationis*.
[4] St. John V. 19.   [5] *Ibid.*

that the Son's acts are to be compared with a pupil's work in likeness to or imitation of his master, or that such things as the Father has first formed in their spiritual essence are made by the Son in bodily material;[1] yet how can these opinions be reconciled with the Gospel, which says, not that the Son does like things, but that he does the same things 'in like manner'?[2]

13. There remains the inquiry, what is the 'image of his goodness'? Here, I think, we do well to adopt the same line of reasoning which we used above in regard to the image formed in a mirror. The original goodness is undoubtedly the Father; and from this is born the Son, who is in every respect an image of the Father, and who may also without any doubt be properly called an 'image of his goodness'.

GREEK

In the same way,[3] therefore, I consider that in the case of the Saviour it would be right to say that he is an image of God's goodness, but not goodness itself. And perhaps also the Son, while being good, is yet not good purely and simply. And just as he is the image of the invisible God, and in virtue of this is himself God, and yet is not he of whom Christ himself says, 'that they may know thee, the only true God'; so he is the image of the goodness, and yet not, as the Father is, good without qualification.

LATIN

For there is no other second goodness existing in the Son, besides that which is in the Father. So the Saviour himself rightly says in the Gospel that 'none is good save one, God the Father',[4] the purpose of this statement being to make it understood that the Son is not of some other 'goodness', but of that alone which is in the Father; whose image he is rightly called, because he neither springs from any other source than from original goodness itself,—for if that were so, there would seem to be a different goodness in the Son from that which is in the Father—nor has the goodness that is in him any dissimilarity or divergence from that of the Father. Accordingly we ought

---

[1] See Origen, *Comm. in Cant.* iii. 'Perhaps as God made man in his own image and likeness, he also created all other creatures in the likeness of other heavenly forms.' It looks as if the opinion expressed in the text above belongs really to Origen, and Rufinus is rejecting it.

[2] St. John V. 19.

[3] Frag. 6, Koetschau, from Justinian, *Ep. ad Mennam* (Mansi IX. 525). Rufinus has abbreviated and changed the sense of the original. See too Jerome, *Ep. ad Avitum* 2 : 'God the Father almighty he (i.e. Origen) calls good, and of perfect goodness. The Son is not good, but is a kind of breath and image of goodness, so that he is not called good absolutely, but with an addition, such as the good shepherd, etc.'

[4] St. Mark X. 18.

not to imagine that there is some kind of blasphemy, as it were, in the saying that 'none is good save one, God the Father',[1] as if these words were to be taken as a denial that either Christ or the Holy Spirit is good; but, as we said before,[2] the original goodness must be believed to reside in God the Father, and from him both the Son and Holy Spirit undoubtedly draw into themselves the nature of that goodness existing in the fount[3] from which the one is born and the other proceeds.

If then there are any other things called good in the scriptures, such as an angel, or a man, or a slave, or a treasure, or a good heart, or a good tree,[4] all these are so called by an inexact use of the word, since the goodness contained in them is accidental and not essential. And it would be a long business, demanding another time and another work, to collect all the titles of the Son of God, such for example as the true light, or the door, or righteousness, or sanctification, or redemption, and countless others,[5] and to explain for what reasons either in regard to his powers or his moral qualities each of these names is given to him. Let us rest content with those we have already discussed, and go on to inquire into the remaining parts of our subject in their proper order.

---

[1] St. Mark X. 18.
[2] See p. 27.
[3] See Ch. I. 6, p. 10.
[4] For 'good angel' see Tobit V. 21 and 2 Macc. XV. 23; 'good man', St. Matt. XII. 35; 'good slave', St. Matt. XXV. 21; 'good treasure', St. Matt. XII. 35; 'good heart', St. Luke VIII. 15; 'good tree', St. Matt. VII. 17.
[5] Origen makes such a collection in his *Comm. in Ioh.* I. 21-24.

CHAPTER III

THE HOLY SPIRIT

1. We come, therefore, to the investigation, in as brief a manner as possible, of the subject of the Holy Spirit. Now all who in any way believe in the existence of Providence admit that God, who created and set in order the entire creation, is unbegotten,[1] and they recognise him to be the parent of the universe. And we are not alone in declaring that he has a Son. For although this may seem marvellous and incredible to those who are considered to be philosophers, whether of Greek or barbarian race, yet there are some even of them who appear to have held a belief in his existence, for they admit that all things were created by the word or reason of God.[2] We, however, in conformity with our faith in that doctrine which we hold for certain to be divinely inspired, believe that there is no possible way of explaining and bringing to man's knowledge the higher and diviner teaching about the Son of God, except by means of those scriptures which were inspired by the Holy Spirit, namely, the gospels and the writings of the apostles, to which we add, according to the declaration of Christ himself,[3] the law and the prophets. But no one except those who are familiar with the law and the prophets, or those who profess their belief in Christ, could have even a suspicion of the personal existence of the Holy Spirit. For although no one is able to speak worthily of God the Father, still it is possible to gain some notion of him from our experience of the visible creation and from the instinctive thoughts of the human mind; and, moreover, it is possible for such knowledge to be confirmed from the holy scriptures. And in regard to the Son of God, although 'no one knoweth the Son save the Father',[4] yet again from the divine scriptures the mind of man is directed how to think of him too; and this not only from the New, but also from the Old Testament, through those deeds done by holy men which allude figuratively to Christ, and from which we can learn both his divine nature and the human nature which he assumed.

2. Of the existence of the Holy Spirit, however, we are taught in many passages of scripture. For instance, David says in the

---

[1] See Ch. II. 6, p. 19 above.
[2] The doctrine of the Logos, the Reason or Thought of God immanent in creation, was first expressed by Heracleitus (c. 500 B.C.). Plato, in the *Timaeus*, 34 B, describes the World-soul which the Creator put within the body of the universe to be the source of life and reason.
[3] See St. Luke XXIV. 25-27: St. John V. 39, 46.
[4] St. Matt. XI. 27.

fiftieth psalm, 'And take not thy Holy Spirit from me';[1] and in
Daniel it is said, 'The Holy Spirit, who is in thee'.[2] But in the
New Testament we have proofs in abundance, as when the Holy
Spirit is related to have descended upon Christ,[3] and when the
Lord breathed on his apostles after the resurrection and said,
'Receive the Holy Spirit';[4] and the angel says to Mary, 'The
Holy Spirit shall come upon thee',[5] and Paul teaches us that
'no one can say that Jesus is the Lord except in the Holy
Spirit',[6] and in the Acts of the Apostles 'through the laying on
of the apostles' hands the Holy Spirit was given'[7] in baptism.
From all of which we learn that the person of the Holy Spirit
is of so great authority and dignity that saving baptism is not
complete except when performed with the authority of the whole
most excellent Trinity, that is, by the naming of Father, Son
and Holy Spirit;[8] and that the name of the Holy Spirit must
be joined to that of the unbegotten God the Father and his
only-begotten Son. Who, then, is not amazed at the tremendous
majesty of the Holy Spirit, when he hears that 'he who shall
speak a word against the Son of man' may hope for forgiveness,
but 'he who shall blaspheme against the Holy Ghost has no
forgiveness, either in this present world or in the world to
come'?[9]

3. It is proved by many declarations throughout the whole
of scripture that the universe was created by God and that there
is no substance which has not received its existence from him;
which refutes and dismisses the doctrines falsely taught by some,
that there is a matter which is co-eternal with God,[10] or that
there are unbegotten souls, in whom they would have it that
God implanted not so much the principle of existence as the
quality and rank of their life.[11] Moreover in that little book

---

[1] Ps. LI. (Sept. L.) 13.
[2] Dan. IV. 6 (Theodotion) : see IV. 9, English version.
[3] See St. Matt. III. 16 and parallels.
[4] St. John XX. 22.
[5] St. Luke I. 35.
[6] I Cor. XII. 3.
[7] Acts VIII. 18.
[8] See St. Matt. XXVIII. 19.
[9] St. Matt. XII. 32.
[10] This is a Gnostic doctrine, taught by Marcion among others. Tertullian, *Adv. Marc. I.* xv. 'If, then, he constructed the world out of some
underlying material that was unborn and uncreated and contemporaneous
with God, as Marcion believes the Creator did, ...'
[11] See Origen, *Con. Cels.* IV. 30. 'We shall not, however, imitate him
(i.e. Celsus) nor speak after his style about the philosophers who declare
that they know the nature of the universe and argue with one another
whether . . . souls are unbegotten and not created by God but simply
arranged in order by him and changed from one body to another, or whether
they are originated at the same time as the body and then either endure for
ever or pass away.' Origen's own opinion, according to Rufinus (*Apol. ad*

composed by Hermas, called 'The Shepherd, or the Angel of Repentance',[1] it is thus written: 'First of all, believe that God is one, who created and set in order all things; who, when nothing existed before, caused all things to be; who contains all things, but himself is contained by none.'[2] Similar statements are also made in the book of Enoch.[3] But up to the present we have been able to find no passage in the holy scriptures which would warrant us in saying that the Holy Spirit was a being made or created, not even in that manner in which we have shown above that Solomon speaks of wisdom, nor in the manner in which the expressions we have dealt with, such as life, or word, or other titles of the Son of God, are to be understood. The 'Spirit of God', therefore,

GREEK

Following[4] the same reasoning we believe that everything whatever except the Father and God of the universe is created.

LATIN

who 'moved upon the waters', as it is written, in the beginning of the creation of the world,[5] I reckon to be none other than the Holy Spirit, so far as I can understand; which indeed I have demonstrated in my exposition of these passages,[6] not, however, according to their literal but according to their spiritual meaning.

4. Now some of our predecessors have observed that in the New Testament, whenever the Spirit is mentioned without its qualifying adjective, the expression should be understood to refer to the Holy Spirit; as for instance, 'the fruit of the Spirit is love, joy, peace'[7] and the rest. And here again: 'seeing ye began in the Spirit, are ye now made perfect in the flesh?'[8] We, however, think that this peculiar use may be observed in the Old Testament also, as when it says, 'he that giveth spirit

---

Anastas, 6) was as follows: 'Some maintain that souls were created long ago, when God made all things of nothing, and that now he simply arranges them in bodies according to his own judgment. This is the opinion of Origen and certain other Greeks.' See below pp. 72-74.

[1] The second title occurs in Hermas, *Vis.* V. 8, and in Clem. Alex. *Strom.* I. 85, 4 (Stählin ii, 55, 12 f.)

[2] Hermas, *Mand.* 1.

[3] Enoch, Ch. II. 5.

[4] Frag. 7, Koetschau, from Justinian, *Ep. ad Mennam* (Mansi IX. 528). Justinian's letter contains also the following sentence: 'that he (i.e. Origen) called the Holy Spirit a created being, as well as the Son, and included them in the number of the other created beings; and accordingly he terms them "ministering creatures".' Koetschau inserts these last two words in the text. Rufinus has omitted the heretical statements.

[5] See Gen. I. 2, 1.   [7] Gal. V. 22.

[6] Not extant.   [8] Gal. III. 3.

to the people who are upon the earth, and spirit to them that walk thereon'.[1] For undoubtedly every one who walks upon the earth, that is to say, every earthly and corporeal being, is a partaker of the Holy Spirit, which he receives from God. And

GREEK	LATIN
my Hebrew master[2] used to say that the two six-winged seraphim in Isaiah[3] who cry one to another and say, Holy, holy, holy is the Lord of hosts, were the only-begotten Son of God and the Holy Spirit. And we ourselves think that the expression in the song of Habakkuk, 'In the midst of the two living creatures thou shalt be known'[4] is spoken of Christ and the Holy Spirit.	my Hebrew master used to say that the two seraphim, which are described in Isaiah[3] as having six wings each and as crying one to another and saying, Holy, holy, holy is the Lord of hosts, were to be understood to mean the only-begotten Son of God and the Holy Spirit. And we ourselves think that the expression in the song of Habakkuk, 'In the midst of the two animals' (or the two living creatures) 'thou shalt be known',[4] should be understood to refer to Christ and the Holy Spirit.

LATIN

For all knowledge of the Father, when the Son reveals him, is made known to us through the Holy Spirit. So that both of these, who in the words of the prophet are called 'animals' or 'living beings', are the cause of our knowledge of God the Father. For as it is said of the Son that 'no one knoweth the Father but the Son, and he to whom the Son willeth to reveal him',[5] so in the same way does the apostle speak of the Holy Spirit; 'God hath revealed them unto us by his Spirit: for the Spirit searcheth all things, even the deep things of God.'[6] Again, when in the gospel the Saviour is referring to the divine and deeper doctrines which his disciples could not yet receive, he speaks to the apostles as follows: 'I have yet many things to say unto you, but ye cannot receive them now; howbeit when the comforter is come, even the Holy Spirit, who proceedeth from the Father, he shall teach you all things, and bring to

---

[1] Is. XLII. 5.
[2] Frag. 8. Justinian, *Ep. ad. Mennam* (Mansi IX. 528). The passage is also adversely commented on by Antipater of Bostra, in John of Damascus, *Sacra Parallela* II. 771 (Migne P. G. 96, p. 505). It seems to suggest that the Son and the Spirit are creatures. But see below p. 311.
[3] Is. VI. 2 f.   [5] St. Matt. XI. 27.
[4] Habak. III. 2 (Sept.)   [6] I Cor. II. 10.

your remembrance all that I have said unto you'.[1] So then we must understand that as the Son, who alone knows the Father, reveals him to whom he will, in the same way also the Holy Spirit, who alone 'searcheth even the deep things of God',[2] reveals God to whom he will. For 'the Spirit breathes where he willeth'.[3]

We must not suppose, however, that the Spirit knows God as we do, through the revelation of the Son. For if the Holy Spirit knows the Father by this means, he passes from ignorance to knowledge; and it is certainly as impious as it is foolish to confess that he is the Holy Spirit and then to ascribe ignorance to him. For even if we grant that something else existed before the Holy Spirit, yet it was not by a process of development that he came to be the Holy Spirit; as if one should dare to say that at the time when he was not yet the Holy Spirit he did not know the Father, but that after he had gained this knowledge he became the Holy Spirit. That could not be, for the Holy Spirit would never have been included in the unity of the Trinity, that is, along with God the unchangeable Father and with his Son, unless he had always been the Holy Spirit.[4] Of course, these terms that we use, such as 'always' or 'has been', or any similar ones that bear a temporal significance, must be interpreted with reservations and not pressed; for they relate to time, but the matters of which we are now speaking, though described in temporal language for the purposes of discussion, in their essential nature transcend all idea of time.

5. Nevertheless it seems right to inquire into the reason why he who is 'born again through God'[5] to salvation has need of both Father and Son and Holy Spirit and will not obtain salvation apart from the entire Trinity, and why it is impossible to become partaker of the Father or the Son without the Holy Spirit. In discussing these points it will undoubtedly be necessary to describe the activity which is peculiar to the Holy Spirit and that which is peculiar to the Father and Son.

GREEK

The God[6] and Father, who holds the universe together, is superior to every being that exists, for he imparts to each

---

[1] St. John XVI. 12 f.; XIV. 26.
[2] 1 Cor. II. 10.
[3] Or, 'The Spirit (or wind) bloweth where it listeth.' St. John III. 8.
[4] Cp. Origen In Num. Hom. XI. 8. 'I think therefore that the Holy Spirit is holy without ever having been made holy. For there did not come to him from some external source a holiness which he did not previously possess, but he always was holy, and never experienced a beginning of holiness.'
[5] 1 St. Peter I. 3.
[6] Frag. 9, Koetschau, from Justinian, Ep. ad Mennam (Mansi IX. 524). The passage is omitted by Rufinus, but we have a Latin version of it in Jerome, Ep. ad Avitum 2; 'The Son also, he says, is less than the Father,

one from his own existence that which each one is; the Son, being less than the Father, is superior to rational creatures alone (for he is second to the Father); the Holy Spirit is still less, and dwells within the saints alone. So that in this way the power of the Father is greater than that of the Son and of the Holy Spirit, and that of the Son is more than that of the Holy Spirit, and in turn the power of the Holy Spirit exceeds that of every other holy being.

LATIN

I am of opinion, then, that the activity of the Father and the Son is to be seen both in saints and in sinners, in rational men[1] and in dumb animals, yes, and even in lifeless things and in absolutely everything that exists; but the activity of the Holy Spirit does not extend at all either to lifeless things, or to things that have life but yet are dumb, nor is it to be found in those who, though rational, still lie in wickedness[2] and are not wholly converted to better things. Only in those who are already turning to better things and walking in the ways of Jesus Christ, that is, who are engaged in good deeds and who abide in God,[3] is the work of the Holy Spirit, I think, to be found.

6. That the activity of the Father and the Son is to be found both in saints and in sinners is clear from the fact that all

---

being second to him; and the Holy Spirit is inferior to the Son and dwells in all the saints. And in this order the power of the Father is greater than that of the Son and of the Holy Spirit; and in turn the power of the Son is greater than the Holy Spirit and so too the power of the Holy Spirit is greater than that of all other beings who are called holy.' Origen explains his meaning somewhat more fully in *Con. Cels.* V. 29 and VIII. 15. In the former passage he calls the Son a 'second God' in the sense that in him are contained all virtues and all reason, which virtues and reason dwelt pre-eminently in the soul of Jesus. In the latter he declares that Christians 'say that the Son is not stronger than the Father but inferior to him'. Origen's doctrine, which is susceptible of a strictly orthodox interpretation, may be illustrated from Justin, I *Apol.* 13 (Christ is regarded as God 'in the second place'); from a fragment in Leont. Byzant. *De Sectis,* Act. X. 4 (Migne P. G. 86. 1, p. 1264); and from Hilary, *De Trin.* III. 12, IX. 56, XII. 54 and *Tract. in Ps.* cxxxviii, 17. Compare also the practical teaching of the Church Catechism, 'First I learn to believe in God the Father, who hath made me and all the world; secondly in God the Son, who hath redeemed me and all mankind; and thirdly in God the Holy Ghost, who sanctifieth me and all the elect people of God.'

[1] *In hominibus rationalibus.* Semler suggests *omnibus* for *hominibus.* Koetschau, however, thinks that the text needs further emendation and proposes the following: 'the activity of the Father and the Son is to be seen in all rational beings, both saints and sinners; that of the Father in dumb animals also, yes, and even. . . . . ' But Rufinus may well have written the text as it stands, in his keen desire to avoid anything like Origen's subordination of the Son.

[2] 1 St. John V. 19.

[3] See 1 Cor. IV. 17, Eph. II. 10, 1 St. John IV. 13.

rational beings are partakers of the word of God, that is, of
reason, and so have implanted within them some seeds, as it
were, of wisdom and righteousness, which is Christ. And all
things that exist derive their share of being from him who
truly exists, who said through Moses, 'I am that I am';[1] which
participation in God the Father extends to all, both righteous
and sinners, rational and irrational creatures and absolutely everything that exists.   Certainly the apostle Paul shows that all have
a share in Christ, when he says, 'Say not in thy heart, who
shall ascend into heaven? that is, to bring Christ down; or who
shall descend into the abyss? that is, to bring Christ back
again from the dead.   But what saith the scripture?   The word
is nigh thee, even in thy mouth and in thy heart.'[2]   By this he
indicates that Christ is 'in the heart' of all men, in virtue of
his being the word or reason, by sharing in which men are
rational.

Moreover that passage in the Gospel which says, 'If I had
not come and spoken unto them they had not had sin, but now
they have no excuse for their sin',[3] clearly refers to those who
have come to the age of reason, up to which time a man does
not 'have sin', but from whence onward he becomes responsible
for sin; and it reveals how men are said to 'have sin' when they
share in the word or reason, that is to say, from the time when
they become capable of knowledge and understanding, as soon
as the reason implanted within them has taught them the distinction between good and evil; and when once they have begun
to know what is evil then, if they do it, they render themselves
responsible for sin.   This is the meaning of the saying that men
'have no excuse for their sin' from the time that the divine word
or reason has begun to reveal within their heart the distinction
between good and evil, to warn them that they must avoid and
beware of evil; and it is also the meaning of that other saying,
'To him that knoweth good and doeth it not, to him it is sin'.[4]

Again, the gospel teaches that no men are without communion
with God, when the Saviour speaks as follows, 'The kingdom
of God cometh not with observation; neither shall they say, Lo
here! or, there! but the kingdom of God is within you'.[5]
Further, we must see whether perhaps the same meaning does
not attach to what is written in Genesis, 'And he breathed into
his face the breath of life, and man became a living soul'.[6]   If
this breath of life is understood to have been given to men in
general, then all men have a share in God.   But if we are to
understand the expression as referring to the Spirit of God, in
view of the fact that Adam is found to have uttered certain

---

[1] Exod. III. 14.   [4] St. James IV. 17.
[2] Rom. X. 6-8.   [5] St. Luke XVII. 20, 21.
[3] St. John XV. 22.   [6] Gen. II. 7.

prophecies,[1] then the breath of life may be regarded as given not universally but only to the saints.

7. Finally, at the time of the flood, when 'all flesh had corrupted God's way,'[2] it is written that God said, as if speaking of unworthy men and sinners, 'My spirit shall not remain in those men for ever, because they are flesh'.[3] Here it is clearly shown that God's spirit is taken away from all the unworthy. It is also written in the Psalms; 'Thou wilt take away their spirit and they will die, and return to their earth; thou wilt send forth thy spirit and they shall be created, and thou wilt renew the face of the earth',[4] which passage clearly points to the Holy Spirit who, after sinners and the unworthy have been taken away and destroyed, creates for himself a new people and 'renews the face of the earth', when through the grace of the Spirit men 'put off the old man with his doings'[5] and begin 'to walk in newness of life'.[6] And this is why the passage fitly applies to the Holy Spirit, because he will dwell not in all men, nor in those who are flesh, but in those whose 'earth has been renewed'. Finally, it was for this reason that the Holy Spirit was bestowed through the laying on of the apostles' hands after the grace and renewal of baptism.[7] Moreover our Saviour after the resurrection, when 'old things had now passed away and all things had become new',[8] being himself 'the new man'[9] and the 'firstborn from the dead',[10] says to the apostles, who were also renewed by faith in his resurrection, 'Receive the Holy Spirit'.[11] This is doubtless what our Saviour Lord himself was pointing out in the gospel, when he said that 'new wine could not be put into old wineskins'[12] and commanded that new wineskins be made, that is, that men should walk 'in newness of life'[13] in order to receive the new wine, the newness of the Holy Spirit's grace.

Thus, therefore, the working of the power of God the Father and God the Son is spread indiscriminately over all created beings, but a share in the Holy Spirit is possessed, we find,

---

[1] Cp. Origen, *Comm. in Cant.* II. 'Adam also is reckoned among the prophets, because he prophesied the "great mystery" in regard to Christ and the Church.' See Eph. V. 32. Also Clem. Alex. *Strom.* I. 135, 3 (Stählin II 84. 5). 'Before the law Adam uttered prophecies in regard to the woman and in regard to the naming of the animals.'

[2] Gen. VI. 12.

[3] Gen. VI. 3.

[4] Ps. CIII. 29, 30 (Eng. vers. CIV.).

[5] Col. III. 9.

[6] Rom. VI. 4.

[7] See Acts VIII. 18, Tit. III. 5.

[8] 2 Cor. V. 17.

[9] Eph. II. 15.

[10] Col. I. 18.

[11] St. John XX. 22.

[12] St. Matt. IX. 17 and parallels.

[13] Rom. VI. 4.

by the saints alone. Accordingly it is said, 'No man can say that Jesus is the Lord except in the Holy Spirit.'[1] Even the apostles themselves are scarcely at the last counted worthy of hearing the words, 'Ye shall receive power, when the Holy Spirit is come upon you'.[2] It follows logically from this, I think, that 'he who has sinned against the Son of Man is worthy of forgiveness',[3] because he who is a sharer in the word or reason seems, if he ceases to live according to reason, to have fallen into ignorance or folly and so to deserve forgiveness; whereas he who has once been counted worthy to share in the Holy Spirit and then turns back again is by this very act and deed said to have blasphemed against the Holy Spirit.[4]

Let no one indeed imagine from what we have said about the Holy Spirit being bestowed on the saints alone, while the blessings and activities of the Father and the Son extend to both good and evil, just and unjust,[5] that we are hereby exalting the Holy Spirit above the Father and the Son or claiming that his dignity is greater than theirs; for this by no means follows. What we have been describing is the peculiar grace and work of the Holy Spirit. But more, nothing in the Trinity can be called greater or less,[6] for there is but one fount of deity, who upholds the universe by his word and reason, and sanctifies 'by the spirit of his mouth' all that is worthy of sanctification, as it is written in the Psalm, 'By the word of the Lord were the heavens established, and all their power by the spirit of his mouth.'[7]

There is, however, a special activity of God the Father, beyond that which he exercised on all things in giving them natural life. There is also a special ministry of the Lord Jesus Christ towards those on whom he confers the natural gift of reason, by means of which well-being is bestowed upon them in addition to mere existence. There is yet another grace of the Holy Spirit bestowed upon such as are worthy, a grace ministered indeed through Christ, but put into operation by the Father in proportion to the merits of those who become capable or receiving it. This is most clearly pointed out by the apostle Paul, when he is explaining that the power of the Trinity is one and the same, in the passage where he says, 'There are diversities of gifts, but the same spirit; and there are diversities

---

[1] 1 Cor. XII. 3.

[2] Acts I. 8.

[3] See St. Matt. XII. 32.

[4] See St. Matt. XII. 31, 32; St. Mark III. 29.

[5] See St. Matt. V. 45.

[6] Koetschau (following Schnitzer, who regarded the passage from 'But more' to 'spirit of his mouth' as interpolated by Rufinus) points out that this sentence contradicts the Greek fragment on p. 33. The probability would seem to be that Rufinus has modified some such phrase as 'there is no separation in the Trinity' (see p. 37) into what appears above.

[7] Ps. XXXIII. 6.

of ministrations, but the same Lord; and there are diversities of workings, but the same God, who worketh all things in all. But to each one is given the manifestation of the spirit as is profitable.'[1] Here we are most clearly shown that there is no separation in the Trinity,[2] but that this which is called the 'gift of the spirit' is ministered through the Son and worked by God the Father. And yet 'all these worketh that one and the self-same spirit, dividing to each man as he will'.[3]

8. This then, is the testimony we bear to the unity of Father, Son and Holy Spirit. Let us now return to the original plan of our discussion.[4] God the Father bestows on all the gift of existence; and a participation in Christ, in virtue of his being the word or reason, makes them rational. From this it follows that they are worthy of praise or blame, because they are capable alike of virtue and of wickedness. Accordingly there is also available the grace of the Holy Spirit, that those beings who are not holy in essence may be made holy by participating in this grace. When therefore they obtain first of all their existence from God the Father, and secondly their rational nature from the Word, and thirdly their holiness from the Holy Spirit, they become capable of receiving Christ afresh in his character of the righteousness of God,[5] those, that is, who have been previously sanctified through the Holy Spirit; and such as have been deemed worthy of advancing to this degree through the sanctification of the Holy Spirit obtain in addition the gift of wisdom by the power of the working of God's Spirit. This is what I think Paul means when he says that 'to some is given the word of wisdom, to others the word of knowledge, by the same spirit'.[6] And while pointing out the distinction of each separate gift he refers them all to the fount of the universe when he says, 'There are diversities of workings, but one God, who worketh all things in all.'[7]

Thus the working of the Father, which endows all with existence, is found to be more glorious and splendid, when each one, through participation in Christ in his character of wisdom and knowledge and sanctification, advances and comes to higher degrees of perfection; and when a man, by being sanctified through participation in the Holy Spirit, is made purer and holier, he becomes more worthy to receive the grace of wisdom and knowledge, in order that all stains of pollution and ignorance may be purged and removed and that he may make so great an advance in holiness and purity that the life which he received from God shall be such as is worthy of God, who gave it to be pure and perfect, and that that which exists shall be as

---

[1] 1 Cor. XII. 4-7.
[2] See note p. 37 above.
[3] 1 Cor. XII. 11.
[4] See Gr. Frag. pp. 33-34 above.
[5] See 1 Cor. I. 30.
[6] 1 Cor. XII. 8.
[7] 1 Cor. XII. 6.

worthy as he who caused it to exist. Thus, too, the man who is such as God who made him wished him to be, shall receive from God the power to exist for ever and to endure for eternity. That this may come to pass, and that those who were made by God may be unceasingly and inseparably present with him who really exists, it is the work of wisdom to instruct and train them, and lead them on to perfection, by the strengthening and unceasing sanctification of the Holy Spirit, through which alone they can receive God.

In this way, then, through the ceaseless work on our behalf of the Father, the Son and the Holy Spirit, renewed at every stage of our progress, we may perchance just succeed at last in beholding the holy and blessed life; and when after many struggles we have been able to attain to it we ought so to continue that no satiety of that blessing may ever possess us; but the more we partake of its blessedness, the more may the loving desire for it deepen and increase within us, as ever our hearts grow in fervour and eagerness to receive and hold fast the Father, the Son and the Holy Spirit. But if at any time satiety should possess the heart of one of those who have come to occupy the perfect and highest stage, I do not think that such a one will be removed and fall from his place all of a sudden. Rather must he decline by slow degrees, so that it may sometimes happen, when a slight fall has occurred, that the man quickly recovers and returns to himself. A fall does not therefore involve utter ruin, but a man may retrace his steps and return to his former state and once more set his mind on that which through negligence had slipped from his grasp.

CHAPTER IV

LOSS, OR FALLING AWAY

To show what is this loss, or fall, of those who live negligently, it seems not unreasonable to make use of an illustration.
Suppose a man has gradually become skilled in the science or
art, let us say, of geometry or medicine, up to the point of
reaching perfection, having trained himself for a long time by
instructions and exercises so as to acquire completely the knowledge of the aforesaid art. It could surely never happen that
such a man should lie down to sleep with all this skill and wake
up without it. It is not to the point to bring forward or take
account here of accidents which happen through some injury or
weakness, for these do not apply in the case we have proposed
as an illustration. According to that, so long as the geometrician
or doctor in question occupies himself in the studies and rational
instructions relating to his art, a knowledge of the subject will
remain with him. If, however, he loses interest in these exercises and neglects to work, then through this negligence his
knowledge is gradually lost, a few details at first, then more,
and so on until after a long time the whole vanishes into oblivion
and is utterly erased from his memory. Yet if, in the first stages
of his fall, when the negligence which threatens to ruin him
has not gone far, he is aroused and without delay returns to
himself, it is certainly possible to recover that which had but
recently been lost and to renew the knowledge which by that
time had been only slightly erased from his mind. Let us now
apply this to those who have devoted themselves to the knowledge
and wisdom of God, to learn and labour about whom surpasses
all other studies in ways beyond comparison; and let us consider, in the light of our illustration, what is involved in the
acquisition of this knowledge and what in its loss, especially
bearing in mind what the apostle says of those who are perfect,
that they shall behold the glory of the Lord 'face to face' 'by
revelations of mysteries'[1] * * * * * * * *
(All[2] rational creatures who are incorporeal and invisible, if they
become negligent, gradually sink to a lower level and take to

[1] It is evident that Rufinus has omitted a considerable section at this
point, for in his text there is no discussion of 'what is involved in the
acquisition of this knowledge, and what in its loss'. Fragments of the
missing section are found in Jerome and are inserted into the text here
by Koetschau. For the N.T. allusions see 1 Cor. XIII. 2 and Rom. XVI.
25.
[2] See Jerome *Con. Joh. Hieros.* 16, 'We wish to know . . . whether
the doctrine of Origen is true, who said that all rational creatures . . . ' and
as above.

themselves bodies suitable to the regions into which they descend; that is to say, first, ethereal bodies, and then aereal. And when they reach the neighbourhood of the earth they are enclosed in grosser bodies, and last of all are tied to human flesh[1] '* * * It is[2] a mark of extreme negligence and sloth for any soul to descend and to lose its own nature so completely as to be bound, in consequence of its vices, to the gross body of one of the irrational animals.)'

2. But[3] in our desire to explain the divine blessings which are bestowed upon us by the Father, the Son and the Holy Spirit, that Trinity which is the fount of all holiness, we have somewhat digressed from our subject in these last remarks; for when the question of the soul had arisen, we felt we ought to deal with it here, seeing that we were discussing the cognate topic of our rational nature. But the subject of rational nature as a whole, with its divisions into three genera and species, will be more conveniently considered in its proper place.[4] And with God's permission, through Jesus Christ and the Holy Spirit, we shall so consider it.

3. This blessed[5] and ruling power, therefore, that is, the power that exercises control of all things, we call the Trinity. This is the good God and kindly Father of all, at once beneficent power and creative power, that is, the power that does good and creates and providentially sustains. And it is absurd and impious to suppose that these powers of God have been at any time in abeyance for a single moment. Indeed, it is unlawful even to entertain the least suspicion that these powers, through which chiefly we gain a worthy notion of God, should at any time have ceased from performing works worthy of themselves and have become inactive. For we can neither suppose that these powers which are in God, nay, which are God, could have been thwarted from without, nor on the other hand, when nothing

---

[1] This doctrine of the descent of the soul is found in Plato, *Phaedrus* 246 B-D, a passage clearly referred to by Origen in *Con. Cels.* IV. 40. Jerome says (*Con. Joh. Hieros.* 19), in connexion with this doctrine: 'What you admire so much we long ago despised when we found it in Plato.' Koetschau refers also to the doctrine of Carpocrates, the Gnostic, as set forth in Irenaeus *Adv. Haer.* 1, XXV. 4. But there is no resemblance between the ethical system of Origen and the antinomian theories of Carpocrates beyond the fact that both are based on the idea of transmigration.

[2] See Jerome *Ep ad. Avitum* 3, 'When he comes to deal with rational creatures and says that they have descended into earthly bodies through negligence, he adds the following: It is a mark of extreme negligence. . . .' and as above. Jerome says also in *Con. Joh. Hieros.* 19 that 'Origen used Jacob's ladder to teach that rational creatures descend gradually to the lowest step, namely, to flesh and blood.' This may also belong here.

[3] We return to Rufinus at this point.

[4] i.e. in Ch. V. (p. 44 ff.).

[5] This section, to the end of Ch. IV., is found in one MS. only and has been obliterated from another. See Koetschau's ed., p. 65, note on l. 8.

stood in their way, can we believe that they were reluctant to act and perform works worthy of themselves or that they feigned impotence. We can therefore imagine no moment whatever when that power was not engaged in acts of well-doing. Whence it follows that there always existed objects for this well-doing, namely, God's works or creatures, and that God, in the power of his providence, was always dispensing his blessings among them by doing them good in accordance with their condition and deserts. It follows plainly from this, that at no time whatever was God not Creator, nor Benefactor, nor Providence.

4. Yet in this matter human intelligence is feeble and limited, when it tries to understand how during the whole of God's existence his creatures have existed also, and how those things, which we must undoubtedly believe to have been created and made by God have subsisted, if we may say so, without a beginning. Since then there is this conflict in our human thoughts and reasonings, and the soundest arguments on either side oppose and rebut one another, each bending the mind of the thinker into its own direction, this truth, which can be confessed without any risk to piety, presents itself as appropriate to the small and narrow capacity of our mind, namely, that God the Father always existed, and that he always had an only-begotten Son, who at the same time, according to the explanation we have given above, is called Wisdom. This is that Wisdom in whom God delighted when the world was finished,[1] in order that we might understand from this that God ever rejoices. In this Wisdom, therefore, who ever existed with the Father, the Creation was always present in form and outline, and there was never a time when the pre-figuration of those things which hereafter were to be did not exist in Wisdom.

5. It is probably in this way that, so far as our weakness allows, we shall maintain a reverent belief about God, neither asserting that his creatures were unbegotten and coeternal with him nor on the other hand that he turned to the work of creation to do good when he had done nothing good before. For the saying that is written, 'In wisdom hast thou made all things,'[2] is a true one. And certainly if 'all things have been made in wisdom', then since wisdom has always existed, there have always existed in wisdom, by a pre-figuration and pre-formation, those things which afterwards have received substantial existence. This is, I believe, the thought and meaning of Solomon when he says in Ecclesiastes: 'What is it that hath been made? The same that is to be. And what is it that hath been created? The same that is destined to be created. And there is nothing fresh under the sun. If one should speak of anything and say, Behold, this is new: it already hath been, in the ages that were before

---

See Prov. VIII. 30 (Latin text in Lactantius, *Inst. Div.* IV. 6).
[2] Ps. CIV. (Sept. CIII.) 24.

us'.[1] If then particular things which are 'under the sun' have already existed in the ages which were before us—since 'there is nothing fresh under the sun'—then

GREEK	LATIN
all genera[2] and species have for ever existed, and some would say even individual things; but either way, it is clear that God did not begin to create after spending a period in idleness.	undoubtedly all genera and species have for ever existed, and possibly even individual things; but either way, the fact is made clear that God did not begin at a certain time to be Creator, when he had not been such before.

[1] Eccl. I. 9, 10.
[2] Frag. 10, from Justinian, *Ep. ad Mennam* (Mansi IX. 528.)

CHAPTER V

RATIONAL NATURES

1. After this brief discussion which we have conducted to the best of our ability on the subject of the Father, the Son and the Holy Spirit, our next task is to say a few words about rational natures, their species, orders and functions. We shall include not only the holy and the wicked powers, but also those who occupy a middle position between the good and the bad and are still involved in struggle and conflict. We find in the holy scriptures very many names of certain orders and functions both of the holy powers and of the opposite kind. First we shall mention these names themselves, and then we shall attempt, so far as we are able, to investigate their meaning.

There are certain holy angels of God whom Paul calls 'ministering spirits, appointed to minister on behalf of those who shall receive the inheritance of salvation'.[1] Also, in the writings of the same Saint Paul we find him giving the names, from what source I know not, of certain 'thrones, dominions, principalities and powers';[2] and after enumerating these, as if he thought there were yet other rational functions and orders beyond those already mentioned, he says of the Saviour, 'Who is above every principality and authority and power and dominion, and every name that is named not only in this world, but also in the world to come'.[3] Here he plainly shows that besides those beings he has mentioned there are certain others, which may be named indeed in this world, but yet have not on the present occasion been enumerated by him, and which perhaps were not known to any other person; and there are others still, which cannot be named in this world, but will be named in the world to come.

2. Then in the next place we must know that every being which is endowed with reason and yet fails to adhere to the ends and ordinances laid down by reason, is undoubtedly involved in sin by this departure from what is just and right. Every rational creature is therefore susceptible of praise and of blame; of praise, if in accordance with the reason which he has in him he advances to better things; of blame, if he departs from the rule and course of what is right, in which case he is also rightly subject to pains and penalties. We must believe this to be true even of the devil himself and of those who are with him and are called his angels. But the titles of these beings must now

---

[1] Heb. I. 14.   [2] Col. I. 16.   [3] Eph. I. 21.

be explained, in order that we may know who they are with whom our discussion has to deal.

The name Devil, and Satan, and Wicked one, is mentioned in many places of scripture, and he who bears it is also described as being the enemy of God. Certain 'angels of the devil'[1] are also named, and in addition a 'prince of this world';[2] but whether this latter is the devil himself or some other has not yet been clearly proclaimed. There are also certain 'princes of this world' mentioned, who have a wisdom which is to be destroyed;[3] but whether these princes are the same as those principalities 'against whom our wrestling is',[4] or whether they are different, no one, it seems to me, can easily decide. After the principalities there is also a mention of certain powers, against whom we wrestle and maintain a struggle, as we do also against the 'princes of this world' and the 'rulers of this darkness'; and certain 'spiritual hosts of wickedness in the heavenly places'[5] are also mentioned by Paul. And what are we to say of the 'evil spirits' and 'impure daemons'[6] who are mentioned in the gospels? Then again, there are some who are included under the common title of 'heavenly beings', but who are said to bend the knee, or to be destined to bend the knee, at the name of Jesus; and others again who are 'earthly' or from 'under the earth',[7] all of whom Paul enumerates in order.

And in a place where we have been discussing the subject or rational natures it would certainly not be right to keep silence about ourselves, the race of men, who as you know are called 'rational animals'. Nor must we pass over this point, as if it were unimportant, that even in regard to us men there are references to certain different classes, as when it is said that 'the Lord's portion is his people Jacob, Israel is the cord of his inheritance',[8] whereas other nations are said to be the portion of the angels, as, 'when the Most High divided the nations and dispersed the sons of Adam, he fixed the bounds of the nations according to the number of the angels of God'.[9] Therefore, along with all the other rational natures, the constitution of the human soul must also be examined.

3. Such, then, are the many important names of orders and functions that are given us, and behind them it is certain that there are real existences. We must now inquire whether God, the Founder and Creator of all things, made some of these beings so holy and blessed that they could admit nothing at all that

---

[1] St. Matt. XXV. 41; Rev. XII. 7.
[2] St. John XII. 31; XIV. 30; XVI. 11.
[3] See 1 Cor. II. 6.
[4] See Eph. VI. 12.
[5] Ibid.
[6] See St. Luke VII. 21; IV. 33.
[7] Phil. II. 10.   [8] Deut. XXXII. 9.   [9] Deut. XXXII. 8.

was contrary to this nature, and others in such a way that they could become capable both of virtue and of wickedness; or whether we are to suppose that he made some to be altogether incapable of virtue, and others who can admit no wickedness whatever but can only remain in a state of blessedness, and others still who can admit either of these conditions. To begin our inquiry from the names themselves, let us consider whether the 'holy angels', from the time they first existed, always were holy, and are holy, and will be holy, and neither have ever admitted nor could ever admit an occasion of sin.

Then in the next place, let us also consider whether those who are called holy 'principalities' began from the first moment of their creation by God to exercise their 'principality' over others who had been made subject to them, and whether the latter were created in this condition and made for the very purpose of being subject and subordinate. Similarly, in regard to those who are called 'powers', let us consider whether they were created in this condition and for this very purpose, that they might exercise power, or whether it is some prize or reward of virtue that they have come to this power and dignity. Moreover, in regard to those who are called 'thrones' or 'seats', let us consider whether they were counted worthy of their seat and secure possession of blessedness from the time their personality first emerged, so that they enjoy it solely by the will of the Creator, and whether those who are called 'dominions' have had this dominion not conferred upon them as a reward for their progress but freely bestowed as a privilege of their creation, so that it is in some way a part of their nature and inseparable from them.

Now if we accept the view that the holy angels and holy powers and blessed seats and glorious virtues and splendid dominions possess their powers and dignities and glories as part of their essence, it will seem to follow undoubtedly that those beings which have been mentioned in connexion with the opposite functions must be regarded in the same way. Thus those principalities 'against whom our wrestling is' must be held not to have departed from good of their own free will and after that to have adopted the determination to resist and oppose everything good, but to have possessed this determination as part of their essence from the beginning. Similarly in regard to the powers and virtues, the evil that is in them will not be later than or subsequent to their first existence. Those, too, whom scripture has termed 'rulers and princes of the darkness of the world', inherit this realm of darkness which they rule over and possess, not as a result of perversity of will but from the necessity of their creation. Similar reasoning will force us to the same conclusion in regard to the 'spiritual hosts of wickedness' and the 'evil spirits' and 'impure daemons'.

But if this is an absurd belief to hold of the bad and opposing powers—and it certainly is absurd that the cause of their wickedness should be separated from the determination of their own will and ascribed, as something unavoidable, to their Creator—how can we fail to come to a similar conclusion in regard to the good and holy powers, namely, that goodness is not in them as part of their essence. Essential goodness is found, as we have plainly shown,[1] solely in Christ and the Holy Spirit, and of course in the Father also. For the nature of the Trinity has been shown to contain nothing that is compound, which might appear to allow these good qualities to belong to it as accidental consequences. We conclude, then, that the position of every created being is the result of his own work and his own motives, and that the powers above mentioned, which appear as holding sway or exercising authority or dominion over others, have gained this superiority and eminence over those whom they are said to govern or on whom they exercise their authority, not by some privilege of creation but as the reward of merit.

4. Yet in questions of such importance and difficulty we do not wish to base our assertions merely on a correct train of reasoning and to compel the assent of our hearers by conjectural inferences alone. Let us see, therefore, whether we can obtain any statements from the holy scriptures, by the authority of which these conclusions may be more credibly upheld. First we shall bring forward what holy scripture contains on the subject of the evil powers; and after that, with the help of such light as the Lord shall be pleased to bestow upon us, we shall make inquiry about the rest of the powers, our object being, in matters of so great difficulty, to get as near to the truth as possible and to shape our belief according to the rule of piety.

Now we find in the prophet Ezekiel two prophecies addressed to the prince of Tyre, the first of which might appear, before one had heard the second, to be spoken of some man who was prince of the Tyrians. For the present, therefore, we shall take nothing from the first one. But since the second is most evidently of such a kind that it cannot possibly refer to a man, but must be understood of some higher power, which had fallen from higher places and been cast down to lower and worse ones, we shall adduce that as an illustration which most clearly proves that these opposing and wicked powers were not so formed and created by nature, but came from better conditions and changed for the worse; and that the blessed powers also are not of such a nature as to be unable to admit qualities the opposite of their own, supposing one of them should desire to do so and should become negligent and fail to guard with the utmost caution the blessedness of his condition. For when he who is called the

---

[1] See Ch. II. 13 (p. 27 f.).

'prince of Tyre'[1] is related to have been 'among the holy ones' and 'without stain' and set 'in the paradise of God', 'adorned with a crown of honour and beauty', how, I ask, can we suppose such a being to have been inferior to any of the holy ones? He is described as having been 'a crown of honour and beauty' and as having walked 'in the paradise of God' 'without stain'. How then can anyone possibly suppose that such a being was not one of those holy and blessed powers which, dwelling as they do in a state of blessedness, we must believe are endowed with no other honour than this?

But let us now see what the actual words of the prophecy teach us. 'The word of the Lord', it says, came unto me, saying, Son of man, take up a lamentation for the prince of Tyre, and say unto him, Thus saith the Lord God: Thou wert a signet of likeness and a crown of honour in the delights of the paradise of God. Thou wast adorned with every fine stone and gem, and wast clothed with sardius and topaz and emerald and carbuncle and sapphire and jasper, set in gold and silver, and with agate and amethyst and chrysolite and beryl and onyx; with gold also didst thou fill thy treasuries and thy store-houses in thy midst. From the day thou wast created with the cherubim, I placed thee in the holy mount of God. Thou wast in the midst of the fiery stones, thou wast stainless in thy days, from the day thou wast created until the time that iniquities were found in thee; from the multitude of thy commerce thou didst fill thy storehouses with iniquity, and thou didst sin and wast cast wounded out of the mount of God. A cherub drove thee forth from the midst of the fiery stones. Thy heart was lifted up at thine honour; thy knowledge was corrupted with thy beauty; for the multitude of thy sins I have cast thee down to the earth in the presence of kings. I have given thee for a show and a laughing-stock because of the multitude of thy sins and thine iniquities. By thy commerce thou hast polluted thy holy places. And I will bring forth fire from the midst of thee and it shall devour thee, and I will give thee for ashes and cinders on the earth in the sight of all that see thee; and all who knew thee among the nations shall mourn over thee. Thou hast been made a destruction, and thou shalt exist no more for ever.'[2]

Who is there that, hearing such sayings as this, 'Thou wast a signet of likeness and a crown of honour in the delights of the paradise of God', or this, 'from the time thou wast created with the cherubim, I placed thee in the holy mount of God', could possibly weaken their meaning to such an extent as to suppose them spoken of a human being, even of a saint, not to mention the prince of Tyre? Or what 'fiery stones' can he think of, 'in the midst' of which any man could have lived?

---

[1] See Ezek. XXVIII. 11-19.   [2] Ezek. XXVIII. 11-19.

Or who could be regarded as 'stainless' from the very 'day he was created', and yet at some later time could have acts of unrighteousness found in him and be said to be 'cast forth into the earth'? This certainly indicates that the prophecy is spoken of one who, not being in the earth, was 'cast forth into the earth', whose 'holy places' also are said to be 'polluted'.

These statements, therefore, from the prophet Ezekiel concerning the prince of Tyre, must relate, as we have shown, to an adverse power, and they prove in the clearest manner that this power was formerly holy and blessed, and that he fell from this state of blessedness and was cast down into the earth 'from the time that iniquity was found in him', and that his fallen condition was not due to his nature or creation. We consider, therefore, that these statements refer to some angel, to whom had been allotted the duty of supervising the Tyrian people, whose souls also were apparently committed to his care. But what Tyre, or what souls of Tyrians we ought to understand— whether it be the city which is situated in the territory of the province of Phoenicia, or some other city of which the one we know on earth is a figure, and whether the souls are those of the actual Tyrians, or of the inhabitants of that Tyre which we understand spiritually,—there seems no need to inquire in this place. For we should appear to be investigating, in a casual manner, matters whose importance and obscurity certainly demand a work and treatment of their own.

5. Again, we are taught by the prophet Isaiah the following facts about another opposing power. He says : 'How has Lucifer, who arose in the morning, fallen from heaven. He who assailed all the nations is broken and dashed to the earth. Thou saidst indeed in thy heart, I will ascend into heaven; above the stars of heaven I will place my throne; I will sit upon a lofty mountain above the lofty mountains which are toward the north; I will ascend above the clouds; I will be like the Most High. But now shalt thou be cast down to the lower world, and to the foundations of the earth. All who see thee shall be amazed over thee and say : This is the man that afflicted the whole earth, that moved kings, that made the whole round world a desert, that destroyed cities and did not loose those who were in chains. All the kings of the nations sleep in honour, each one in his own house; but thou shalt be cast forth upon the mountains, as an accursed dead man, with the many dead that have been pierced through with swords and have descended to the lower world. As a garment clotted and stained with blood will not be clean, so too shalt thou not be clean, because thou hast ruined my land and killed my people. Thou shalt not abide henceforth for ever, thou most wicked seed. Make ready thy sons for slaughter for the sins of their father, that they rise not up and possess the earth by inheritance and fill it with wars. And I will rise

up against them, saith the Lord of Sabaoth, and I will cause their name to perish and their remnant and their seed.'[1]

It is most clearly proved by these words that he who formerly was Lucifer and who 'arose in the morning' has fallen from heaven. For if, as some suppose, he was a being of darkness, why is he said to have formerly been Lucifer or light-bearer? Or how could he 'rise in the morning', who had in him no light at all? Moreover the Saviour teaches us about the devil as follows: 'Lo, I see Satan fallen as lightning from heaven'.[2] So he was light once. Further, our Lord, who is the truth, compared even the power of his own glorious advent to lightning, in the words: 'For as the lightning shineth from one end of heaven even to the other, so shall also the coming of the Son of Man be'.[3] Yet he also compares Satan to lightning, and says that he fell from heaven, in order to show thereby that he was in heaven once, and had a place among the holy ones, and a share in that light in which all the holy ones share, in virtue of which the angels become 'angels of light'[4] and the apostles are called 'the light of the world'[5] by the Lord.

In this way, then, even Satan was once light, before he went astray and fell to this place, when 'his glory was turned into dust',[6] which is the peculiar mark of the wicked, as the prophet also says. And so he is called the 'prince of this world',[7] for he exercises his princely power over those who are obedient to his wickedness, since 'this whole world' (and here I take 'world' to mean this earthly place) 'lieth in the evil one',[8] that is, in this apostate. That he is an apostate, or fugitive,[9] the Lord also says in Job, in the following words, 'Thou wilt take with a hook the apostate dragon',[10] that is, the fugitive dragon. And it is certain that the dragon means the devil himself.

The opposing powers, then, are called by the name of 'fugitives' and are said to have been at one time 'stainless'. But to be stainless is a quality which belongs essentially to none except the Father, Son and Holy Spirit; for holiness is in every created being an accidental quality, and what is accidental may also be lost. These opposing powers, however, were once stainless and dwelt indeed among those that have continued stainless until now. All this shows that no one is stainless by essence

[1] Is. XIV. 12-22.
[2] St. Luke X. 18.
[3] St. Matt. XXIV. 27.
[4] 2 Cor. XI. 14.
[5] St. Matt. V. 14.
[6] See Is. XIV. 11, 12.
[7] St. John XII. 31; XVI. 11.
[8] 1 St. John V. 19.

[9] Rufinus transliterates the Greek ἀποστάτης and then gives the Latin equivalent *refuga,* runaway, fugitive, or exile.
[10] Job XL. 20.

or by nature, nor is any one polluted essentially. Consequently it lies with us and with our own actions whether we are to be blessed and holy, or whether through sloth and negligence we are to turn away from blessedness into wickedness and loss; the final result of which is, that when too much progress, if I may use the word, has been made in wickedness, a man may descend to such a state (if any shall come to so great a pitch of negligence) as to be changed into what is called an opposing power.[1]

[1] Jerome's version of this passage should be compared with the above, which Koetschau regards as unfaithful to the original. See Jerome, *Ep. ad Avitum* 3. 'Moved by these considerations we believe that as a result of their own free will some are included in the number of the saints and those who serve God, while others of their own fault have departed from holiness and descended to such a pitch of negligence as to be changed into opposing powers.'

CHAPTER VI

THE END OR CONSUMMATION

1. An end or consummation is clearly an indication that things are perfected and consummated. This fact is a timely reminder to us, that if a man is seized with a desire to read and learn about these matters that are so hard and difficult to understand, he must bring with him a perfect and instructed mind. Otherwise, if he has had no experience in inquiries of this kind, they may perhaps appear to him to be vain and superfluous; or else, if he has a mind full of prejudice and preoccupations in other directions, he may think these inquiries are heretical and contrary to the faith of the Church, not so much because he is convinced by reason as because he decides according to his own prejudices. Now we ourselves speak on these subjects with great fear and caution, discussing and investigating rather than laying down fixed and certain conclusions. For we have previously pointed out what are the subjects on which clear doctrinal statements must be made, and such statements we made, I think, to the best of our ability, when speaking of the Trinity.[1] Now, however, we are dealing, as well as we can, with subjects that call for discussion rather than for definition.

The end of the world and the consummation will come when every soul shall be visited with the penalties due for its sins. This time, when everyone shall pay what he owes, is known to God alone. We believe, however, that the goodness of God through Christ will restore his entire creation to one end, even his enemies being conquered and subdued. For so says the holy scripture: 'The Lord said unto my Lord, Sit thou on my right hand, until I make thine enemies the footstool of thy feet'.[2] And if it is not very evident what the prophetic language here means, let us learn from Paul the Apostle, who says more openly, 'Christ must reign, till he hath put all his enemies under his feet'.[3] But if even this clear declaration of the Apostle is not sufficient to inform us what is the meaning of 'putting enemies under his feet', hear further what he says in the words that follow: 'For all things must be made subject to him'.[4] What then is this 'subjection', by which 'all things must be made subject' to Christ? In my opinion it is the same subjection by which we too desire to be subjected to him, and by which the apostles and all the saints who have followed Christ were subject to him. For the word subjection, when used of

---

[1] See Preface 3-10 (pp. 2-6).
[2] Ps. CX. 1 (Sept. CIX. 1).
[3] 1 Cor. XV. 25.
[4] 1 Cor. XV. 27, 28.

our subjection to Christ, implies the salvation, proceeding from Christ, of those who are subject; as David also said, 'Shall not my soul be subject to God? For of him cometh my salvation'.[1]

2. Seeing, then, that such is the end, when 'all enemies shall have been subjected to Christ', when 'the last enemy shall be destroyed, that is, death', and when 'the kingdom shall be delivered up to God and the Father by Christ, to whom all things have been subjected',[2] let us, I say, from such an end as this, contemplate the beginning of things. For the end is always like the beginning; as therefore there is one end of all things, so we must understand that there is one beginning of all things, and as there is one end of many things, so from one beginning arise many differences and varieties, which in their turn are restored, through God's goodness, through their subjection to Christ and their unity with the Holy Spirit, to one end, which is like the beginning.[3] I refer to all those who, by 'bending the knee in the name of Jesus',[4] have through this very fact displayed the sign of their subjection. These are they who dwell 'in heaven and on earth and under the earth',[5] the three terms indicating the entire universe, that is, all those beings who started from one beginning but were drawn in various directions by their own individual impulses and were distributed throughout the different ranks of existence in accordance with their merit; for in them goodness does not reside essentially, as it does in God and his Christ and in the Holy Spirit. For only in this Trinity, which is the source of all things, does goodness reside essentially. Others possess it as an accident, liable to be lost, and only then do they live in blessedness, when they participate in holiness and wisdom and in the divine nature itself.

GREEK	LATIN
In the case[6] of those who do not pay sleepless attention to themselves, changes of condition take place, more quickly or	But if they are careless and indifferent about this participation, then each becomes the cause of his own lapse or fall,

<hr/>

[1] Ps. LXII. 1 (Sept. LXI. 1).

[2] See 1 Cor. XV. 24-27.

[3] Again Rufinus has altered Origen, considerably weakening his precise statements. See Jerome *Ep. ad Avitum* 3. 'Once again a beginning arises from the end and an end from the beginning, and all things are so changed that one who is now a man may in another world become a daemon, while a daemon, if he lives negligently, may be bound to a grosser body, that is, may become a man. Thus,' continues Jerome, 'he mixes up everything, so that one may be changed from an archangel into a devil, and on the other hand a devil may turn into an angel.'

[4] Phil. II. 10.

[5] *Ibid.*

[6] Frag. 11. Justinian, *Ep. ad Mennam* (Mansi IX. 528). A comparison of the two columns will show how freely Rufinus has dealt with Origen's work, omitting some passages and expanding others.

GREEK

more slowly, and to a greater or less extent, according to the individual fault. So, arising out of this fault, by a divine judgment corresponding to the better or worse movements of each and in accordance with merit, one will have in the future order of things the rank of angel; or the power of a ruler; or authority over certain beings; or a throne over subjects; or lordship over slaves.

LATIN

one more quickly and another more slowly, one to a greater and another to a lesser extent, by the fault of his own personal slothfulness. Now, as we have said, the particular fall or lapse by which each one departs from its original state is capable of exhibiting the greatest diversity, corresponding to the movements of the mind and will, so that one recedes but slightly, another more seriously, to lower things. Here then we see the just judgment of God's providence, that diversity of conduct is taken into account and each is treated according to the deserts of his departure and defection from goodness. Certain of those, indeed, who have continued in that beginning which we have described as being like the end that is to come, have allotted to them in the ordering and arrangement of the world, the rank of angel, others that of powers, others that of principalities, others that of authorities (clearly in order to exercise authority over those who 'need to have authority above their head');[1] while others have the rank of thrones, the duty of judging and ruling those who need this, and others have lordship, doubtless over slaves. All these privileges the divine providence, by a fair and just judgment, has conferred upon them as a reward for their merit and for the progress they have made in imitating and participating in God.

---

[1] See 1 Cor. XI. 10.

GREEK

Others, however, who have not been utterly cast out, will have a subordinate position assigned them below those above mentioned. And thus, generally speaking, from among those who have been set under the rulers and authorities and thrones and lordships, even from these the human race will one day be constituted in the world in unity. . . .

LATIN

Those, however,[1] who have moved from their state of primal blessedness, yet not beyond the possibility of return, have been made subject to the rule and governance of those holy and blessed orders whom we have just described; and if they make use of the help of these and become reformed by their precepts and salutary discipline, they may return and be restored to their state of blessedness. It is probably from among these, so far as I am able to judge, that the order of our human race was constituted, in the hope of restoring it in the age to come, or in the ages beyond that, when there shall be the 'new heaven and new earth',[2] of which Isaiah speaks, to that unity

LATIN

which the Lord Jesus promises when he prays to God the Father for his disciples, 'I pray not for these alone, but also for all who shall believe on me through their word, that they all may be one; as I, Father, am in thee, and thou art in me, that so they may be one in us';[3] and again when he says, 'That they may be one, as we are one, I in them, and thou in me, that they also may be perfected in one'.[4] The Apostle Paul also confirms this when he says, 'Till we all come to the unity of the faith, to a perfect man, to the measure of the stature of the fulness of Christ';[5] and the same apostle also exhorts us, who even now in the present life have been placed in the Church, in which we see an imitation of the future kingdom, to strive after the same pattern of unity, when he says, 'That ye all say the same things, and that there be no divisions among 'you, but that ye be

---

[1] Cp. Jerome *Ep. ad Avitum* 3. 'Those, however, who have descended, but whose movement has not involved them in utter ruin, will be made subject to the care and rule and governance of the principalities, powers, thrones and dominions; and perhaps out of these the human race will one day be constituted in one of the worlds that will be made when, as Isaiah says, there shall be a "new heaven and a new earth".'

[2] Is. LXV. 17.

[3] St. John XVII. 20, 21.

[4] St. John XVII. 22, 23.

[5] Eph. IV. 13.

perfected in one and the same mind and in one and the same judgment'.[1]

3. We must know, however, that some of those[2] who fell from that beginning of which we have spoken above, have given themselves over so completely to a life of unworthiness and wickedness, that they are not only regarded as unworthy of this instruction and training whereby through the flesh the human race, aided by the heavenly powers, is being instructed and trained, but on the contrary become adversaries and opponents of those who are being so trained and disciplined. The result is that all our mortal life is full of struggles and conflicts, since we are resisted and thwarted by those who can see no way back to the better state from which they fell, those, namely, who are called 'the devil and his angels',[3] and other orders of wicked beings whom the apostle enumerates among the opposing powers.

GREEK	LATIN
But[4] I think that, from among those that have been made subject to the worse kind of rulers and authorities and world-powers, in each world or in certain worlds, there are some who, by reason of their good deeds and their desire to be transferred from these powers, will speedily attain manhood *	But whether among those orders that live under the chieftainship of the devil and conform to his wickedness there are some who will one day in the ages to come succeed in turning to goodness

by reason of the power of free-will which is in them, or whether it be true that long-continued and deep-rooted wickedness turns

---

[1] I Cor. I. 10.

[2] See Jerome, *Ep. ad Avit.* 3. 'Those, however, who do not deserve to return to their former state by passing through a human life, will become the 'devil and his angels' and the worst kind of daemons, and will be appointed to different tasks in one of the many worlds according to their varying degrees of merit.'

[3] See above p. 44 ff.

[4] Frag. 12 (Koetschau) from Justinian, *Ep. ad Mennam* (Mansi IX. 529) Rufinus has shortened the original. There is another paraphrase of this passage of Origen in Jerome, *Ep. ad Avitum* 3 : 'the daemons themselves and the rulers of the darkness in any world or worlds, if they desire to turn to better things, become men and so revert to their original condition, in order that being disciplined by the punishments and torments which they endure for a long or short period while in the bodies of men they may in time reach the exalted rank of the angels. It follows logically from this that any rational creature can develop out of any other, not once or suddenly but over and over again ; that we may become angels or, if we live carelessly, daemons, and on the other hand daemons, if they desire to possess virtue, may attain the dignity of angels.' No opinion of Origen's was more vehemently opposed than this one which gave daemons and lost men a chance of restoration. See Rufinus *Apol.* I. 10 and Augustine, *De Civ. Dei* XXI, 17 ; also pp. 40-41 above.

at last from a habit into a kind of nature, you, reader, must judge; whether, that is, this portion of the creation shall be utterly and entirely out of harmony even with that final unity and concord, both in the ages that are 'seen' and 'temporal' and in those that are 'not seen' and eternal.[1] But in the meantime, alike in these ages that are 'seen' and 'temporal' and in those that are 'not seen' and 'eternal',[2] all those beings are arranged in a definite order proportionate to the degree and excellence of their merits. And so it happens that some in the first, others in the second, and others even in the last times, through their endurance of greater and more severe punishments of long duration, extending, if I may say so, over many ages, are by these very stern methods of correction renewed and restored, first by the instruction of angels and afterwards by that of powers yet higher in rank, so that they advance through each grade to a higher one, until at length they reach the things that are 'invisible' and 'eternal', having traversed in turn, by some form of instruction, every single office of the heavenly powers. It appears to follow from this, in my opinion, that every rational nature can, in the process of passing from one order to another, travel through each order to all the rest, and from all to each, while undergoing the various movements of progress or the reverse in accordance with its own actions and endeavours and with the use of its power of free will.

4. Now Paul says that there are some things that are 'seen' and 'temporal', while besides these there are others that are 'not seen' and 'eternal'. We ask therefore in what sense those that are 'seen' are 'temporal'? Does it mean that in all those periods and ages to come, in which the dispersion and division of the one beginning is to be restored to one and the same end and likeness, there will exist nothing whatever corresponding to this present world? Or is it rather that while the form of the things that are 'seen' passes away, their substance is by no means destroyed? Now Paul seems to confirm the latter explanation when he says; 'the form of this world shall pass away'.[3] Moreover David seems to indicate the same truth when he says; 'The heavens shall perish, but thou shalt remain; and they all shall grow old as a garment, and as a cloak thou shalt change them, as a garment they shall be changed'.[4] For if the heavens shall be 'changed', certainly that which is 'changed' does not perish; and if 'the form of this world passes away', it is not by any means an annihilation or destruction of the material

---

[1] Rufinus leaves the salvation of the devil and his angels an open question, though Origen had asserted it as a fact. See Jerome *Ep. ad Pamm. et Ocean.* 7 (Origen teaches that) 'after many ages and the one restoration of all things Gabriel will be in the same state as the devil, Paul as Caiaphas and virgins as prostitutes.'

[2] See 2 Cor. IV. 18.   [3] 1 Cor. VII. 31.   [4] Ps. CII. 26.

substance that is indicated, but the occurrence of a certain change of quality and an alteration of the outward form.

Isaiah too, when he says in prophecy that 'there shall be a new heaven and a new earth',[1] undoubtedly suggests a similar thought. For the renewal of 'heaven and earth' and the transmutation of the 'form of this world' and the alteration of the 'heavens' will undoubtedly be accomplished in readiness for those who are journeying along the way which we have indicated above,[2] making for that end, namely, blessedness, to which we are told that even God's enemies themselves are to be subjected, the end in which God is said to be 'all' and 'in all'.[3] And if any-one thinks that in this 'end' material or bodily nature will utterly perish, he can provide no answer whatever to my difficulty, how beings so numerous and mighty can exist and live their life without bodies; since we believe that to exist without material substance and apart from any association with a bodily element is a thing that belongs only to the nature of God, that is, of the Father, the Son and the Holy Spirit. Perhaps somebody else will say that in the end every bodily substance will be so pure and refined that we must think of it as being like the ether, as it were of a heavenly purity and clearness.[4] But exactly how it will be is known to God alone, and to those who through Christ and the Holy Spirit are the 'friends'[5] of God.

[1] Is. LXV. 17. [2] See p. 57. [3] See 1 Cor. XV. 24, 25, 28.
[4] Jerome's version of this is as follows (*Ep. ad Avitum* 4). 'Bodily substances will utterly disappear, or at any rate in the end of all things bodies will be similar to our air and sky or to any clearer and purer body that can be conceived.'
[5] St. John XV. 15; St. James II. 23.

CHAPTER VII

THINGS CORPOREAL AND INCORPOREAL

1. In the preceding chapters, after the place in which we set forth to the best of our ability the doctrine of the Father, the Son and the Holy Ghost, we have dealt with and discussed the subject of rational natures.[1] We have treated this subject in a general way, rather by logical inference than by precise dogmatic statement. Let us now see what are the matters which we ought to discuss in the following pages according to our doctrine, that is, according to the faith of the Church.

All souls and all rational natures, whether holy or wicked, were made or created. All these are incorporeal in respect of their proper nature, but though incorporeal they were nevertheless made. For all things were made by God through Christ, as John teaches in general terms in the Gospel when he says: 'In the beginning was the Word, and the Word was with God, and the Word was God. The same was in the beginning with God. All things were made through him, and without him nothing was made.'[2] Further, the apostle Paul enumerates created things by their kinds and numbers and ranks with the object of proving that all things were made through Christ. For he says: 'All things were created in him, things in the heaven and things on earth, things visible and invisible, whether thrones, dominions, principalities or powers, all were created through him and in him, and he is before all creatures, and he is the head.'[3] Plainly, then, he declares that all things were made and created 'in Christ' and 'through Christ', whether they are 'visible', that is, corporeal, of 'invisible' which I take to be none other than the incorporeal and spiritual powers. Now it is these creatures, whom he has spoken of in general terms as being either corporeal or incorporeal, that he enumerates, as it seems to me, under their various kinds in the words that follow, namely, 'thrones, dominions, principalities, authorities and powers.'

2. Let these remarks serve as an introduction to our present purpose, which is to come in due order to an inquiry about the sun, moon and stars by the method of inference. We ask whether these bodies ought to be reckoned among the 'principalities' by reason of the fact that they are said to have been made to exercise rulership, that is principality, over day and night;[4] or whether we must suppose that they possess only that 'rule over day and night' which is involved in their office of giving

---

[1] Origen refers to Chs. V. and VI.
[2] St. John I. 1-3.
[3] Col. I. 16-18.
[4] See Gen. I. 16.

light and are not princes belonging to the order and office of the
'principalities'. Now when it is said that 'all things were made
through him'[1] and 'in him were created all things, whether,
things in the heaven or things on earth',[2] we cannot doubt that
those bodies which are 'in the firmament' (this being another
name for heaven), in which those luminaries are said to have
been 'set',[3] are to be numbered among the heavenly things.
Then again, since the course of our discussion has clearly revealed
that all things were made or created, and that among the things
that were made there is nothing which does not admit of good and
evil and have a capacity for either, how shall we regard as
reasonable the opinion held by some even of our own people
about the sun, moon and stars, that these are unchangeable and
incapable of becoming the opposite of what they are? Some too
have entertained this belief about the holy angels, and there are
heretics who even apply it to certain souls, which are called by
them 'spiritual natures'.[4]

First, then, let us see what reason itself can discover about
the sun, moon and stars, namely, whether it is correct to suppose,
as some do, that they are exempt from the possibility of change;[5]
and so far as we can let us first employ statements from the holy
scriptures. Now Job appears to show that not only is it possible
for the stars to be subject to sins, but that they are in fact 'not
clean' from the pollution of sin. For he writes as follows:
'The stars also are not clean in his sight'.[6] This is certainly
not meant to refer to the brightness of their body, as if, for
example, one were to say that a certain garment was not clean.
Were it to be understood thus, an injurious reflexion would
undoubtedly be cast upon the Creator by the charge that there
was something unclean in the brightness of their body. For if
the stars are unable either by their own diligent efforts to assume
for themselves a clearer body or by their slackness a less pure

---

[1] St. John I. 3.   [2] Col. I. 16.   [3] See Gen. I. 17.

[4] This was a Gnostic doctrine. Some men are by nature 'spiritual',
possessing a spark of the divine life. Others, at any rate according to
the earlier Gnostic teaching, are earthly and incapable of salvation. See
Hastings, *Encyclopaedia of Religion and Ethics,* Art. Gnosticism (E. F.
Scott), Vol. VI, p. 235.

[5] It was a widespread opinion that the stars were living beings. Plato
regarded them as divine (*Timaeus* 40 B). The Stoics held the same view
(Cicero, *De Natura Deorum* II. 15, 39). Philo (*De Mundi Opif.* 24) says
that they are pure and divine beings, but susceptible only of virtue, and
not of evil. Origen probably introduced a new idea in regard to the stars
when, in order to fit them into his theory of the continual progress or
relapse of all rational creatures, he argued that they were capable of
sin.

[6] Job XXV. 5. Origen quotes this passage again in his *Comm. in
Ioh.* I. 35, but there he more wisely adds: 'unless indeed this statement
is hyperbolical'.

one, why are they blamed for being 'not clean', since they would receive no praise even if they were clean?

3. To make this point more clearly understood we must inquire, first, whether it is right to think of the sun, moon and stars as living and rational beings; next, whether their souls came into existence along with their bodies or at some previous time; and further, whether we are to understand that after the consummation of this age their souls will be released from their bodies and, just as we cease from this life, so will they cease from the work of giving light to the world. It is true that to inquire into these matters seems somewhat daring, yet impelled as we are by a keen desire to ascertain the truth, we see nothing unreasonable in examining and testing, by the grace of the Holy Spirit, all that lies within our power.

We think, therefore, that they may be called living beings from the fact that they are said to receive commands from God;[1] for commands are not usually given to any but living and rational creatures. Now the scripture says * * * commandment:[2] 'I have given precepts to all the stars'.[3] What then are these precepts? Surely that each of the stars in its own order and its own courses should supply the world with brightness to the extent of what has been bestowed upon it. Now those which are called planets move in one kind of course, those called fixed stars in another. Here we have a most evident reminder of the fact that no movement can take place in any body which does not possess life, nor can living beings exist at any time without movement. And since the stars move with such majestic order and plan that never have we seen their course deflected in the slightest degree, is it not the height of stupidity to say that such order, such exact observance of rule and plan, is accomplished by things without reason? In Jeremiah indeed the moon is even called by the title 'queen of heaven'.[4] But if the heavenly bodies are living and rational beings we shall doubtless observe among them instances of progress and relapse; for the statement of Job, 'the stars are not clean in his sight',[5] appears to me to suggest some such idea as this.

4. We must now consider whether these beings, whom the course of our discussion has shown to be living and rational, would appear to have been endowed with life and bodies simultaneously, at the time when, as the scripture says, 'God made two great lights, the greater light to rule the day and the lesser

---

[1] Origen in *Con. Celsum* V. 11 expresses his belief that the 'sun, moon and stars pray to God who is over all through his Only-begotten'.

[2] Koetschau concludes that there is an omission in the text at this point, relying on Rufin. Palaest. *De Fide* 19, where it is stated that Origen quotes 'the prophet David', i.e. Ps. CIII. 18, as well as Is. XLV. 12.

[3] Is. XLV. 12.   [4] Jerem. XLIV. 17-19, 25.   [5] Job XXV. 5.

light to rule the night; he made the stars also',[1] or whether
it was not so, but that God put the spirit into them from without after their bodies were made.[2] My own opinion is that the
spirit was put into them from without; nevertheless it will be
worth while to prove this from the scriptures. We shall see that
it is easy to prove this assertion by inference, but more difficult if we appeal to the witness of the scriptures. Now by inferences it may be shown to be true in the following way. If
the soul of a man, which while it remains the soul of a man is
certainly inferior, can be proved not to have been formed with
the body but separately, and placed in the body from without,
much more will this be the case with the souls of those who
are called 'heavenly beings'.

Now with regard to man, how could it be possible that the
soul of him who 'supplanted his brother in the womb',[3] that is,
Jacob, was formed at the same time as his body? Or how
could the soul or formative principle of him who, while still
lying in his mother's womb, was filled with the Holy Spirit,
have been formed at the same time as his body? I mean John,
who 'leaped in his mother's womb' and tossed himself about
with great joy because the voice of Mary's salutation had sounded
in the ears of his mother Elizabeth.[4] How could the soul and
formative principle of him who 'before he was fashioned in the
womb' is said to have been 'known by God' and 'before he
came to the birth was sanctified by him',[5] have been formed at
the same time as his body? Otherwise it would appear that
God fills some men with the Holy Spirit regardless of justice
and their merits and sanctifies them when they have done nothing
to deserve it. And if that were so, how should we avoid the
difficulty expressed in that passage in which it is said, 'Is there
unrighteousness with God? God forbid.'[6] Or this, 'Is there
respect of persons with God?'[7] For this is the consequence of
that line of argument which maintains that souls come into
existence at the same time as their bodies.

(The sun[8] also, and the moon and the rest of the heavenly
bodies are living beings; and moreover, just as we men for

---

[1] Gen. I. 16.   [2] See above p. 4.   [3] Gen. XXV. 22-26.
[4] See St. Luke I. 41, 44.   [5] See Jerem. I. 5.   [6] Rom. IX. 14.
[7] Rom. II. 11.
[8] Koetschau inserts in the text this passage from Jerome, *Ep. ad Avitum* 4.
He follows Schnitzer in placing it here because Jerome definitely associates it with the quotation from Romans VIII. 20, 21, which occurs at
the beginning of paragraph 5. The passage is clearly meant to give a
true representation of the original, though not perhaps in a strict translation. In the quotation which follows it (see p. 65 n. 2) Jerome claims
to give Origen's own words. In another passage (Jerome, *Con. Ioh.
Hieros.* 17) he gives Origen's doctrine as follows: 'the sun itself and the
moon and the whole host of the stars are souls of creatures once rational
and incorporeal, but now subject to vanity, that is to fiery bodies, which

certain sins have been enveloped in these bodies of ours, which are gross and heavy, so the lights of heaven have been given bodies of one sort or another to enable them to provide more or less light, while the daemons, for greater offences, have been clothed with aereal bodies).

GREEK	LATIN
And that[1] the soul of the sun is older than the covering which serves it for a body can, I think, be logically shown from a comparison of the sun with man, and after that from the scriptures.	So far, then, as we can draw inferences from a comparison with the conditions of human life, it follows, I think, that whatever is shown by reason and scriptural authority to be true for men ought much more to be regarded as true in the case of the heavenly beings.

LATIN

5. But let us see whether we can find in holy scripture any passages that refer strictly to the heavenly beings themselves. Paul the apostle speaks as follows: 'the creation was subjected to vanity, not of its own will, but by reason of him who subjected it in hope, because the creation itself also shall be delivered from the bondage of corruption into the liberty of the glory of the sons of God.'[2] To what 'vanity', pray, was the creation subjected, and what 'creation' is meant, and how 'not of its own will', and with what 'hope'; how, too, shall 'the creation itself be delivered from the bondage of corruption'? Moreover the same apostle says elsewhere: 'the expectation of the creation waiteth for the revealing of the sons of God'.[3] And again elsewhere: 'not only so, but the creation itself groaneth and travaileth together in pain until now'.[4] The question arises, 'What is its groaning, and what its pains?' But first let us see what is the 'vanity' to which the creation was subjected. My own opinion is, that this is nothing else than the possession of bodies, for even though the bodies of the stars are composed of ether, they are nevertheless material. This, it seems to me, is the reason why Solomon arraigns the whole bodily universe as being in a way burdensome and as impeding the activity of spirits, thus: 'Vanity of vanities, all is vanity, said the Preacher; all

---

we in our ignorance and simplicity call the lights of the world'. Justinian also (*Ep. ad Mennam—Mansi* IX. 513) charges Origen with saying that 'the sky and the sun and moon and stars and the waters above the heavens are living and rational powers'. Rufinus has apparently toned down the original and changed its order, but he does not seem to have omitted much at this point.

[1] Frag. 13, Koetschau, from Justinian, *Ep. ad Mennam.* (Mansi IX. 532).

[2] Rom. VIII. 20, 21.   [3] Rom. VIII. 19.

[4] Rom. VIII. 23, 22.

is vanity'.[1] 'For', he adds, 'I looked and I saw all things that are under the sun, and behold, all is vanity.'[2]

This then is the 'vanity' to which the creation was subjected, and above all that creation which is certainly the greatest thing in this world and which holds a distinguished pre-eminence by reason of its function. That is, the sun, moon and stars are said to have been subjected to vanity, because they were clothed with bodies and set to perform the task of giving light to the human race. And this creation, scripture says, was subjected to vanity 'not of its own will'.[3] For it did not undertake a service to vanity by the exercise of free-will, but in obedience to the wish of him who was subjecting it, because he who subjected it promised those who were being given over unwillingly to vanity that on the fulfilment of their splendid work of service they should be delivered from this bondage of corruption and vanity, when the time of redemption 'of the glory of the sons of God' should have come. Having received this hope, and looking for the fulfilment of this promise, the entire creation now in the meantime 'groans together' with us (for it even has sympathy with those whom it serves) and 'is in pain together', while in patience it hopes for what has been promised.[4]

Consider also the following passage, and see whether this other saying of Paul may not perhaps apply to these beings who not willingly, but in obedience to the will of him who subjected them and with the hope of promises to come were subjected to vanity. 'I could desire,' he says, 'to be dissolved (or "to depart") and be with Christ; for it is far better.'[5] For I think

GREEK	LATIN
For I consider[6] that the sun might say that it was a finer thing to be dissolved and be with Christ; for it is very far better. And whereas Paul adds: 'But to abide in the flesh is more needful for your sakes',[7] the sun might say: 'To abide in this heavenly body is more needful for the sake of the revealing of the children of God'. And the same may be said of the moon and the rest of the heavenly bodies.	that the sun too might say, 'I could desire to be dissolved (or "to depart") and be with Christ; for it is far better.' And whereas Paul adds: 'But to abide in the flesh is more needful for your sakes',[7] the sun might say: 'To abide in this heavenly and shining body is more needful for the sake of the revealing of the sons of God.' The same may well be believed and said of the moon and stars.

[1] Eccl. I. 2.   [2] Eccl. I. 14.   [3] Rom. VIII. 20.
[4] See Rom. VIII. 21, 22.   [5] Phil. I. 23.
[6] Frag. 14, Koetschau, from Justinian, *Ep. ad Mennam* (Mansi IX. 532).
[7] Phil. I. 24.

LATIN

Let us now see what is meant by the 'freedom of the creation' and its 'deliverance from bondage'.[1] (When[2] at the end and consummation of the world souls and rational creatures have been released as it were from their bars and prisons by the Lord, some of them by reason of indolence will move but slowly, while others by earnest effort will speed along in brisk flight. And since all have free will and of their own accord can acquire either virtues or vices, the former will be in a much worse condition than they are now, while the latter will arrive at a a better state. For differences of movement and will in either direction will lead to different states; that is, angels may become men or daemons, and on the other hand daemons may become men or angels.) When Christ 'shall have delivered up the kingdom to God, even the Father',[3] then those living beings, because they have before this been made part of Christ's kingdom, shall also be delivered up along with the whole of that kingdom to the rule of the Father; so that, when 'God shall be in all',[4] they also, since they are a part of all, may have God even in themselves, as he is in all things.

---

[1] See Rom. VIII. 21.

[2] The passage in brackets is inserted here by Koetschau, following Schnitzer, from Jerome, *Ep. ad Avitum* 4. Jerome prefaces this passage with the statement: 'lest any one should suppose that what we say is our own, let us quote his very words.'

[3] 1 Cor. XV. 24.   [4] 1 Cor. XV. 28.

CHAPTER VIII

THE ANGELS

1. A similar course of reasoning must be applied to the angels. We must not suppose that it is the result of chance that a particular duty is assigned to a particular angel; the work of curing and healing, for instance, to Raphael; the supervising of wars to Gabriel; the task of attending to the prayers and supplications of mortals to Michael.[1] We must believe that they have obtained these duties for no other reason except their own individual merits and that they entered upon them as a reward for the zeal and virtue they displayed before the construction of this world; after which event this or that kind of duty was assigned to each member of the order of archangels, while others were counted worthy of being enrolled in the order of angels and to act under this or that archangel, or under this or that leader or chief of his order. All this, as we have said, was arranged not by chance or at random, but by the most appropriate and righteous judgment of God, being settled in accordance with merit, God himself deciding and approving. Thus to one angel would be entrusted the Church of Ephesus, to another the Church of Smyrna;[2] this angel would be Peter's, that Paul's;[3] and so on through the entire number of those 'least ones' who are in the Church it would be decided which of the angels, who daily 'see the face of God,'[4] must be attached to each, and also which angel it must be who was to encamp 'around them that fear God'.[5] Certainly we must suppose that all these duties are not performed by accident or chance, nor because the angels were naturally created for them, lest in so doing we should charge the Creator with partiality. Rather must we believe that they were conferred in accordance with merit and virtue and with the activity and ability of each individual spirit, by God the most righteous and impartial governor of all things.[6] *   *   *   *

---

[1] For the names of the archangels and their tasks, see Enoch ch. XL.
[2] Rev. II. 1, 8.   [3] See Acts XII. 7-15; XXVII. 23-4.
[4] See St. Matt. XVIII. 10.   [5] See Ps. XXXIV. 7.
[6] The text of Rufinus continues on p. 68. But a long passage dealing with the creation and fall of souls has been omitted here. For evidence we have not only the considerable fragments which immediately follow, but also indications in Jerome, *Ep. ad Ephes.* I., where reference is made to 'those who suppose that before the creation of the world souls dwelt with the angels and the other powers in the heavenly Jerusalem'; and in Jerome, *Apol.* ii. 8, 'some suppose that souls were made long ago, that is, at the time when God created all things out of nothing; but that now by his own judgment he has ordained that they should be born in the body. This is the opinion of Origen and other Greeks'. See Int. pp. xxvii-xxviii.

GREEK

God[1] did not begin to create minds * * before the ages[2] minds were all pure, both daemons and souls and angels, offering service to God and keeping his commandments. But the devil, who was one of them, since he possessed free-will, desired to resist God, and God drove him away. With him revolted all the other powers. Some sinned deeply and became daemons, others less and became angels; others still less and became archangels; and thus each in turn received the reward for his individual sin. But there remained some souls who had not sinned so greatly as to become daemons, nor on the other hand so very lightly as to become angels. God therefore made the present world and bound the soul to the body as a punishment. For God is no 'respecter of persons',[3] that among all these beings who are of one nature (for all the immortal beings are rational) he should make some daemons, some souls and some angels; rather is it clear that God made one a daemon, one a soul and one an angel as a means of punishing each in proportion to its sin. For if this were not so, and souls had no pre-existence, why do we find some new-born babes to be blind, when they have committed no sin, while others are born with no defect at all? But it is clear that certain sins existed before the souls, and as a result of these sins each soul receives a recompense in proportion to its deserts. They are[4] sent forth from God as a punishment, that they must undergo on earth a first judgment. That is why the body is called a frame, because the soul is enclosed within it.[5]

But when[6] they had revolted from their former blessedness they were endowed with bodies in consequence of the fall from their first estate which had taken place in them, and allotted to

---

[1] God did not . . . . to p. 68 'his right hand'. Frag. 15 Koetschau. The passage is a composite one, made up from sources which will be indicated in these notes. The first sentence is from Antipater of Bostra in John of Damascus, Sacra Parallela ii. 770 (Migne P. G. 96, p. 501).

[2] 'Before the ages' . . . to 'deserts', from Leontius Byz. De Sectis, Act. X. 5 (Migne P. G. 86 i., pp. 1264-5).

[3] Acts X. 34.

[4] 'They are sent forth . . . .' to end of paragraph, is from Epiphanius, Haer. lxiv. 4 (Migne P. G. 41, pp. 1076-7).

[5] The play upon words is between δέμας, the body (i.e. 'the frame or stature of man', Liddell & Scott), and δεδέσθαι, to be bound. In Justinian's Ep. Synod. (Mansi IX. 536) this fancied derivation is attributed to Plato, but incorrectly. Plato called the body a 'tomb' (σῶμα, σῆμα, Crat. 400 BC; Gorg. 493 A) and spoke of the soul as being 'bound' to it (διαδεδεμένην Phaedo 82 E).

[6] This sentence is formed by Koetschau out of two passages from Antipater of Bostra in John of Damascus, Sacra Parallela, ii. 770 and 771. (Migne P. G., 96, pp. 504, 505).

various ranks. So from being 'minds' they have become angels, archangels   *   *   *   *   *   *

LATIN

Just as the daemons,[1] sitting by the altars of the Gentiles, used to feed on the steam of the sacrifices, so also the angels, allured by the blood of the victims which Israel offered as symbols of spiritual things, and by the smoke of the incense, used to dwell near the altars and to be nourished on food of this sort *   *   *

GREEK

But when they fell away,[2] as the New Testament says,[3] from their unity with God, they were given the rule and lordship over those who had fallen lower still and were also 'sent forth to minister to those who are to inherit salvation',[4] though they themselves had fallen from this salvation and were in need of one to lead them back * * * He did not wish to command them to return to their original perfect blessedness, for when commanded they are, according to the prophet, 'mighty in strength to do his word' and 'to hear the voice of his words';[5] and the Spirit's testimony cannot lie[6] * * * They were zealous for the sake of those who had lost the 'good seed'[7] sown by the Lord and they sought to be entrusted by the Lord with the restoration of these, although they themselves had cast away the purity of the first seed. But if they are 'mighty in strength'[8] to do the will of God, and if they seek the destruction of the impious, this is a sign that it is on account of their good-will towards God that they stand before him[9] and serve him and are at his right hand.

LATIN

Concerning those who maintain that spiritual natures are of different kinds.[10]

2. (We must take care)[11] not to fall into the silly and impious fables of those who pretend that spiritual natures, both those belonging to the heavenly orders and those that form the human race, are of different kinds and were therefore originated by

---

[1] For this Latin fragment see Theophil. Alex. *Ep. Synod.* 2 (Migne P. L. 22, p. 763).

[2] 'But when . . . ' to end of Greek quotation. A series of sentences extracted from Antipater of Bostra in John of Damascus, *Sacra Parallela* ii. 770-771 (Migne P. G. 96, pp. 504, 505).

[3] Perhaps a reminiscence of Jude 6.   [4] Heb. I. 14.

[5] Ps. CIII. 20.   [6] See St. John V. 32, X. 35

[7] St. Matt. XIII. 24.   [8] Ps. CIII. 20.

[9] See St. Luke I. 19.

[10] In some MSS. this title has been incorporated into the text. It is at this point that we return to Rufinus.

[11] Words such as these appear to be missing from the text.

different creators. For while it seems absurd, and indeed is absurd, that the differing natures of rational beings should be attributed to one and the same creator, nevertheless the objectors are ignorant of the cause of these differences. They say that it seems illogical for one and the same creator, quite apart from any reason of merit, to confer on some the authority to rule, while others are subjected to rulers, or to assign principalities to some, while others are made subject to princes. All such opinions, however, are met and refuted by the line of reasoning we have set forth above,[1] in which the cause of the diversity and variety among these beings is shown to be derived not from any unfairness on the part of the Disposer but from their own actions, which exhibit varying degress of earnestness or laxity according to the goodness or badness of each.

But to help us perceive more readily that this is the truth about the heavenly beings, let us take examples from human life, both past and present, in order that by logical inference from things visible we may behold even the invisible.[2] Our opponents will admit that Paul and Peter were undoubtedly men of 'spiritual nature'.[3] When therefore we find that Paul did much that was contrary to religion, in having 'persecuted the church of God',[4] and that Peter committed so grave a sin as to affirm with an oath, when questioned by the maid that kept the door, that he did not know who Christ was,[5] how comes it that such men, who according to our opponents are spiritual, should have fallen into sins like these? I ask the more insistently because they are in the habit of quoting over and over again the saying, 'A good tree cannot bring forth evil fruit'.[6] Well, if we grant that 'a good tree cannot bring forth evil fruit', and yet by their own admission Paul and Peter were certainly sprung from the root of a good tree, how can they be imagined to have brought forth fruit so evil as this? And if they return the answer which they generally contrive, that it was not Paul who persecuted but some unknown person who was in Paul, and not Peter who denied but sometimes else who denied in Peter, then why did Paul say, if he had done no sin, that 'I am not worthy to be called an apostle, because I persecuted the church of God'?[7] And why does Peter himself 'weep bitterly'[8] for the sin of another? This shows how foolish are all their reasonings.

3. Our contention is, however, that among all rational creatures there is none which is not capable of both good and evil. But it does not necessarily follow that, because we say

---

[1] See p. 45 ff.   [2] Rom. I. 20.   [3] I Cor. II. 13-16.
[4] I Cor. XV. 9; Gal. I. 13.
[5] St. Matt. XXVI. 69-74; St. John XVIII. 17.
[6] St. Matt. VII. 18; St. Luke VI. 43.
[7] I Cor. XV. 9.   [8] St. Matt. XXVI. 75; St. Luke XXII. 62.

there is no nature which cannot admit evil, we therefore affirm that every nature has admitted evil, that is, has become evil. Just as we may say that every human nature possesses the capacity to become a sailor, and yet this will not result in every man becoming a sailor; or again that it is possible for every man to learn the art of grammar or medicine, and yet this does not prove that every man is either a doctor or a schoolmaster: so when we say that there is no nature which cannot admit evil, we do not necessarily indicate that every nature has actually done so; nor on the other hand will the statement that there is no nature which may not admit good prove that every nature has admitted what is good. Our opinion is that not even the devil himself was incapable of good, but the fact that he could admit good did not lead him to desire it or to take pains to acquire virtue. For, as we learn from the passages we quoted out of the prophets, he was at one time good, when he dwelt 'in the paradise of God', 'in the midst of the cherubim' [1] Just as, therefore, he

GREEK	LATIN
But[2] it has been shown that the devil was not created as such, but that he fell to this state as a result of his own wickedness. It is clear, therefore, that they too came to their state as a result of their own goodness.	had in himself the power of admitting either good or evil, and falling away from good he turned with his whole mind to evil, so also there are other created beings who, while possessing the power to choose either, by the exercise of free will flee from evil and cleave to the good.

There is therefore no nature which may not admit good or evil, except the nature of God, which is the source of all good, and that of Christ; for Christ is wisdom, and wisdom certainly cannot admit folly; and he is righteousness, and assuredly righteousness will never receive unrighteousness; and he is word or reason, which certainly cannot become irrational; further, he is light, and we are sure that 'darkness does not comprehend'[3] the light. In like manner also the nature of the Holy Spirit, which is holy, does not admit pollution, for it is holy by nature or essence.

But if any other nature is holy, it is so because it is made holy by the reception or inspiration of the Holy Spirit; the

---

[1] Ezek. XXVIII. 13 f.
[2] Frag. 16, Koetschau, from Antipater of Bostra in John of Damascus, *Sacra Parallela* ii. 771 (Migne P. G. 96, p. 505).
[3] St. John I. 5.

possession of this quality does not arise from its own nature, but is an accidental addition to it, and being an addition it can also become separated and lost. So too righteousness may be possessed as an accident, and accordingly this also may be lost. And even the wisdom which we possess is still accidental, in spite of the fact that it lies within our own power to become wise through personal effort and merit, when we pay due attention to wisdom; and that while we continue to display the requisite zeal we shall always have a share in wisdom, which share will be greater or less in proportion to the merit of our conduct and the degree of our zeal. For the kindness of God, as is worthy of him, incites and attracts all things to that blessed end, when 'all sorrow and sadness and sighing shall flee away'[1] and disappear.

4. So far then as I can see, the foregoing discussion has sufficiently proved that it is not from any random or chance circumstances that the principalities hold their princedoms or the other orders are assigned their respective offices, but that each has obtained his degree of dignity in proportion to his own merits, though it is not our business to know or to inquire what the actual deeds were through which they earned their entrance into a particular order. It is enough for us, to enable us to establish the impartiality and justice of God, to be certain of this, that in accordance with the statement of the apostle Paul 'there is no respect of persons with God',[2] who on the contrary dispenses all his gifts in proportion to the merits and progress of each recipient. No angelic office, therefore, exists except as a reward of merit, nor do authorities wield their authority except as a result of their progress, nor do those who are called thrones, that is, authorities for judging and ruling, administer their functions except as a reward of merit, nor do the dominions exercise dominion but by merit; for this supreme and most excellent order of rational creatures in the heavenly places is thus arranged in a glorious variety of offices.

We must think of the opposing powers in precisely the same way. These have become attached to their particular place or office, so as to be 'principalities', or 'powers', or 'rulers of the darkness of the world', or 'spiritual hosts of wickedness',[3] or 'malignant spirits', or 'impure daemons',[4] not because they hold it essentially nor because they were so created; on the contrary, these ranks in wickedness have been assigned to them in proportion to their bad conduct and the progress they have made in wrong-doing. Thus there exists that other order of rational creatures, who have so utterly abandoned themselves to wickedness that they lack the desire, rather than the power, to return,

---

[1] Is. XXXV. 10.   [2] Rom. II. 11.
[3] See Eph. VI. 12.   [4] See St. Luke VII. 21 ; IV. 33.

so long as the frenzy of their evil deeds is a passion and a delight.

The third order of rational creatures is composed of those spirits who are judged fit by God to replenish the human race. These are the souls of men, some of whom, in consequence of their progress, we see taken up into the order of angels, those, namely, who have been made 'sons of God' or 'sons of the resurrection';[1] or those who forsaking the darkness have loved the light and have been made 'sons of the light';[2] or those who, after winning every fight and being changed into 'men of peace', become 'sons of peace'[3] and 'sons of God'; or those who, by mortifying their members which are upon the earth[4] and rising superior not only to their bodily nature but even to the wavering and fragile movements of the soul itself, have 'joined them-selves to the Lord',[5] being made wholly spiritual, so as to be always 'one spirit',[6] with him, judging each individual thing in company with him, until they reach the point when they become perfect 'spiritual men' and 'judge all things', because their mind is illuminated in all holiness through the word and wisdom of God, while they themselves are utterly incapable of being judged by any man.[7]   *   *   *   *   *

GREEK

Whole[8] nations of souls are stored away somewhere in a realm of their own, with an existence comparable to our bodily life,

---

[1] St. Luke XX. 36; Rom. VIII. 14.   [2] St. Luke XVI. 8.
[3] St. Matt. V. 9; St. Luke X. 6.   [4] Col. III. 5.
[5] 1 Cor. VI. 17.   [6] Ibid.   [7] See 1 Cor. II. 15.

[8] Frag. 17a, Koetschau, a composite passage from Gregory of Nyssa, *De Anima et Resurr.* (Migne, P. G. 44, pp. 112 C-113 D) and *De Hom. Opificio* c. 28 (Migne, P. G. 44, p. 250). This passage describes Origen's teaching on the pre-existence of souls, and the successive bodies which they receive as they fall or rise in the scale of being. Koetschau's argu-ments for including it in the text of Origen are given in his introduction, pp. 117-118. Briefly they are as follows. Jerome (*Ep. ad Avitum* 4) asserts that Origen 'argued at very great length' (*sermone latissimo disputavit*) that angels or human souls or daemons might for serious offences be con-demned to inhabit the bodies of beasts, or even of fishes. The quotation from Justinian, *Ep. ad Mennam* (see p. 74, n. 2) is in accord with this. But nothing of the kind is found in Rufinus. On the contrary, he sum-marily dismisses the doctrine of transmigration, as one that ought not to be accepted, being supported by false interpretations of scripture. Gregory of Nyssa, however, who regarded Origen as in some respects his theological master, has a passage in which he says that 'it is the opinion of some of our predecessors, who composed works on First Principles, that before their bodies were made souls existed as a kind of nation in a realm of their own' (*De Hom. Opificio* c. 28). The allusion is clearly to Origen. In another work (*De Anima et Resurr.*) Gregory says, 'I have heard from those who hold these opinions (i.e. on transmigration) that whole nations of souls are stored away somewhere in a realm of their own . . .' The repetition of the last phrase connects the two passages. As the second

but in consequence of the fineness and mobility of their nature they are carried round with the whirl of the universe.* * * There the representations of evil and of virtue are set before them; and so long as a soul continues to abide in the good it has no experience of union with a body.[1] * * * But[2] by some inclination towards evil these souls lose their wings and come into bodies, first of men; then through their association with the irrational passions, after the allotted span of human life they are changed into beasts; from which they sink to the level of insensate nature. Thus that which is by nature fine and mobile, namely the soul, first becomes heavy and weighed down, and because of its wickedness comes to dwell in a human body; after that, when the faculty of reason is extinguished, it lives the life of an irrational animal; and finally even the gracious gift of sensation is withdrawn and it changes into the insensate life of a plant. From this condition it rises again through the same stages and is restored to its heavenly place. * * * On earth[3] by means of virtue souls grow wings and soar aloft, but when in heaven their wings fall off through evil and they sink down and become earthbound and are mingled with the gross nature of matter.

For if[4] a soul has been torn away from the more exalted realm through some wickedness and after having once tasted the life of the body again becomes a man, then, since life in the flesh is admittedly far more subject to passion than the eternal and bodiless life, it follows of necessity that the soul which comes into such a life, in which the occasions of sin are more numerous, comes also into the midst of greater wickedness and is rendered more subject to passion than before. Now passion in a human soul is a likening to the irrational. And when the soul has become closely associated with the irrational it descends to the nature of the brutes; and once it has taken the road of wickedness it never ceases in its advance towards further wickedness, not even when found in the irrational state. For the cessation of evil-doing means the beginning of an impulse towards virtue; and among irrational beings virtue does not exist. Thus

---

one goes on to give an account of the fall of the souls, it is reasonable to suppose that it corresponds to the *sermo latissimus* of Jerome, though not perhaps literally. The thought is Platonic in origin, based upon *Phaedrus* 245-249.

[1] The passage beginning 'there the representations. . . .' and ending at 'body' is taken from Gregor. Nyss., *De Hom. Opificio* c. 28 (*init*), where it follows the statement that 'some of our predecessors, who composed works on First Principles' (i.e. Origen), have believed that souls pre-existed in a realm of their own.

[2] This passage continues from 'whirl of the universe' above. Gregor. Nyss. *De Anima et Resurr.* 112 C.

[3] Gregor. Nyss. *De Anima et Resurr.* 113 CD.

[4] This passage forms part of Koetschau's Frag. 17a and is taken from Gregory of Nyssa, *De Hom. Opificio* c. 28.

the soul will of necessity continually be changed for the worse, ever advancing towards what is more degraded and always discovering something worse than the nature in which it now is. And just as the sensible nature is lower than the rational, so too there is a further fall from this to the insensible.[1]

GREEK	LATIN
When the soul[2] falls away from the good and inclines towards evil it becomes more and more involved in this. Then, unless it turns back, it is rendered brutish by its folly and bestial by its wickedness * * and it is carried towards the conditions of unreason and, so to speak, of the watery life. Then, as befits the degree of its fall into evil, it is clothed with the body of this or that irrational animal.	We think[3] that those opinions, which some are accustomed unnecessarily to inquire into and uphold, to the effect that souls depart so far from their true selves as to forget their rational nature and dignity and to sink down into the condition of irrational animals, like beasts or cattle, ought certainly not to be accepted. In support of these

LATIN

opinions they are accustomed to quote certain alleged proof passages out of the scriptures; the fact, for instance, that a beast to which a woman has unnaturally prostituted herself is deemed equally guilty with the woman and is ordered to be stoned with

[1] The quotation from Gregory of Nyssa ends here.
[2] Frag. 17b, Koetschau, from Justinian, *Ep. ad Mennam* (Mansi IX. 529). Rufinus' text continues here from p. 72. Compare with it Jerome, *Ep. ad Avitum* 4: 'At the end (i.e. of Book I.) he argues at very great length that an angel, or a human soul, or a daemon (all of which he maintains are of a single nature though diverse in their wills) may through exceedingly great carelessness be reduced to the condition of an irrational beast; and that sooner than endure the pain of their punishments and the torment of the fire they may choose to become dumb creatures and to dwell in seas or rivers or to take the body of this or that animal; so that we have to fear not only the assumption of the bodies of quadrupeds, but even of fishes.' It must be remembered, however, that Origen put forward these opinions not as settled dogmas, but as speculations devised to answer problems of human thought. He stated this specifically, according to Jerome, who continues the above quotation as follows: 'Then at the end, to avoid the charge of holding the Pythagorean doctrine of transmigration, after this wicked discussion in which he has wounded the soul of his reader, he says, These arguments must not, in our opinion, be taken as dogmas, but as inquiries and conjectures, intended to show that the problems have not been completely overlooked.' Rufinus has inserted an altered version of this caveat on p. 75.
[3] Rufinus' text continues here from p. 72 above. What he says is precisely the opposite of what Origen wrote.

her;[1] or that a 'bull that gores' is commanded to be stoned:[2] or further, that Balaam's ass spoke, when 'God opened its mouth' and the 'dumb beast of burden, answering with human voice, reproved the madness of the prophet'.[3] For our part we beg leave to mention these things not as fixed doctrines, but as opinions to be discussed and then rejected. This is our sole reason for mentioning them, namely, that we should not appear to have refused to discuss any question that has been raised. But at the proper place and time we will refute and drive away this perverse doctrine, and then show how the passages which they quote out of the holy scriptures ought to be understood.

[1] See Levit. XX. 16.   [2] See Exod. XXI. 29.
[3] See Num. XXII. 28-30 and 2 Pet. II. 16.

BOOK II

CHAPTER I

THE WORLD AND THE CREA- | THE WORLD.
TURES IN IT.[1]

LATIN

1. Although the whole discussion in the preceding book has been concerned with the world and its arrangement, I think that we ought now to follow this up by dealing with a few particular questions about the world itself; for instance, about its beginning and its end; and about the events which occur between the beginning and the end by the ordering of divine providence; and about those which are supposed to occur before or after that period.

In this inquiry one fact appears clear at the outset. The entire constitution of the world is various and diverse; for it consists of rational beings, and others more divine, and of bodies of different kinds; and besides these, of dumb animals, that is, wild beasts, cattle, birds and all creatures that live in water; then secondly, of places, such as heaven or the heavens, earth, water, and also the air which is between these two, or that which men call the aether; and finally of all things which spring or grow out of the earth.

GREEK	LATIN
Now[2] since the world is so very varied and comprises so great a diversity of rational beings,	Seeing then that the world contains this great variety, and that even among rational beings there is great diversity,—which indeed we must suppose to be the object for which all the other variety and diversity exists—what cause can be given to account for the existence of the world, especially when we bear in mind that end in which, as we argued in the preceding
what else can we assign as the cause of its existence	

---

[1] The Greek chapter heading is taken from Photius, *Bibl. Cod.* 8.

[2] Frag. 18 (Koetschau), from Justinian *Ep. ad Mennam* (Mansi IX. 529), Rufinus has reproduced it in an enlarged form.

GREEK

LATIN

book,[1] all things shall be restored to their original state? If our argument there is admitted to be sound, what other cause can we imagine to account for the great diversity of this world except the variety and diversity of the motions and declensions of those who fell away from that original unity and harmony in which they were at the first created by God?

except the diversity in the fall of those who decline from unity in dissimilar ways?

LATIN

These beings, disturbed and drawn away from that state of goodness, and then tossed about by the diverse motions and desires of their souls, have exchanged the one undivided goodness of their original nature for minds that vary in quality according to their different tendencies.

2. But God who, by the unspeakable skill of his wisdom, transforms and restores all things, whatever their condition, to some useful purpose and the common advantage of all, recalls these very creatures, so different from each other in mental quality, to one harmony of work and endeavour; so that, diverse though the motions of their souls may be, they nevertheless combine to make up the fulness and perfection of a single world, the very variety of minds tending to one end, perfection. For there is one power which binds and holds together all the diversity of the world and guides the various motions to the accomplishment of one task, lest so immense a work as the world should be dissolved by the conflicts of souls. It is for this reason, we think, that God, the parent of all things, in providing for the salvation of his entire creation through the unspeakable plan of his word and wisdom, has so ordered everything that each spirit or soul, or whatever else rational existences ought to be called, should not be compelled by force against its free choice to any action except that to which the motions of its own mind lead it,—for in that case the power of free choice would seem to be taken from them, which would certainly alter the quality of their nature itself—and at the same time that the motions of their wills should work suitably and usefully together to produce the harmony of a single world, some being in need of help, others able to give help, others again to provide struggles and conflicts for those who are making progress, whose diligence

[1]See Bk. I, Ch. VI. 2 (p. 53 above).

will be accounted the more praiseworthy and whose rank and position recovered after their victory will be held the more securely, as it has been won through difficulty and toil.

3. Although therefore the whole world is arranged in diverse parts and functions, we must not suppose that its condition is one of discord and self-contradiction; but as our 'one body' is composed of 'many members'[1] and is held together by one soul, so we should, I think, accept the opinion that the universe is as it were an immense, monstrous animal, held together by the power and reason of God as by one soul.[2] This truth is, I believe, referred to by holy scripture in the following passage spoken through the prophet, 'Do not I fill heaven and earth, saith the Lord'?[3] And again, 'Heaven is my throne, and earth is the footstool of my feet';[4] and in what the Saviour said, when he tells us not to swear, 'neither by heaven, for it is the throne of God, neither by the earth, for it is the footstool of his feet';[5] and further, in what St. Paul says in his oration to the Athenians, 'in him we live and move and have our being'.[6] For how do we 'live and move and have our being in God' except through the fact that he binds and holds together the universe by his power? And how is heaven the 'throne of God' and earth the 'footstool of his feet', as the Saviour himself declares, except through the fact that alike in heaven and in earth God's power fills all things, as he says, 'Do not I fill heaven and earth, saith the Lord'?[7] I do not think, therefore, that anyone will find it difficult to admit, from the passages we have quoted, that God, the parent of all things, fills and holds together the entire universe with the fulness of his power.

And now, since the argument of the preceding discussion has shown that the diverse motions of rational creatures and their varying opinions have given rise to the diversity of this world, we must see whether it may not be appropriate that the world should have a conclusion similar to its beginning.[8] Now there is no doubt that its end must be looked for in much diversity and variety, and this variety, when found to exist at the end of this world, will in its turn provide causes and occasions of diversity in that other world which is to come after this; for clearly the end of this world is the beginning of the world to come.

4. If the course of our discussion has revealed this to be the case, it seems to follow that, as the diversity of the world cannot exist apart from bodies, we should discuss the question of bodily nature. It is evident from the observation of ordinary things that bodily nature admits of diverse and various changes,

---

[1] See 1 Cor. XII. 12.
[2] The theory of the World-soul comes from Plato, *Timaeus* 30 AB. See Zeller, *Plato and the Older Academy*, Ch. VII. 3 (p. 341, Eng. Trans. 1876).
[3] Jerem. XXIII. 24.   [4] Is. LXVI. 1.   [5] St. Matt. V. 34 f.
[6] Acts XVII. 28.   [7] Jerem. XXIII. 24.   [8] See above, p. 53.

to such an extent that it can undergo every kind of transformation; for example, wood turns into fire, fire into smoke
and smoke into air; and even oil, a liquid, changes into fire.[1]
Do not also articles of food whether used by men or by animals,
exhibit the same fact of change? For whatever it is that we
take as food, it turns into the substance of our body. Moreover
it would not be difficult to explain the way in which water
changes into earth or air, and air again into fire, or fire into
air or air into water; in the present place, however, it is enough
simply to mention these facts, as our purpose is to discuss the
question of bodily matter. Now by matter we mean that which
underlies bodies, namely, that from which they take their
existence when qualities have been applied to or mingled with
them.[2] We speak of four qualities, heat, cold, dryness, wetness.
These qualities, when mingled with the *hyle* or matter (which
matter is clearly seen to have an existence in its own right apart
from these qualities we have mentioned), produce the different
kinds of bodies. But although, as we have said, this matter
has an existence by its own right without qualities, yet it is
never found actually existing apart from them.

In regard then to this matter, which is so great and wonderful as to be sufficient for all the bodies in the world, which God
willed to exist, and to be at the call and service of the Creator
in all things for the fashioning of whatever forms and species he
wished, receiving into itself the qualities which he had willed
to bestow upon it, I cannot understand how so many distinguished men have supposed it to be uncreated, that is, not made
by God himself the Creator of all things, but in its nature and
power the result of chance.[3] I wonder, too, how such men can
find fault with those who deny that God is the Maker of this
universe or that he providentially cares for it, and can charge
them with impiety for believing that so great a work as the
world exists without a Maker or Sustainer, when they themselves are guilty of a like impiety in saying that matter is uncreated and co-eternal with the uncreated God. Their theory is
as follows: if we suppose for the sake of argument that matter
did not exist, then, they say, since God could not make anything when nothing existed, he would undoubtedly have been
idle, having no matter on which to work; but they believe that
this matter was at his hand by chance, and not by his own pro-
vision, and they think that this thing which was discovered by

[1] See Zeller, *Aristotle and the Earlier Peripatetics,* Ch. IX. B. (Eng.
trans. 1897, pp. 482-5).

[2] See Plato, *Timaeus* 51 A. 'The mother and receptive basis of the
visible and sensible world is neither earth, nor air, nor fire, nor water, nor
anything derived from these nor anything from which they are derived, but
an invisible and formless substance, capable of receiving all.'

[3] See Zeller, *Plato and the Older Academy,* Ch. VII. 1. (Eng. trans.
1876, pp. 293 ff.).

chance was able to suffice him for so immense a work and for
the exercise of his mighty power, so as to subserve the plan of
all his wisdom and be separated and formed into a world.   This
seems to me to be very absurd and characteristic of men who are
utterly ignorant of the power and intelligence ot an uncreated
being.

But in order to look more carefully into the plan of things,
let it be granted that for a little while matter did not exist, and
that God, when nothing existed before, caused to exist the things
which he desired.   What shall we think?   Would God have
created a matter that should be better or greater or of a kind
other than that which he did produce from his own power and
wisdom, in order that things which before were not might exist?
Or would he have created it worse and inferior?   Or would he
have created it like to and the same as that matter which these
men call uncreated?   I think anyone can easily discern that
neither a better nor an inferior matter could have assumed the
forms and species of the world, but only such a matter as that
which did assume them.   How then will it seem anything but
impious to call that uncreated which, if we believe it to be made
by God, is found beyond a doubt to be exactly the same as
that which is said to be uncreated?

5. To obtain scriptural authority for believing that this is
so, hear how the doctrine is confirmed in the book of Maccabees,
where the mother of the seven martyrs is exhorting one of her
sons to endure the tortures.   She says: 'I pray you, my son,
look at heaven and earth and all that is in them, and when you
see all this, remember that God made it when it did not exist'.[1]
Further, in the book of The Shepherd, in the first commandment,
it says as follows: 'First of all believe that God is one, who
created and set in order all things and caused the universe to
exist out of nothing'.[2]   Perhaps also that passage which occurs
in the Psalms refers to this doctrine: 'He spake and they were
made; he commanded and they were created'.[3]   For the statement 'he spake and they were made' seems to point to the
substance of things that exist, whereas 'he commanded and they
were created' seems to be spoken of the qualities by which the
substance itself was moulded into form.

[1] 2 Macc. VII. 28.   [2] Hermas, *Mand.* I. 1. See p. 2 above.
[3] Ps. CXLVIII. 5.

CHAPTER II

THE PERPETUITY OF BODILY NATURE

1. At this point some are wont to inquire whether, as the Father begets an only begotten Son and brings forth a Holy Spirit, not as beings who did not exist before, but in the sense that the Father is the origin and source of the Son or the Holy Spirit and no thought of before or after can be entertained in respect of them, some similar kinship or close connexion may not be understood to exist also between rational natures and bodily matter. In order to examine this question with due care and completeness they are wont to direct the beginning of their discussion to the inquiry whether this bodily nature, which supports the lives and upholds the movements of spiritual and rational minds, will last eternally like them or whether in fact it will be destroyed and utterly perish. And that this may be determined more precisely a previous inquiry seems necessary, namely, whether it is possible for rational beings to endure altogether without bodies when they have reached the height of holiness and blessedness,—a thing which to me indeed seems very difficult and well-nigh impossible—or whether it is necessary that they should always be joined to bodies. If then anyone could show a reason whereby it was possible for them to do without bodies of any kind, the consequence would seem to be that just as bodily nature was created out of nothing after a space of time and brought into being from non-existence, so too it might cease to exist when the need it had served had passed away.

2. But if it is impossible by any means to maintain this proposition, namely, that any being, with the exception of the Father, Son and Holy Spirit, can live apart from a body, then logical reasoning compels us to believe that, while the original creation was of rational beings, it is only in idea and thought that a material substance is separable from them, and that though this substance seems to have been produced for them or after them, yet never have they lived or do they live without it; for we shall be right in believing that life without a body is found in the Trinity alone.[1] Now as we have said above, material substance possesses such a nature that it can undergo every kind of transformation. When therefore it is drawn down to lower beings it is formed into the grosser and more solid condition

---

[1] See Bk. I. Ch. II. 2 (p. 15 above). In Bk. I. Ch. VII. 1, (p. 59 above) Origen says that all rational beings are, so far as their essential nature goes, incorporeal. It is their fall which causes them to assume bodies; see Ch. IV. 1 (pp. 40-41 above). Rufinus has probably modified this passage.

of body and serves to distinguish the visible species of
this world in all their variety. But when it ministers to more
perfect and blessed beings, it shines in the splendour of 'celestial
bodies'[1] and adorns either the 'angels of God' or the 'sons of
the resurrection'[2] with the garments of a 'spiritual body'.[3] All
these beings go to make up the diverse and varied condition of
the one world.

If you wish to discuss these questions more fully, it will be
necessary to examine the divine scriptures very intently and
diligently, with all reverence and fear of God, to see whether
there can perchance be found in them any secret and hidden
meaning, anything spoken in deep or veiled language (the Holy
Spirit making the meaning clear[4] to those who are worthy) about
matters such as these, after more testimonies have been collected
that bear on this particular point.

[1] 1 Cor. XV. 40. [2] See St. Luke XX. 36; St. Matt. XXII. 30.
[3] 1 Cor. XV. 44. [4] The phrase is taken from Heb. IX. 8.

CHAPTER III

THE BEGINNING OF THE WORLD AND ITS CAUSES

1. It remains to inquire next, whether there was another world before the one which now exists;[1] and if there was, whether it was of the same kind as the present world, or slightly different or inferior; or whether there was no world at all, but something like that 'end' which we understand will exist at the conclusion of all things, 'when the kingdom is delivered up to God, even the Father';[2] and whether this 'end' was in its turn the end of another world, obviously of that which preceded the beginning of the present one, and whether it was the varying falls of intellectual beings which provoked God to form a world of such variety and diversity as this.

Further, I think that the following point also calls for similar inquiry, whether after this world there will be a course of healing and improvement, very severe no doubt and full of pain to those who have refused to obey the word of God, yet a process of instruction and rational training through which those who in this present life have devoted themselves to these pursuits and, being made purer in mind, have attained here and now to a capacity for divine wisdom, may advance to a richer understanding of truth; and whether after this the end of all things follows immediately. Or again, whether for the correction and improvement of those who need it there will be yet another world, either similar to the one that now exists, or better than it, or possibly much worse; and how long will the world that comes after this exist, of whatever sort it be, or whether it will exist at all; and if there will ever be a time when there will be no world anywhere, or if there ever was a time when there was

---

[1] With this paragraph compare Jerome, *Ep. ad Avitum* 5. 'In the second book he (i.e. Origen) asserts that there are innumerable worlds, not, in the manner of Epicurus, many similar worlds existing at one time, but that after the end of one world comes the beginning of another. A world existed before this world of ours, and another in turn will exist after it, and another after that, and others in constant succession. But he is in doubt whether there will ever be a world similar in every respect to another world, so that the two would appear to differ in no particular, or whether it is certain that there will never be one world quite like another and totally indistinguishable from it.' In Theophilus of Alexandria's Paschal letter, translated by Jerome in his *Ep.* 96, we also find the following : 'Nor does any man die over and over again, as Origen dared to write, in his desire to establish that most impious doctrine of the Stoics by the authority of the divine scriptures.' Rufinus has carefully avoided giving the views that Origen really expressed.

[2] 1 Cor. XV. 24.

no world at all; or if there have been, or shall be, many worlds; or if it will ever happen that one world will turn out to be equal to another and similar in all respects and indistinguishable from it.[1]

2. To make it the more clear, then, whether bodily matter exists but for a space of time and whether, just as it did not exist before it was made, so it will be again resolved into non-existence, let us first see if it can possibly happen for any being to live without a body. For if any being can live without a body, then it is possible for all things to exist without bodies, since our previous chapter has shown that all things work towards one end.[2] But if all things can exist without bodies, doubtless bodily substance will cease to exist when there is no use for it.[3] Yet how are we to understand the words spoken by the apostle in the passage where he discusses the resurrection of the dead? For he says, 'This corruptible must put on incorruption and this mortal must put on immortality. But when this corruptible shall have put on incorruption and this mortal shall have put on immortality, then shall come to pass the saying that is written: Death is swallowed up in victory. O death, where is thy victory. O death, where is thy sting? The sting of death is sin, and the strength of sin is the law'.[4] Some such meaning as the following seems to be suggested by the apostle. When he speaks of 'this corruptible' and 'this mortal', with the air of one who is as it were touching and displaying something, to what else can it apply except bodily matter? This matter of the body, then, which now is corruptible, shall put on incorruption when a perfect soul, instructed in the doctrines of incorruption, has begun to use it.

And I would not have you be surprised that we should use the metaphor of bodily clothing to describe a perfect soul, which on account of the word of God and his wisdom is here called

---

[1] Photius (*Bibl. Cod.* 109) says that Clement, Origen's predecessor at Alexandria, 'talked marvels about transmigrations of souls and about many worlds having existed before Adam'.

[2] See above Bk. II. Ch. I., 2. (p. 77).

[3] See Jerome, *Ed. ad Avitum* 5. 'If,' he says (i.e. Origen), 'as the course of the argument forces us to admit, all things have lived without bodies, then all bodily existence will be swallowed up, and that which was once created out of nothing will be resolved into nothing. And a time will come when its use will once again be necessary.' So Theophilus Alex. in Jerome *Ep.* 96: 'For if, according to the error of Origen, bodily nature is empty and transient . . .' and the same author in Jerome *Ep.* 92: 'What shall I say about the resurrection of the dead, in regard to which he (i.e. Origen) most clearly blasphemes, declaring that after a succession of many ages our bodies will gradually be resolved into nothing and vanish into thin air; and, lest we should think this a trifle, he adds that the resurrection body will be not only corruptible but mortal.' Other similar passages occur in these two letters. Rufinus has again modified the outspoken views of Origen and omitted much.

[4] Cor. XV. 53-56.

'incorruption'. For indeed Jesus Christ himself, who is the Lord and Creator of the soul, is said to be the 'clothing' of the saints, as the apostle says, 'Put ye on the Lord Jesus Christ'.[1] As therefore Christ is the clothing of the soul, so by an intelligible kind of reasoning the soul is said to be the clothing of the body; for it is an ornament of the body, covering and concealing its mortal nature. When therefore the apostle says, 'This corruptible must put on incorruption', it is as if he said, 'This body, with its corruptible nature, must receive the clothing of incorruption, that is, a soul that possesses in itself incorruption, by virtue of the fact that it has put on Christ, who is the wisdom and the word of God.' And when this body, which one day we shall possess in a more glorious form, shall have become a partaker of life, it will then, in addition to being immortal, become also incorruptible. For whatever is mortal is on that very account also corruptible, but we cannot say that what is corruptible is also mortal. For instance, we call a stone or a log corruptible, but it will not follow that we also call them mortal, for they have never lived. But since the body partakes of life, we call it mortal because the life can be and is separated from it, while in another sense we also call it corruptible.

A wonderful insight is therefore revealed in the following words of the holy apostle. Referring in the first place to bodily matter in general, that matter which, in whatever form it is found, whether carnal as now or as hereafter in the subtler and purer form which is called spiritual, the soul always makes use of, he says, 'This corruptible must put on incorruption'. In the second place, referring to the body in particular he says, 'This mortal must put on immortality'. Now what else can this 'incorruption' and 'immortality' be except the wisdom and word and righteousness of God, which mould and clothe and adorn the soul? This is the meaning of the saying that the corruptible puts on incorruption and the mortal puts on immortality. For now, although we may make great progress, still since 'we know in part and we prophesy in part' and even those things which we seem to understand are seen 'through a glass darkly',[2] 'this corruptible' does not yet 'put on incorruption', nor is 'this mortal' encompassed with 'immortality'; and since undoubtedly this training of ours in the body extends over a very long period, namely, up till the time the bodies themselves with which we are encompassed are found worthy of incorruption and immortality by reason of the word and wisdom and perfect righteousness of God, on this account it is said that 'this corruptible must put on incorruption and this mortal must put on immortality'.

3. Nevertheless, those who believe[3] that rational creatures can ever lead a life apart from the body may at this point raise

---

[1] Rom. XIII. 14.   [2] See 1 Cor. XIII. 9, 12.
[3] i.e. Origen: see quotation from Jerome in the note that follows.

such questions as the following. If it is true that 'this corruptible shall put on incorruption and this mortal shall put on immortality' and that in the end 'death shall be swallowed up', this is nothing else but a declaration that material nature is to be destroyed; for it is on material nature that death can have its effect,[1] during the time that those who are in the body have their powers of mind blunted, as it appears, by the nature of bodily matter. If, however, they exist apart from the body, they will then escape all the trouble that comes from this kind of disturbance. But since they could not of a sudden escape from all bodily clothing, they must first be supposed to abide in bodies more pure and subtle, which have in addition the property of not being conquered by death or pierced by 'death's sting',[2] so that finally when material nature has gradually ceased to be, death may be 'swallowed up' and destroyed 'in the end', and all its sting entirely blunted through the divine grace, which the soul has become capable of receiving and has thereby proved itself worthy of obtaining 'incorruption' and 'immortality'. And then all will indeed be able to say, 'O death, where is thy victory? O death where is thy sting. The sting of death is sin'.[3] If therefore these conclusions appear logical,[4] it follows that we must believe that our condition will at some future time be incorporeal; and if this is admitted, and it is said that all must be subjected to Christ, it is necessary that this incorporeal condition shall be the privilege of all who come within the scope of this subjection to Christ, since

GREEK

But if[5] what has been subjected to Christ shall in the end be subjected also to God,[6] then all

LATIN

all who have been subjected to Christ will in the end be subjected also to God the Father,[6]

---

[1] See Jerome, *Ep. ad Avitum* 5. 'And in the words that follow (Origen says); if, as has been proved by reason and by the authority of the scriptures, this corruptible shall put on incorruption and this mortal shall put on immortality, and death shall be swallowed up in victory and corruption in incorruption, then perhaps also the whole of bodily nature will be destroyed, for on this alone can death have its effect.'

[2] 1 Cor. XV. 55, 56.

[3] *Ibid.*

[4] For the passage beginning here see Jerome, *Ep. ad Avitum* 5: 'And a little further on (Origen says); if these opinions are not contrary to the faith, perhaps we shall one day live without bodies. And if he who is perfectly subjected to Christ must be understood to be without a body, and all are to be subjected to Christ, then we too shall exist without bodies, when we have become perfectly subjected to him.'

[5] Frag. 19 (Koetschau), from Justinian *Ep. ad Mennam* (Mansi IX. 529).

[6] See Jerome *Ep. ad Avitum* 5 (following the passage last quoted): 'If all shall be subjected to God, then all will lay aside their bodies; and

GREEK | LATIN

GREEK

will lay aside their bodies; and I think that there will then be a dissolution of bodily nature into non-existence, to come into existence a second time if rational beings should again fall.

LATIN

to whom it is said that Christ will deliver up the kingdom. Thus it appears that then even the use of bodies will cease; and if this happens, bodily nature returns to non-existence, just as formerly it did not exist.

But let us see what those who make these assertions have to face. It will be seen to be a necessity that, if bodily nature were to be destroyed, it must be restored and created a second time. For it is apparently possible that rational creatures, who are never deprived of the power of free-will, may once again become subject to certain movements. This power is

LATIN

granted them by God lest, if they held their position for ever irremovably, they might forget that they had been placed in that final state of blessedness by the grace of God and not by their own goodness. These movements would again undoubtedly be followed by a variety and diversity of bodies, out of which a world is always composed; for it could never exist except as a result of variety and diversity, and this can in no way be produced apart from bodily matter.

4. Moreover, as for those who maintain that worlds similar to each other and in all respects alike sometimes come into existence, I do not know what proofs they can bring in support of this theory. For if it is said that there is to be a world similar in all respects to the present world, then it will happen that Adam and Eve will again do what they did before, there will be another flood, the same Moses will once more lead a people numbering six hundred thousand out of Egypt, Judas also will twice betray his Lord, Saul will a second time keep

then the entire universe of bodily things will be dissolved into non-existence; but, if necessity should demand it a second time, it would come into existence again in the event of the fall of rational creatures. For God has given souls over to struggle and conflict, in order that they may understand that their complete and final victory has been attained not by their own strength but by the grace of God. I think, therefore, that on account of the variety of causes worlds become diverse, and that the errors of those who maintain their similarity are hereby shattered.' The words 'If all . . . . rational creatures' agree with Frag, 19.

the clothes of those who are stoning Stephen, and we shall say that every deed which has been done in this life must be done again.[1] I do not think that this can be established by any reasoning, if souls are actuated by freedom of choice and maintain their progress or the reverse in accordance with the power of their own will. For souls are not driven on some revolving course which brings them into the same cycle again after many ages, with the result that they do or desire this or that, but they direct the course of their deeds towards whatever end the freedom of their individual minds may aim at.

What these men say, however, is the same as if one were to maintain that if a bushel of corn were poured out on the ground it could happen that on two occasions the grains would fall in exactly the same positions, so that each single grain would lie the second time next to that grain besides which it was thrown at the first, and the bushel would be scattered in the same order and with the same marks as formerly. Certainly this is an utterly impossible thing to happen with the innumerable grains of a bushel, even if they were to be poured out again and again without ceasing for countless ages. It seems to me, then, impossible that the world could be restored again a second time with the same order and the same number of births, deaths and actions; but worlds may exist that are diverse, having variations by no means slight, so that for certain clear causes the condition of one may be better, while another for different causes may be worse, and another intermediate. What may be the number or measure of these worlds I confess I do not know; but I would willingly learn, if any man can show me.

5. This world, however, which is itself called an 'age',[2] is said to be the end of many ages. Now the holy apostle teaches that Christ did not suffer in the age that was before this, nor yet in the age before that; and I do not know whether it is in my power to enumerate all the previous ages in which he did not suffer. I will, however, quote the statements of Paul from which I have arrived at this point of knowledge. He says: 'But now once at the consummation of the ages he has been manifested to put away sin by the sacrifice of himself.'[3] He says that Christ has become a 'sacrifice' once, and that 'at the consummation of the ages he has been manifested to put away sin'.[4] But after the present age, which is said to have been

[1] Cp. Origen *Con. Celsum* IV. 67, 68 : V. 20, 21. The identical recurrence of things in cycles was a Stoic doctrine. See Hicks, *Stoic and Epicurean*, pp. 33 ff., and Arnold, *Roman Stoicism*, p. 193.
[2] Wisdom XIII. 9 (Sept. and R. V. marg.).
[3] Hebr. IX. 26.
[4] Jerome, in his *Apology* I. 20, says that 'your Origen allows himself to assert that Christ has often suffered and will often suffer, on the ground that what was beneficial once will be beneficial always'. Compare Book IV. Ch. III, 14 (26), on p. 310 below.

made for the consummation of other ages, there will yet be further 'ages to come'; for we learn this plainly from Paul himself when he says, 'that in the ages to come he might show the exceeding riches of his grace in kindness towards us'.[1] He did not say, 'in the age to come'; nor, 'in two ages'; but, 'in the ages to come'. I think, therefore, that the indications of this statement point to many ages.

If, however, there is something greater than the ages,—so that among created beings we think of ages, but among those who exceed and surpass visible created beings, something still greater—which will perhaps exist at the 'restitution of all things',[2] when the universe reaches its perfect end, then possibly that period in which the consummation of all things will happen is to be understood as something more than an age. In regard to this I am influenced by the authority of holy scripture, which says, 'For an age, and still more'.[3] Now when it says 'still more', undoubtedly it wishes something more than an age to be understood. And see whether that saying of the Saviour, 'I will that, where I am, these also may be there with me' and, 'as I and thou are one, that they also may be one in us',[4] does not seem to point to something more than an age or ages, perhaps even more than the 'ages of the ages',[5] to that period, namely, when all things are no longer in an age, but 'God is all and in all'.[6]

6. Now that we have discussed to the best of our ability these questions about the system of the world, it seems not inappropriate to inquire into the meaning of the actual term 'world'; for it is a term which is frequently shown in the holy scriptures to possess different significations. That which in Latin we speak of as *mundus,* in Greek is called *kosmos;* and *kosmos* signifies not only the world, but also an ornament. For instance in Isaiah, where a reproving speech is addressed to the 'chief daughters of Sion'[7] and the prophet says, 'Instead of an ornament of gold for thy head thou shalt have baldness on account of thy works',[8] he uses for ornament the same word as for world, namely, *kosmos.* It is said also that a representation of the world was to be seen on the garment of the high priest, as we find in the Wisdom of Solomon when it says, 'Upon the long garment was the entire world'.[9] This earth of ours together with its inhabitants is also called the world, as when the scripture says, 'The whole world lieth in the evil one'.[10] Clement indeed, a disciple of the apostles, mentions those whom

---

[1] Eph. II. 7.   [2] Acts III. 21.
[3] This is a misinterpretation of 'from this time forth and for evermore', Ps. CXV. 18; CXXI. 8; CXXV. 2.
[4] St. John XVII. 24, 21.   [5] Gal. I. 5; 1 Tim. I. 17.
[6] 1 Cor. XV. 28.   [7] See Is. III. 17.   [8] Is. III. 24.
[9] Wis. XVIII. 24.   [10] 1 St. John V. 19.

the Greeks call 'people of the opposite earth', and speaks of
other parts of the world which none of our people can reach,
nor can any of those who live there cross over to us; and these
parts themselves he called 'worlds,' when he says, 'The ocean
is impassable to men, and the worlds beyond it are governed
by the same ordinances of God the Ruler'.[1]

This universe which consists of heaven and earth is also
called a world, as Paul says, 'The fashion of this world will
pass away.'[2] Our Lord and Saviour indeed alludes to yet another
world, which it is difficult to describe and depict in actual truth,
beyond this visible one. For he says, 'I am not of this world;[3]
and the words, 'I am not of this world', suggest that he was
of some other world. We have already said that it is difficult
for us to explain this other world; and for this reason, that if
we did so, there would be a risk of giving some men the impression that we were affirming the existence of certain imaginary
forms which the Greeks call 'ideas'. For it is certainly foreign
to our mode of reasoning to speak of an incorporeal world that
exists solely in the mind's fancy or the unsubstantial region of
thought; and how men could affirm that the Saviour came from
thence or that the saints will go thither[4] I do not see.

There is no doubt, however, that the Saviour alludes to
something more glorious and splendid than this present world,
and invites and exhorts all who believe in him to direct their
course towards it. But whether that world, which he wishes us to
know of, is one that stands widely apart and separate from this
in space and quality and glory, or whether, as seems to me
more likely, it excels in quality and glory but is nevertheless
contained within the limits of this world, is uncertain, and in
my opinion an unsuitable subject for the mind and thoughts of
men. But from what Clement appears to allude to when he
says, 'The ocean, which is impassable to men, and the worlds
beyond it',[5] where he uses the plural 'worlds' and indicates that
they are all directed and ruled by the same providence of the
most high God, he would seem to throw out to us some germs
of an opinion such as this, that the entire universe of things
that exist, both celestial and supercelestial, earthly and infernal
may be spoken of in a general way as a single perfect world,
within which or by which those other worlds that are in it
must be supposed to be contained.

---

[1] The 'people of the opposite earth' are the Greek *antichthones*. See
Clem. *Ad Cor.* XX. 5, 8. 'The unsearchable places of the abysses and the
unfathomable realms of the lower world are controlled by the same ordinances. . . . The ocean, which men cannot pass, and the worlds beyond it,
are ruled by the same injunctions of the Master.' (Kirsopp Lake's translation, Loeb Classical Library, *Apostolic Fathers,* Vol. I. p. 45).
[2] 1 Cor. VII. 31.   [3] St. John XVII. 14, 16.
[4] See St. John XVII. 24.   [5] 1 Clem. *Ad Cor.* XX. 8.

Accordingly there are some who would apply the term world'
to the spheres of the moon and the sun and the heavenly bodies
called 'planets' or wanderers; and further, they would maintain
that the uppermost sphere itself, which they call 'fixed', is
rightly termed a world. Finally they appeal to the book of the
prophet Baruch to bear witness to this assertion, because in it
there are very clear indications of the seven worlds or heavens.[1]
They would maintain, however, that above the sphere which they
call 'fixed' there is another; and that, just as in our system the
heaven contains all things that are under it, so this sphere, with
its immense size and indescribable span, encloses the vast extent
of all the other spheres in its yet more magnificent circuit, so
that all things are within it as this earth of ours is under the
heaven.[2] They believe that this sphere is called in the holy
scriptures the 'good land' and the 'land of the living',[3] and that
it has its own heaven, the one we have before spoken of, in which
the names of the saints are said to be written, or to have been
written, by the Saviour.[4] This heaven it is which contains and
encloses that 'earth' which the Saviour in the gospel promises
to the 'meek' and gentle.[5] Further, they would say that this
earth of ours, which was formerly called 'dry land', took its
new name from that earth, just as our firmament was called
'heaven' after the designation of that heaven.[6] But we have
treated more fully of such opinions in the place in which we
inquired into the meaning of the passage, 'In the beginning God

---

[1] The Greek *Apocalypse of Baruch* is an account of the journey of
Baruch through five heavens. But both M. R. James (*Texts and Studies,*
Vol. V., p. li, 1897) and R. H. Charles (*Apoc. and Pseudep. of O. T.*
Vol. II., p. 527) regard the work as being incomplete in the form in which
we have it; so that probably when Origen read it there were seven heavens
described. It is called 4 Baruch by James and 3 Baruch by Charles, and
is probably a Christian redaction of a Jewish work dating from early in
the 2nd century.

[2] Koetschau quotes the following parallels. Cicero, *De Repub.* VI. 17
(*Somn. Scip.* 4). 'All things are bound together by nine circles or spheres,
one of which, the outside one, is the heavenly sphere, which embraces all
the rest.' Gregor. Nyss. *In Hexaëm.* (Migne, P. G. 44 p. 117). 'On account
of the limitless extent of the sphere of the fixed stars the great wisdom of
God established in the middle of the entire span the nature of the sun, to
be the basis of earthly things.'

[3] See Exod. III. 8; Deut. VIII. 8; Jerem. XI. 19; Ps. XXVII. 13;
CXLII. 5.

[4] See St. Luke X. 20.   [5] See St. Matt. V. 4.

[6] See Gen. I. 10, 8 and Origen *In Psalm. Hom.* II. 4. 'There is also
that other earth, of which the scripture speaks, the one that flows with
milk and honey, which the Saviour in the Gospels promises to the meek,
when he says: "Blessed are the meek, for they shall possess the earth".
This earth which we inhabit is in its true designation called the "dry land".
just as the heaven which we behold is properly called the firmament. But
the firmament takes the name of heaven from the appellation of that other
heaven, as the scripture teaches in Genesis.'

made the heaven and the earth'.[1] For it was shown that there is another 'heaven' and another 'earth' besides the firmament, which is said to have been made after the second day, and the 'dry land', which was afterwards called 'earth'.

Certainly what some say of this world, that it is corruptible because it was made, and yet does not go to corruption because the will of God, who made it and preserves it from being mastered by corruption, is stronger and more powerful than corruption, may more rightly be believed of that world which we have above called a 'fixed' sphere, because by the will of God it is in no way 'subject to corruption',[2] for the reason that it has not admitted the causes of corruption. For indeed it is a world of saints and of those who have been completely purified and not of the wicked, as our world is. Now we must see whether the apostle may not have been thinking of that world when he said, 'While we look not at the things which are seen, but at the things which are not seen : for the things which are seen are temporal; but the things which are not seen are eternal. But we know that if the earthly house of this our tabernacle be dissolved, we have a building from God, a house not made with hands, eternal in the heavens'.[3] For when it is said elsewhere, 'Because I shall see the heaven, the works of thy fingers',[4] and when God said through the prophet about all visible things that 'My hand made all these',[5] he declares that that 'eternal house' which he promises to the saints in heaven was not 'made with hands', which undoubtedly signifies a difference in creation between the 'things which are seen' and the 'things which are not seen'. Now the phrase 'things which are not seen' does not mean the same as 'things which are invisible'. For the things which are invisible are not only not seen, but do not even possess a nature which admits of their being seen; they are what the Greeks have called *asomata* or incorporeal.[6] But the things of which Paul said, 'they are not seen', possess a nature which admits of their being seen; he is explaining, however, that they are not yet seen by those to whom they are promised.

7. We have outlined, then, to the best of our knowledge, these three opinions[7] about the end of all things and the supreme

---

[1] This is not found in Origen *In Gen. Hom.* I. 1, 2. See the previous note.

[2] See Rom. VIII. 20, 21.

[3] 2 Cor. IV. 18, V. 1.

[4] Ps. VIII. 3 A. V. and R. V. The reading above is that of VIII. 4 in Vulg. and Sept.

[5] See Is. LXVI. 2.

[6] See Book I, Preface 8 (p. 5 above).

[7] Compare Jerome *Ep. ad Avitum* 5, 6. 'Three notions of the end are suggested to us, from which the reader is invited to discover the truest and best. Either we shall live without a body, when by being subjected to Christ we shall be subjected to God, and God shall be all in all; or

blessedness. Each of our readers must judge for himself, with
all care and diligence, whether one of them may be approved
and adopted. We have said that either we must suppose it
possible to lead a bodiless existence, after 'all things have been
subjected to Christ' and through Christ to God the Father, when
God shall be 'all and in all';[1] or that when the universe has
been subjected to Christ and through Christ to God, with whom
it becomes 'one spirit'[2] in view of the fact that rational beings
are spirits, then also the bodily substance itself, being united to
the best and purest spirits, will be changed, in proportion to
the quality or merits of those who wear it, into an ethereal
condition, according to the apostle's saying, 'and we shall be
changed',[3] and will shine with light; or else that when the fashion
of those things which are seen passes away[4] and all their corruptible nature has been banished and purified, and the entire
condition of the world we know, in which the spheres of the
planets are said to be, is left behind and superseded, there exists
above that sphere which is called 'fixed' an abiding place for the
pious and blessed, in as it were a 'good land' and a 'land of the
living', which the 'meek' and gentle will receive for an inheritance. To this land or earth belongs that heaven which, with its
more magnificent circuit, surrounds and confines it, and this is
the true heaven and the first to be so called.

In this heaven and earth the end and perfection of all things
may find a safe and most sure abode. There, for instance, those
who have for their offences endured the sharp reproof of punishments by way of purgation and have fulfilled and discharged
every obligation may be found worthy of a dwelling-place in the
earth; while those who have been obedient to the word of God
and have already here by their submission shown themselves
receptive of his wisdom may be said to gain the kingdom of
that heaven or heavens. Thus a worthier fulfilment may be found
for the saying, 'Blessed are the meek, for they shall inherit the
earth', and 'Blessed are the poor in spirit, for they shall inherit
the kingdom of heaven,'[5] and for what was said in the psalm,

else, just as what is subjected to Christ will with Christ himself be subjected to God and joined into one compact union, so every substance will
be resolved into its highest condition and changed into ether, which is of
a purer and simpler nature; or else, that that sphere which we have
above called the 'fixed' sphere, and all that is comprised within its span,
shall be dissolved into nothing, but that the further sphere, by which the
lower zone is itself contained and bounded, will be called the "good land",
while yet another sphere, which revolves around this same land and is
called heaven, will serve as a dwelling-place for the saints. In talking
like this (Jerome adds), is he not most plainly following the errors of the
nations and foisting the ravings of philosophers on the simplicity of the
Christian faith?'

[1] See 1 Cor. XV. 27, 28.   [2] 1 Cor. VI. 17.
[3] 1 Cor. XV. 52.   [4] See 1 Cor. VII. 31; 2 Cor. IV. 18.
[5] See St. Matt. V. 5, 3.

'He shall exalt thee, that thou shalt inherit the earth'.[1] For we speak of descending to this earth, but of being 'exalted' to that one, which is on high. In this way, therefore, there seems to be opened a road for the progress of the saints from that earth to those heavens, so that they would appear not so much to remain permanently in that earth as to dwell there in the hope of passing on, when they have made the requisite progress, to the inheritance of the 'kingdom of heaven'.

[1] Ps. XXXVII. 34.

CHAPTER IV

GREEK	LATIN
THAT THERE IS ONE GOD OF THE LAW AND THE PROPHETS AND THAT THE GOD OF THE OLD AND NEW COVENANTS IS THE SAME.[1]	THAT THE GOD OF THE LAW AND THE PROPHETS, AND THE FATHER OF OUR LORD JESUS CHRIST, IS ONE.

LATIN

1. Now that we have, to the best of our ability, discussed these matters briefly in order, it follows from the plan which we adopted at the beginning that we proceed to refute those who think that the Father of our Lord Jesus Christ is a different God from him who gave Moses the sayings of the law and sent the prophets, and who is the God of the fathers Abraham, Isaac and Jacob.[2] For it is of prime necessity that we should be firmly grounded in this article of our faith. We will consider, then, that statement which occurs frequently in the gospels and is attached to various acts of our Lord and Saviour: 'That it might be fulfilled which was spoken through "this or that" prophet,'[3] where it is evident that these are prophets of that God who made the world. From this follows the conclusion that he who sent the prophets himself foretold what was to be foretold of Christ, and there is no doubt that it was the Father of Christ, and not some different being, who foretold these things. Further, the fact that illustrations are frequently drawn from the Old Testament by the Saviour and his apostles can only indicate that they both attach authority to the ancient writers. And further, the fact that when urging his disciples to the exercise of kindness, the Saviour says, 'Be ye perfect, as your heavenly Father is perfect, who bids his sun rise on the good and on the evil, and sends rain on the just and on the unjust,'[4] suggests even to a man of the smallest intelligence this most obvious meaning, that he is putting before his disciples

---

[1] The Greek title of this chapter is taken from Photius *Bibl. Cod.* 8.

[2] This was the doctrine held by Marcion, a heretical Christian teacher of the earlier half of the second century. He was puzzled by the character attributed to God in the Old Testament anl declared that, although that God might be just, he could not be regarded as good or as the Father whom Jesus revealed. See Eusebius, *Hist. Eccl.* IV. 11 and Tertullian, *Con. Marc.* passim. Many of the Gnostics adopted the same doctrine, as a means of overcoming the difficulties of the Old Testament and fitting it into their systems.

[3] See St. Matt. II. 15; IV. 14; VIII. 17.

[4] St. Matt. V. 48, 45.

as a pattern for imitation no other God than the maker of heaven and the giver of the rain.

Again, when he says that those who pray must say, 'Our Father, who art in heaven',[1] what does he appear to be indicating, if not that God must be sought for in the better parts of the world, that is, of his own creation? When, too, in laying down those most admirable rules about oaths he says that we are not to swear, 'neither by heaven, because it is God's throne, nor by the earth, because it is the footstool of his feet',[2] does he not appear to be in most open agreement with the words of the prophet, 'Heaven is my throne, and the earth is the footstool of my feet.'[3] Further, when he cast out of the temple those who were selling 'oxen and sheep and doves' and overturned the 'tables of the moneychangers' and said, 'Take these things hence; and make not my Father's house a house of merchandise',[4] he was undoubtedly calling that God his Father, to whose name Solomon had built the magnificent temple.

Again, the saying, 'Have ye not read what was said by God to Moses; I am the God of Abraham and the God of Isaac and the God of Jacob; he is not the God of the dead, but of the living',[5] teaches us most clearly that he called the God of the patriarchs, because they were holy and living men, 'the God of the living', the same God indeed who had said in the prophets, 'I am God, and there is no God beside me'.[6] For if the Saviour, knowing that he who is written of in the law is the God of Abraham, and that it is the same God who says, 'I am God, and there is no God beside me', confesses that this very God who, as the heretics suppose,[7] is ignorant that there is another God above him, is the Father, he is absurdly declaring that being to be the Father who is ignorant of the existence of a higher God. If, however, God is not ignorant, but is deceiving us when he says, 'There is no God beside me', it is a greater absurdity still, to think that the Saviour should confess that his Father was a liar. From all these considerations the mind is led to this conclusion, that the Saviour knows no other Father except God the founder and creator of all things.

2. It would be a long business if we were to gather out of every passage in the gospels the proofs by which we are taught that the God of the law and the gospels is one and the same. Let us, however, touch briefly on the Acts of the Apostles, where Stephen and the apostles direct their prayers to that God 'who made heaven and earth' and who 'spoke by the mouth of his

---

[1] St. Matt. VI. 9.   [2] See St. Matt. V. 34, 35.
[3] Is. LXVI. 1.   [4] See St. John II. 14-16.
[5] St. Matt. XXII. 31, 32.   [6] Is. XLVI. 9.
[7] Basileides (see Hippolytus, *Philosophum,* VII. 23) and Valentinus (*ibid.* VI. 33). The Valentinians maintained that the Creator of the world made the statement (Is. XLVI. 9) in ignorance : see Irenaeus, in Epiphanius; Oehler, *Corpus haeres.* II. i., p. 348.

holy prophets', calling him 'the God of Abraham, Isaac and Jacob', the God who led his people out of the land of Egypt.[1] These expressions undoubtedly direct our minds to faith in the Creator and implant an affection for him in those who have piously and faithfully accepted this truth about him; in accordance with the words of the Saviour himself who, when he was asked what was 'the greatest commandment in the law', answered, 'Thou shalt love the Lord thy God with all thy heart and with all thy soul and with all thy mind.' And a second is like unto it: 'Thou shalt love thy neighbour as thyself'; to which he added, 'On these two commandments hang all the law and the prophets'.[2] How is it, I ask, that he commends to the man whom he was instructing and leading on to discipleship this commandment above all others, as a means undoubtedly of kindling affection for the God of the old law, since both commandments had been previously laid down by the law in those very words?

Nevertheless, let it be granted in spite of all these most evident proofs that it is about some other and unknown God that the Saviour says, 'Thou shalt love the Lord thy God with all thy heart', and the rest. Now if the law and the prophets come, as they say,[3] from the Creator, that is, from another God than him whom they call good, how can it be logical to add as he does, 'On these two commandments hang the law and the prophets'. For how can that which is strange and foreign to God depend upon him? And when Paul says, 'I give thanks to my God, whom I serve from my forefathers with a pure conscience',[4] he shows with perfect clearness that in coming to Christ he did not come to any new God. For what other 'forefathers' of Paul can we think of except those of whom he says, 'Are they Hebrews? So am I. Are they Israelites? So am I.'[5]

Further, does not the introduction to his Epistle to the Romans show precisely, to all who know how to understand Paul's letters, the very same thing, namely, what God Paul is preaching? For he says, 'Paul a servant of Jesus Christ, called to be an apostle, separated unto the gospel of God, which he promised before by his prophets in the holy scriptures concerning his Son, who was born of the seed of David according to the flesh, but foreordained to be the Son of God with power, according to the spirit of sanctification and the resurrection from the dead of Jesus Christ our Lord',[6] and the rest. There is also the passage which says, 'Thou shalt not muzzle the mouth of the ox when he

[1] See Acts IV. 24, 25; III. 13; V. 30; VII. 2, 32, 34.
[2] St. Mark XII. 28, 30, 31; St. Matt. XXII. 36, 37, 39, 40.
[3] Koetschau refers to Origen, *In Jerem. hom.* XII. 5. 'The heretics say: "You see what the Creator is like. He is the God of the prophets, who says, I will not spare nor have compassion to save them from destruction. How can this God be good"?' See Jerem. XIII. 14.
[4] 2 Tim. I. 3.   [5] 2 Cor. XI. 22.   [6] Rom. I. 1-4.

treadeth out the corn. Is it for the oxen that God careth? Or saith he it altogether for our sake? Yea, for our sake it was written, because he that plougheth ought to plough in hope, and he that thresheth to thresh in hope of partaking.'[1] Here he shows clearly that God who gave the law says the words 'Thou shalt not muzzle the mouth of the ox when he treadeth out the corn' for our sake, that is, for the sake of the apostles, and that his care was not for the oxen but for the apostles, who were preaching the gospel of Christ. In other passages, too, Paul himself appropriates a promise of the law, speaking as follows: 'Honour thy father and mother, which is the first commandment with promise, that it may be well with thee, and thou mayest live long in the land, the good land, which the Lord thy God will give thee.'[2] In these words Paul undoubtedly declares that the law, and the God of the law, and his promises, are pleasing to him.

3. But since the supporters of this heresy are sometimes wont to beguile the hearts of very simple people by certain fallacious sophistries, I think it not unreasonable to bring forward the points raised in their arguments and to refute their deceit and falsehoods. They say that it is written, 'No man hath seen God at any time';[3] yet the God whom Moses proclaims was seen by Moses himself and before that by his fathers, whereas the God who is announced by the Saviour has been seen by no one at all. Let us then ask them this question, whether the Being, whom they profess to be God and who they say is different from God the Creator, is visible or invisible. If they should say that he is visible, they will not only be proved to be in opposition to that passage of scripture which says of the Saviour that he is 'the image of the invisible God, the firstborn of all creation',[4] but besides this, they will run into the absurdity of saying that God has a body.[5] For in no other way can anything be seen except by its shape and size and colour, which are properties of bodies. And if God is declared to be a body, then, since every body is made of matter, we shall find that God is made of matter too; and if so, then, since matter is undoubtedly corruptible, God will according to them be corruptible. Again, we will ask them this question also. Is matter made or uncreated, that is, not made? If they should say that it is unmade, that is, uncreated, we shall inquire whether one part of matter is God, and another part the world. But if they should answer that matter is made, it will follow undoubtedly that they confess that he whom they call God is made, which certainly neither their reason nor ours will admit.[6]

---

[1] I Cor. IX. 9, 10.   [2] Eph. VI. 2, 3, cited from Exod. XX. 12.
[3] St. John I. 18.   [4] Col. I. 15.
[5] Compare with this I Pref. 9 (p. 6 above).
[6] Compare with this Bk. II., I. 4 (p. 79 above).

But they will say, 'God is invisible.' Now what are you to do? If you say that he is invisible by nature, then he ought not to be visible even to the Saviour.[1] Yet in spite of this God the Father of Christ is said to be seen; for Christ says, 'He who hath seen the Son hath seen the Father also'.[2] This certainly involves you in serious difficulties, whereas we interpret it more correctly as referring not to sight but to understanding. For he who has understood the Son has understood the Father also. It is in this manner then that we must suppose Moses to have seen God, not by looking at him with eyes of flesh, but by understanding him with the vision of the heart and the perception of the mind, and even this in part only. For it is well-known that he, that is, the one who gave the oracles to Moses, says, 'Thou shalt not see my face, but my back'.[3] Certainly these statements must be understood by the aid of that symbolism which is appropriate to the understanding of divine sayings, and those old wives' fables, which ignorant people invent on the subject of the front and back parts of God, must be utterly rejected and despised. Nor indeed must anyone suppose that we have entertained some impious thought in saying that the Father is not visible even to the Saviour, but he must consider the exact meaning of the terms we use in controverting the heretics. For we have said that it is one thing to see and be seen, another to perceive and be perceived or to know and be known. To see and be seen is a property of bodies, which it would certainly not be right to apply either to the Father or to the Son or to the Holy Spirit in their relations one with another. For the Trinity by its nature transcends the limits of vision, although it grants to those who are in bodies, that is, to all other creatures, the property of being seen one by another. But incorporeal, and above all intellectual nature is capable of nothing else but to know and be known, as the Saviour himself declares when he says, 'No one knoweth the Son save the Father, neither doth any know the Father save the Son, and he to whom the Son willeth to reveal him.'[4] It is clear, then, that he did not say, 'No one seeth the Father save the Son', but 'No one knoweth the Father save the Son'.

4. If, however, they think that in those statements which are made in the Old Testament to the effect that God is angry or repents, or is subject to any other human emotion, they are provided with material for refuting us with the assertion that God must be believed to be entirely without passion and destitute of all these emotions, we must show them that similar statements are to be found even in the parables of the gospel, as

[1] See Jerome, *Ep. ad Avitum* 6. 'In the same book he (i.e. Origen) says: Grant that God is invisible. If then he is invisible by nature, he will not be visible even to the Saviour.'
[2] St. John XIV. 9.   [3] Exod. XXXIII. 23.   [4] St. Matt. XI. 27.

when it says that God 'planted a vine' and 'let it out to husbandmen', which husbandmen killed the servants who were sent to
them, and when at last the Son was sent they put him to death
too, wherefore God is said to have become angry and to have
taken away the vineyard from them and to have delivered the
wicked husbandmen to destruction and given the vineyard to
others who would 'render him the fruits in their season'.[1] Again,
in the case of those citizens who, when the father of the house-
hold set out to 'receive for himself a kingdom', 'sent messengers
after him saying, We will not have this man to reign over us',
on the father's return after having obtained his kingdom he
was angry, and commanded them to be slain before him and
their city to be burnt by fire.[2] For ourselves, however, whenever we read of the anger of God, whether in the Old or the
New Testament, we do not take such statements literally, but
look for the spiritual meaning in them, endeavouring to understand them in a way that is worthy of God. But we dealt with
these points, according to our poor ability, when expounding that
verse of the second Psalm in which it says, 'Then shall he speak
unto them in his wrath, and trouble them in his fury', where
we showed, as best we could, in what way this ought to be
understood.[3]

---

[1] See St. Matt. XXI. 33-41.   [2] See St. Luke XIX. 12-27.
[3] See Ps. II. 5. We do not possess the explanation to which Origen
here refers. In his *Hom. in Jerem.* XVIII. 6 he says: 'If you hear of the
anger of God and the wrath of God, do not suppose that this anger and
wrath are passions of God.'

CHAPTER V

THE JUST AND THE GOOD

1. But some are influenced by the fact that the leaders of this heresy appear to have made for themselves a distinction, saying that the just is one thing and the good another, and have applied this distinction even to the divine nature, asserting that the Father of our Lord Jesus Christ is a good God but not just, whereas the God of the law and prophets is just but not good.[1] I think it necessary, therefore, to answer this point as briefly as I can.

They reckon, then, that goodness is that sort of disposition by which one is led to do good to all, even when the recipient of the benefit is unworthy and does not deserve our kindness. But, as it appears to me, they have not rightly applied this definition, for they think that no good is done to him who is visited with any sorrow or hardship. Justice, however, they suppose to be the sort of disposition which renders to every man according to his deserts. Yet here again they do not rightly interpret the meaning of their own definition. For they think that justice is to do evil to the evil and good to the good; that is, according to their meaning, that one who is just will not show himself well disposed to the evil, but will behave towards them with a kind of hatred;[2] and they collect all the stories they can find in the Old Testament to support this view, such for example, as the story of the flood and the punishment of those who are said to have been drowned in it,[3] or how Sodom and Gomorrah were destroyed by a devastating rain of fire and brimstone,[4] or how all the children of Israel died in the desert on account of their sins, so that not one of those who had set out from Egypt was found to enter the promised land except Joshua and Caleb.[5] From the New Testament, however, they gather those sayings of pity and gentleness which the Saviour uttered when teaching his disciples and in which he is found to declare that 'none is good save one, God the Father'.[6] Relying on this they have dared to call the Father of our Saviour Jesus Christ the good God, but to say that the God of the world is a different being, whom they are pleased to term just, but not good.

---

[1] The protagonist of this view was Marcion, whose teaching is described and combated in Tertullian, *Adv. Marcionem.*
[2] See Plato *Repub.* 331 E-336 A.   [3] See Gen. VII. 4, 21-23.
[4] See Gen. XIX. 24, 25.   [5] See Num. XIV. 11-24, 30.
[6] See St. Mark X. 18; St. Luke XVIII. 19.

2. Now first, of all we must, I think, demand of these people an answer to the following question. How, according to their own definition, can they show the Creator to be just in punishing according to their deserts those who perished at the time of the flood, or the men of Sodom, or those who set out from Egypt, when we sometimes see far more wicked and heinous crimes committed than those for which the above mentioned people were destroyed, but do not yet see every sinner paying the just penalty of his deeds? Will they say that he who once was just has now become good? Or will they prefer to adopt this opinion, that he is just now, but patiently bears with man's offences, whereas then he was not even just, when he exterminated innocent children and babes at the breast along with monstrous and impious giants?[1]

But they believe as they do because they are ignorant how to interpret any passage except literally. If this is not so, let them show how it is just, in a literal sense, for the sins of the parents to be visited on the heads of the children, and on the children's children after them, to the third and fourth generation?[2] We, however, do not understand such sayings in a literal sense, but as Ezekiel taught when he uttered his well-known 'proverb',[3] we inquire what is the inner meaning of the proverb. Further, they ought also to explain this, how he can be just and one who 'rewards every man according to his deserts',[4] when he punishes earthly-minded men and the devil, though they have committed nothing deserving of punishment; for if, as these men say, they were beings of an evil and ruined nature, they could not do anything good. And as for their calling him a judge, he would seem to be a judge not so much of deeds as of natures, if it be a fact that an evil nature cannot do good nor a good nature evil.

Then in the next place, if he whom they call good is good to all, undoubtedly he is good even to those who are destined to perish. Why then does he not save them? If he is unwilling, then he will not be good; if he is willing but cannot, he will not be almighty. On the other hand let them hear from the gospels how the Father of our Lord Jesus Christ 'prepares fire for the devil and his angels'.[5] How can a work like that, so punitive and sorrowful, be associated with the good God according to their interpretation? Further, the Saviour himself, the Son of the good God, openly declares that 'if signs and wonders had been done in Tyre and Sidon they would have repented long ago, sitting in sackcloth and ashes'.[6] Yet when he came quite near to those very towns and had entered into

---

[1] Gen. VI. 1-7, 17 and VII. 21 ff. Origen is fully alive to the problem of undeserved suffering.
[2] Exod. XX. 5, XXXIV. 7; Deut. V. 9.   [3] See Ezek. XVIII. 2, 3.
[4] Ps. LXII. 12.   [5] St. Matt. XXV. 41.   [6] St. Matt. XI. 21.

their 'borders',[1] why, I ask, did he decline to enter their actual
territories and show their people an abundance of 'signs and
wonders', if it had been certain that as a result of such actions
they would 'repent in sackcloth and ashes'? As he certainly
does not do this, without doubt he is abandoning to destruction
men whom his very remark in the gospels shows not to have
been of an evil and ruined nature; for he points out that they
could have repented.

Moreover, in one of the gospel parables, when 'the king
enters in to see the guests' who had been invited, he sees 'one
not wearing a wedding garment' and says to him, 'Friend,
how camest thou in hither not having on a wedding garment?'
Then he says to the servants, 'Bind him hand and foot and
cast him forth into the outer darkness; there shall be weeping
and gnashing of teeth'.[2] Let them tell us; who is this 'king'
who entered in to see the guests, and finding one in mean garments commands him to be bound by his servants and thrust
into the outer darkness? Is it indeed he whom they call 'just'?
If so, why had he ordered 'good and bad' to be invited, and not
directed his servants to inquire into their merits? This conduct
certainly indicates the disposition not, as they say, of one who
is merely just and who 'rewards according to merit',[3] but of
one who shows impartial kindness to all. If, however, it is
necessary to understand this passage as referring to the good
God, that is, either to Christ or to the Father of Christ, what
more is there to object to even in the just God? Nay, what
action is there which they can charge against the God of the
law comparable to this, that he commanded the man, who had
been invited by the servants sent by himself to call both good
and bad, to be bound hand and foot and flung into the outer
darkness, because of the mean garments he was wearing?

3. These arguments, which we have drawn from the authority
of the scriptures, ought to suffice for the refutation of those
points which the heretics are accustomed to urge. It will not
seem unfitting, however, if we discuss the matter with them in
a few words from the standpoint of logical reasoning also. Let
us ask them, therefore, whether they know what theory of
virtue and wickedness is held by men, and whether it seems
logical to speak of virtues in God, or, as they think, in these
two gods. Let them also answer this question: if they think
that goodness is one virtue, which I take it they will undoubtedly
admit, what do they say about justice? They will certainly
never be so foolish, I think, as to deny that justice is a virtue.
Therefore, if a virtue is something good, and justice is a virtue,
undoubtedly justice is goodness. If, however, they should say
that justice is not something good, the alternative is either

[1] See St. Matt. XV. 22.
[2] See St. Matt. XXII. 11-13.   [3] See Ps. LXII. 12.

something bad, or something indifferent. Now I consider it
would be stupid to answer men who said that justice was something bad; I should appear to be answering either senseless
arguments or men of unsound mind. For how could that be
something bad, which, as even our opponents will admit, can
render good to those who are good? But if they should say
it is a thing indifferent, it follows that, since justice is indifferent,
then temperance and prudence and the rest of the virtues will also
be accounted indifferent. What then shall we reply to Paul when
he says, 'If there be any virtue, if there be any praise, think
on these things, which ye both learned and received and heard
and saw in me'.[1]

Let them, therefore, search the divine scriptures and tell us
what the various virtues are, and not hide behind this statement
of theirs that the God who 'renders to each man according to
his desert' renders ill to the evil out of hatred towards them;
when the truth is that those who have sinned need severer remedies
for their cure, and it is for this reason that he brings upon
them the afflictions which, though aiming at improvement, seem
at the moment to convey a sense of pain. They do not read
what is written about the hope of those who perished in the flood,
of which hope Peter in his first epistle speaks as follows: 'Because
Christ was put to death in the flesh, but quickened in the spirit;
in which he went and preached to the spirits who were held in
prison, who were aforetime disbelieving, when the long-suffering
of God waited in the days of Noah, while the ark was a prepar-
ing, wherein few, that is eight souls, were saved by water, as
also by a like figure baptism now saves you.'[2]

And in regard to Sodom and Gomorrah, let them tell us
whether they believe the words of the prophets to come from
God the Creator, from him, that is, who is related to have
'rained upon them a shower of fire and brimstone'.[3] What does
the prophet Ezekiel say of them? 'Sodom shall be restored to
her former estate'.[4] And when God afflicts those who deserve
punishment, how else is it except for their good? It is he who
says to the Chaldaeans: 'Thou hast coals of fire; sit upon them.
They shall be a help to thee'.[5] Further, let them hear what
is related in the seventy-seventh psalm, which is ascribed to
Asaph, about those who fell in the desert; it says, 'When he
slew them, then they sought him'.[6] It does not say that some
sought him after others had been killed, but that those who
were slain perished in such a manner that when put to death
they sought God. From all these illustrations it is plain that
the just and good God of the law and the gospels is one and
the same, and that he does good with justice and punishes in

---

[1] Phil. IV. 8, 9.
[2] 1 St. Peter III. 18-21.
[3] Gen. XIX. 24.
[4] Ezek. XVI. 55.
[5] Is. XLVII. 14, 15 (Sept.).
[6] Ps. LXXVIII. 34.

kindness, since neither goodness without justice nor justice without goodness can describe the dignity of the divine nature.

Let us add also the following remarks, which are necessitated by their subtle arguments. If the just is different from the good, then since evil is the opposite of good and unjust of just, undoubtedly the unjust will be different from the evil; and as the just man according to you is not good, so neither will the unjust man be evil; and again, as the good man is not just, so also the evil man will not be unjust. And how can it be anything but absurd that the good God should have an opponent who is evil, whereas the just God, whom they say is inferior to the good one, has no opponent? For Satan is called evil, but there is no other corresponding to him who is called unjust. What then shall we do? Let us retrace the steps of our argument to the point from which we started. They will not be able to say that the evil man is not unjust and the unjust man not evil? If, however, in these opposites injustice is inseparably associated with evil and evil with injustice, then undoubtedly the good man will be inseparably associated with the just and the just with the good; so that as we call evil and injustice one and the same wickedness, we should hold goodness and justice to be one and the same virtue.

4. But once again they recall us to the words of scripture, quoting that famous question of theirs. They say: it is written that 'a good tree cannot bring forth evil fruit, neither can an evil tree bring forth good fruit; for a tree is known by its fruit.'[1] What do you make of this, they say? What sort of a tree the law is, is shown by its fruits, that is, by the words of its precepts. For if the law is found to be good, undoubtedly we shall believe that he who gave it is a good God; if, however, it is just rather than good, we shall think of God as a just lawgiver. But Paul the apostle says in no roundabout terms, 'The law then is good, and the commandment holy and just and good'.[2] It is plain from this that Paul had not learned the doctrines of those who separate the just from the good, but had been instructed by that God and illuminated by the spirit of that God who is at the same time both 'holy and good and just', and that it was through his spirit that he spoke when he said that 'the commandment of the law is holy and just and good'. And in order to show the more clearly that goodness was in the commandment to a greater degree than justice and holiness, in repeating the passage he used goodness alone instead of the three words, when he says, 'Is then that which is good death to me? God forbid'.[3] He knew, of course, that goodness

[1] See Hippolytus' Epitome of the teaching of Marcion and Cerdo in *Philosophum.* X. 19, where the above saying is quoted. For the saying itself see St. Matt. VII. 18; XII. 33.
[2] Rom. VII. 12.   [3] Rom. VII. 13.

is the general term for the virtues, while justice and holiness are particular kinds of goodness; and so, where in his former words he had mentioned the general together with the particular, in repeating the passage he fell back on the general term alone.

Further, in the words that follow Paul says, 'Sin worked death in me through that which is good'.[1] Here he includes in the general term that which before he had described by means of the particular terms. It is in this way also that we must understand the saying, 'the good man out of the good treasure of his heart brings forth good, and the evil man out of his evil treasure brings forth evil';[2] for here, too, good and evil are taken in the general sense, the term 'good man' undoubtedly indicating both justice and temperance, prudence and piety and everything which can be spoken of or understood as good. Similarly also does it speak of the 'evil man', who undoubtedly would be unjust and impure and everything else that in different ways disfigures the 'evil man'. For just as nobody thinks anyone to be an evil man, nor can he be evil, apart from these works of wickedness, so it is certain that nobody will be thought to be good apart from the opposite virtues.

There still remains to them the passage in the gospel, which they think is as it were specially given to them for a shield, where the Lord said, 'None is good save one, God the Father'.[3] This, they say, is the proper description of the Father of Christ, who is a different being from God the creator of all things, to which creator Christ gave no title indicating goodness. Let us see, therefore, whether in the Old Testament the God of the prophets and the creator of the world and the lawgiver is not spoken of as good. What is it that is said in the Psalms, 'How good is God to Israel, to the upright in heart!'[4] and, 'Let Israel now say that he is good, that his mercy endureth for ever.'[5] And in the Lamentations of Jeremiah it is written, 'The Lord is good to those who wait for him, to the soul that seeketh him.'[6] As then God is frequently called good in the Old Testament, so too the Father of our Lord Jesus Christ is called just in the gospels. Indeed, in the gospel according to John our Lord himself when praying to the Father says, 'O just Father, the world hath not known thee'.[7] And lest they should say

---

[1] Rom. VII. 13.   [2] St. Luke VI. 45.

[3] See St. Mark X. 18; St. Luke XVIII. 18. For the use made of this text see Hippolytus, *Philosophum.* VII. 31. Prepon, a disciple of Marcion, said that 'the just' was a third principle, intermediate between good and evil. Marcion himself, according to Hippolytus, said that Christ, in order to be a mediator, had to be free from all connexion not only with evil but even with good, and adduced this text in support of his doctrine. The Naassenes (*ibid.* V. 7) used the same text to support their doctrine that the primal seed, the generative cause of all existence, was alone good.

[4] Ps. LXXIII. 1.   [5] Ps. CXVIII. 2.
[6] Lam. III. 25.   [7] St. John XVII. 25.

that it was the creator of the world whom our Lord, because he had taken human flesh, called Father, and that it was he whom he termed just, they are prevented by the sentence which immediately follows; for he says, 'The world hath not known thee'. For according to them it is only the good God whom the world does not know; it most certainly recognises its founder, as the Lord himself says, 'The world loves what is its own'.[1] Clearly, then, he whom they think to be the good God is said in the gospels to be just. And when time permits we shall be able to collect still more passages where in the New Testament the Father of our Lord Jesus Christ is called just, and where in the Old Testament the creator of heaven and earth is called good, so that the heretics, convinced by the multitude of proofs, may at length perchance blush for shame.

[1] St. John XV. 19.

CHAPTER VI

GREEK	LATIN
THE INCARNATION OF THE SAVIOUR.[1]	THE INCARNATION OF CHRIST.

LATIN

1. Now that these points have been discussed, it is time to resume our inquiry into the incarnation of our Lord and Saviour, how he became man and dwelt among men. We have considered, to the best of our small ability, the divine nature, from a contemplation of his own works rather than from our feelings, and while beholding his visible creatures we have also by faith contemplated those that are invisible. For human frailty can neither see everything with the eyes nor comprehend everything by reason, since we men are beings weaker and frailer than all other rational creatures, those that dwell in heaven or above the heavens surpassing us in excellence. Our next task is to inquire about him who stands midway between all these creatures and God, that is, the Mediator,[2] whom the apostle Paul declares to be the 'firstborn of all creation'.[3] And when we see what is related in the holy scriptures of his majesty, and perceive that he is called the 'image of the invisible God' and the 'firstborn of all creation', and that 'in him were created all things visible and invisible, whether thrones or dominions or principalities or powers, all were created through him and in him, and he is before all, and in him all things consist',[4] who is the 'head of all', having as his head only God the Father, as it is written, 'the head of Christ is God';[5] and when we see too that it is written, 'No man knoweth the Father save the Son, nor doth any know the Son save the Father'[6]—for who can know what 'wisdom' is, except him who brought it into being; or who knows for certain what 'truth' is, except the Father of truth; who indeed could trace out the universal nature of his 'Word' and of that God who is from God except God alone 'with whom the Word was'?[7]—we ought to hold it as certain that none else save the Father alone knows this Word (or reason, if he should be so called), this wisdom, this truth, of whom it is written, 'I suppose that not even the world itself could contain the books which should be written,'[8] about the glory, that is, and about the

---

[1] For the Greek title see Photius, *Bibl. Cod.* 8.
[2] See 1 Tim. II. 5.   [3] Col. I. 15.   [4] See Col. I. 15-17.
[5] See 1 Cor. XI. 3.   [6] St. Matt. XI. 27.   [7] See St. John I. 1.
[8] St. John XXI. 25.

majesty of the Son of God. For it is impossible to put into writing all that belongs to the Saviour's glory.

When, therefore, we consider these great and marvellous truths about the nature of the Son of God, we are lost in the deepest amazement that such a being, towering high above all, should have 'emptied himself'[1] of his majestic condition and become man and dwelt among men, a fact which is evidenced by the 'grace poured upon his lips'[2] and by the witness which the heavenly Father bore him,[3] and confirmed by the signs and wonders and mighty deeds which he did. And before that personal appearance which he manifested in the body, he sent the prophets as heralds and messengers of his coming; while after his ascension into the heavens he caused the holy apostles, unlearned and ignorant men from the ranks of tax-gatherers or fishermen but filled with his divine power, to travel throughout the world, in order to gather together out of every nation and all races a people composed of devout believers in him.

2. But of all the marvellous and splendid things about him there is one that utterly transcends the limits of human wonder and is beyond the capacity of our weak mortal intelligence to think of or understand, namely, how this mighty power of the divine majesty, the very word of the Father, and the very wisdom of God, in which were created 'all things visible and invisible',[4] can be believed to have existed within the compass of that man who appeared in Judaea; yes, and how the wisdom of God can have entered into a woman's womb and been born as a little child and uttered noises like those of crying children; and further, how it was that he was troubled, as we are told, in the hour of death, as he himself confesses when he says, 'My soul is sorrowful even unto death';[5] and how at the last he was led to that death which is considered by men to be the most shameful of all,—even though on the third day he rose again.

When, therefore, we see in him some things so human that they appear in no way to differ from the common frailty of mortals, and some things so divine that they are appropriate to nothing else but the primal and ineffable nature of deity, the human understanding with its narrow limits is baffled, and struck with amazement at so mighty a wonder knows not which way to turn, what to hold to, or whither to betake itself. If it thinks of God, it sees a man; if it thinks of a man, it beholds one returning from the dead with spoils after vanquishing the kingdom of death. For this reason we must pursue our contemplation with all fear and reverence, as we seek to prove how the reality of each nature exists in one and the same person, in such a way that nothing unworthy or unfitting may be thought to reside in that divine and ineffable existence, nor on the other

---

[1] Phil. II. 7.   [2] Ps. XLV. 3.   [3] St. Matt. III. 17; St. Luke III. 22.
[4] Col. I. 16.   [5] St. Matt. XXVI. 38; St. Mark XIV. 34.

hand may the events of his life be supposed to be the illusions caused by deceptive fantasies.[1] But to utter these things in human ears and to explain them by words far exceeds the powers we possess either in our moral worth or in mind and speech. I think indeed that it transcends the capacity even of the holy apostles; nay more, perhaps the explanation of this mystery lies beyond the reach of the whole creation of heavenly beings. It is then in no spirit of rashness, but solely in response to the demands of our inquiry at this stage, that we shall state in the fewest possible words that we may term the content of our faith concerning him rather than anything which needs to be proved by arguments of human reason, bringing before you our suppositions rather than any clear affirmations.

3. The only-begotten Son of God, therefore, through whom, as the course of our discussion in the previous chapters has shown, 'all things visible and invisible were made',[2] according to the teaching of scripture both made all things and 'loves what he made'.[3] For since he is the invisible 'image' of the 'invisible God',[4] he granted invisibly to all rational creatures whatsoever a participation in himself, in such a way that each obtained a degree of participation proportionate to the loving affection with which he had clung to him. But whereas, by reason of the faculty of free-will, variety and diversity had taken hold of individual souls, so that one was attached to its author with a warmer and another with a feebler and weaker love, that soul of which Jesus said, 'No man taketh from me my soul',[5] clinging to God from the beginning of the creation and ever after in a union insepara-ble and indissoluble, as being the soul of the wisdom and word of God and of the truth and the true light, and receiving him wholly, and itself entering into his light and splendour, was made with him in a pre-eminent degree one spirit, just as the apostle promises to them whose duty it is to imitate Jesus, that 'he who is joined to the Lord is one spirit'.[6] This soul, then, acting as a medium between God and the flesh (for it was not possible for the nature of God to mingle with a body apart from some medium), there is born, as we said, the God-man, the medium being that existence to whose nature it was not contrary to assume a body. Yet neither, on the other hand, was it contrary to nature for that soul, being as it was a rational existence, to receive God, into whom, as we said above,

---

[1] i.e. as the various docetic heresies asserted.
[2] Col. I. 16.   [3] See Wis. XI. 24.   [4] Col. I. 15.
[5] See Jerome *Ep. ad Avitum* 6 'And lower down he (i.e. Origen) says, No other soul, which has descended into a human body, has revealed in itself so pure and genuine a likeness to its former condition as that of which the Saviour says, No man taketh my soul from me, but I lay it down of myself.' For the text see St. John X. 18.
[6] 1 Cor. VI. 17.

it had already completely entered by entering into the word and wisdom and truth.

It is therefore right that this soul, either because it was wholly in the Son of God, or because it received the Son of God wholly into itself, should itself be called, along with that flesh which it has taken, the Son of God and the power of God, Christ and the wisdom of God; and on the other hand that the Son of God, 'through whom all things were created', should be termed Jesus and the Son of man. Moreover the Son of God is said to have died, in virtue of that nature which could certainly admit of death, while he of whom it is proclaimed that 'he shall come in the glory of God the Father with the holy angels' is called the Son of man.[1] And for this reason, throughout the whole of scripture, while the divine nature is spoken of in human terms the human nature is in its turn adorned with marks that belong to the divine prerogative. For to this more than to anything else can the passage of Scripture be applied, 'They shall both be in one flesh, and they are no longer two, but one flesh'.[2] For the Word of God is to be thought of as being more 'in one flesh' with his soul than a man is with his wife. Moreover what could more appropriately be 'one spirit'[3] with God than this soul, which joined itself so firmly in love to God as to be worthy of being called 'one spirit' with him?

GREEK

It was[4] on this account also that the man became Christ, for he obtained this lot by reason of his goodness, as the prophet bears witness when he says, 'Thou hast loved righteousness and hated iniquity; wherefore God hath anointed thee, thy God with the oil of gladness above thy fellows.'[5] It was appropriate that he who had never been separated from the Only-begotten should be called

LATIN

4. To prove that it was the perfection of his love and the sincerity of his true affection which gained for him this inseparable unity with God, so that the taking up of his soul was neither accidental nor the result of personal preference, but was a privilege conferred upon it as a reward for its virtues, listen to the prophet speaking to it thus; 'Thou hast loved righteousness and hated

---

[1] This is an example of the principle called the *Communicatio idiomatum,* by which qualities that are in strictness only applicable to the divine nature are sometimes predicated of the human, and *vice versa.* For the quotation see St. Matt. XVI. 27; St. Mark VIII. 38; St. Luke IX. 26.

[2] See St. Matt. XIX. 5, 6, from Gen. II. 24.

[3] See 1 Cor. VI. 17.

[4] Frag. 20 (Koetschau) from Justinian, *Ep. ad Mennam* (Mansi IX. 528). The translation 'God hath anointed thee' might almost be rendered 'God hath made thee Christ', or 'the Anointed one', which would bring out Origen's meaning more clearly. Rufinus has omitted the last sentence.

[5] Ps. XLV. 7.

GREEK   LATIN

by the name of the Only-be- | iniquity; wherefore God hath
gotten and glorified together | anointed thee, thy God with the
with him. | oil of gladness above thy
                                                              | fellows.'[1]

LATIN

As a reward for its love, therefore, it is anointed with the
'oil of gladness', that is the soul with the word of God is made
Christ; for to be anointed with the oil of gladness means nothing else but to be filled with the Holy Spirit. And when he
says, 'above thy fellows', he indicates that the grace of the
Spirit was not given to it as to the prophets, but that the
essential 'fulness' of the Word of God himself was within it,
as the apostle said, 'In him dwelleth all the fulness of the godhead
bodily'.[2] Finally, this is the reason why he not only said,
'Thou hast loved righteousness', but added, 'and hated iniquity'.
For to hate iniquity is the same thing which the scripture says
of him: 'He did no sin, neither was guile found in his mouth;'[3]
and again, 'He was tempted in all points like as we are, yet
without sin'.[4] Further, the Lord himself says, 'which of you
convicteth me of sin?'[5] And again he says of himself, 'Lo, the
prince of this world cometh and findeth nothing in me'.[6] All
of which shows that no consciousness of sin existed in him.
And the prophet, in order the more clearly to point out this
fact, that the consciousness of iniquity had never entered his
mind, says, 'Before the boy could know how to call for his
father or mother, he turned himself from iniquity'.[7]

5. But if the above argument, that there exists in Christ a
rational soul, should seem to anyone to constitute a difficulty,
on the ground that in the course of our discussion we have often
shown that souls are by their nature capable of good and evil,[8]
we shall resolve the difficulty in the following manner. It cannot be doubted that the nature of his soul was the same as that
of all souls; otherwise it could not be called a soul, if it were not
truly one. But since the ability to choose good or evil is within
the immediate reach of all, this soul which belongs to Christ so
chose to love righteousness as to cling to it unchangeably and
inseparably in accordance with the immensity of its love; the
result being that by firmness of purpose, immensity of affection
and an inextinguishable warmth of love all susceptibility to change
or alteration was destroyed, and what formerly depended upon
the will was by the influence of long custom changed into nature.
Thus we must believe that there did exist in Christ a human

---

[1] Ps. XLV. 7.   [2] Col. II. 9.   [3] 1 Peter II. 22.
[4] Heb. IV. 15.   [5] St. John VIII. 46.   [6] St. John XIV. 30.
[7] Is. VIII. 4; VII. 16.   [8] See above Bk. I. 8, 3 (p. 69).

and rational soul, and yet not suppose that it had any susceptibility to or possibility of sin.

6. To explain the matter more fully it will not appear absurd
if we use an illustration, although on so high and difficult a
subject there is but a small supply of suitable examples. However, if we may use this one without offence, the metal iron is
susceptible of both cold and heat. Suppose then a lump of iron
be placed for some time in a fire. It receives the fire in all its
pores and all its veins, and becomes completely changed into
fire, provided the fire is never removed from it and itself is not
separated from the fire. Are we then to say that this, which is
by nature a lump of iron, when placed in the fire and ceaselessly burning can ever admit cold? Certainly not; it is far
truer to say of it, what indeed we often detect happening in
furnaces, that it has been completely changed into fire, because
we can discern nothing else in it except fire. Further, if anyone
were to try to touch or handle it, he would feel the power of
the fire, not of the iron. In this manner, then, that soul which,
like a piece of iron in the fire, was for ever placed in the word,
for ever in the wisdom, for ever in God, is God in all its acts
and feelings and thoughts; and therefore it cannot be called
changeable or alterable, since by being ceaselessly kindled it
came to possess unchangeability through its unity with the word
of God. And while, indeed, some warmth of the Word of God
must be thought to have reached all the saints, in this soul we
must believe that the divine fire itself essentially rested,
and that it is from this that some warmth has come to all
others.

The very fact, too, that it says, 'God anointed thee, thy God
with the oil of gladness above thy fellows',[1] shows that that
soul is anointed with the 'oil of gladness', that is, with the
word of God and with wisdom, in one way, and his 'fellows',
that is, the holy prophets and apostles, in another. For the
latter are said 'to have run in the odour of his ointments',[2] but
that soul was the vase containing the ointment itself, of whose
glowing effluence all the prophets and apostles became worthy
partakers. As therefore the odour of the ointment is one thing
and the substance of the ointment another, so Christ is one thing
and his fellows another. And as the vessel which contains the
substance of the ointment can by no means admit any foul smell,
whereas it is possible for those who share in its odour, if they
move a little farther away from its glowing effluence, to admit
any foul smell that meets them, so it was impossible for Christ,
who is like the vase itself in which the substance of the ointment
lay, to admit an odour of an opposite kind, whereas his fellows

---

[1] Ps. XLV. 7.   [2] See Song of Songs I. 3 (Vulg.).

will be partakers and receivers of his odour in proportion to their nearness to the vase.

7. I think, too, that the prophet Jeremiah understood what is the nature of the wisdom of God in him, which was also the nature he had assumed for the salvation of the world, when he said: 'The breath of our countenance is Christ the Lord, of whom we said that we shall live under his shadow among the nations.'[1] For just as the shadow of our body is inseparable from the body and unswervingly undertakes and performs the movements and gestures of the body, so I think the prophet wished to allude to the action and movement of Christ's soul, which was inseparably attached to him and performed everything in accordance with his own movement and volition, and that it was this which he called the shadow' of Christ the Lord, under which shadow we were to 'live among the nations'. For the nations which imitate that soul through faith and so reach salvation, live in the mystery of this assumption. Moreover when David says, 'Be mindful of my reproach, O Lord, wherewith they have reproached me in the stead of thy Christ',[2] he appears to me to allude to the same thing. And what else does Paul mean when he says, 'Our life is hid with Christ in God'.[3] Also in another place he says, 'Do you seek a proof of him who speaks in me, that is, Christ?'[4] Yet again, he says that Christ is 'hid in God'.[5] Unless the meaning of this expression be something like that which, as we said above, was indicated by the prophet in the phrase 'the shadow of Christ', it probably exceeds the comprehension of the human mind.

We see moreover many other statements in the divine scriptures which bear upon the interpretation of the word 'shadow'; such as that in the gospel according to Luke, where Gabriel says to Mary, 'The Spirit of the Lord shall come upon thee and the power of the Highest shall overshadow thee'.[6] The apostle also, speaking in regard to the law, says that they who hold to the circumcision of the flesh 'serve a copy and shadow of the heavenly things'.[7] And in another place it says, 'Is not our life on the earth a shadow?'[8] If then both the law which is on the earth is a 'shadow', and we are to live among the nations in the 'shadow of Christ', we must consider whether the truth of all these shadows will not be learned in that revelation when, no longer 'through a mirror and in a riddle' but 'face to face',[9] all the saints shall be counted worthy to behold the glory of God and the causes and truth of things. And seeing that a pledge of this truth has already been received through the Holy Spirit[10] the apostle said, 'Even if we have formerly

---

[1] Lam. IV. 20.   [2] Ps. LXXXIX (Vulg. LXXXVIII) 51, 52.
[3] Col. III. 3.   [4] 2 Cor. XIII. 3.   [5] ? Eph. III. 9.
[6] St. Luke I. 35.   [7] Heb. VIII. 5.   [8] See Job VIII. 9.
[9] See 1 Cor. XIII. 12.   [10] See 2 Cor. V. 5.

known Christ after the flesh, yet henceforth we know him so no more'.[1]

In the meantime, these are the thoughts which occur to us at the moment in our discussion of such very difficult subjects as the incarnation and deity of Christ. If there be anyone who can discover something better and prove what he says by clearer statements out of the holy scriptures, let his opinion be accepted in preference to mine.

[1] 2 Cor V. 16.

CHAPTER VII

GREEK   LATIN

THAT IT WAS THE SAME SPIRIT | THE HOLY SPIRIT.
WHO WAS IN MOSES AND THE
REST OF THE PROPHETS AND IN
THE HOLY APOSTLES.[1]

LATIN

1. After the first discussions which, as the subject demanded, we entered into at the beginning concerning the Father, the Son and the Holy Spirit, it seemed that we ought to go back again and prove that the same God was creator and founder of the world and Father of our Lord Jesus Christ, that is, that there is one and the same God of the law, the prophets and the gospels. Then also in regard to Christ, who had previously been shown to be the word and wisdom of God, we had to demonstrate in the succeeding chapters how he became man. Our remaining task is to return as briefly as possible to the subject of the Holy Spirit.

It is time, therefore, for us to discuss to the best of our ability a few points about the Holy Spirit, whom our Lord and Saviour in the gospel according to John called the Paraclete.[2] Now just as it is the same God himself and the same Christ himself, so also it is the same Holy Spirit himself who was in the prophets and the apostles, that is, both in those who believed in God before the coming of Christ and in those who have taken refuge in God through Christ. We have heard of heretics who have dared to say that there are two Gods or two Christs, but we have never heard it maintained by anyone that there are two Holy Spirits.[3] For how could they affirm this from the scriptures, or what distinction could they make between one Holy Spirit and the other, even supposing it were possible to discover any definition or description of the Holy Spirit? For granting that Marcion or Valentinus can draw distinctions

---

[1] For the Greek title see Photius *Bibl. Cod.* 8.

[2] St. John XIV. 16 etc.

[3] In the Apostolic Canons (49) it is enacted that anyone who baptizes into 'three unoriginated beings, or three sons, or three paracletes' shall be deprived of his office. Origen, too, in another place mentions some who affirmed the existence of two Holy Spirits: see *In Ep. ad Titum Frag.* (Lomm. V. 287 f.) 'Moreover if there are any who say that it was one Holy Spirit who was in the prophets, but another who was in the apostles of our Lord Jesus Christ, they commit one and the same offence of impiety as those who, so far as in them lies, cut and rend the nature of the deity, by saying that there is one God of the law and another of the gospels.'

in regard to deity and describe the nature of the good as one thing and the nature of the just as another, what reasonings or devices will warrant their introducing distinctions into the Holy Spirit? I think they can find nothing that points to any distinction whatsoever.

2. Now we are of opinion that every rational creature receives without any difference a share in the Holy Spirit just as in the wisdom of God and the word of God.[1] I see, however, that the special coming of the Holy Spirit to men is declared to have happened after Christ's ascension into heaven rather than before his coming into the world. Before that time the gift of the Holy Spirit was bestowed on prophets only and on a few others among the people who happened to have proved worthy of it; but after the coming of the Saviour it is written that 'the saying was fulfilled which was spoken by the prophet Joel', namely, that 'it shall come to pass in the last days, that I will pour out my spirit upon all flesh and they shall prophesy';[2] which indeed is similar to that other saying, 'All nations shall serve him'.[3]

Through the grace of the Holy Spirit, then, along with many other results, this most splendid fact is revealed, that whereas the truths written in the prophets and the law of Moses were formerly understood by very few, namely by the prophets alone, and scarcely anywhere was there one out of the whole people who could get beyond the literal meaning and perceive something greater, that is, could detect a spiritual sense in the law and prophets, now there are innumerable multitudes of believers who, although unable to explain logically and clearly the process of their spiritual perception, have yet almost to a man the firm conviction that circumcision ought not to be understood literally, nor the Sabbath rest, nor the pouring out of an animal's blood, nor the fact that oracles were given by God to Moses on these points; and there is no doubt that this discernment is suggested to them all by the power of the Holy Spirit.[4]

---

[1] See above Bk. I. 3, 5 (p. 34), where the Spirit's operation is said to extend to the saints alone. The Spirit is given potentially to all, but his effective working is confined to the saints, of Old and New Testament times alike.

[2] Acts II. 16, 17 (Joel II. 28).   [3] Ps. LXXII. 11.

[4] The basis of this 'spiritual' interpretation of the Old Testament is given in *Con. Celsum* VII. 34. 'Walking' with God, having 'ears to hear', or having our 'eyes' opened, are clearly metaphorical expressions, which make nonsense when interpreted literally. Origen, however, with other writers of the school of Alexandria, uses this poetical phraseology to justify an arbitrary treatment of passages where a literal interpretation is demanded. A merely literal interpretation, even of a plain historical narrative, was despised on the ground that it indicated inferiority of spiritual capacity in the commentator. See Origen, *In Matt. Comm. ser.* 27 'for the spiritual and prophetic meaning of scripture is veiled beneath the outward narrative, so that all scripture may be understood literally by inferior readers, but in a mystical way by the spiritual and the perfect.'

3. But just as there are many ways of apprehending Christ, who although he is wisdom, does not exert or possess the power of wisdom in all men, but only in those who apply themselves to wisdom in him; nor, although he is called a physician, does he act as such towards all men, but only towards those who have realised their feeble and sick condition and fly to his compassion in the hope of obtaining health; so, too, I think, is it the case with the Holy Spirit, in whom is every manner of gift. For to some is granted by the Spirit the word of wisdom, to others the word of knowledge, to others faith; and thus to each individual man who is able to receive him the same Spirit becomes and is apprehended as the very thing of which he, who has been deemed worthy to partake of him, stands in need.[1]

These divisions and distinctions are unperceived by those who, hearing him called in the gospels the Paraclete,[2] but not considering from what work or activity he takes this name, have likened him to some common spirits or other and by so doing have tried to disturb the churches of Christ even to the point of arousing no small dissensions among the brethren. But the gospel shows him to be of such power and majesty that it says the apostles could not yet receive those truths which the Saviour wished to teach them until the time 'when the Holy Spirit should come',[3] who would pour himself into their souls and to enlighten them concerning the nature and faith of the Trinity. The men in question, however, owing to the poverty of their understanding, which renders them not only incapable of logically setting forth the truth themselves, but unable even to pay proper attention to what is said by us, have entertained low and unworthy views of his deity and so delivered themselves over to errors and deceits under the malign influence of some spirit of error rather than the wise precepts of the Holy Spirit, according to the saying of the apostle, 'Following the doctrine of daemon spirits, who forbid to marry', 'to the ruin and destruction of many', and 'urging to abstain from meats',[4] in order that by the outward show of stricter observances they may lead astray the souls of the innocent.

4. We must know, therefore, that the Paraclete is the Holy Spirit, who teaches truths greater than can be uttered by the voice, truths which are, if I may so say, 'unspeakable', and which 'it is not lawful for a man to speak',[5] that is, which cannot be indicated in human language. For the phrase 'not lawful' was spoken, we believe, by Paul as the equivalent of 'not possible', as in the place where he says, 'all things are lawful, but all things do not edify'.[6] Those things, that is, which are

[1] See 1 Cor. XII. 8, 9.   [2] St. John XIV. 16 etc.
[3] St. John XVI. 12-14.
[4] See 1 Tim. IV. 1, 3 and St. Luke II. 34 (Vulg.).
[5] 2 Cor. XII. 4.   [6] 1 Cor. X. 23.

within our power because we can have them, he speaks of as being 'lawful' for us.   But the Paraclete, who is called the Holy Spirit, is so called from his work of 'consolation' (*paraclesis* being termed in Latin *consolatio*); for anyone who has been deemed worthy to partake of the Holy Spirit, when he has learned his unspeakable mysteries, undoubtedly obtains consolation and gladness of heart.   Since by the Spirit's guidance he has come to know the reasons for all things that happen, and why and how they happen, his soul can never be in any way disquieted or admit any feeling of sadness;[1] nor is it in anything affrighted, for it clings to God's word and wisdom and 'in the Holy Spirit calls Jesus Lord'.[2]

We have made mention, then, of the Paraclete and to the best of our ability have explained how we ought to think about him.   But in the epistle of John our Saviour is also called a 'paraclete', when it says, 'If any man sin, we have a paraclete with the Father, Jesus Christ the righteous, and he is the propitiation for our sins'.[3]   Let us then consider whether perhaps this title 'paraclete' means one thing when applied to the Saviour and another when applied to the Holy Spirit.   Now in regard to the Saviour 'paraclete' seems to mean intercessor; for in Greek it bears both meanings, comforter and intercessor, but according to the phrase that follows, in which it says that 'he is the propitiation for our sins',[3] it seems that in the case of the Saviour the word 'paraclete' must be understood rather in the sense of intercessor, for he is said to intercede with the Father 'for our sins'.   When used of the Holy Spirit, however, the word 'paraclete' ought to be understood as 'comforter', because he provides comfort for the souls to whom he opens and reveals a consciousness of spiritual knowledge.[4]

---

[1] See St. John XIV. 26, 27.   [2] See 1 Cor. XII. 3.
[3] 1 St. John II. 1, 2.
[4] Origen appears to have overlooked Rom. VIII. 26, 27.

CHAPTER VIII

THE SOUL[1]

1. After this, the course of our inquiry demands that we should deal in a general way with the soul, beginning with souls of a lower and rising to those of a higher order. No one, I suppose, will doubt that all living creatures whatever, even those that live in water, have souls. This view is supported by the general opinion of men and confirmed in addition by the authority of holy scripture, when it says that 'God made great whales and every soul of the living creatures that swim, which the waters brought forth after their kind'.[2] It is confirmed also, from the common light of reason, by those who lay down a definition of the soul in precise terms. For soul is defined thus, as an existence possessing imagination and desire, which qualities can be expressed in Latin, though the rendering is not so apt as the original, by the phrase, capable of feeling and movement.[3] This may be said of all living creatures, including those that live in water, and the same definition of soul may be shown to apply to birds also. Scripture, too, adds the authority of another pronouncement when it says, 'Ye shall not eat the blood, for the soul of all flesh is its blood, and ye shall not eat the soul with the flesh';[4] in which it most plainly describes the blood of all living creatures as their 'soul'. And if, in regard to the saying that 'the soul of all flesh is its blood', anyone should now raise the question of bees, wasps and ants, as well as those creatures that live in water, oysters, cockles and the rest, which have no blood and yet are most clearly seen to be living creatures, we must reply that the same force which in others is due to the energy of the red blood is exerted in creatures of this kind by that fluid which exists in them, though it be of a different colour; for it matters not at all what colour it is, so long as the substance is endowed with life. As for beasts of burden and cattle, however, even common opinion has no hesitation in admitting that they possess souls. Nevertheless the teaching of scripture is clear, when God says, 'Let the earth bring forth the living soul after its kind, four-footed beasts and creeping things and beasts of

---

[1] The title in Greek is found in Photius, *Bibl. cod.* 8.

[2] Gen. I. 21.

[3] See Aristotle, *De anima* 3, 9, 1. 'The soul of living creatures is defined by its two powers, that of discernment, which is a function of thought and perception, and that of movement in space'. Philo, *Legis. alleg.* II. 7 (71) 'Soul is a nature that possesses imagination and desire.' See also Tertullian, *De anima* 14-16.

[4] See Levit. XVII. 14.

the earth after their kind'.[1] Then in regard to man, although
no one has any doubt nor could anyone raise a question about
it, yet the divine scripture declares that 'God breathed into his
face the breath of life, and man became a living soul.'[2]

It remains for us to inquire concerning the order of angels,
whether they too possess souls or are souls, and also concerning
the other divine and heavenly beings including the opposing
powers.   Nowhere do we find any authority of divine scripture
for saying that either angels or any other divine beings who are
God's 'ministering spirits'[3] possess souls or are called souls;
and yet they are believed by very many to be endowed with souls.
But in regard to God we find it written as follows: 'And I will
put my soul upon that soul that has eaten blood, and I will root
it out from among my people'.[4]   And again elsewhere: 'Your
new moons and sabbaths and great days I will not accept.   Your
fasts and holidays and feast days my soul hateth'.[5]   And in the
twenty-first psalm it speaks thus of Christ—for it is certain that
this psalm is composed in the person of Christ, as the gospel
bears witness[6]—'But thou, Lord, be not far from my help, look
to my defence; deliver my soul from the sword, my beloved one
from the hand of the dog.'[7]   There are, however, many other
testimonies to the soul that Christ had when he dwelt in the flesh.

2. But all question about the soul of Christ is removed when
we consider the nature of the incarnation.   For just as he truly
had flesh, so also he truly had a soul.   As for that, indeed, which
is called in the scriptures the 'soul of God',[8] it is difficult both to
think and to state how it ought to be understood; for at the
same time we declare that the nature of God is simple and has
no intermixture of any additional substance.   Still, however we
are to think of it, the fact remains that it is apparently called
'the soul of God'.   In regard to Christ, however, there is no
doubt.   And on that account I see no absurdity in holding or
expressing some similar view concerning the holy angels and
the other heavenly powers, if we grant that the above-mentioned
definition of the soul appears to apply to them.   For who can
rationally deny that they are capable of feeling and of movement?
If then the definition, that an existence which is rationally
capable of feeling and movement is called a soul, appears to be
correct, the same definition appears to apply to the angels also.
For what else is there in them but rational feeling and movement?
And things which have one definition have also undoubtedly the
same substance.   The apostle Paul indeed intimates that there
is a kind of soul-like man, whom he says 'cannot receive the

---

[1] Gen. I. 24.   [2] Gen. II. 7.   [3] Heb. I. 14.
[4] Levit. XVII. 10.   [5] Is. I. 13, 14.
[6] See St. Mark XV. 34 and parallels.
[7] Ps. XXII. (Eng. Vers.) 20, 21.
[8] Is. I. 14; XLII. 1, etc.

things of the Spirit of God',[1] but to whom the doctrine of the Spirit of God appears foolish, and he cannot understand it because it is 'spiritually discerned'. Also in another place he says: 'It is sown a soul-like body' and rises a 'spiritual body',[2] thus showing that at the resurrection of the just there will be nothing soul-like in those who have been counted worthy of the life of the blessed.

On this account we ask whether there is not some substance which, in so far as it is soul, is imperfect. But whether it is imperfect for this reason, that it falls away from perfection, or whether it was so made by God, we shall inquire when each separate point begins to be discussed in order. For if the soul-like man 'does not receive the things of the Spirit of God', and just because he is soul-like cannot receive the knowledge of a better nature, namely the divine, here is perhaps the reason why Paul, in his desire to teach us plainly what it is through which we can understand the things of the Spirit, that is, spiritual things, joins and associates the mind rather than the soul with the Holy Spirit. For this is what I suppose him to indicate when he says, 'I will pray with the spirit, I will pray with the mind also. I will sing a psalm with the spirit, I will sing a psalm with the mind also'.[3] He does not say, I will pray with the soul, but with the spirit and the mind; not, sing with the soul, but sing with the spirit and the mind.

3. But perhaps it will be asked: If it is the mind, which with the spirit prays and sings, and the mind also which receives perfection and salvation, how is it that Peter says, 'Receiving the end of our faith, the salvation of our souls'?[4] If the soul neither prays nor sings with the spirit, how shall it hope for salvation? Or, if it should attain to blessedness, will it no longer be called a soul? Let us see whether, perhaps, this point may be answered in the following manner, that

GREEK	LATIN
just as[5] the Saviour came to save that which was lost,[6] but when the lost is saved, it is no longer lost; so, if he came to save the soul, as he came to save that which was lost, the soul when saved remains a soul no longer. We must further	just as the Saviour came to save that which was lost,[6] and then when it is saved, that which was said to be lost is not lost; so also perhaps that which is being saved is called a soul, but when it has been saved it will be called by the name of its more

[1] See 1 Cor. II. 14. The word translated 'natural' is in Greek *psychikos*, from *psyche*, soul.
[2] 1 Cor. XV. 44.   [3] 1 Cor. XIV. 15.   [4] 1 St. Peter I. 9.
[5] Frag. 21, Koetschau, from Justinian, *Ep. ad Mennam* (Mansi IX. 532). Jerome, *Ep. ad Avitum* 6, also quotes the same passage, following the Greek more closely than Rufinus.
[6] See St. Luke XIX. 10.

GREEK

inquire whether, as there was a time when that which has been lost was not lost, and there will be a time when it will not be lost, so also there was a time when the soul was not a soul and there will be a time when it will not be a soul.

LATIN

perfect part. Some, too, will think that this point can be added, that just as that which was lost, undoubtedly existed before it was lost, when it was something, I know not what, other than lost, and just as there will also certainly be a time when it will not be lost; so the soul, which is said to have become lost, will apparently have been something at a time when it was not yet lost and may have been called a soul from the fact of its becoming lost, but when delivered from its lost condition it can once again be that which it was before it became lost and was called a soul.

LATIN

Further, certain careful investigators have concluded that an interpretation of no slight importance is suggested by the very meaning of the word soul as indicated in its Greek form. For a divine saying speaks of God as a fire, saying, 'Our God is a consuming fire'.[1] Moreover, Scripture also speaks as follows concerning the nature of the angels: 'Who maketh his angels spirits and his ministers a burning fire';[2] and elsewhere, 'The angel of the Lord appeared in a flame of fire in a bush'.[3] In addition we have received a command to be 'fervent in spirit',[4] by which expression undoubtedly the word of God is proved to be hot and fiery. Further, the prophet Jeremiah hears from him who gave him the oracles, 'Behold, I have put my words in thy mouth as fire'.[5]

As therefore God is 'fire' and the angels 'a flame of fire' and the saints are all 'fervent in spirit', so on the contrary those who have fallen away from the love of God must undoubtedly be said to have cooled in their affection for him and to have become cold. For the Lord also says, 'Because iniquity has multiplied, the love of the many shall grow cold'.[6] And further, all those things, whatever they may be, which in the holy scripture are likened to the adverse power, you invariably find to be cold. For the devil is called a 'serpent' and a 'dragon',[7] and what can be found

---

[1] Heb. XII. 29 (Deut. IV. 24; IX. 3).
[2] Heb. I. 7 (Ps. CIV. 4).   [3] Exod. III. 2.   [4] Rom. XII. 11.
[5] Jerem. V. 14.   [6] St. Matt. XXIV. 12.
[7] See Rev. XII. 9; XX. 2.

colder than these? Again, a dragon, an allusion, certainly, to one of the wicked spirits, is said to reign in the waters, while a prophet declares him to live in the sea.[1]   And elsewhere a prophet says, 'I will draw my holy sword upon the dragon, the flying serpent, upon the dragon, the crooked serpent, and it shall slay him';[2] and again it says, 'Even though they hide from mine eyes and descend into the depth of the sea, there will I command the dragon and he shall bite them'.[3]   In Job also he is said to be the 'king of all things which are in the waters'.[4]   A prophet declares that 'evils shall be kindled from the north upon all who dwell on the earth'.[5]   Now the north wind is described in the scriptures as cold, as it is written in Wisdom, 'the cold north wind'.[6]   This then must undoubtedly be understood of the devil. If therefore the things which are holy are termed fire and light and fervent things while their opposites are termed cold, and the love of sinners is said to grow cold, we must ask whether perhaps even the word soul, which in Greek is *psyche,* was not formed from *psychesthai,* with the idea of growing cold after having been in a diviner and better state, and whether it was not derived from thence because the soul seems to have grown cold by the loss of its first natural and divine warmth and on that account to have been placed in its present state with its present designation.[7]

GREEK

For[8] when the prophet says, 'Before I was humbled, I went wrong',[9] the saying is uttered in the person of the soul itself, to the effect that formerly in heaven it 'went wrong', before it was 'humbled' in the body.   And when it says, 'Turn unto thy rest, O my soul',[10] it means that he who has played a manly part here in good deeds turns to the former 'rest' by reason of the righteousness of his conduct.

---

[1] See Ezek. XXIX. 3; XXXII. 2.   [2] Is. XXVII. 1.   [3] Amos IX. 3.
[4] See Job XLI. 25 (26) Sept.   [5] See Jerem. I. 14.
[6] Ecclus. XLIII. 20. Origen calls Ben Sira's book by the name of Wisdom in *Comm. in Ioh.* Frag. 74 and 136 (Koetschau).
[7] Aristotle (*De anima* I. 2, 405b) mentions this etymological explanation of the word: 'others say that the soul is the cold element, so called from breathing and cooling (*katapsyxis*).' See also Plato, *Cratylus* 399 D-E and Tertullian, *De anima* 25 and 27.
[8] Fragment 22, Koetschau, from Epiphanius, *Haer.* 64, 4. Cp. Jerome, *Con. Ioh. Hieros. c.* 7: 'The second point' (i.e. taken from the *De Principiis*) 'is that souls are bound in this body as in a prison, and that before the man was formed in paradise, these souls dwelt among the rational creatures in the heavens.' Wherefore afterwards, in order to console itself, the soul says in the Psalms, 'Before I was humbled, I went wrong; and, Turn unto thy rest, O my soul; and, Bring my soul out of prison; and other similar utterances.' Rufinus has omitted most of this passage.
[9] Ps. CXIX. 67.   [10] Ps. CXVI. 7.

LATIN

Finally, see whether you can easily find in the holy scriptures a place where the soul is described in real terms of praise. Expressions of blame, on the contrary, occur frequently, as here: 'An evil soul destroys him that possesses it',[1] and, 'The soul that sinneth it shall die'.[2] For after it has been said, 'All souls are mine; as the soul of the father, so the soul of the son is mine',[3] it certainly seems to follow that he would say, 'The soul that doeth righteousness, it shall be saved, and the soul that sinneth, it shall die'. Yet in this instance we see that he has associated with the soul the fact of blame, but as to anything worthy of praise he is silent. We must see,[4] therefore, whether perchance, as we said was made clear by its very name, the *psyche* or soul was so called from its having cooled from the fervour of the righteous[5] and from its participation in the divine fire, and yet has not lost the power of restoring itself to that condition of fervour in which it was at the beginning. Some such fact the prophet appears to point to when he says, 'Turn unto thy rest, O my soul'.[6] All these considerations seem to show that when the mind departed from its original condition and dignity it became or was termed a soul, and if ever it is restored and corrected it returns to the condition of being a mind.

GREEK

(ii) [*If anyone shall say that*][7] the creation of all rational creatures consisted of minds bodiless and immaterial without any number or name, so that they all formed a unity by reason of the identity of their essence and power and energy and by their union with and knowledge of God the Word; but that they were seized with weariness of the divine love and contemplation, and changed for the worse, each in proportion to his inclination in this direction; and that they took bodies, either fine in substance or grosser, and became possessed of a name, which accounts for the differences of names as well as of bodies among the higher powers; and that thus the cherubim, with the rulers and authorities, the lordships, thrones and angels and all the other

---

[1] Ecclus. VI. 4.   [2] Ezek. XVIII. 4.   [3] Ezek. XVIII. 4.

[4] Koetschau points out that the passage beginning here and ending with the words 'it returns to the condition of being a mind' (below) are a brief summary of what is contained in the following Greek Fragments and the citation from Jerome *Ep. ad Avitum*: see pp. 125-127.

[5] See p. 124 above.   [6] Ps. CXVI. 7; and cp. p. 124 above.

[7] This and the following paragraphs are the Anathemas (ii. to via) against Origen, decreed by the Second Council of Constantinople in 553. Though they cannot be taken as literal extracts from the *De Principiis*, they express the teaching of this work, doubtless for the most part in Origen's own words. Cp. the Anathemas at the end of Justinian, *Ep. ad Mennam* (Mansi IX. 533). Koetschau marks these extracts as Frag. 23a.   See Mansi IX. 396-397.

heavenly orders came into being and received their names, [*let him be anathema*]   *   *   *   *   *   *

(iii) [*If anyone shall say that*] the sun, the moon and the stars themselves belonged to the same unity of rational beings, and have become what they now are through a declension towards the worse, [*let him be anathema*] *   *   *   *   *   *

(iv) [*If anyone shall say that*] the rational beings who grew cool in respect of the divine love and were in consequence called souls were for a punishment clothed with the grosser bodies possessed by us and were given the name of men, while those who proceeded to the extremity of evil-doing were clothed with cold and murky bodies and became what are called daemons or 'spiritual hosts of wickedness'[1] [*let him be anathema*]   *   * The soul[2] received its body as a result of former sins, by way of punishment or vengeance   *   *   *   *   *

(v) [*If anyone shall say that*] the soul-like condition comes from the angelic and archangelic condition, and the daemonic and human from the soul-like; and that conversely from the human come angels and daemons, and that each order of the heavenly powers is made up either wholly from those below or from those above, or else both from those above and those below   [*let him be anathema*]   *   *   *   *   *   *

(via) [*If anyone shall say that*] the race of daemons appears two-fold, being composed of human souls and of higher spirits that have fallen to this condition, and that out of all the original unity of rational beings one mind remained steadfast in the divine love and contemplation, and that he, having become Christ and king of all rational beings, created all bodily nature, both heaven and earth and the things that are between them * * [*let him be anathema*]   *   *   *   *   *   *

Those rational[3] beings who sinned and on that account fell from the state in which they were, in proportion to their particular sins were enveloped in bodies as a punishment; and when they are purified they rise again to the state in which they formerly were, completely putting away their evil and their bodies.   Then again a second or a third or many more times they are enveloped in different bodies for punishment.   For it is probable that different worlds have existed and will exist, some in the past and some in the future   *   *   Along with[4] the falling away and the cooling from life in the spirit came what is now called soul, which is capable nevertheless of an ascent to the state in which it was at the beginning.   This I think is spoken of by the

---

[1] Eph. VI. 12.
[2] This sentence is inserted here by Koetschau from Justinian, *Ep. ad Mennam* (Mansi IX. 512 E).
[3] Justinian, *Ep. ad Mennam* (Mansi 489-492).
[4] Justinian, *Ep. ad Mennam* (Mansi IX. 529), Frag 23 b, Koetschau.

prophet in the passage, 'Turn unto thy rest, O my soul';[1] so that this becomes wholly mind.

LATIN

Mind[2] when it fell was made soul, and soul in its turn when furnished with virtues will become mind. This we can find by considering the soul of Esau,[3] who was condemned in a later life for ancient sins. And in regard to the heavenly bodies we must conclude that the sun's soul, or whatever it ought to be called, did not begin to exist at the time the world was made, but at a time before it entered that shining and burning body. Let us think in a similar way of the moon and the stars, that although they have unwillingly been compelled to be 'subject to vanity'[4] as a result of causes long past, yet it is in the hope of future reward that they do not their own will, but the will of the Creator, by whom they have been appointed to these duties.

4. Now[5] if this is so, it seems to me that the departure and downward course of the mind must not be thought of as equal in all cases, but as a greater or less degree of change into soul, and that some minds retain a portion of their original vigour, while others retain none or only a very little. This is the reason why some are found right from their earliest years to be of ardent keenness, while others are duller, and some are born extremely dense and altogether unteachable. This statement of ours, however, that mind is changed into soul, or anything else that seems to point in that direction, the reader must carefully consider and work out for himself; for we must not be supposed to put these forward as settled doctrines, but as subjects for inquiry and discussion.

The reader must also take this point into consideration, that of the passages in the gospels which concern the soul of the Saviour, it is noticeable that some refer to it under the name of soul and others under the name of spirit. When scripture wishes to indicate any suffering or trouble that affected him, it does so under the name soul, as when it says: 'Now is my soul troubled',[6] and 'My soul is sorrowful even unto death',[7] and 'No one taketh my soul from me, but I lay it down of myself'.[8] On the other hand he commends 'into his Father's hands' not his soul but his spirit;[9] and when he says the 'flesh is weak' he does not say the 'soul' is 'willing' but the 'spirit';[10] from which it appears as

---

[1] Ps. CXVI. 7. See p. 124 f. above.
[2] Latin quotation taken from Jerome, *Ep. ad Avitum* 6. It is preceded by the words: 'And after much discussion he (i.e. Origen) deals with the question of the soul and speaks as follows. . .'
[3] See Malachi I. 2, 3.   [4] Rom. VIII. 20.
[5] At this point we return to Rufinus.   [6] St. John XII. 27.
[7] St. Matt. XXVI. 38 and parallels.   [8] St. John X. 18.
[9] See St. Luke XXIII. 46.
[10] St. Matt. XXVI. 41 and parallels.

if the soul were a kind of medium between the weak flesh and
the willing spirit.

5. But perhaps someone may meet us with those objections
of which we ourselves have given warning in our own arguments,
and may say, 'How then is mention made even of God's soul?'[1]
To him we shall reply as follows.   Just as in all bodily expressions
that are applied to God, such as his fingers or hands or arms
or eyes or mouth or feet, we do not mean these parts of the
human body, but we indicate by such bodily terms certain of
God's powers,[2] so also we must suppose that there is some other
object which is indicated by this term, the soul of God.   And if
it is lawful for us to dare to say anything further on such a
subject, the 'soul of God' may perhaps be understood to mean
his only-begotten Son.   For as the soul, implanted throughout
the whole body, is the source of all movement and directs every
operation of the body, so also the only-begotten Son of God,
who is his word and wisdom, is in close touch and association
with every power of God, being implanted in him.   And perhaps
it is as an indication of this mystery that God is spoken of or
described in the scriptures as a body.[3]

We must consider, indeed, whether perhaps there may not
be this additional reason for understanding God's soul to mean
his only-begotten Son, namely, that it was he who came 'to this
place of affliction' and 'descended into the vale of tears' and into
the place of our humiliation, as it says in the Psalm: 'Because
thou hast humiliated us in the place of affliction'.[4]   Finally, I
know some who, in expounding the passage which is spoken by
the Saviour in the gospel, 'My soul is sorrowful even unto death',[5]
have interpreted it of the apostles, whom he might have termed
his soul because they were better than the rest of his body.   For
they say that 'the multitude of believers is called his body',[6]
and that the apostles, because they are better than the remaining
multitude, ought to be regarded as his soul.

These points about the rational soul we have brought forward
to the best of our ability rather as matters for discussion by our
readers than as definite and settled doctrines.   As for the souls
of cattle and other dumb creatures, let those remarks suffice
which we have made above in general terms.[7]

---

    [1] See p. 121 above.
    [2] See Origen Comm. in Ioh. XIII. 22 'When we find eyes, eyelids and
ears, hands, arms and feet ascribed to God, yes and even wings, we alle-
gorise these terms, despising those who invest God with a form like that
of man.'
    [3] In his De Oratione XXIII. 3 Origen shows that he is alluding to
such passages as Gen. III. 8 and Ps. XI. 4.
    [4] See Ps. XLIII. 20 (Sept.) and LXXXIV. 6.
    [5] St. Matt. XXVI. 38 and parallels.
    [6] See 1 Cor. XII. 27; Eph. IV. 12; V. 30.
    [7] See above Book II. Ch. VIII. 1. (p. 120).

CHAPTER IX

THE WORLD, AND THE MOVEMENTS OF RATIONAL CREATURES BOTH GOOD AND EVIL, AND THE CAUSES OF THESE MOVEMENTS

1. Now, however, let us return to the order which we fixed upon for our discussion and contemplate the beginning of creation, so far as it is possible for the mind to contemplate the beginning of God's creative work.

GREEK

In the beginning,[1] as we contemplate it, God created by an act of his will as large a number of intelligent beings * * * as he could control. For we must maintain that even the power of God is finite, and we must not, under pretext of praising him, lose sight of his limitations. For if the divine power were infinite, of necessity it could not even understand itself, since the infinite is by its nature incomprehensible. He made therefore just as many as he could grasp and keep in hand and subject to his providence. In the same way he prepared just as much matter as he could reduce to order * * *

LATIN

We must suppose, therefore, that in the beginning God made as large a number of rational and intelligent beings, or whatever the before-mentioned minds ought to be called, as he foresaw would be sufficient. It is certain that he made them according to some definite number fore-ordained by himself; for we must not suppose, as some would, that there is no end of created beings, since where there is no end there can neither be any comprehension nor limitation. If there had been no end, then certainly created beings could neither have been controlled nor provided for by God. For by its nature whatever is infinite will also be beyond comprehension * * * *

LATIN

Moreover when the scripture says that God created all things 'by number and measure',[2] we shall be right in applying the

[1] Frag. 24 Koetschau, from Justinian *Ep. ad Mennam* (Mansi IX. 489 and 525). Rufinus has toned down Origen's daring assertion that God's power has limits. Cp. Theophilus Alex. *Ep pasch.* II. 17 (in Jerome *Ep.* CXVIII) 'Origen says: God made as many beings as he could grasp and hold in subjection to himself and control by his providence'. Also Rufinus Palaest. *De fide* 17 'Origen. . . who spoke thus: God did not make all the beings whom he wished to make, but only those whom he could hold together and grasp.'

[2] Wis. XI. 20.

term 'number' to rational creatures or minds for this very reason, that they are so many as can be provided for and ruled and controlled by the providence of God; whereas 'measure' will correspondingly apply to bodily matter, which we must believe to have been created by God in such quantity as he knew would be sufficient for the ordering of the world. These then are the objects which we must believe were created by God in the beginning, that is, before everything else. And it is this truth which we may suppose to be indicated also in that beginning which Moses somewhat obscurely introduces when he says, 'In the beginning God made the heaven and the earth'.[1] For it is certain that these words refer not to the 'firmament' nor to the 'dry land', but to that heaven and earth from which the names of the ones we see were afterwards borrowed.[2]

2. But since these rational beings, which as we said above[3] were made in the beginning, were made when before they did not exist, by this very fact that they did not exist and then began to exist they are of necessity subject to change and alteration. For whatever may have been the goodness that existed in their being, it existed in them not by nature but as a result of their Creator's beneficence. What they are, therefore, is something neither their own nor eternal, but given by God. For it did not always exist, and everything that is given can also be withdrawn and taken away. But the cause of the withdrawal will lie in this, that the movements of their minds are not rightly and worthily directed. For the Creator granted to the minds created by him the power of free and voluntary movement, in order that the good that was in them might become their own, since it was preserved by their own free will; but sloth and weariness of taking trouble to preserve the good, coupled with disregard and neglect of better things, began the process of withdrawal from the good. Now to withdraw from the good is nothing else than to be immersed in evil; for it is certain that to be evil means to be lacking in good. Hence it is that in whatever degree one declines from the good, one descends into an equal degree of wickedness. And so each mind, neglecting the good either more or less in proportion to its own movements, was drawn to the opposite of good, which undoubtedly is evil. From this source, it appears, the Creator of all things obtained certain seeds and causes of variety and diversity, in order that, according to the diversity of minds, that is, of rational beings (which diversity they must be supposed to have produced from the causes we have stated above) he might create a world that was various

---

[1] Gen. I. 1.
[2] See Gen. I. 6-10 and above Bk. II. Ch. III. 6 (p. 91 f.); also *Con. Celsum* VI. 59.
[3] See above Bk. I., Ch. VIII. 3 f. (p. 69).

and diverse.   What we mean by various and diverse it is now our wish to explain.[1]

3. By the world we now mean all that is above the heavens, or in them, or on the earth, or in what are called the lower regions, or any places that exist anywhere; together with the beings who are said to dwell in them.   All this is called the world.   In this world some creatures are said to be 'supercelestial',[2] that is, placed in the more blessed abodes and clothed with the brighter and more heavenly bodies; and among these many differences are revealed, as for instance when the apostle said, 'There is one glory of the sun, another glory of the moon, and another glory of the stars, for one star differeth from another star in glory.'[3]

Some creatures, however, are called 'earthly',[4] and among these, too, that is, among men, there are no small differences, for some are barbarians, others Greeks, and of the barbarians some are wilder and fiercer, whereas others are more gentle. Some moreover employ laws of the highest excellence, others poorer and ruder ones, while others follow inhuman and savage customs rather than laws.   Some men are from the very moment of their birth in a humble position, brought up in subjection and slavery, placed under lords and princes and tyrants; whereas others are brought up with more freedom and under more rational influences.   Some have healthy bodies, others from their earliest years are invalids; some are defective in sight, others in hearing and speech; some are born in such a condition, others lose the use of one faculty or another soon after birth or else suffer a like misfortune when fully grown.   But what purpose is there in my unfolding and enumerating the tragic tale of human miseries, from which some are free while others are involved in them, when every man can weigh and ponder over all these matters for himself?[5]   There are also certain invisible powers, to which the management of things upon earth is entrusted; and we must believe that among these, too, no small differences exist, just as is found to be the case among men. The apostle Paul indeed intimates that there are also certain

---

[1] With this paragraph cp. Origen, *In Ioh*. II. 13. 'The evil or the wicked is opposite to the good, and not-being is opposite to being; from which it follows that the wicked and the evil are not-being.'   Also *Con. Celsum* IV. 70. 'For admitted that God, while preserving each individual's free-will, makes use of the evil of wicked men in the administration of the world, so disposing them as to conduce to the benefit of the whole, nevertheless such men are deserving of blame. . . ' See also Origen *In Num. hom*. XIV. 2 (Lomm. X. 162). Theophilus of Alexandria, *Ep. pasch.* II. 10 (in Jerome, *Ep*. 98) says that Origen affirmed that 'it was through the negligence and movement and descent of the higher rational creatures that God was led to create this world of diversity.'

[2] See *Con. Celsum* III. 42, 80: V. 4: VI. 59.

[3] 1 Cor. XV. 41.   [4] 1 Cor. XV. 40.

[5] See above p. 102 and n. 1.

'infernal' powers[1] and among these in like manner a condition
of variety must undoubtedly be looked for. As for dumb
animals and birds and creatures that live in water, it seems
superfluous to inquire about them, since it is certain that they
should be regarded as of contingent and not primary importance.

4. Now we are told that all things which were made, were
made through Christ and in Christ, as the apostle Paul most
clearly intimates when he says, 'For in him and through him
were all things created, whether things in heaven or things on
earth, visible and invisible, whether thrones or dominions or
principalities or powers; all were created through him and in
him'.[2] Moreover John in the gospel reveals precisely the same
when he says, 'In the beginning was the Word, and the Word
was with God, and the Word was God; the same was in the
beginning with God. All things were made through him, and
without him was nothing made'.[3] Further, in the Psalms it is
written, 'Thou hast made all things in wisdom'.[4]

Seeing then that Christ, as he is the Word and wisdom, is
also 'righteousness',[5] it will follow undoubtedly that those things
which were made in the Word and in wisdom may be said also
to have been made in that 'righteousness' which Christ is; whence
it will be apparent that in the things which were made there
was nothing unrighteous, nothing accidental, but all will be shown
to be such as the principle of equity and righteousness demands.
How then this great variety and diversity of things can be
understood to be most righteous and equitable it is, I am sure,
impossible for human thought or speech to explain, unless as
prostrate suppliants we beseech the Word himself, the 'wisdom
and righteousness',[6] who is the only-begotten Son of God, that
he, pouring himself by his grace into our minds, may deign to
enlighten what is dark, to open what is shut, to reveal what is
secret; which he will do if only we are found seeking, or asking,
or knocking so worthily as to deserve to receive when we seek,
to find when we ask and to have the door opened in response to
our knock.[7] Relying, therefore, not on our own intelligence,
but on the help of that wisdom which made all things, and
that righteousness which we believe to be implanted in all created
beings, even though we are for the moment unable to declare
the answer, we shall nevertheless, trusting in his mercy, endeavour
to search out and discover how the great variety and diversity
of the world is consistent with the whole principle of righteousness. I say principle, of course, in a general sense; for only
an ignorant man would demand a special justification for every
single case and only a fool would offer to give it.

[1] The inhabitants, presumably, of the 'lower parts of the earth.' Eph.
IV. 9.
[2] Col. I. 16. [3] St. John I. 1. [4] Ps. CIV. 24. [5] See 1 Cor. I. 30.
[6] See 1 Cor. I. 30. [7] See St. Matt. VII. 7, 8; St. Luke XI. 9, 10.

5. But when we say that the world is arranged in this variety, in which as we have explained above it was made by God,[1] the God whom we call good and righteous and absolutely fair, the following objection is wont to be raised by many, and particularly by those who come from the schools of Marcion, Valentinus and Basilides and who assert that souls are in their natures diverse. They ask how it is consistent with the righteousness of God who made the world that on some he should bestow a habitation in the heavens, and not only give them a better habitation, but also confer on them a higher and more conspicuous rank, favouring some with a 'principality', others with 'powers', to others again allotting 'dominions',[2] to others presenting the most magnificent seats in the heavenly courts, while others shine with golden light and gleam with starry brilliance, there being 'one glory of the sun, another glory of the moon, and another glory of the stars, for one star differeth from another star in glory'.[3] To sum it up briefly, they ask what reason there could be, supposing that God the Creator lacks neither the will to desire what is good and perfect nor the power to produce it, that when creating rational natures, that is, beings of whose existence he himself is the cause, he should make some of higher rank and other of second and third and many still lower and less worthy degrees?

Finally, they raise an objection on the score of the differences that exist among men on the earth. Some, they say, inherit at birth a happier lot, as for example the one who springs from Abraham and is born by promise,[4] and the other, the child of Isaac and Rebecca who, while yet lying in the womb, supplants his brother and is said, before he is born, to be loved by God;[5] and, speaking generally, one man is born among the Hebrews, with whom he finds instruction in the divine law, another among the Greeks who are themselves men of wisdom and no small learning, another among the Ethiopians, whose custom is to feed on human flesh, others among the Scythians, where parricide is practised as if sanctioned by law, or among the Taurians, where strangers are offered in sacrifice.[6] If then, they ask us, this great diversity and these various and different conditions of birth, in which certainly the power of free-will has no place—for a man does not choose for himself either where or in what nation or what state of life he shall be born,—if, they say, all this is not caused by a diversity in the natures of souls, that is, a soul with an evil nature is destined for an evil nation and a good one for a good nation, what alternative is there but

---

[1] See above, Bk. I. Ch. V. 3 and VIII. 2, pp. 45 f. and 68 f.
[2] See Col. I. 16.   [3] See 1 Cor. XV. 41.
[4] See Gen. XVII. 16; Gal. IV. 23.
[5] See Gen. XXV. 21-26; Rom. IX. 10-13.
[6] Cp. Origen *Con. Celsum* V. 27, 34.

to suppose that it is the result of accident or chance? Now if this were admitted, we should no longer believe the world to have been made by God nor to be ruled by his providence, and consequently it would seem that no judgment of God on every man's deeds is to be looked for. But in this matter what is clearly the truth of things is for him alone to know who 'searches all things, even the deep things of God'.[1]

6. We, however, speaking simply as men, will, in order not to nourish the insolence of the heretics by being silent, to the best of our ability reply to their objections with such arguments as may occur to us, as follows. We have frequently shown in the preceding chapters, by declarations which we were able to quote from the divine scriptures, that God the Creator of the universe is both good and just and omnipotent.[2] Now when 'in the beginning'[3] he created what he wished to create, that is rational beings, he had no other reason for creating them except himself, that is, his goodness. As therefore he himself, in whom was neither variation nor change nor lack of power, was the cause of all that was to be created, he created all his creatures equal and alike, for the simple reason that there was in him no cause that could give rise to variety and diversity. But since these rational creatures, as we have frequently shown and will show yet again in its proper place,[4] were endowed with the power of free will, it was this freedom which induced each one by his own voluntary choice either to make progress through the imitation of God or to deteriorate through negligence. This, as we have said before,[5] was the cause of the diversity among rational creatures, a cause that takes its origin not from the will or judgment of the Creator, but from the decision of the creature's own freedom. God, however, who then felt it just to arrange his creation according to merit, gathered the diversities of minds into the harmony of a single world, so as to furnish, as it were, out of these diverse vessels or souls or minds, one house, in which there must be 'not only vessels of gold and silver, but also of wood and of earth, and some unto honour and some unto dishonour.'[6]

These were the reasons, as I think, which gave rise to the diversity of this world, wherein divine providence arranges all creatures individually in positions corresponding to the variation in their movements and the fixed purpose of their minds. For this reason the Creator will not appear to have been unjust when, according to the above principles, he placed everyone in a position proportionate to his merit; nor will the happiness

---

[1] I Cor. II. 10.
[2] See above Bk. II. Chs. IV. and V. (pp. 95 ff.).   [3] Gen. I. 1.
[4] See above Bk. I. Ch. V. 3, VI. 3, VIII. 3 (pp. 45 f., 56 f., and 69 f.) and Bk. III. (pp. 157 ff.).
[5] See p. 130 above.   [6] 2 Tim. II. 20.

or unhappiness of anyone's birth, or any condition whatever that may fall to his lot, be supposed to be due to chance; nor will it be believed that there are different creators or souls that are diverse by nature.

7. But even holy scripture does not seem to me to be altogether silent on the nature of this secret, as when the apostle Paul, arguing on the subject of Esau and Jacob, says: 'For when they were not yet born and had done nothing either good or evil, that the purpose of God which was formed according to election might stand, not from works but from him who called them, it was said that the elder should serve the younger, as it is written, Jacob I loved, but Esau I hated'.[1] And after this he addresses himself and says: 'What shall we say then? Is there unrighteousness with God?' And in order to give us an occasion of inquiring into these matters and discovering how they are not outside all reason, he replies to himself and says, 'God forbid'.[2] For, as it appears to me, the same question which faces us in connexion with Esau and Jacob may also be raised in regard to all the heavenly beings and all creatures on earth and in the lower regions; and, it seems to me, just as it says there, 'When they were not yet born and had done nothing either good or evil', so, too, can it be said about all the rest. For 'when they were not yet' created 'and had done nothing either good or evil, that the purpose of God according to election might stand',[3] then, as certain men think, some were made heavenly, others of the earth and others of the lower regions, 'not from works', as the aforesaid men think, 'but from him who called them'.[4] 'What then shall we say', if this is so? 'Is there then unrighteousness with God? God forbid'.[5]

As, therefore, when the scriptures are examined with much diligence in regard to Esau and Jacob, it is found that there is 'no unrighteousness with God' in its being said of them, before they were born or had done anything, in this life of course, that 'the elder should serve the younger', and as it is found that there is no unrighteousness in the fact that Jacob supplanted his brother even in the womb, provided we believe that by reason of his merits in some previous life Jacob had deserved to be loved by God to such an extent as to be worthy of being preferred to his brother, so also it is in regard to the heavenly creatures, provided we note that their diversity is not the original condition of their creation, but that for antecedent causes a different position of service is prepared by the Creator for each one in proportion to the degree of his merit, which depends on the fact that each, in being created by God as a mind or rational spirit, has personally gained for, himself, in accordance with the movements of his mind and the disposition of his heart, a greater or

---

[1] Rom. IX. 11-13.   [2] Rom. IX. 14.
[3] Rom. IX. 11-13.   [4] Rom. IX. 11.   [5] Rom. IX. 14.

less share of merit, and has rendered himself either lovable or
it may be hateful to God. We must also note, however, that
some beings who are of higher merit are ordained to suffer with
the rest and to perform a duty to those below them, in
order that by this means they themselves may become sharers
in the endurance of the Creator, according to the Apostle's own
words, 'The creature was made subject to vanity, not willingly,
but by reason of him who subjected it, in hope.'[1]

Bearing in mind, then, this sentiment, 'Is there unrighteousness with God? God forbid',[2] which the apostle uttered when
expounding the birth of Esau and Jacob, I think it right that
the same sentiment should be employed in considering the case
of all creatures, since, as we said above, the righteousness of
the Creator ought to be apparent in all. And this, it appears
to me, will only be shown with real clearness, if each being,
whether of heaven or earth or below the earth, may be said to
possess within himself the causes of diversity antecedent to his
birth in the body. For all things were created by the Word of
God and by his wisdom, and were set in order through the
operation of his righteousness; and in his gracious compassion
he provides for all and exhorts all to be cured by whatever
remedies they may, and incites them to salvation.

8. As, then, without any doubt it will happen in the day of
judgment that the good will be separated from the evil and the
righteous from the unrighteous and every individual soul will by
the judgment of God be allotted to that place of which his
merits have rendered him worthy, a point which, if God will,
we shall prove in the pages that follow,[3] so also in the past
some such process, I think, has taken place. For we must
believe that God rules and arranges the universe by judgment
at all times. And the teaching of the apostle, when he says
that 'in a great house there are not only vessels of gold and
silver, but also of wood and of earth, and some unto honour,
and some unto dishonour', with the additional words, 'if a man
purge himself, he shall be a vessel unto honour, sanctified and
meet for the master's use, prepared unto every good work',[4]
undoubtedly proves this point, that whoever purges himself when
placed in this life, will be prepared for every good work in the
future, whereas he who does not purge himself will be, in accordance with the extent of his impurity, a 'vessel unto dishonour',
that is, an unworthy one.

In this way it is possible for us to understand that even
before the present life there were rational vessels, either wholly

---

[1] Rom. VIII. 20. This sentence, though contrary to Origen's system
considered in a strictly logical way, shows that he was not unmindful of
the nobility and necessity of sacrifice.

[2] Rom. IX. 14.　　　　　　　　　　[3] See the next chapter.

[4] 2 Tim. II. 20, 21.

purged or less so, that is, vessels which had purged themselves or had not, and that from this circumstance each vessel received, according to the measure of its purity or impurity, its place or region or condition in which to be born or to fulfil some duty in this world. All these, down to the very least, God supervises by the power of his wisdom and distinguishes by the controlling hand of his judgment; and thus he has arranged the universe on the principle of a most impartial retribution, according as each one deserves for his merit to be assisted or cared for. Herein is displayed in its completeness the principle of impartiality, when the inequality of circumstances preserves an equality of reward for merit. But the grounds of merit in each individual are known with truth and clearness only to God, together with his only-begotten Word and Wisdom and his Holy Spirit.

GREEK	LATIN
RESURRECTION AND PUNISH-MENT.[1]	THE RESURRECTION AND THE JUDGMENT.

LATIN

1. But since our discourse has reminded us of the judgment to come and of retribution and the punishment of sinners, in accordance with the threatenings of the holy scriptures and the contents of the Church's teaching[2] to the effect that at the time of the judgment 'eternal fire' and 'outer darkness' and a 'prison' and a 'furnace' and other similar things have been prepared for sinners,[3] let us see what we ought to believe about these matters also.

Now to approach them in the requisite order we must first, it seems to me, begin a discussion on the resurrection, in order to learn what it is that shall come either to punishment or to rest and blessedness. On this matter we have already argued more fully in the other books which we have written on resurrection[4] and have shown what were our views about it. Now, however, for the sake of logical continuity in this treatise, it seems not unreasonable to repeat a few of the arguments from our former works, particularly because some make this objection to the faith of the church, that our beliefs about the resurrection are altogether foolish and silly.[5]

The chief objectors are the heretics, who must, I think, be answered in the following manner. If they admit, with us, that there is a resurrection of the dead, let them answer this question : 'What was it that died? Was it not a body?' If so, there will be a resurrection of the body. Then again, let them say whether they believe that we are to possess bodies, or not. I submit

---

[1] The Greek title is taken from Photius, *Cod.* 8, p. 4, where, as Koetschau rightly points out, it is incorrectly written as two separate titles, 'Concerning Resurrection. Concerning Punishment.'

[2] See above p. 4.

[3] See St. Matt. XXV. 41, VIII. 12; 1 Peter III. 19.

[4] Only small fragments of these works are extant. See the edition of Lommatzsch XVII. 55-64. Origen's views on the Resurrection are clearly set forth in the *Con. Celsum* V. 17-19, VII. 32 and VIII. 49-50. His endeavour to uphold a spiritual doctrine of the resurrection body was misinterpreted by Methodius, Jerome and others as an attack upon the Church's faith.

[5] Rufinus, (*Apol. in Hieron.* II. 4) claims that in his translation of the *First Principles* he had adhered to the teaching of the Church in the passages dealing with the 'resurrection of the flesh'.

that, seeing that the apostle Paul says, 'It is sown a natural body, it will rise again a spiritual body',[1] these men cannot deny that a body rises or that in the resurrection we are to possess bodies. What then? If it is certain that we are to possess bodies, and if those bodies which have fallen are declared to rise again—and the expression 'rise again' could not properly be used except of that which had previously fallen—then no one can doubt that these bodies rise again in order that at the resurrection we may once more be clothed with them. The one thing, therefore, is bound up with the other. For if bodies rise again, undoubtedly they rise again as a clothing for us, and if it is necessary, as it certainly is, for us to live in bodies, we ought to live in no other bodies but our own. And if it is true that they rise again and do so as 'spiritual', there is no doubt that this means that they rise again from the dead with corruption banished and mortality laid aside; otherwise it would seem vain and useless for a man to rise from the dead in order to die over again. Finally, this can be the more clearly understood by carefully observing what is the quality of the 'natural body' which, when sown in the earth, can reproduce the quality of a 'spiritual body'. For it is from the natural body that the very power and grace of the resurrection evokes the spiritual body, when it transforms it from dishonour to glory.

2. Since the heretics, however, think themselves most learned and wise, we shall ask them whether every body has some form, that is, whether it is fashioned in some shape? If they say there is a body which is not fashioned in some shape, they will show themselves the most ignorant and foolish of men; for no one, except an utter stranger to all learning, will deny that a body has a shape.[2] But if they give the logical answer and say that every body is fashioned in some definite shape, we shall inquire of them whether they can explain and describe to us the shape of a 'spiritual body'; which they certainly will in no way be able to do. Further, we shall ask them for an explanation of the differences among those who rise again. How will they prove the truth of the saying: 'there is one flesh of birds, another of fishes; there are also bodies celestial and bodies terrestrial; but there is one glory of heavenly beings, another of earthly, one glory of the sun, another glory of the moon, another glory of the stars, for one star differeth from another star in glory; so also is the resurrection of the dead'?[3] Let them show us, therefore, that the differences of glory among those who rise are comparable to these gradations among the heavenly

[1] I Cor. XV. 44.
[2] See Methodius, *De Resurr.* 25, 2. According to Methodius, Origen taught that in the resurrection men would have the same form as previously, but not a form of flesh.
[3] I Cor. XV. 39-42.

bodies; and if by any means they have tried to think out some system along the lines of the differences among the heavenly bodies, we shall request them also to mark the differences in the resurrection indicated by the comparison drawn from earthly bodies.

We indeed understand the matter thus : the apostle, when he wished to describe how great were the differences among those who rise in glory, that is, the saints, drew a comparison from the heavenly bodies, saying, 'One glory of the sun, another glory of the moon, another glory of the stars.' When, on the other hand, he wished to teach us the differences among those who shall come to the resurrection without being purified in this life, that is, as sinners, he draws an illustration from earthly creatures and says, 'One flesh of birds, another of fishes'. For heavenly things are worthy of being compared with the saints, and earthly with sinners. Let this be said in opposition to those who deny the resurrection of the dead, that is, the resurrection of bodies.

3. We now direct the discussion to some of our own people, who either from poverty of intellect or from lack of instruction introduce an exceedingly low and mean idea of the resurrection of the body. We ask these men in what manner they think that the 'natural body' will, by the grace of the resurrection, be changed and become 'spiritual'; and in what manner they believe that what is 'sown in weakness' will be 'raised in power', and what is sown 'in dishonour' is to 'rise in glory', and what is sown 'in corruption' is to be transformed into 'incorruption'?[1] Certainly if they believe the apostle, who says that the body, when it rises in glory and in power and in incorruptibility, has already become spiritual, it seems absurd and contrary to his meaning to say that it is still entangled in the passions of flesh and blood, seeing that he says plainly, 'Flesh and blood shall not inherit the kingdom of God, neither shall corruption inherit incorruption.'[2] Further, how do they take the passage in which the apostle says, 'We shall all be changed'?[3] This change, the character of which we have before spoken of,[4] we must certainly look forward to, and we are undoubtedly right in expecting it to consist in some act that is worthy of the divine grace; for we believe that it will be a change of like character to that

---

[1] See 1 Cor. XV. 42-44.
[2] 1 Cor. XV. 50. According to Photius, *Ep.* I. 8, 15 (Migne P. G. 102, p. 645), Origen and his followers expressed themselves more clearly than Rufinus will allow on the spiritual nature of the Resurrection. 'They will have it that our bodies do not rise with our souls, but that the latter rise without bodies, thus giving the name resurrection to I do not know what. For it should be a resurrection of that which has fallen and died, and not of something which exists and remains in incorruption for ever, such as the soul is.'
[3] 1 Cor. XV. 51.   [4] See above p. 139.

in which, as the apostle describes it, 'a bare grain of wheat or of some other kind' is sown in the earth, but 'God giveth it a body as it pleased him',[1] after the grain of wheat itself has first died.[2]

So must we suppose that our bodies, like a grain of corn, fall into the earth, but that implanted in them is the life-principle which contains the essence of the body; and although the bodies die and are corrupted and scattered, nevertheless by the word of God that same life principle which has all along been preserved in the essence of the body raises them up from the earth and restores and refashions them, just as the power which exists in a grain of wheat refashions and restores the grain, after its corruption and death, into a body with stalk and ear.[3] And so in the case of those who shall be counted worthy of obtaining an inheritance in the kingdom of the heavens, the life-principle before mentioned, by which the body is refashioned, at the command of God refashions out of the earthly and natural body a spiritual body, which can dwell in the heavens; while to those who have proved of inferior merit, or of something still meaner than this, or even of the lowest and most insignificant grade, will be given a body of glory and dignity corresponding to the dignity of each one's life and soul; in such a way, however, that even for those who are to be destined to 'eternal fire' or to 'punishments'[4] the body that rises is so incorruptible, through the transformation wrought by the resurrection, that it cannot be corrupted and dissolved even by punishments.[5] *   *   *

4. If then this is the character of the body which rises from the dead, let us now see what is the meaning of the threatened 'eternal fire'.[6] Now we find in the prophet Isaiah that the fire by which each man is punished is described as belonging to himself. For it says, 'Walk in the light of your fire and in the flame which you have kindled for yourselves'.[7] These words

---

[1] 1 Cor. XV. 37, 38.   [2] See St. John XII. 24.

[3] See Origen, Con. Celsum V. 23. 'We do not, therefore, maintain that the body which has undergone corruption returns to its original nature, any more than the grain of wheat which has undergone corruption returns to the condition of a grain of wheat. What we say is that, just as over the grain of wheat there arises a stalk, so there is implanted in the body a certain life-principle, from which, not being corruptible, the body arises in incorruption.' See also Con. Celsum V. 18, 19 and VII. 32.

[4] See St. Matt. XXV. 41, 46.

[5] Koetschau assumes a gap here to allow for certain statements made by Origen which Rufinus does not give. See Anathema X of the Second Council of Constantinople : '[If anyone shall say that] the Lord's body after the resurrection was ethereal and spherical in shape, and that after the resurrection all other men's bodies will be the same, and that when the Lord has put away his own body and all men have done likewise, then the nature of bodies will disappear into nonexistence, [let him be anathema].' Also Justinian, Ep. ad Mennam. Mansi IX 516 D. 'He (i.e. Origen) says that in the resurrection the bodies of men will rise spherical.'

[6] See St. Matt. XXV. 41, 46.   [7] Is. L. 11.

seem to indicate that every sinner kindles for himself the flame
of his own fire, and is not plunged into a fire which has been
previously kindled by some one else or which existed before him.
Of this fire the food and material are our sins, which are called
by the apostle Paul wood and hay and stubble.[1]   And I think
that just as in the body an abundance of eatables or food that
disagrees with us either by its quality or its quantity gives rise
to fevers differing in kind and duration according to the degree
in which the combination of noxious elements supplies material
and fuel for them—the quality of which material, made up of the
diverse noxious elements, being the cause which renders the
attack sharper or more protracted—so when the soul has gathered
within itself a multitude of evil deeds and an abundance of sins,
at the requisite time the whole mass of evil boils up into punishment and is kindled into penalties; at which time also the mind
or conscience, bringing to memory through divine power all things
the signs and forms of which it had impressed upon itself at
the moment of sinning, will see exposed before its eyes a kind
of history of its evil deeds, of every foul and disgraceful
act and all unholy conduct.   Then the conscience is harassed
and pricked by its own stings, and becomes an accuser and witness
against itself.

This, I think, was what the apostle Paul felt when he said,
'Their thoughts one with another accusing or else excusing them,
in the day when God shall judge the secrets of men, according to
my gospel, by Jesus Christ'.[2]   From which we understand that
in the very essence of the soul certain torments are produced
from the harmful desires themselves that lead us to sin.[3]

5. But to prevent your thinking that this explanation of
the matter is somewhat difficult to grasp, we can consider the
effect of those faults of passion which often occur in men, as
when the soul is burnt up with the flames of love, or tormented
by the fires of jealousy or envy, or tossed about with furious
anger, or consumed with intense sadness; remembering how some

---

[1] See 1 Cor. III. 12.   [2] Rom. II. 15, 16.
[3] Origen's doctrine of the purifying nature of 'eternal fire', stated in
this and the succeeding paragraphs, is also described in *Con. Celsum* V.
16 and VI. 25, 26. Jerome *Ep. ad Avitum* 7, says : 'As for the fire of
Gehenna and the torments, with which holy scripture threatens sinners,
Origen does not make them consist in punishments, but in the conscience
of sinners, when by the goodness and power of God the whole memory
of our offences is placed before our eyes. The entire crop of our sins
springs up as it were from seeds which have remained hidden in the soul,
and every shameful and impious act that we have done is represented in an
image before our eyes, so that the mind, beholding its former acts of self-
indulgence is punished by a burning conscience and stung by the pricks
of remorse.' So also *Comm. in Ep. ad Ephes.* III. 5 and *Apol. adv. Rufin.*
II. 7. Cp. Clement of Alexandria, *Strom.* VII. 6, 34 (Stahlin III. 27, 5-8).
'We, however, maintain that the fire purifies not flesh, but sinful souls ; for
we call it not the all-devouring and tormenting, but the discerning fire.'

men, finding the excess of these ills too heavy to bear, have
deemed it more tolerable to submit to death than to endure
such tortures.   You will ask, indeed, whether for men who have
been entangled in the ills which arise from the above-mentioned
faults and have been unable all the time they were in this life
to secure for themselves any amelioration and have so departed
from this world, it will be a sufficient punishment that they
should be tortured by the long continuance in them of those
harmful desires, whose deadly poison was in this life assuaged
by no healing remedy; or whether when these desires have been
changed they will be tormented by the stings of a general
punishment.

Now I think that another species of punishment may be
understood to exist; for just as, when the limbs of the body are
loosened and torn away from their respective connexions, we
feel an intense and excruciating pain, so when the soul is found
apart from that order and connexion and harmony in which it
was created by God for good action and useful experience and
not at concord with itself in the connexion of its rational movements, it must be supposed to bear the penalty and torture of
its own want of cohesion and to experience the punishment due
to its unstable and disordered condition.   But when the soul,
thus torn and rent asunder, has been tried by the application of
fire, it is undoubtedly wrought into a condition of stronger inward
connexion and renewal.

6. There are many other matters, too, which are hidden from
us, and are known only to him who is the physician of our souls.
For if in regard to bodily health we occasionally find it necessary
to take some very unpleasant and bitter medicine as a cure for
the ills we have brought on through eating and drinking, and
sometimes, if the character of the ill demands it, we need the
severe treatment of the knife and a painful operation, yes, and
should the disease have extended beyond the reach even of these
remedies, in the last resort the ill is burnt out by fire, how much
more should we realise that God our physician, in his desire to
wash away the ills of our souls, which they have brought on
themselves through a variety of sins and crimes, makes use of
penal remedies of a similar sort, even to the infliction of a
punishment of fire on those who have lost their soul's health.

Allusions to this are found also in the holy scriptures.   For
instance, in Deuteronomy the divine word threatens that sinners
are to be punished with 'fevers and cold and pallor', and tortured
with 'feebleness of eyes and insanity and paralysis and blindness
and weakness of the reins'.[1] And so if anyone will gather at
his leisure from the whole of scripture all the references to
sufferings which in threats against sinners are called by the names

[1] See Deut. XXVIII. 22, 28, 29.

of bodily sicknesses, he will find that through them allusion is
being made to either the ills or the punishments of souls. And
to help us understand that as physicians supply aids to sufferers
with the object of restoring them to health through careful treatment, so with the same motive God acts towards those who have
lapsed and fallen into sin, there is proof in that passage in which,
through the prophet Jeremiah, God's 'cup of fury' is commanded
'to be set before all nations' that 'they may drink it and become
mad and spew it out'.[1] In this passage there is a threat which
says, 'If anyone refuse to drink, he shall not be cleansed';[2] from
which certainly we understand that the fury of God's vengeance
ministers to the purification of souls.

Isaiah teaches that even the punishments which are said to be
inflicted by fire are meant to be applied as a help, when he speaks
thus about Israel: 'The Lord will wash away the filth of the
sons and daughters of Sion, and will purge away the blood from
the midst of them by the spirit of judgment and the spirit of
burning'.[3] And of the Chaldaeans he speaks thus: 'Thou hast
coals of fire, sit upon them; they shall be to thee for a help',[4]
and in other places he says: 'The Lord shall sanctify them in
burning fire',[5] and in the prophet Malachi it speaks as follows:
'The Lord shall sift and refine his people as gold and silver; he
shall refine and purify and pour forth purified the sons of Judah'.[6]

7. Moreover, the saying in the gospel about unjust stewards,
who must be 'cut asunder' and 'their portion placed with the
unbelievers',[7] as if the portion which was not theirs were to be
sent somewhere else, undoubtedly alludes to some sort of punishment, as it seems to me, which falls on those whose spirit has
to be separated from their soul. Now if we are to understand
this spirit as belonging to the divine nature, that is, as being
the Holy Spirit, we shall perceive that the passage relates to
the gift of the Holy Spirit. It tells us that when, whether
through baptism or the grace of the Spirit, the 'word of wisdom'
or the 'word of knowledge'[8] or of any other endowment has
been given to a man as a gift and not rightly used, that is to
say, either 'hidden in the earth' or 'bound up in a napkin',[9]
the gift of the Spirit will surely be withdrawn from his soul, and
the portion which remains, namely the essence of the soul, will
be placed with the unbelievers, cut asunder and separated from
that Spirit with whom, by joining itself to the Lord, it ought
to have been 'one spirit'.[10]

[1] See Jerem. XXV. 15, 16, 27.   [2] See Jerem. XXV. 28, 29.
[3] Is. IV. 4.   [4] Is. XLVII. 14, 15 (Sept.) and see above p. 104.
[5] See Is. LXVI. 16, 17.   [6] Mal. III. 3.
[7] See St. Luke XII. 42-46.   [8] See 1 Cor. XII. 8.
[9] See St. Matt. XXV. 25; St. Luke XIX. 20.
[10] See 1 Cor. VI. 17.

If, however, we are to understand the spirit as being not the Spirit of God but the nature of the soul itself, then that portion of it will be called the better, which was made in the 'image and likeness' of God,[1] whereas the other portion will be that which afterwards through the misuse of free will was received in a condition contrary to the nature of its original purity; and this portion, as being the friend and beloved companion of the material body, is visited with the fate of the unbelievers. But the cutting asunder may also be understood in a third sense, namely, that whereas each of the faithful, though he be the least in the Church, is we are told attended by an angel who is declared by the Saviour always to 'behold the face of God the Father',[2] this angel of God, who was certainly one with him over whom he was set, is to be withdrawn from him if by disobedience he becomes unworthy; and in that case 'his portion', that is the portion consisting of his human nature, being torn asunder from God's portion, is to be numbered with the unbelievers, seeing that he did not faithfully observe the warnings of the angel allotted to him by God.[3]

3. The 'outer darkness',[4] too, is in my opinion not to be understood as a place with a murky atmosphere and no light at all, but rather as a description of those who through their immersion in the darkness of deep ignorance have become separated from every gleam of reason and intelligence. We must also see whether possibly this expression does not mean that just as the saints will receive back the very bodies in which they have lived in holiness and purity during their stay in this life, but bright and glorious as a result of the resurrection, so, too, the wicked, who in this life have loved the darkness of error and the night of ignorance, will after the resurrection be clothed with murky and black bodies, in order that this very gloom of ignorance, which in the present world has taken possession of the inner parts of their mind, may in the world to come be revealed through the garment of their outward body. (Perhaps,[5] however, the 'gloom and darkness'[6] should be taken to mean this coarse and earthly body, through which at the end of this world each man that must pass into another world will receive the beginnings of a fresh birth) * * * The expression 'prison'[7] must be thought of in a similar way.   *   *   *   *   *

---

[1] See Gen. I. 26.   [2] See St. Matt. XVIII. 10.

[3] See St. Luke XII. 46.   [4] St. Matt. VIII. 12 etc.

[5] This passage, taken from Jerome, *Ep. ad Avitum* 7, has been omitted by Rufinus. Jerome adds: 'In so speaking he clearly supports the doctrine of transmigration taught by Pythagoras and Plato.'

[6] See St. Matt. VIII. 12 etc.

[7] 1 St. Peter III. 19 and p. 138 above. This sentence belongs to Rufinus.

GREEK

There[1] is a resurrection of the dead, and there is punishment, but not everlasting. For when the body is punished the soul is gradually purified, and so is restored to its ancient rank * * For all wicked men, and for daemons, too, punishment has an end, and both wicked men and daemons shall be restored to their former rank.

LATIN

Let these remarks,[2] which we have made at this point, to preserve the order of our discourse, in the fewest possible words, suffice for the present.

---

[1] Fragment 25, Koetschau, the first part taken from Leont. Byz. *De Sectis,* Act. X. 6 (Migne P. G. 86 I, 1265), and the second (beginning, 'For all wicked men . . . .') from Justinian, *Ep. ad Mennam* (Mansi IX. 517). Rufinus has omitted the explicit denial of everlasting punishment.

[2] This concluding sentence is from Rufinus.

CHAPTER XI

THE PROMISES[1]

1. Let us now consider briefly what we ought to believe about the promises.

It is certain that no living creature can be altogether inactive and immovable, but that it is eager for every kind of movement and for continual action and volition; and it is clear, I think, that this nature resides in all living beings. Much more then must a rational being such as man be always engaged in some movement or activity. And if a man forgets himself and is unaware of what befits him, his whole purpose centres round bodily experiences and in all his movements he is occupied with the pleasures and lusts of the body. If, however, he is one who strives to care or provide for the common good, he applies himself either to serving the State or obeying the magistrates or to whatever else may seem to be clearly of benefit to people generally. But if there be a man who can discern something better than these activities, which appear to be connected with the body, and can give diligent attention to wisdom and knowledge, he will undoubtedly direct all his efforts towards studies of this sort, with the object of learning, through inquiry into truth, what are the causes and reason of things.[2] As therefore in this life one man decides that the highest good is the pleasure of the body, another the service of the State, and another devotion to studies and learning, so we seek to know whether in that life which is the true one, the life which is said to be 'hid with Christ in God',[3] that is, in the eternal life, there will be for us any such order or condition of existence.

2. Now some men, who reject the labour of thinking and seek after the outward and literal meaning of the law, or rather give way to their own desires and lusts, disciples of the mere letter, consider that the promises of the future are to be looked for in the form of pleasure and bodily luxury.[4] And chiefly on this account they desire after the resurrection to have flesh of such a sort that they will never lack the power to eat and drink and to do all things that pertain to flesh and blood, not following the teaching of the apostle Paul about the resurrection of a

---

[1] For the title see Acts XXVI. 6 and Heb. VI. 12. The Latin agrees with the Greek title, to be found in Photius, *Bibl. Cod.* 8.

[2] See Virgil, *Georgics* II. 490.

[3] See Col. III. 3.

[4] These simple folk (Lat. *simpliciores*), who took the Scriptures literally, are further described in Origen, *In Matt.* XVII. 35 (Lomm. IV. 167 f.) and *In Cant. Proleg.* (Lomm. XIV. 295).

'spiritual body'.[1] Consequently they go on to say that even after the resurrection there will be engagements to marry and the procreation of children, for they picture to themselves the earthly city of Jerusalem about to be rebuilt with precious stones laid down for its foundations and its walls erected of jasper and its battlements adorned with crystal; it will also have an outer wall composed of different precious stones, namely, jasper, sapphire, chalcedony, emerald, sardius, onyx, chrysolite, chrysoprase, hyacinth and amethyst.[2] Then, too, they suppose that 'aliens' are to be given them to minister to their pleasures, and that they will have these for 'plowmen' or 'vinedressers' or 'wall-builders',[3] so that by them their ruined and fallen city may be raised up again; and they consider that they are to receive the 'wealth of nations' to live on and that they will have control over their riches, so that even the camels of Midian and Ephah will come and bring them 'gold, incense and precious stones'.[4]

All this they try to prove on prophetic authority from those passages of scripture which describe the promises made to Jerusalem; where it is also said that 'they who serve God shall eat and drink, but sinners shall hunger and thirst', and that 'the righteous shall enjoy gladness, but confusion shall possess the wicked'.[5] From the New Testament, too, they quote the Saviour's saying, in which he makes a promise to his disciples of the gladness that wine brings; 'I will not drink of this cup until the day that I drink it new with you in my Father's kingdom'.[6] They add also the following, that the Saviour calls those blessed, who now hunger and thirst, and promises them that they shall be filled;[7] and they quote from the scriptures many other illustrations, the force of which they do not perceive must be figurative and spiritual. Then, too, after the fashion of what happens in this life, and of this world's positions of dignity or rank or supreme power, they consider that they will be kings and princes, just like the corresponding earthly rulers, relying on the saying in the gospel, 'Thou shalt have authority over five cities'.[8] And, to speak briefly, they desire that all things which they look for in the promises should correspond in every detail with the course of this life, that is, that what exists now should exist again. Such are the thoughts of men who believe indeed in Christ, but because they understand the divine scriptures in a Judaistic sense, extract from them nothing that is worthy of the divine promises.

3. Those, however, who accept a view of the scriptures which accords with the meaning of the apostles, do indeed hope that

---

[1] I Cor. XV. 44.
[2] See Rev. XXI. 10-21; Is. LIV. 12; Ezek. XXVIII. 13.
[3] See Is. LXI. 5; LX. 10.   [4] See Is. LXI. 6; LX. 5, 6.
[5] See Is. LXV. 13, 14.   [6] St. Matt. XXVI. 29.
[7] See St. Matt. V. 6; St. Luke VI. 21.
[8] See Jerem. XVII. 25; St. Luke XIX. 19.

the saints will eat; but they will eat the 'bread of life',[1] which
is to nourish the soul and enlighten the mind with the food of
truth and wisdom and to cause it to drink from the cup of
divine wisdom, as the divine scripture says: 'Wisdom has prepared her table, she has slain her victims, she has mingled her
wine in the bowl and cries with a loud voice, Turn in to me and
eat the bread which I have prepared for you, and drink the
wine which I have mingled for you'.[2] The mind, when nourished
by this food of wisdom to a whole and perfect state, as man was
made in the beginning, will be restored to the 'image and likeness'[3] of God; so that, even though a man may have departed
out of this life insufficiently instructed, but with a record of
acceptable works, he can be instructed in that Jerusalem, the
city of the saints, that is, he can be taught and informed and
fashioned into a 'living stone', a 'stone precious and elect',[4]
because he has borne with courage and endurance the trials of
life and the struggles after piety. There, too, he will come to
a truer and clearer knowledge of the saying already uttered here,
that 'man does not live by bread alone, but by every word that
proceedeth out of the mouth of God'.[5] Moreover, the princes
and rulers must be understood to be those who both rule over
the souls of lower condition and also instruct and teach them
and initiate them into things divine.

4. But if these considerations seem scarcely able to produce
a worthy desire in minds that hope for literal promises, let us
continue our inquiry a little, and see how an eager longing for
the reality of things is natural to us and implanted in our soul;
so that we may at last be able, by following out a spiritual
view of scripture, to describe as it were the true forms of the
'bread of life' and the quality of that 'wine' and the characteristics
of the 'principalities'.[6] As, then, in those arts, which are accomplished by manual labour, the design, the why or how
or for what uses a thing is made, lies in the mind, but its
practical efficacy is unfolded through the help of the work of our
hands, so we must believe that in regard to God's works, which
have been made by him, their design and meaning remain a
secret. Now when our eye sees the works of the craftsman, if
it observes an article which has been made with unusual skill,
immediately the mind burns to discover of what sort it is and
how and for what uses it was made. Much more, and beyond
all comparison, does the mind burn with unspeakable longing
to learn the design of those things which we perceive
to have been made by God. This longing, this love has, we
believe, undoubtedly been implanted in us by God; and as the eye

[1] St. John VI. 35.   [2] See Prov. IX. 2-5.
[3] Gen. I. 26.   [4] See 1 Peter II. 4-6.
[5] St. Matt. IV. 4 (Deut. VIII. 3).
[6] See St. John VI. 35; Prov. IX. 2, 5; St. Luke XIX. 17, 19.

naturally demands light and vision and our body by its nature
desires food and drink, so our mind cherishes a natural and
appropriate longing to know God's truth and to learn the causes
of things.

Now we have not received this longing from God on the
condition that it should not or could not ever be satisfied; for
in that case the 'love of truth'[1] would appear to have been
implanted in our mind by God the Creator to no purpose, if its
gratification is never to be accomplished. So when even in this
life men devote themselves with great labour to sacred and
religious studies, although they obtain only some small fragments out of the immeasurable treasures of divine knowledge,[2]
yet [they gain this advantage,][3] that they occupy their mind
and understanding with these questions and press onward in their
eager desire. Moreover they derive much assistance from the
fact that by turning their mind to the study and love of truth
they render themselves more capable of receiving instruction in
the future. For when a man wishes to paint a picture, if he
first sketches with the faint touch of a light pencil the outlines
of the proposed figure and inserts suitable marks to indicate
features afterwards to be added, this preliminary drawing with
its faint outline undoubtedly renders the canvas more prepared to
receive the true colours. So it will be with us, if only that faint
form and outline is inscribed 'on the tablets of our heart'[4] by
the pencil of our Lord Jesus Christ. This is perhaps the reason
why it is said, 'To every one that hath shall be given and added'.[5]
It is clear, then, that to those who have now in this life a kind
of outline of truth and knowledge there shall be added in the
future the beauty of the perfect image.

5. Such was, I think, the 'desire' indicated by him who said,
'I am in a strait between two, having a desire to depart and be
with Christ; for this is far better'.[6] He knew that when he
had gone back to Christ he would learn more clearly the reasons
for all things that happen on earth, that is, the reasons which
account for man, for his soul or his mind, or whichever of these
constitutes man,[7] and what is the meaning of the 'ruling spirit',
and of the 'spirit who works', and of the 'living spirit',[8] and
of the grace of the Holy Spirit which is given to the faithful.
Then also he will understand the significance of the name Israel,
and of the diversity of races; and also of the twelve tribes contained in Israel, and of the people of each several tribe. He

---

[1] See 2 Thess. II. 10.   [2] See Col. II. 2, 3.
[3] The sentence is not complete in Latin, and Koetschau suggests inserting the words *lucri habent et,* which are translated above.
[4] See 2 Cor. III. 3.   [5] St. Matt. XXV. 29.
[6] Phil. I. 23.
[7] See above Bk. II. Ch. VIII. 3, 4, (p. 122 ff.).
[8] These titles are probably suggested by passages such as Eph. II. 2;
1 Cor. XII. 6, 11; Rom. VIII. 2.

will also understand the reasons for the priests and Levites and
for the different priestly orders, and whose type it was that was
seen in Moses; and he will learn, too, what is the true meaning
in God's sight of the jubilees and the weeks of years.   Further,
he will see the reason of the feast days and the holy days and
will perceive the causes of all the sacrifices and purifications.
He will observe the reason for the cleansing after leprosy and
for the different kinds of leprosy, and the meaning of the purification of those who suffer an emission of seed.   He will learn
about the good powers, what they are, and their greatness and
qualities, and likewise about the opposite kind, and the explanation
of the love which the former bear towards mankind and of the
persistent jealousy of the latter.[1]   He will perceive what is the
reason of souls[2] and the meaning of the diversity among animals,
whether those that live in water, or birds, or beasts; and for
what cause each genus is divided into so many species; and
what purpose of the Creator or what indication of his wisdom
is concealed in each individual thing.   Further, he will learn the
reason why certain properties are attached to certain roots and
herbs; and what is the reason of the fallen angels, and for what
cause they are allowed to flatter in some respects those who do
not despise them with complete faith and to exist for the purpose
of deceiving and leading men astray.   He will learn the judgment of divine providence about each individual thing; about
things which happen to men, that they happen not by chance
or accident, but by a reason so carefully thought out, and so
high above us, that it does not overlook even the number of the
hairs of our head, and that not of the saints only but probably
of all men; the scope of which providence extends even to the
'two sparrows'[3] which are sold for a penny, whether 'sparrows'
is to be understood spiritually or literally.   For now in this
present life we seek, but there we shall see plainly.[4]

6. All this leads us to suppose that no small interval of time
may pass before the reason merely of things on earth can be
shown to worthy and deserving men after their departure from
life, in order that through their acquaintance with it all and the
grace of full knowledge they may enjoy an indescribable gladness.

So then, if the air between heaven and earth is not devoid of
living and even rational beings, as the apostle said, 'Wherein
in times past ye walked according to the course of this world,
according to the prince of the power of this air, the spirit who
now worketh in the children of disobedience',[5] and again, 'We
shall be caught up in the clouds to meet Christ in the air, and so
shall we ever be with the Lord',[6] we must suppose that the saints

---

[1] See above Bk. I. Ch. V. (p. 44 ff.).
[2] See above Bk. II. Ch. VIII. (p. 120 ff.).
[3] See St. Matt. X. 30, 31.   [4] See 1 Cor. XIII, 12.
[5] Eph. II. 2.   [6] 1 Thess. IV. 17.

will remain there for some time, until they learn the reason of the ordering of all that goes on in the air, in its two-fold form. By two-fold form I mean, for example; when we were on earth we saw animals or trees and we perceived the differences among them and also the very great diversity among men. But when we saw these things we did not understand the reasons for them; but this alone was suggested to us by the very diversity of what we saw, that we should search out and inquire for what reason all these were created diverse and arranged in such variety; and if we have cherished on earth a zeal and love for this kind of knowledge, there will be given to us after death an acquaintance with and understanding of that reason, if indeed the matter turns out as we should wish. When therefore we have comprehended that in its fulness, we shall comprehend in two-fold form the things we saw on earth.

We may speak in some such way also about the abode in the air. I think that the saints as they depart from this life will remain in some place situated on the earth, which the divine scripture calls 'paradise'.[1] This will be a place of instruction and, so to speak, a lecture room or school for souls, in which they may be taught about all that they had seen on earth and may also receive some indications of what is to follow in the future; just as when placed in this life they had obtained certain indications of the future, seen indeed 'through a glass darkly', and yet truly seen 'in part',[2] which are revealed more clearly and brightly to the saints in their proper times and places. If anyone is 'pure in heart'[3] and of unpolluted mind and well-trained understanding he will make swifter progress and quickly ascend to the region of the air, until he reaches the kingdom of the heavens, passing through the series of those 'abiding places',[4] if I may so call them, which the Greeks have termed spheres, that is, globes, but which the divine scripture calls heavens. In each of these he will first observe all that happens there, and then learn the reason why it happens; and thus he will proceed in order through each stage, following him who has 'entered into the heavens, Jesus the Son of God',[5] and who has said, 'I will that, where I am, they also may be with me'.[6] Further, he alludes to this diversity of places when he says, 'In my Father's house are many abiding-places'.[7] He himself, however, is everywhere and runs through all things; nor are we any longer to

---

[1] See Gen. II. 8 etc. (Sept.); St. Luke XXIII. 43.
[2] See 1 Cor. XIII. 12.   [3] St. Matt. V. 8.
[4] See St. John XIV. 2. The Greek idea of the heavens was that of a series of revolving spheres, beginning with that of the moon and ending with the sphere of the fixed stars (see par. 7 below). Philo says (*De somniis* I. 22) that the lower air nearest the earth is the home of disembodied souls.
[5] Heb. IV. 14.   [6] St. John XVII. 24.   [7] St. John XIV. 2.

think of him as being confined within those narrow limits in
which he once lived for our sakes, that is, not as being in that
circumscribed condition which was his when he dwelt on earth
among men in a body like ours, so that it was then possible
to think of him as being enclosed in some one place.

7. When the saints have reached the heavenly places, then
they will see clearly the nature of the stars, one by one, and
will understand whether they are living creatures or whatever
may be truth about them.[1] They will also perceive the other
reasons for God's works, which he himself shall reveal to them.
For now he will show to them, as to sons, the causes
of things and the perfection of his creation, teaching them
why one star is placed in its particular position in the sky
and why it is separated from another by so great an
interval of space; what would happen, for example, if it were
nearer or farther away; or if this star had been greater than
that, how the entire universe would not retain its identity but
everything would be changed into another form.   And when they
have gone through everything connected with the reason of the
stars and with those ways of life that exist in heaven they will
come to 'the things which are not seen',[2] or to those whose
names alone we have as yet heard, and to the things 'invisible'.[3]
That there are many of these we learn from Paul the apostle,
but what they are or what differences exist among them we
cannot even guess with our feeble intellect.

And so the rational being, growing at each successive stage,
not as it grew when in this life in the flesh or body and in the
soul, but increasing in mind and intelligence, advances as a
mind already perfect to perfect knowledge, no longer hindered
by its former carnal senses, but developing in intellectual power,
ever approaching the pure and gazing 'face to face',[4] if I may
so speak, on the causes of things.[5]   And it attains perfection,
first that perfection by which it rises to this condition, and
secondly that by which it remains therein, while it has for the
food on which it feeds the problems of the meaning of things
and the nature of their causes.   For as in this bodily life of ours
we grew first of all bodily into that which we now are, the
increase being supplied in our early years merely by a sufficiency
of food, whereas after the process of growth has reached its

---

[1] See above Bk. I., Ch. VII. 3 (p. 59 ff.).

[2] 2 Cor. IV. 18.   [3] See Rom. I. 20; Col. I. 16.

[4] See 1 Cor. XIII. 12. Jerome's paraphrase of this passage is as follows
(Ep. ad Avitum 7): 'And at the end of the second book, in the course of
his argument about our final perfection, he says : When we have progressed
so far that we are no longer flesh and bodies, and possibly not even souls,
but mind and understanding come to perfection and not blinded by any
cloud of disturbing passions, we shall see rational and spiritual beings "face
to face".'

[5] See above p. 147.

limit we use food not in order to grow but as a means of preserving life within us; so, too, I think that the mind, when it has come to perfection, still feeds on appropriate and suitable food in a measure which can neither admit of want nor of superfluity. But in all respects this food must be understood to be the contemplation and understanding of God, and its measures to be those that are appropriate and suitable to this nature which has been made and created. These measures will rightly be observed by every one of those who are beginning to 'see God', that is, to understand him through 'purity of heart'.[1]

---

[1] See St. Matt. V. 8.

BOOK III

PREFACE OF RUFINUS

The two former books on 'First Principles' I translated not merely at your request, but at your urgent demand, during the days of Lent. But since in those days, my devout brother Macarius, you were living near me and were more at leisure than you are now, I also worked the more. These latter two, however, I have been slower in interpreting, seeing that you have paid me fewer visits from the furthermost part of the city to press forward the work. Now if you remember what I mentioned in my former preface,[1] that certain people would be angry if they did not hear us speak some evil of Origen, this came to pass immediately, as I think you discovered. But if those daemons who incite the tongues of men to evil speaking were so incensed against that work, in which he had not yet fully laid bare their secrets, what do you suppose will happen to this, in which he has revealed all the dark and hidden ways by which they creep into the hearts of men and deceive weak and feeble souls? At once you will see everything in confusion, dissensions aroused, clamour raised throughout the city, and condemnation called down upon the man who strove to dispel the diabolical darkness of ignorance by the light of the gospel lamp. Let such things, however, be counted of small moment by everyone who desires, while preserving unimpaired the rule of the Catholic faith, to be trained in divine instruction.

But this I must needs mention, that, as I did in the former books, so in these also I have taken care not to translate such passages as appeared to be contrary to the rest of Origen's teaching and to our own faith, but to omit them as forgeries interpolated by others.[2] If, however, he appeared to say anything of a novel kind about rational creatures, then, seeing that the essence of the faith is not involved in this, for the sake of knowledge and discussion, on occasions when perchance we had to reply to certain heresies in a similar order, I have not omitted such statements, either in these or in the former books, except perhaps where he wished to repeat in the later books what had been said in the former; in which case I have thought it right for the sake of brevity to cut out some of these repetitions.

Anyone who reads these books with a desire to advance in knowledge and not to raise objections will do better to have them explained to him by skilled teachers. For it is absurd to

[1] See Preface, Bk. I. p. xlii. [2] See Preface, Bk. I. p. xli.

have the fictitious songs of the poets and the ridiculous tales in the comedies explained by grammarians, while anyone thinks he can learn without master or interpreter the things which are written about God and the heavenly powers and the entire universe, in which every wicked error whether of pagan philosophers or of heretics is refuted. This is how it comes about that when the discussions concern things difficult and obscure men choose rather to condemn them rashly and ignorantly, than to learn their meaning by study and diligence.

CHAPTER I

GREEK

FREE WILL[1]

FREE WILL

1. Such we believe should be our beliefs about the divine promises, when we apply our understanding to the contemplation of that eternal and never-ending age and contemplate its unspeakable joy and blessedness.

1. Since the teaching of the church includes the doctrine of the righteous judgment of God, a doctrine which, if believed to be true, summons its hearers to live a good life and by every means to avoid sin—for it assumes that they acknowledge that deeds worthy of praise or of blame lie within our own power—let us now discuss separately a few points on the subject of free will, a problem of the utmost possible urgency. And in order to understand what free will is we must explain its meaning, that when this has been made clear the precise question may lie before us.

Since the teaching of the church includes the doctrine of a future righteous judgment of God, a belief in which summons and persuades men to live a good and blessed life and in every way to avoid sin, and since by this the fact is undoubtedly indicated that it lies within our own power to devote ourselves to a life worthy either of praise or of blame, I consider it necessary in consequence to discuss a few points on the subject of our free will, inasmuch as this question has been dealt with in no unworthy manner by very many writers. And in order the more easily to understand what free will is, let us inquire what is the nature of will and of desire.

2. Of things that move some have the cause of their movement within themselves, while others are moved solely from

2. Of things that move some have the causes of their movements within themselves, while others receive them from

---

[1] This chapter, marked as Frag. 26, Koetschau, is preserved in Ch. XXI. of the *Philocalia*, a collection of extracts from Origen's works made by Gregory and Basil. See the Edition of J. A. Robinson, Cambridge 1893, p. 152 ff.

GREEK

without.[1] Those, for example, moved solely from without are portable things, such as logs of wood and stones and all matter that is held together simply by its own constitution. Let the view that would regard the flux of bodies as motion be excluded from the present discussion, since there is no need of this for our purpose. Things that have the cause of their movement in themselves are animals and plants and in a word everything that is held together by its nature or by soul. Among these they say are included even metals; and in addition fire is self-moved and perhaps also springs of water. But while all these have the cause of their movement within themselves, some are said to be moved out of themselves, others from within themselves; non-living things out of themselves, living things from within themselves.

LATIN

without. Those, for example, moved solely from without are all lifeless things, such as stones, logs of wood and other things of this kind, which are held together simply by the constitution of their material or by their physical structure. We must of course exclude for the present the view that regards it as motion when bodies dissolve in corruption; for this has no bearing on our immediate purpose. Other things have the cause of their movement in themselves, as animals, trees and all things which are held together either by natural life or by soul. Among these some think that even the veins of metals should be reckoned; and, in addition, fire must be supposed to be self-moved and perhaps also springs of water. But of these which have the cause of their movements within themselves, some are said to be moved out of themselves, others from within themselves; and they are so divided because those which have life but no soul move out of themselves, those which have soul from within themselves.

[1] A similar passage is found in Origen, *De Oratione* VI. 1. 'Of things that move some derive their movement from without, such as non-living things and things that are held together simply by their own constitution, as well as things that are moved by nature and soul when occasionally these move not as such but in a manner similar to that of things held together simply by their own constitution. For instance, stones hewn from the quarry and logs which have lost their power of growth are held together simply by their own constitution and derive their movement from without; and so also do the bodies of animals and the portable fruits of plants which, when changed in position by anyone, change not like animals or plants but like stones or logs which have lost the power of growth. And even if these latter move in virtue of the fact that all bodies are in a state of flux as they decay, nevertheless this movement in the process of decay is inseparably connected with the former kind. A second class of things comprises those that are moved by their inherent nature or soul, which are said, by those

GREEK | LATIN

Now living things are moved from within themselves when there arises within them an image which calls forth an impulse. And again in certain animals images arise which call forth impulses, the imaginative nature setting the impulse in ordered motion; for instance, in the spider, an image of weaving a web arises and the impulse to weave it follows, the insect's imaginative nature inciting it to accomplish this task in an orderly manner, and beyond this imaginative nature the insect possesses nothing else. So in the bee there is an impulse to produce a honeycomb.

These latter move when there comes to them an image, that is, a kind of desire or incitement, which impels them to move towards an object. Again, there exists in certain animals such an image, that is, a desire or feeling, which by a natural instinct impels and excites them to ordered and complex motion; as we see in spiders, which by an image, that is, a desire and longing to weave a web, are excited to accomplish in an orderly manner the work of weaving, some natural movement undoubtedly calling forth the impulse to do this kind of work; nor do we find that this insect has any other feeling beyond the natural longing to weave a web. So, too, the bee is impelled to fashion honeycombs and to gather, as they call it, aerial honey.

3. The rational animal, however, has something besides its imaginative nature, namely reason, which judges the images. Some it rejects, others it approves of, the object being that the creature may be guided in accordance with these latter images. So it happens that, since there are in the nature of reason possibilities of contemplating good and evil, by following out which and contemplating them both we are led to

3. But while the rational animal has in itself these natural movements, it has also, to a greater extent than the other animals, the faculty of reason, by means of which it can judge and discern between the natural movements, disapproving of and rejecting some and approving of and accepting others. So by the judgment of this reason the movements of men may be guided and directed towards an approvable life.

---

who use words in a very precise manner, to be moved out of themselves. A third kind of movement is that observed in animals, which is called movement from within themselves. And I think that the movement of rational creatures is movement through themselves.' The Greek prepositions used are ἐξ (out of), ἀπὸ (from within) and διὰ (through). For the sources of this fragment of Origen's teaching on Physics see Clem. Alex. *Stromata* II. xx. 110 (Stählin II. 173, 17 ff.) and Von Arnim, *Chrysippi Frag. Phys.* 714.

choose good and avoid evil, we are worthy of praise when we devote ourselves to the practice of good, and of blame when we act in the opposite way.

We must not forget, however, that the greater part of the nature assigned to every rational creature is in the animals in varying degree, some having more and some less; so that the instinct in hunting dogs and in war horses comes near, if I may say so, to reason itself. To be subject, then, to a particular external impression which gives rise to such or such an image is admittedly not one of the things lying within our power; but to decide to use what has happened either in this way or in that is the work of nothing else but the reason within us, which, as the alternatives appear, either influences us towards the impulses that incite to what is good and seemly or else turns us aside to the reverse.

From which it follows that, since the nature of this reason in man includes a faculty of distinguishing between good and evil, and when man has done this he possesses also the power of choosing that which he has approved of, he is rightly deemed worthy of praise when he chooses what is good, and of blame when he follows what is base and evil.

We must, however, by no means forget that in certain dumb animals, as for instance clever dogs or war horses, there is found a more complex movement than in the rest, so that some men think that these are moved by a kind of rational intelligence. But we must believe that this results not so much from reason as from an instinctive and natural movement bestowed in especially large measure for purposes of this kind.[1] But, as we were saying, since the rational animal is thus constituted, we men are liable to meet with and receive from without, whether through sight or hearing or the other senses, certain impressions which urge and excite us to good movements or the reverse. Now inasmuch as these come from without, it certainly does not lie within our power to avoid meeting and receiving them; but to judge and determine how we ought to use them when they come is the work and business of that reason which is in us, that is of our own judgment. For by the judg-

---

[1] Rufinus' qualification of Origen's bold statement will be noticed.

GREEK   LATIN

ment of this reason we use the stimuli that meet us from without for whatever purpose the reason itself may approve, directing our natural movements at its bidding to courses that are good or the reverse.

4. But if anyone should say that the impression from without is of such a sort that it is impossible to resist it whatever it may be, let him turn his attention to his own feeling and movements and see whether there is not an approval, assent and inclination of the controlling faculty towards a particular action on account of some specious attractions.

4. But if anyone should say that those impressions from without that call forth our movements are of such a sort that it is impossible to resist them, whether they incite us to good or to evil, let him who thinks thus turn his attention for a little while to himself, carefully examining his own inner movements, and see whether he does not find that, when the attraction of any desire strikes him, nothing is accomplished until the assent of the soul is gained and the bidding of the mind indulges the wicked suggestion. It is as if an appeal were being made on certain plausible grounds from two different sides to a judge dwelling within the tribunal of our heart, in order that when the grounds have been first stated the sentence to act may proceed from the judgment of reason.

For instance, when a woman displays herself before a man who has determined to remain chaste and to abstain from sexual intercourse and invites him to act contrary to his purpose, she does not become the absolute cause of the abandonment of that purpose. The truth is that he is first entirely delighted with the sensation and lure of the pleasure and has no wish to resist it nor to strengthen his previous determina-

Suppose, for instance, that when a man has determined to live a chaste and continent life and to abstain from all sexual intercourse, a woman appears before him and invites and entices him to do something contrary to his purpose, that woman does not become the true and absolute cause or necessity of his perverse conduct, since it is in his power, by calling to mind his resolution, to bridle the incite-

GREEK   LATIN

tion; and then he commits the licentious act. On the other hand the same experiences may happen to one who has undergone more instruction and discipline; that is, the sensations and incitements are there, but his reason, having been strengthened to a higher degree and trained by practice and confirmed towards the good by right doctrines, or at any rate being near to such confirmation, repels the incitements and gradually weakens the desire.

ments to lust and to restrain the delights of the attraction that allures him by the stern rebukes of virtue, so that all desire for the pleasure is put to flight and the firmness and constancy of his determination endures. Finally, if allurements of this kind occur to men of greater learning who have grown strong in divine instruction, they at once remember who they are, calling to mind what they studied and learnt long ago and guarding themselves by the stay of this most holy doctrine; and thus they refuse and reject every attraction the incitement offers and repel the opposing evil desires by the help of the reason implanted within them.

5. But to throw the blame for what so happens to us on external things and to free ourselves from censure, declaring that we are like stocks and stones, which are dragged along by agents that move them from without, is neither true nor reasonable, but is the argument of a man who desires to contradict the idea of free will. For if we were to ask such a one what free will was, he would say it consisted in this, that when I proposed to do a certain thing no external cause arose which incited me to do the opposite.

5. Since then it is established by a kind of natural evidence that these things are so, is it not gratuitous to refer the causes of our deeds to what happens to us from without and to remove the blame from ourselves, in whom the entire cause lies, that is, to say that we are like stocks and stones, which have no movement within them but receive the causes of their movement from without? This indeed is neither a true nor a proper assertion, but one invented for the sole purpose of denying the freedom of the will; unless we are to suppose that free will could consist in this, that nothing which happens to us from without could incite us to good or evil.

Again, to throw the blame simply on our constitution is absurd, for education can take

But if anyone should refer the causes of our faults to the natural unruly constitution of

GREEK

the most intemperate and savage of men and, if they will follow her exhortation, can change them, so that the alteration and change for the better is very great, the most licentious men often becoming better than those who formerly seemed not to be such by their very nature, and the most savage changing to such a degree of gentleness that those who had never at any time behaved savagely yet seem to be savage in comparison with him who has changed to gentleness. We see others also most steady and respectable men, who by perversion to lower ways fall from their respectability and steadiness and change into a condition of licentiousness, often beginning such conduct in middle life and plunging into disorder after the season of youth, which so far as its nature goes is unstable, has passed. Reason therefore shows that external things do not lie within our power; but to use them in this way or the other, since we have received reason as a judge and investigator of the way in which we ought to deal with each of them, that is our task.

6. That it is our own task to live a good life, and that God asks this of us not as his work nor as a thing which comes to

LATIN

the body, this can be shown to be contrary to the experience of all education. For how many do we see who, when they have previously lived· an uncontrolled and intemperate life and have been the captives of luxury and lust, and are then perchance incited by the word of teaching and instruction to lead a better life, undergo so great a change that instead of being given to luxurious and disgraceful conduct they become sober and exceedingly chaste, and instead of being fierce and savage they become exceedingly mild and gentle? So on the other hand we see quiet and respectable men who, when they have become associated with turbulent and shameless people, have their 'good manners corrupted by evil conversations'[1] and are turned into men of the same sort as those who are steeped in every kind of wickedness. This sometimes happens to men of mature age, so that they prove to have lived more chastely in youth than when advanced years have granted them the opportunity of a freer life. The result of our reasoning, therefore, is to show that things which happen from without are not in our power, but to use them well or badly, when that reason which is within us discerns and decides how we ought to use them, this lies within our power.

6. But in order to confirm by the authority of the Scriptures the results of our reasoning, namely, that to live rightly or

---

[1] See 1 Cor. XV. 33.

GREEK

us from somebody else, nor, as some think, from fate, but as our own task, the prophet Micah will bear witness when he says, 'It hath been told thee, O man, what is good, and what doth the Lord require of thee but to do justice and to love mercy and to be ready to walk with thy God?'[1]

And Moses says, 'I have set before thy face the way of life and the way of death. Choose the good and walk in it'.[2] And Isaiah: 'If ye are willing and obey me, ye shall eat the good of the land. But if ye are unwilling and disobey me, a sword shall devour you. For the mouth of the Lord hath spoken it.'[3] And in the Psalms: 'If my people had hearkened unto me, and if Israel had walked in my ways, I would have humbled their enemies to nothing and laid my hand upon those that afflict them',[4] where the 'hearkening' and 'walking in the ways' of God are assumed to be in the people's power.

When, too, the Saviour says, 'I say unto you, that ye resist not him that is evil',[5] and 'Whosoever is angry with his brother shall be in danger of the judgment',[6] and 'Whosoever looketh upon a woman to lust after her hath committed adultery already

LATIN

otherwise is our task and not a thing that depends on external causes, nor, as some think, on the irresistible pressure of fate, Micah the prophet will bear witness when he says in these words, 'It hath been told thee, O man, what is good, and what doth the Lord require of thee but to do justice and to love mercy and to be ready to walk with the Lord thy God?'[1]

And Moses speaks thus, 'I have set before thy face the way of life and the way of death. Choose the good and walk in it'.[2] And Isaiah says, 'If ye are willing and hearken to me, ye shall eat the good of the land. But if ye are unwilling and do not hearken, a sword shall devour you. For the mouth of the Lord hath spoken it'.[3] And in the Psalms it is written, 'If my people had hearkened unto me, and if Israel had walked in my ways, I would have humbled their enemies to nothing . . . . .',[4] by which he shows that the 'hearkening' and 'walking in the ways' of God were in the people's power.

Further, when the Saviour says, 'But I tell you not to resist him that is evil',[5] and 'Whosoever is angry with his brother shall be in danger of the judgment',[6] and 'Whosoever looketh upon a woman to lust after her hath committed adul-

---

[1] Micah VI. 8.   [2] Deut. XXX. 15, 19.
[3] Is. I. 19, 20.
[4] Ps. LXXXI. 13, 14. The end of the quotation may have dropped out of the Latin text by accident.
[5] St. Matt. V. 39.   [6] St. Matt. V. 22.

GREEK

in his heart',[1] and in any other commandment he gives, he tells us that it lies in our power to observe the injunctions and that we shall with good reason be 'in danger of the judgment' if we transgress them.

This is why he also says, 'Every one who heareth these words of mine and doeth them shall be likened to a wise man who built his house upon the rock',[2] and the words that follow; but 'he that heareth and doeth them not is like a foolish man who built his house upon the sand',[3] and what follows. And when he says to those on the right hand, 'Come to me, ye blessed of my father', and the words that follow, 'for I was hungry and ye gave me to eat; I was thirsty and ye gave me to drink',[4] with the utmost clearness he gives the promises as to men who are worthy of being praised, whereas on the contrary he says to the others as to men who are blameworthy in comparison with the former, 'Depart, ye cursed, into the everlasting fire.'[5]

Let us see how Paul also reasons with us as being men of free will and ourselves responsible for our destruction or salvation. 'Or despisest thou', he says, 'the riches of his goodness and forbearance and long-

LATIN

tery with her already in his heart,'[1] and in any other commandments he gives, what else does he indicate but that it lies in our power to observe what is commanded, and that for this reason we are rightly brought 'in danger of the judgment' if we transgress what we certainly have power to observe?

This is why he also says, 'Everyone who heareth these words of mine and doeth them is like a wise man who built his house upon the rock',[2] and the rest; and also, 'He that heareth them and doeth them not is like a foolish man who built his house upon the sand,'[3] and the rest. Further, what he says to those on the right hand, 'Come to me, all ye blessed of my father,' and the rest, 'for I was hungry and ye gave me to eat; I was thirsty and ye gave me to drink',[4] plainly shows that the issue lay with themselves, whether to be counted worthy of praise for keeping the commandments and receiving the promises, or to be counted worthy of blame like the others, whose desert was to hear and receive the opposite, to whom it is said, 'Depart, ye cursed, into the everlasting fire'.[5]

Let us see how Paul the apostle also speaks to us as having the power of choice and as having in ourselves the causes of our salvation or destruction. 'Or despisest thou the riches of his goodness and forbearance

---

[1] St. Matt. V. 28.
[2] St. Matt. VII. 24.
[3] St. Matt. VII. 26.

[4] St. Matt. XXV. 34, 35.
[5] St. Matt. XXV. 41.

GREEK | LATIN

GREEK

suffering, not knowing that the goodness of God leadeth thee to repentance? but after thy hardness and impenitent heart treasurest up for thyself wrath in the day of wrath and revelation and righteous judgment of God, who will render to every man according to his works : to them that by patience in well-doing seek for glory and honour and incorruption, eternal life; but unto them that are factious and obey not the truth, but obey unrighteousness, shall be wrath and indignation, tribulation and anguish, upon every soul of man that worketh evil, of the Jew first and also of the Greek; but glory and honour and peace to every man that worketh good, to the Jew first and also to the Greek'.[1] Indeed, there are in the scriptures ten thousand passages which with the utmost clearness prove the existence of free will.

7. But since certain sayings from both the Old and the New Testaments incline us to the opposite conclusion, namely, that it is not in our power whether we keep the commandments and are saved or transgress them and are lost, let us bring forward some of these sayings and see what is the explanation of

LATIN

and longsuffering, not knowing that the goodness of God leadeth thee to repentance? but after thy hardness and impenitent heart treasurest up for thyself wrath in the day of wrath and revelation of the righteous judgment of God, who will render to every man according to his works; to them that by patience in well-doing seek for glory and honour and incorruption, eternal life; but unto them that are factious and obey not the truth, but obey unrighteousness, shall be wrath and indignation, tribulation and anguish, upon every soul of man that worketh evil, of the Jew first and also of the Greek; but glory and honour and peace to every man that worketh good, to the Jew first and also to the Greek'.[1] And you can find many other, yes, innumerable passages in the holy scriptures, which clearly show that we have the power of free will. For it would be absurd that we should have commandments given, the keeping of which is to save us and the transgression to condemn, if we do not possess the power to keep them.

7. But since there are found in the divine scriptures certain sayings so laid down that the opposite conclusion appears capable of being understood from them, let us bring them forward and discuss them by the rule of piety[2] and give the explanations of them. Thus from the few sayings that we now

---

[1] Rom. II. 4-10.
[2] A characteristic addition of Rufinus. Cp. Bk. III. Ch. 5, 3 (p. 238).

GREEK | LATIN

them. Thus from the ones we bring forward, any person who in a similar way selects for himself all the sayings that seem to destroy free will may consider our arguments in explanation of them.

Now many have been troubled by the story of Pharaoh, in dealing with whom God says several times, 'I will harden Pharaoh's heart'.[1] For if he is hardened by God and through being hardened sins, he is not himself responsible for the sin; and if this is so, Pharaoh has no free will. And someone will say that in the same way those who are lost have no free will and will not be lost on their own account. Also the saying in Ezekiel, 'I will take away their stony hearts and will put in them hearts of flesh, that they may walk in my statutes and keep my judgments',[2] might lead one to suppose that it was God who gave the power to walk in the commandments and to keep the judgments, by his removing the hindrance, the stony heart, and implanting something better, the heart of flesh.

Let us look also at the saying in the gospel, the answer which the Saviour gives to those who ask why he speaks to the multitude in parables.[3] 'That seeing they may not see,' he

explain, the meaning of the other similar sayings which appear to rule out the power of free will may become clear.

Now many are troubled by the words spoken to Pharaoh by God, who says several times, 'I will harden Pharaoh's heart'.[1] For if he is hardened by God and through being hardened falls into sin, he himself is not the cause of his sin. And if this is so, Pharaoh will appear not to have free will, and consequently men will assert that this example shows that all others who perish do not find the cause of their loss in their own free will. Also the saying in Ezekiel, 'I will take away their stony hearts and will put in them hearts of flesh, that they may walk in my statutes and keep my judgments',[2] might lead one to suppose that it was God who gave the power to walk in his commandments and to keep his judgments, if it was he who removed the stony heart, which hindered them from keeping the commandments, and who implanted in them the better and more sensitive one, which is here called a heart of flesh.

Let us look also at the nature of the saying with which the Lord and Saviour in the gospel gives answer to those who asked him why he spoke to the multitude in parables.[3] He

[1] Exod. IV. 21, VII. 3.   [2] Ezek. XI. 19, 20.
[3] See St. Matt. XIII. 10.

GREEK

says, 'and hearing they may hear and not understand, lest haply they should be converted and it should be forgiven them.'[1] And further, the saying by Paul, that it is 'not of him that willeth nor of him that runneth, but of God that hath mercy';[2] and elsewhere, 'Both to will and to do are of God';[3] and elsewhere, 'So then he hath mercy on whom he will, and whom he will he hardeneth. Thou wilt say to me then, Why doth he yet find fault; for who hath resisted his will?'[4] And, 'The persuasion is of him that calleth',[5] and not of us.

And again, 'Nay but, O man, who art thou that repliest against God? Shall the thing formed say to him that formed it, Why didst thou make me thus? Or hath not the potter a right over the clay, from the same lump to make one part a vessel unto honour, and another unto dishonour?'[6] These passages are in themselves sufficient to disturb ordinary people with the thought that man is not a free agent, but that it is God who saves and destroys whom he will.

8. Let us begin therefore with the statements made about Pharaoh, that he was hardened by God in order that he might not let the people go. Along with this we shall examine also the apostle's saying, 'So then

LATIN

says, 'That seeing they may not see, and hearing they may hear and not understand, lest haply they should be converted and it should be forgiven them.'[1] And further, what was said by Paul the apostle, that it is 'not of him that willeth nor of him that runneth, but of God that hath mercy';[2] and elsewhere, 'Both to will and to do are of God';[3] and again elsewhere, 'So then he hath mercy on whom he will, and whom he will he hardeneth. Thou wilt say to me, therefore, why then doth he yet find fault; for who resisteth his will?'[4]

'O man, who art thou that repliest against God? Doth the thing formed say to him that formed it, Why didst thou make me thus? Or hath not the potter a right over the clay, from the same lump to make one vessel unto honour, and another unto dishonour?'[6] These passages and others like them seem to have no small effect on ordinary people, so that they hesitate to believe that each man has freedom over his own will, but think that it depends on the will of God whether a man is saved or lost.

8. Let us begin therefore with the statements made to Pharaoh, who is said to have been hardened by God in order that he might not let the people go. Along with this we shall also deal with that word of the

---

[1] St. Mark IV. 12.
[2] Rom. IX. 16.
[3] See Phil. II. 13.
[4] Rom. IX. 18, 19.
[5] See Gal. V. 8. This quotation is missing, probably by accident, from the text of Rufinus.
[6] Rom. IX. 20, 21.

GREEK

he hath mercy on whom he will, and whom he will he hardeneth.'[1] Now these passages are used by some of the heretics, who practically destroy free will by bringing in lost natures, which cannot receive salvation, and on the other hand saved natures, which are incapable of being lost.[2] Pharaoh, they say, having a lost nature, is in consequence hardened by God, who has mercy on the spiritual men but hardens the earthly.

Let us see, then, what they mean. We shall ask them whether Pharaoh was of an earthly nature. When they answer, we shall say that a man with an earthly nature is completely disobedient to God. But if he is disobedient, what need is there of hardening his heart, and that not once but several times? There is none, unless we assume that it was possible for him to obey and that, since he was not earthly, he would have obeyed completely when put to shame by the portents and signs; but that God, in order to display his mighty works for the salvation of the many, needs Pharaoh to proceed to a further degree of disobedience and hardens his heart on this account.

LATIN

apostle in which he says, 'So then he hath mercy on whom he will, and whom he will he hardeneth.'[1] Now it is on these passages that the heretics chiefly rely, when they say that it is not in our power to be saved, but that the natures of souls are such that they are absolutely lost or saved, and that a soul with an evil nature can by no means become good nor can one with a good nature become evil. So they say that Pharaoh, since he was of a lost nature, was in consequence hardened by God, who hardens those that are of an earthly nature but has mercy on those that are of a spiritual nature.

Let us see, then, what they mean by this assertion; and let us first ask them to tell us whether they mean that Pharaoh had an earthly nature, which they call a lost one. They will doubtless reply: 'An earthly one.' If then he was of an earthly nature he was altogether incapable of believing in God or obeying him, seeing that his nature was opposed to this. But if this disobedience was implanted in him by nature, what further need was there for his heart to be hardened by God, and that not once but several times? There was none, unless we assume that it was possible for him to yield to persuasion. Nor could anyone be said to be hardened by another except a man who in himself was not

---

[1] Rom. IX. 18.
[2] The heretics are the followers of Marcion, Valentinus and Basilides. Cp. Bk. II. Ch. IX, 5 (p. 133).

GREEK   LATIN

hard. But if he was not hard of himself, it follows that he was not of an earthly nature, but of such a sort as to be capable of giving way when amazed by the signs and mighty works. And indeed Pharaoh was necessary to God, in order that for the salvation of the many God might display his power in him during his long resistance and struggle against God's will; and it is on this account that his heart is said to be hardened.

This will be our answer to them in the first place, for the purpose of overthrowing their supposition that Pharaoh was of a lost nature.

Let this be our answer to them in the first place, in order that their supposition that Pharaoh was by nature lost may be overthrown.

We must return them the same answer in regard to the words spoken by the apostle. For whom does God harden? The lost? Why? Because they would obey if they were not hardened? Then would they not clearly be saved otherwise, since they are not of a lost nature? And on whom does he have mercy? Is it on those who are to be saved? But how is there need of a second mercy for those who have once for all been fashioned for salvation and who by their nature are in any case destined to be blessed? The truth is that, since they are in danger of being lost unless they obtain mercy, they obtain mercy in order that they may not incur that of which they are in danger, namely, being lost, but may be in the position of those who are saved. This is our answer to such persons.

Let us also deal with them in a similar way in regard to the words spoken by the apostle Paul. Whom, according to your opinion, does God harden? Is it those who you say are of a lost nature? They would have acted otherwise, I suppose, if they had not been hardened? But if they come to loss through being hardened, they are lost not by nature but by accident. Then again tell us, on whom does God have mercy? Is it on those who are to be saved? But how is there need of a second mercy for those who once for all were destined by nature for salvation and come to blessedness naturally? The truth is, as even their case shows, that it was possible for the men in question to be lost, and the reason why they obtain mercy is that by this means they may not be lost, but may come to salvation and possess the realms of the holy. Let this be our

GREEK

LATIN

answer to those who by fabricated stories bring forward doctrines of natures that are good or evil, that is, spiritual or earthly, which natures, they say, determine the salvation or loss of each individual soul.

9. But to those who think they understand the meaning of 'hardened'[1] we must address the further question: What actually do they mean by saying that God in his working hardens the heart, and with what purpose does he do this? Now they must safeguard the idea of God, who is according to sound doctrine just and good; but if they do not admit that, let it be granted them for the moment that he is merely just. Then let them show how he that is good and just, or he that is merely just, is acting justly when he hardens the heart of a man who as a result of this hardening is lost; and how he that is just can be a cause of the loss and disobedience of those who are punished as a result of their hardening and disobedience.

9. We must now reply to those who would have it that the God of the law is merely just and not good,[1] asking them : In what way do they suppose that the heart of Pharaoh was hardened by God, by what operation or with what purpose in view? For they must safeguard the view and conception of God, who is according to us just and good, but according to them merely just. Then let them show us how God, whom they themselves admit to be just, is acting justly when he hardens a man's heart in order that through this very hardening the man may sin and be lost; and how God's justice can be defended in this case, where God himself is the cause of the loss of those whom by his authority as judge he will hereafter condemn on the very ground that they were hard and unbelieving.

Why, too, does he blame Pharaoh, saying, 'Thou wilt not let my people go; behold, I will smite all the firstborn in Egypt, even thy firstborn',[2] and all the rest that is recorded as being said by God through Moses to Pharaoh? It is incumbent on him who believes that the

Why, too, does he blame Pharaoh, saying, 'If thou wilt not let my people go, behold, I will smite all the firstborn in Egypt, even thy firstborn',[2] and all the rest that is recorded as being said by God through Moses to Pharaoh? It is incumbent on every man who

---

[1] I.e., the Marcionites and other Gnostics. See above Bk. II. Ch. IX. 5 (p. 133).

[2] Exod. IV. 23.

GREEK

scriptures are true and that God is just, if he is a thoughtful man, to take pains to show how God, in using such expressions as these, can be clearly conceived to be just. If, however, anyone should rise up and in a bare-faced manner[1] champion the doctrine that the Creator is evil,[2] we should need other arguments to answer him.

10. But since they admit that they look upon God as being just, and our view is that he is good as well as just, let us consider how one who is good and just could harden Pharaoh's heart. See then whether we cannot prove, through an illustration used by the apostle in the Epistle to the Hebrews, that God has mercy on one and hardens another by a single operation; that it is not his purpose to harden, but that he acts with kindly intent, and that the hardening follows as a result of the substance of evil present in the particular evil person, so that God is said to harden him who is already hardened. 'The land', it says, 'which hath drunk the rain that cometh (oft)[3] upon it, and bringeth forth herbs meet for them for whose sake it is also tilled, receiveth blessing from God;

LATIN

believes the record of the scriptures to be true and desires to show that the God of the law and the prophets is just, to give an explanation of all this, and to show how no diminution of the justice of God is involved in it; for, even if they deny that he is good, still they admit that the Judge and Creator of the world is just. There is, however, another kind of answer for those who assert that a wicked being, namely the devil, is the Creator of this world.[2]

10. But since we acknowledge that the God who spoke by Moses is not only just but also good, let us consider carefully how one who is just and good can rightly be said to harden Pharaoh's heart. Let us see whether perchance we may solve this difficult problem by certain examples and illustrations taken from the apostle Paul, showing that God has mercy on one and hardens another by one and the same operation; that God's actions and desires do not aim at hardening the man who is hardened, but that during the time in which he is displaying kindness and forbearance those who treat his kindness and forbearance with contempt and pride have their heart hardened while the punishment of their misdeeds is being deferred, whereas they who receive his kindness and forbearance as an

[1] Lit. 'with uncovered head', a phrase taken from Plato, *Phaedrus* p. 243 B.
[2] See Book III, Ch. I. 16 (p. 189 below).
[3] This word is missing, probably by accident, from the Greek text. See below p. 173.

GREEK

but if it beareth thorns and thistles, it is rejected and nigh unto a curse, whose end is to be burned.'[1] As regards the rain, then, there is one operation, but the land which has been tilled brings forth fruit, while that which is neglected and barren brings forth thorns.

Now it seems almost irreverent to represent the giver of the rain as saying: 'It is I who made the fruits and the thorns that are in the earth'; yet in spite of this it is true. For if there had been no rain, there would have been neither fruits nor thorns, but after the rain has fallen in due time and measure, both spring up. For it says: 'the land which hath drunk the rain that cometh oft upon it, if it beareth thorns and thistles, is rejected and nigh unto a curse'.[1] So then the blessing of the rain comes also on the inferior land, but this, being neglected and untilled, brings forth thorns and thistles. Thus the marvellous works done

LATIN

opportunity of repentance and amendment obtain mercy. To show our meaning more clearly, we take the illustration used by the apostle Paul in the Epistle to the Hebrews. 'The land which hath drunk the rain that cometh oft upon it, and bringeth forth herbs meet for them by whom it is tilled, shall receive blessing from God; but that which beareth thorns and thistles is rejected and nigh unto a curse, whose end is to be burned'.[1] From these words of Paul which we have quoted it is clearly shown that through one and the same operation of God, by which he bestows rain upon the earth, one piece of land being carefully tilled brings forth good fruits, while another, which is neglected and untilled, produces thorns and thistles.

Now if one were to speak as it were in the person of the showers and say, 'It was I the rain that made the good fruits, and I, too, made the thorns and thistles', although this would seem to be a hard saying it is nevertheless a true one. For if there were no rain, neither fruits nor thorns and thistles would grow; but after the showers have fallen the earth produces both kinds from out of itself. But although the earth has produced both kinds of growth by the blessing of the rain, the diversity of the growth is not to be attributed to the showers, but the blame for an evil crop must fall on those who, when they might have broken

[1] Heb. VI. 7, 8.

GREEK

by God are as it were the rain, while the differing wills of men are like the tilled and the neglected land, though as land they are both of one nature.

LATIN

up the land by frequent ploughing and turned over the dull clods with the heavy mattocks and cut away and rooted out all useless and harmful weeds and cleansed and tilled the fields with all the toil and skill that such cultivation demands and so prepared them for the expected showers, have neglected this and will accordingly reap those most appropriate fruits of their idleness, thorns and thistles. Thus it happens that the goodness and impartiality of the rain visits all lands alike, yet by one and the same operation of the showers that land which has been tilled produces useful fruits with a blessing to its diligent and useful cultivators, whereas that which by the idleness of its cultivators has become hardened brings forth thorns and thistles. Let us therefore take those signs and mighty works which were done by God to be as it were showers provided by him from above. But the purpose and desires of men must be taken to be the land, whether tilled or untilled, which is of one nature as land compared with land, but not of one and the same degree of cultivation.

It follows from this[1] that the will of each person is either hardened by the mighty and wonderful works of God, if it is untilled and fierce and barbarous, so that it becomes

---

[1] This sentence is not in the Greek text as we have it in the *Philocalia*. Robinson (ed. *Philocalia*, Int., p. XXXIII) regards it as a summary of the preceding argument, due to Rufinus alone. Koetschau (see note *ad. loc.*) thinks it is not an addition by Rufinus.

GREEK   LATIN

more savage and thorny than ever, or else it becomes softer and brings itself into obedience with the whole mind, if it has been cleansed from its faults and carefully trained.

11. So, too, if the sun were to utter a voice and say, 'I melt things and dry them up,' when being melted and being dried up are opposites, he would not be speaking falsely in regard to the point in question, since by the one heat wax is melted and mud dried. Thus the one operation which was performed through Moses revealed the hardness of Pharaoh on the one hand, the result of his wickedness, and on the other hand the persuasibility of the mixed Egyptian multitude who joined the Hebrews when they departed.

11. But to prove the matter more clearly it will not be superfluous to employ yet another illustration. For instance, suppose one were to say that the sun binds and loosens, when binding and loosening are opposites. The statement will not, however, be false, for the sun, by one and the same power of its heat, loosens wax and yet dries up and binds together mud. Not that its power operates one way on mud and another way on wax, but that mud is of one quality and wax of another, though indeed according to nature they are one thing because each comes from the earth. So therefore one and the same operation of God, which worked through Moses in signs and wonders, revealed on the one hand the hardness of Pharaoh, which he had developed by the intensity of his wickedness, and on the other hand proclaimed the obedience of those other Egyptians who were mingled among the Israelites and are said to have gone out of Egypt along with them.

And the briefly recorded fact that the heart of Pharaoh experienced a kind of softening when he said: 'But ye shall not proceed far; ye shall go a three days' journey and leave your wives behind',[1] and whatever

Moreover, in regard to the passage which implies that the heart of Pharaoh was gradually being softened, so that on one occasion he said, 'Ye shall not proceed far; ye shall go a three days' journey, but ye shall leave

---

[1] See Exod. VIII. 27, 28.

GREEK

else he spoke when yielding before the marvellous works, makes it clear that these signs had some effect even on him, though they did not entirely accomplish their object. Yet not even this would have happened if the idea held by most people about the words, 'I will harden Pharaoh's heart', rightly represented what was wrought by him, that is, by God.[2]

It is not unreasonable to soften down such expressions even from our common manner of speech.[3] For kind masters often say to servants who have been spoiled by their kindness and forbearance, 'It was I who made you wicked', or 'I am to blame for these serious offences'. We must give heed to the character and force of what is said and not misrepresent it through failing to understand the meaning of the expression.

LATIN

your wives and your children and flocks behind',[1] and any other passages there may be in which he appears to be yielding gradually before the signs and wonders, what else do these indicate except that the power of the signs and wonders had some effect on him, although it did not achieve so much as it ought? For if the hardening had been of such a kind as most people think, we should certainly not have found him yielding even in a few points.[2]

It will not, I think, appear unreasonable to explain even from our common usage the turn and figure of speech which is associated with the expression 'hardening'.[3] For kind masters are often wont to say to servants who have grown more insolent and wicked as a result of patient and gentle treatment, 'It was I who made you this; I have spoiled you; my patience has made you good for nothing; I am the cause of your hard and worthless character, because I do not at once punish you for every single fault according to your deserts.' We must first take note of the turn and figure of the speech

---

[1] See Exod. VIII. 27, 28; X. 9, 11.

[2] Origen deals again with the subject of the 'hardening of Pharaoh's heart' in his *Comm. in Exodum* Ch. X. 27. This is preserved in the *Philocalia*, Ch. XXVII. (ed. Robinson, p. 242). The passage, Origen says, presented great difficulty to many readers. Some thought that God had mercy on some and hardened others purely at random. Others felt that here was one of the mysteries which no ingenuity could penetrate, but which must be accepted by faith. Others went further and supposed two Gods, a just one and a good one. Origen's own solution lies in the thought that God, like a good physician, works for the salvation of all, though sometimes by painful remedies.

[3] This argument is repeated in the *Comm. in Exod.* (see *Philocalia*, Ch. XXVII., ed. Robinson, p. 252, 18 ff.).

GREEK   LATIN

and so come to understand the force of the expression, and not misrepresent a word whose inner meaning we have not carefully investigated.

Accordingly Paul, after clearly examining this question, says to the sinner: 'Or despisest thou the riches of his goodness and forbearance and long suffering, not knowing that the goodness of God leadeth thee to repentance? but after thy hardness and impenitent heart treasurest up for thyself wrath in the day of wrath and revelation of righteous judgment of God'.[1] Now let that which the apostle says to the sinner be applied to Pharaoh, and it will be perceived to be entirely appropriate when addressed to him who 'according to his hardness and impenitent heart was treasuring up for himself wrath', since his hardness would not have been thus proved and made manifest unless the signs had been performed, and performed on so large and grand a scale.

Accordingly Paul the apostle, when clearly dealing with this question, says to the man who remained in sin: 'Or despisest thou the riches of his goodness and forbearance and longsuffering, not knowing that the goodness of God leadeth thee to repentance? but, after thy hardness and impenitent heart treasurest up for thyself wrath in the day of wrath and revelation of the righteous judgment of God'.[1] Let us then take that which the apostle says to the man who lives in sin and apply it to Pharaoh, and see whether you will not find it appropriate when spoken concerning him, for he, 'according to his hardness and impenitent heart,' treasured and stored up for himself 'wrath in the day of wrath', since his hardness would never have been thus proved and made manifest unless signs and wonders of such number and grandeur had followed.

12. But since such statements are hard to believe and are considered to be forced, let us see from the words of the prophets also what is said by those who have experienced the great kindness of God and have lived a good life, but have afterwards fallen into sin. 'Why didst thou make us to err, O Lord, from thy way? Why didst thou harden our heart that we should

12. But if the proofs which we have adduced seem insufficient and the apostolic illustration to be lacking in strength, let us bring forward in addition the witness of prophetic authority and see what the prophets declare about those who by living a good life at the first have deserved to receive very many proofs of God's goodness, but afterwards, as men do, have

[1] Rom. II. 4, 5.

GREEK

not fear thy name? Return for thy servants' sake, the tribes of thine inheritance, that for a little while we may inherit thy holy mountain.'[1] And in Jeremiah: 'Thou didst deceive me, O Lord, and I was deceived; thou wast stronger and didst prevail',[2]

Now the sentence, 'Why didst thou harden our heart, that we should not fear thy name?' spoken by those who are praying for mercy, is spoken in a special sense as follows. Why didst thou spare us so long, not visiting us for our sins, but abandoning us until our transgressions have grown to greatness?

For God abandons most men by leaving them unpunished, in order that from the things that lie within our power the character of each person may be proved

LATIN

fallen into sin. The prophet, making himself one with them, says, 'Why, Lord, didst thou make us to err from thy way? And why didst thou harden our heart that we should not fear thy name? Return for thy servant's sake, the tribes of thine inheritance, that we, too, may receive for a little while some inheritance of thy holy mountain.'[1] And Jeremiah speaks in the same way: 'Thou didst deceive us, O Lord, and we were deceived; thou hast held us and hast prevailed.'[2]

Now the sentence, 'Why, Lord, didst thou harden our heart, that we should not fear thy name', spoken by those who were praying for mercy, must be taken in a special sense, as if it said, Why hast thou spared us so long and not visited us when we sinned, but hast abandoned us, so that our wickedness has grown greater and our freedom to sin has extended because thy punishment ceased? For so a horse,[3] if it does not continually feel the spur of its rider and have its mouth rubbed by the rough bit, becomes hardened. So a young lad, if not continually subdued by flogging, will grow up into an insolent youth, a ready prey to vices.

God therefore abandons and neglects those whom he judges to be unworthy of chastisement. 'For whom the Lord loveth he chasteneth and punisheth; and

---

[1] Is. LXIII. 17, 18.   [2] Jerem. XX. 7.
[3] The illustrations of the horse and the lad are apparently added by Rufinus.

GREEK

and the better ones may become manifest as a result of the test applied to them; while the others remain unnoticed, not indeed by God, for he knows all things before they come to be,[1] but by the rational creation and themselves, in order that they may find the way of healing at a later time; for they would not have known the benefit, unless they had condemned themselves.

This method is of advantage to each, that he may become aware of his own individual

LATIN

scourgeth every son whom he receiveth'.[2] We must suppose from this that those men are already received into the rank and affection of sons, who have deserved to be scourged and punished by God in order that through endurance of trials and tribulations they may be able to say in their own persons, 'Who shall separate us from the love of God which is in Christ Jesus? Shall tribulation or anguish or famine or nakedness or peril or sword?'[3] For through all these is brought out and made manifest the will of each person; and the steadfastness of his perseverance is indicated, not so much to God, who knows all things before they come to be,[1] as to the rational and heavenly powers, who have been appointed as it were helpers and servants of God in the work of bringing to pass the salvation of men.[4] As for the others, who do not yet offer themselves to God with such constancy and affection and are not ready to yield themselves to his service and prepare their souls for trial, these are said to be abandoned by God, that is, not to be instructed, since they are not ready for instruction, their treatment and healing being undoubtedly reserved for a later time.

For these indeed do not know what they obtain from God, unless they first come to the

---

[1] See Susanna V. 42; Ecclus. XLII. 18.

[2] Heb. XII. 6. This quotation and the one that follows are added by Rufinus.

[3] Rom. VIII. 35.   [4] See Bk. I. Ch. VIII. 1 (p. 66 above).

GREEK   LATIN

nature and of the grace of God. The man who is not aware of his own weakness and of the divine grace, even if he receives a benefit before he has had experience of himself or condemned himself, will think that what is supplied to him by the grace of heaven is due to his own good works. This produces conceit and pride, and will prove a cause of his downfall, as we believe happened in the case of the devil, who attributed to himself the privileges which he enjoyed when he lived blamelessly. 'For every one that exalteth himself shall be humbled, and he that humbleth himself shall be exalted.'[1] And observe that for this reason divine things 'have been hidden from the wise and understanding',[2] in order that, as the apostle says, 'no flesh should glory before God',[3] and have been 'revealed unto babes',[4] who after their babyhood have risen to higher things and have remembered that it is not from their own effort so much as from the unspeakable goodness of God that they have reached the uttermost limit of blessedness.

point of desiring to obtain a benefit; which will only happen thus, when a man has previously learned to know himself and to feel what is lacking in himself and to understand from whom he should and can seek the supply of what is lacking. For he who does not first understand his infirmity and sickness is unable to seek a physician; or at any rate the man who has not learned the dangerous nature of his illness will not be grateful to the physician when he has recovered his health. So, too, if a man has not first learned the defects of his soul and the wickedness of his sins and confessed them openly with his own mouth he cannot be cleansed and absolved; otherwise he might be unaware that what he receives is a gift of grace and might think that the divine liberality was a blessing that belonged to him. This would undoubtedly give rise again to arrogance and pride of heart and become once more the cause of his downfall, as we must believe happened in the case of the devil, who thought that the privileges which he enjoyed when he lived blamelessly were his own and not given to him by God. And in him was fulfilled the saying that 'every one that exalteth himself shall be humbled'.[1] It is for this reason, it seems to me, that the divine mysteries

---

[1] St. Luke XIV. 11, XVIII. 14.
[2] St. Matt. XI. 27; St. Luke X. 21.
[3] 1 Cor. I. 29.   [4] St. Matt. XI. 27; St. Luke X. 21.

GREEK

LATIN

have been 'hidden from the prudent and wise',[2] in order, as the scripture says, 'that no flesh should glory before God',[3] and have been 'revealed unto babes'[2], that is, to those who, after becoming infants and babes, or in other words returning to the simplicity of babes, then make progress, and when they reach perfection remember that they have obtained their blessedness not so much by their own virtues as by the grace and mercy of God.

13. The man who is abandoned is abandoned therefore by the divine judgment, and towards certain sinners God is longsuffering, not without reason, but because in regard to the immortality of the soul and the eternal world it will be to their advantage that they should not be helped quickly to salvation but should be brought to it more slowly after having experienced many ills. For physicians also,[1] even though they may be able to heal a man quickly, yet act in a contrary way whenever they suspect the existence of a hidden poison in the body. They do this because they wish to heal the patient more surely, considering it better to let him remain in his fever and sickness for a long time in order that he may regain permanent health, rather than appear to restore him quickly to strength and afterwards to see him relapse and this quicker cure prove only temporary.

13. The man therefore who must needs be abandoned is abandoned by the judgment of God, and God is longsuffering towards certain sinners, though not without a definite reason. For this very fact that he is longsuffering makes for their advantage, since the soul, whose healing and oversight are his concern, is immortal; and being an immortal and eternal thing it is not, even though it be not quickly healed, thereby shut out from salvation, which is only delayed until more convenient times. Moreover it is perhaps expedient for those who have been more deeply infected with the passion of wickedness to attain salvation slowly. For physicians also,[1] when they could very quickly cover the scars of a wound, yet sometimes prevent and defer its immediate healing with a view to ensuring better and sounder health; since they know that it

---

[1] See Origen, *Philocalia*, Ch. XXVII. (ed. Robinson, p. 246, 24 ff. and 251, 22 ff.), and p. 176 above.

[2] St. Matt. XI. 27; St. Luke X. 21.   [3] 1 Cor. I. 29.

GREEK   LATIN

is preferable to cause delay in wounds that fester, and to allow the malignant humour to flow for a while, rather than to hasten to a superficial cure and to shut up within the veins the inflamed and poisonous matter, which when cut off from its usual outlets will undoubtedly creep into the interior of the body and penetrate to the vital parts themselves, so as to bring on not merely bodily disease but actual loss of life.

In the same way God, who knows the secrets of the heart and foreknows the future, perhaps in his longsuffering allows the hidden evil to remain while he draws it out by means of external circumstances, with the object of purifying him who owing to carelessness has received into himself the seeds of sin, that having vomited them out when they come to the surface the sinner, even though he has proceeded far in evil deeds, may in the end be able to obtain purification after his evil life and be renewed. For God deals with souls not in view of the fifty years, so to speak, of our life here, but in view of the endless world.[1] He has made our intellectual nature immortal and akin to himself, and the rational soul is not shut out from healing, as if this life were all.

In the same way also God, who knows the secrets of the heart and foreknows the future, in his great longsuffering allows some things to happen which, coming upon men from without, encourage the passions and faults that are concealed within to emerge and proceed into the light, so that by means of these events men who owing to great negligence and carelessness have received into themselves the roots and seeds of sin may be purified and healed, the seeds being cast up and brought to the surface in order that they may be in a manner vomited forth and dispersed. And thus, even though a man may appear to be involved in very serious evils, suffering convulsions in all his members, he may yet be able in the end to obtain rest and relief, to reach the limit of satiety in his evils and so after many troubles to be restored to his original state. For God deals with souls not in view of the short time of our life here, which is confined to some sixty

[1] See Bk. I. Ch. VI. 3 (p. 57 above).

GREEK   **LATIN**

or a few more years, but in view of the everlasting and eternal age, exercising his providential care over souls that are immortal, just as he himself is eternal and immortal.[1] For he made our rational nature, which he created 'in his own image and likeness',[2] incorruptible, and therefore the soul, which is immortal, is not shut out by the shortness of our present life from the divine healing and remedies.

14. Come then, and let us use the following illustration from the gospel. There is a certain rock, whose surface is covered with a little earth, into which if seeds fall they spring up quickly; but having sprung up, because they have no root, 'when the sun arises they are scorched and wither away'.[3] Now this rock is the soul of man, hardened through carelessness and made stony through evil. For no one's heart was created stony by God, but it becomes such from wickedness.

14. But let us take from the gospels also some illustrations of the matters we speak about. It is related that there is a certain rock covered with a small and scanty depth of earth, into which if seed falls it is said to spring up quickly; but after it has sprung up, because it does not take root deeply, the plant is said 'to be scorched and to wither away' when the sun arises.[3] Now this rock undoubtedly stands for the soul of man, hardened through its own carelessness and made stony by wickedness. For no one has a 'stony heart' created by God, but each person's heart is said to become stony through his own wickedness and disobedience.

If then one were to criticize the farmer for not casting his seed more quickly on the rocky ground, when one saw that other rocky ground which has received seed was flourishing, the farmer would reply: 'I shall sow this ground more slowly, putting in seeds that will be

If then one were to criticize the farmer for not casting his seed more quickly on the rocky ground when one saw that other rocky ground which had received seed was quickly flourishing, the farmer would certainly say in reply: 'I sow this land more slowly for this

[1] See Bk. I. Ch. VI. 3 (p. 57 above).   [2] See Gen. I. 26.
[3] See St. Matt. XIII. 5, 6 and parallels.

GREEK

able to endure, the slower method being better for this ground and safer than is the case with the ground which has received its seed more quickly but superficially'; and we should agree that the farmer spoke reasonably and had acted like a wise man. So, too, the great Farmer of all nature delays the benefit which we should consider quick, for fear lest it should prove superficial.

But it is likely that some one will meet us with the objection, 'Why does some of the seed fall upon the soul that has the superficial soil, that which is as it were a rock?' To this we must answer that it was better for the soul that desired the higher things too hastily and not by the way that led to them to obtain what it desired, in order that when it had condemned itself for this it might patiently endure to receive a long time afterwards the cultivation that is in accordance with nature.

LATIN

reason, that it may retain the seeds it has received. For it is better for ground like this to be sown later, lest perhaps the crop should spring up too rapidly, and coming from the very top of a thin soil should be unable to endure the heat of the sun'. Would not he who at first criticized now acknowledge the reason and skill of the farmer and agree that what formerly seemed to him illogical was in fact done with good reason? In the same way therefore God, who is a most skilful farmer of his entire creation, prevents and delays, undoubtedly till some future time, the restoration of health in cases where we think it should be more quickly restored, for fear lest the cure should prove superficial rather than internal.

But if some one meets us with the objection, 'Why do certain seeds fall upon the rocky ground, that is, upon a hard and rocky soul?' we must answer to this that not even such an event can take place apart from the ordering of divine providence; for unless by this means a knowledge was gained of the great self-condemnation which follows a heedlessness in hearing and a wickedness in examining the divine commands, it would certainly be unknown what useful purpose was served by an orderly training. And so it comes to pass that the soul becomes aware of its fault and casts the blame upon itself and reserves and yields itself up for the process of cultivation that is to follow; that is, the soul sees

GREEK

LATIN

For souls are, so to speak, innumerable, and their habits are innumerable, and equally so are their movements, their purposes, their inclinations and their impulses, of which there is only one perfect superintendent, who has full knowledge both of the times and the appropriate aids and the paths and the ways, namely, the God and Father of the universe. He knows how by means of the great plagues and the drowning in the sea he is leading even Pharaoh; and his superintending care for him does not stop at this point. For when he was drowned he was not destroyed. 'For in the hand of God are both we and our words, and all understanding and knowledge of crafts'.[1] This, then, is a fair defence of the statement that 'Pharaoh's heart was hardened'[2] and of the other statement that 'he hath mercy on whom he will, and whom he will he hardeneth'.[3]

for itself that its faults must first be removed and that it must then undergo instruction in wisdom.

Since, therefore, souls are innumerable, and equally so are their habits, their purposes, their different individual movements, their inclinations and impulses, the variety of which is quite beyond the capacity of the human mind to consider, we must accordingly leave the skill and power and knowledge necessary for their superintendence to God alone, for he only can know the remedies for each individual soul and determine the time for its healing. He, then, who alone, as we have said, is acquainted with the ways of each mortal man, knows by what way he ought to lead even Pharaoh, 'in order that through him his name might be named in all the earth,'[4] chastising him with many plagues and then leading him on to be drowned in the sea. And we must certainly not think that in this drowning the providential care of God for Pharaoh came to an end; for we must not suppose that, because he was drowned, he went immediately out of existence. 'For in the hand of God are both we and our words, and all understanding and knowledge of crafts',[1] as the scripture says. These, then, are the arguments we put forth to the best of our ability, in discussing the passage of scripture in which God is said to have hardened Pharaoh's

---

[1] Wis. VII. 16.
[3] Rom. IX. 18.

[2] See Exod. X. 20.
[4] See Rom. IX. 17 (Exod. IX. 16).

GREEK   LATIN

heart,[2] and the other statement that 'he hath mercy on whom he will and whom he will he hardeneth'.[3]

15. Let us also look at Ezekiel's statement in which he says, 'I will take away from them their stony hearts and I will put in them hearts of flesh, that they may walk in my judgments and keep my ordinances'.[1] Now if God, when he wills, 'takes away the hearts of stone' and implants 'hearts of flesh', so that men keep his ordinances and observe his commandments, it is not in our power to put away wickedness, for the taking away of 'hearts of stone' is nothing else than the removal, from him for whom God wills it, of the wickedness by reason of which a man is hardened. And the insertion of a 'heart of flesh', in order that a man may 'walk in the ordinances of God and keep his commandments', what else is this than to become yielding and unopposed to the truth and to be capable of practising the virtues?

But if God promises to do this, and if we do not lay aside our 'stony hearts' before he takes them away, it is clear that it is not in our power to put away wickedness. And if we ourselves do nothing to implant within us the 'heart of flesh', but it is the work of God, then to live a virtuous life will not be our work, but something due entirely to the divine grace.

15. Let us now also look at the statement of Ezekiel in which he says, 'I will take away from them their stony heart and I will put in them a heart of flesh, that they may walk in my judgments and keep my ordinances.'[1] Now if God, when he wills, takes away the 'heart of stone' and puts in a 'heart of flesh', so that men may keep his ordinances and observe his commandments, it will be seen that it is neither in our power to put away wickedness—for the taking away of a 'heart of stone' would appear to be nothing else than the removal, from him for whom God wills it, of the wickedness by which a man is hardened—nor to insert a 'heart of flesh', that a man may 'walk in God's ordinances and keep his commandments', which indeed is nothing else but to become obedient to God and unopposed to the truth and capable of practising the virtues.

If then God promises to do this, and if, before he takes away our 'stony heart' we are not able of our own selves to lay it aside, it follows that it is not in our power to cast off wickedness, but in God's. And again, if it is not by our own act that there comes into us the 'heart of flesh', if it is the work of God alone, then to live a virtuous life will not be our work,

---

[1] Ezek. XI. 19, 20.   [2] See Exod. X. 20.   [3] Rom. IX. 18.

GREEK

LATIN

but in all respects the work of God's grace.

Now this is what will be said by the man who, arguing from the bare words, would destroy our free will. We, however, shall reply that these words must be understood in the following manner. It is as when a man who suffers from ignorance and want of education, and becomes conscious of his personal defects either from the exhortation of his teacher or from his own reflection, entrusts himself to one whom he believes to be capable of leading him on to education and virtue. When he so entrusts himself, his instructor promises to take away his lack of education and to implant in him education, not as if it counted for nothing in regard to his being educated and escaping from his ignorance that he should have brought himself to be cured, but because the instructor promises to improve one who desires improvement.

Now this is what is said by those who wish to prove by the authority of scripture that nothing lies within our own power. We shall reply to them that these words must not be understood in that sense, but as follows. It is as if an uneducated and uninstructed man, becoming conscious of the disgrace of his condition, whether by being stirred at the exhortation of another or by a desire to rival those who are wise, should entrust himself to one by whom he is confident that he can be carefully trained and competently instructed. If then he, who had formerly hardened himself in ignorance, entrusts himself, as we have said, with full purpose of mind to a master and promises to obey him in everything, the master, on seeing clearly his purpose and determination, will on his part undertake to take away from him his lack of education and to implant in him education, not promising, however, to do this if the disciple withholds his assent and co-operation[1] but only if he offers and pledges himself to entire obedience.

So the divine word promises to take away the wickedness which it calls a 'stony heart', from those who come to it, not if they are unwilling, but if they submit themselves to the physician of the sick; just as in the gospels the sick are found coming to the Saviour and asking

So, too, the divine word promises to take away the 'stony heart' from those who come to it, not indeed from those who do not listen to it, but from those who submit to the precepts of its teaching; just as in the gospels we find the sick coming to the Saviour, asking

[1] Rufinus has misunderstood the Greek.

GREEK

to obtain healing and being healed. And, so to speak, to give sight to the blind is,[1] so far as concerns the request of those who believe they can be healed, a work of the sufferers, but so far as concerns the restoration of sight it is a work of our Saviour. This then is the way by which the word of God promises to implant knowledge in those who come to it, taking away the stony and hard heart, which signifies wickedness, to enable them to walk in the divine commandments and to keep the divine ordinances.

16. After this there is the passage from the gospel, where the Saviour said that he spoke to those that are without in parables for this reason, that 'seeing they may not see and hearing they may not understand, lest they should turn and it should be forgiven them'.[2] Now our opponent will say : 'If when they have heard a clearer message some people certainly do turn, and turn in such a way as to become worthy of the forgiveness of sins, and if the hearing of this clearer message does not rest with them but with their teacher, and he does not proclaim it to them for this reason, lest they should see and understand, then salvation does not lie in their power; and if this is so, we are not free as regards salvation and destruction'.

LATIN

to obtain health and so being healed. And when, for example, the blind are healed[1] and receive sight, it is, so far as concerns the fact that they made request to the Saviour and believed that they could be healed by him, a work of those who were healed; but so far as concerns the fact that their sight was restored, it is a work of the Saviour. In this way also does the divine word promise to give instruction by taking away the stony heart, that is, by banishing wickedness, in order that men may thus be able to walk in the divine ordinances and keep the commandments of the law.

16. After this there comes before us the passage from the gospel, where the Saviour said, 'For this reason I speak to them that are without in parables', 'that seeing they may see and not perceive, and hearing they may hear and not understand, lest haply they should be turned and it should be forgiven them'.[2] In regard to this our opponent will reply: 'If they who hear more clearly are certainly corrected and turned, and turned in such a way as to become worthy of the forgiveness of sins, and if the hearing of this clear message does not rest with them but entirely with their teacher, whose work it is to teach them more openly and clearly, but who says that he does not preach the word to them clearly for this reason,

---

[1] See St. Matt. XI. 5.
[2] See St. Matt. X. 10, 13; St. Mark IV. 11, 12; St. Luke VIII. 10.

GREEK

Now there would be a convincing answer to this, if it were not for the addition, 'lest they should turn, and it should be forgiven them'; namely, that the Saviour did not wish those who would not become noble and good to understand the deeper mysteries, and that this was why he spoke to them in parables. But as it stands, with the words 'lest they should turn, and it should be forgiven them', the answer is more difficult.

In the first place we must note the passage as an argument against the heretics,[1] who hunt out similar passages from the Old Testament, in which there is revealed, as they are bold enough to say, the cruelty of the Creator or his revengeful and punitive attitude, or whatever they choose to call the quality in question, in regard to the wicked; their sole purpose being to deny that there is any goodness in him who formed the world. With the New Testament, however, they do not deal in a similar way, nor even candidly, but pass over statements closely resembling those which they consider open to criticism in the Old Testament.

LATIN

"lest haply they should hear and understand and be turned" and be saved, then their salvation will certainly not rest with themselves; and if this is so, we shall have no freedom as regards either salvation or destruction.'

Now if it were not for the addition, 'lest they should be turned, and it should be forgiven them', there would be a very simple answer, namely, to say that the Saviour did not wish those whom he foresaw would not be good to understand the mysteries of the kingdom of heaven and that he spoke to them in parables on that account. But as it stands, with the addition, 'lest haply they should be turned, and it should be forgiven them', the explanation is rendered more difficult.

And in the first place we must note what a defence this passage furnishes against the heretics,[1] who are accustomed to hunt out from the Old Testament any expressions which may appear to them, as they understand them, to point to some severe and cruel quality in God the Creator, as when he is described as moved with the desire or whatever name they choose to call the quality in question, for vengeance or punishment; their object being to deny that there is any goodness in the Creator. In regard to the gospels, however, they do not pass judgment with the same mental bias or the same feeling, nor do they observe

[1] See Book II, Chs. IV. and V. (pp. 95 ff. above).

GREEK   LATIN

that some such passages as they
condemn and censure in the Old
Testament are to be found also
in the gospels.

For even according to the
gospel the Saviour is clearly
shown, as they themselves assert
in regard to the former writings,
to refrain from speaking plainly
on this account, lest men should
turn, and having turned should
become worthy of the forgiveness of sins; a statement which
of itself is in no way less than
the similar ones from the Old
Testament which are attacked.
If they seek for a defence of the
gospel statement, we must ask
them whether they are not to be
blamed for dealing in different
ways with similar problems; for
they do not take offence at the
New Testament but seek to defend it, whereas in regard to the
Old Testament, in similar passages which they ought to defend equally with those of the
New, they make an attack.
From these considerations we
shall force them to admit that
on account of their resemblances
the scriptures must all be regarded as coming from one God.
But come now, and let us provide, to the best of our ability,
a defence to the question before
us.

17. We said when investigating the case of Pharaoh that
sometimes it does not turn out
to the advantage of those who
are healed that they should be
healed quickly,[1] if, that is, they
have fallen of themselves into
difficulties and are then easily
released from the conditions into

For clearly in this chapter the
Saviour is shown, as they themselves say, not speaking openly
for this reason, lest men should
be turned and when turned
should receive forgiveness of
sins. Now certainly if this is
understood according to the
mere letter, it will be in no
way less than those passages
which are attacked in the Old
Testament. If, however, it
seems, even to them, to call for
an explanation, when passages
of such a sort are found in the
New Testament, it will follow
necessarily that the passages in
the Old Testament which are
attacked shall be cleared from
censure by a similar explanation,
so that by this means the
writings of each Testament may
be proved to come from one
and the same God. But let us
turn, to the best of our ability,
to the question before us.

17. We said before when discussing the case of Pharaoh
that sometimes it does not turn
out to advantage for one to be
healed quickly,[1] especially if the
disease be thereby shut up in the
internal organs and so rage
more fiercely. Therefore God,
who is the perceiver of secret

[1] See p. 181 above.

GREEK

which they have fallen; for despising the evil as being easy of cure and taking no precautions against falling into it they will find themselves in it a second time. In dealing with such persons, therefore, the eternal God, the perceiver of secret things, who knows all things before they come to be,[1] in his goodness refrains from sending them the quicker help and, if I may say so, helps them by not helping them, since this course is for their profit.

It is probable, then, that those 'who are without',[2] concerning whom we are now speaking, were foreseen by the Saviour, according to our supposition, as being not likely to prove steadfast in their conversion, if they were to hear more explicitly the message that was spoken. They were therefore destined by the Lord not to hear the deeper teachings more clearly, lest after having quickly turned and been healed by obtaining forgiveness they should despise the wounds of their wickedness as being slight and easy of cure and should very quickly fall into them again. Perhaps, too, though they had paid the penalty for their former sins which they committed against virtue when they abandoned her, they had not yet fulfilled the appropriate time in which to be themselves abandoned by the divine superintendence and to be filled more and more

LATIN

things and who knows all things before they come to be,[1] in his great goodness delays the healing of such persons and defers the remedy to a more distant time and, if I may say so, heals them by not healing them, lest a premature recovery of health should render them incurable.

It is possible, therefore, in regard to those whom the word of our Lord and Saviour addressed as being 'without',[2] that since he perceived by his power of 'searching the hearts and reins'[3] that they were not yet fit to receive his teaching in clearer terms, he covered up the deeper mysteries of the faith in veiled speech. For he feared that if they were speedily converted and healed, that is, if the forgiveness of their sins were quickly obtained, they might easily fall again into the same disease of sin which they had found could be cured without any difficulty. And if this should happen, no one can doubt that the penalty would be doubled and the quantity of evil continually increased, when there is not only a repetition of sins which had appeared to be forgiven, but even the court of virtue is polluted by the tread

---

[1] Susanna V. 42 and p. 179 above.
[2] St. Mark IV. 11; see 1 Cor. V. 13.
[3] Ps. VII. 10, Sept. (R. V. 9).

GREEK

with the particular evils whose
seeds they had sown and then
afterwards to be called to a more
enduring repentance, such as
would prevent them from quickly falling again into the sins into
which they had previously fallen
when they mocked at the high
worth of noble things and gave
themselves up to all that was
worse.

Those therefore who are
spoken of as being 'without',
plainly by comparison with those
'within',[2] are not altogether far
away from those within, since
while those within hear distinctly, they hear indistinctly
because it is spoken to them
in parables; nevertheless they
hear. But as for the rest of
those who are without, those
called the Tyrians, although it
was foreknown that 'they would
have repented long ago, sitting
in sackcloth and ashes',[3] had the

LATIN

of deceitful-minded and corrupted men, full within of hidden
wickedness. And what remedy
can there ever be for such
persons, who after partaking of
the impure and filthy food of
wickedness have tasted the
pleasure of virtue and received
its sweetness into their mouths
and have then turned over
again to the poisonous and
deadly food of iniquity? Who
doubts that it is better for them
to be put off and abandoned for
a time, in order that if one day
they should happen to have had
their fill of wickedness and be
able to shudder at the filthy
ways in which they now delight,
then at last the word of God
may be effectively revealed to
them, with the result that what
is holy is not given to the dogs
nor pearls cast before swine who
will trample them under their
feet and then turn round and
rend and attack those who have
preached to them the word of
God?[1]

These then are they who are
said to be 'without', doubtless
by comparison with those who
are said to be 'within'[2] and to
hear the word of God more
plainly. Those, however, who
are 'without' also hear the
word, although it is covered up
in parables and darkened by
proverbs. But there are others
besides those who are 'without',
those namely who are called
Tyrians, who do not hear at
all; and in spite of the fact that
the Saviour foreknew that 'they

---

[1] See St. Matt. VII. 6.   [2] See St. Mark IV. 11; 1 Cor. V. 12, 13.
[3] See St. Matt. XI. 21, 22; St. Luke X. 13.

GREEK

Saviour come within their borders, these do not even hear what the others hear, for the reason, probably, that they are much farther distant in respect of merit. The purpose is, however, that at some other time, after it has been 'more tolerable'[1] for them than for those who refused to receive the word, in whose presence he mentioned the Tyrians, these may find a more opportune moment to hear and may experience a more enduring repentance.

See, however, whether in addition to our investigation of the truth we are not striving even more to preserve in every way an attitude of piety towards God and his Christ, since we endeavour to explain completely how in passages of such importance and difficulty relating to the manifold providence of God he is taking thought for the immortal soul.

LATIN

would have repented long ago, sitting in sackcloth and ashes', 'if the mighty works had been done among them which were done among others',[2] yet still they do not hear, not even the things which those 'without' hear. The reason for this is, I believe, that the condition of these people was far inferior and worse in the matter of wickedness than that of those who are said to be 'without', that is, not far from those 'within', and who have deserved to hear the word though only in parables; and that probably their healing was reserved for the time when it will be 'more tolerable' for them 'in the day of judgment'[1] than for those among whom had been performed those mighty works which are recorded. Thus at last, relieved from the weight of their evil deeds they will walk more easily and enduringly in the way of salvation.

But I wish to remind those who read these pages of the following point, namely, that in dealing with most difficult and obscure passages like these we are striving with the utmost earnestness not so much to argue out clearly the solutions of the problems—for this every one will do as the Spirit gives him utterance[3]—but by the cautiousness of our statements to preserve the rule of piety.[4] It is our endeavour to show

---

[1] See St. Matt. XI. 22.
[2] See St. Matt. XI. 21, 22; St. Luke X. 13.   [3] Acts II. 4.
[4] The difference between Rufinus and Origen is well illustrated at this point. Origen is anxious to prove the absolute goodness of God; Rufinus to keep the reader in touch with the faith of the Church. See above Bk. I, Ch. V., 4 (p. 47) and Bk. III, Ch. I., 7 (p. 166).

that the providence of God which governs the universe with justice also rules immortal souls on the most equitable principles in accordance with the merits and motives of each individual. For God's dealings with men are not confined within the life of this age, but a previous state of merit always furnishes the cause of the state that is to follow; and so by an immortal and eternal law of equity and by the control of divine providence the immortal soul is brought to the height of perfection.

If, for instance, one were to inquire in reference to the things which are objected to, namely, that while those who saw wonders and heard divine words are not benefited, the Tyrians would have repented if such things had been done and spoken among them, and were to say, 'Why, pray, did the Saviour preach to such people to their hurt, in order that their sin might be accounted heavier?' —we should answer him thus: that he who knows the hearts of all who find fault with his providence on the ground that they did not believe because it had not given them the chance of seeing what it had allowed others to behold and had not arranged for them to hear what others had heard to their profit, in his desire to prove that the excuse was not reasonable gives them the things which they who blame his administration asked for. The intention is that after they have received these advantages and have been convicted

If, however, one were to attack us in reference to our statement that the word of the preaching was deliberately rejected by certain very depraved and wicked men, and to ask why it was preached to them when the Tyrians, who were certainly despised, are preferable in comparison, especially as the sin of these men was thereby increased and their condemnation rendered more serious by the fact that they heard the word and were not open to believe it, we must answer, it would seem, in the following manner. God, who knows the hearts of all, foreknew the complaints made about his providence particularly by those who say: 'How could we believe, when we neither saw what others saw nor heard what was preached to others? So far are we from being at fault, that those to whom the word was proclaimed and the signs displayed made no delay at all but amazed at the very power of

GREEK

none the less of the utmost impiety in that they have not even then given themselves up to be benefited, they may cease from such audacity, and when their minds have been set free on this point they may learn that God is sometimes long and slow in doing good to men, not allowing them to see and hear things, the seeing and hearing of which merely reveals their sin to be heavier and more grievous if after such great and wonderful experiences they do not believe.

18. Let us also look at the passage, 'So then it is not of him that willeth, nor of him that runneth, but of God that hath mercy'.[1] Now the objectors say: If it is not of him that willeth, nor of him that runneth, but of God that hath mercy, then salvation does not come

LATIN

the miracles became believers.' Wishing therefore to rule out all excuse for complaints of this sort and to show that it was not the delay of the divine providence but the will of each human mind that was the cause of its ruin, God conferred the grace of his benefits even upon unworthy and unbelieving men, in order that 'every mouth may be stopped'[2] and the mind of man may know that the failure is entirely on its own part and in no way due to him. At the same time, when he who has despised the divine benefits conveyed to him is condemned more severely than he who has not deserved to obtain them or hear of them at all, we may understand and know that this too is a mark of the divine mercy and of God's most equitable government, which sometimes delays to give men the opportunity of seeing or hearing the mysteries of the divine power, lest after the power of the miracles has been seen and the mysteries of his wisdom have been heard and known they should despise and neglect them and so be visited with a heavier punishment for this impiety.

18. Let us also look at the saying, 'It is not of him that willeth, nor of him that runneth, but of God that hath mercy'.[1] Now our opponents say: If it is not of him that willeth, nor of him that runneth, but that that man is saved on whom God has mercy, then

---

[1] Rom. IX. 16.

[2] Rom. III. 19.

GREEK

from what lies in our power but from the constitution we have received from him who constituted us what we are or from the will of him who has mercy when he pleases.

We must ask these persons the following question: Is it a good or a bad thing to will what is good? And is it a matter for praise or for blame that one should run with the desire to reach the goal in an eager haste for what is good? If they should say, for blame, they would be answering against all reason, since the saints will and run and clearly in this are doing nothing worthy of blame. But if they should say that it is a good thing to will the good and to run towards it we shall ask them how a lost nature can will better things. That would be like a bad tree bearing good fruit,[1] if to will better things is good. They may answer in a third way that to will the good and to run towards it is one of the things indifferent and neither good nor bad. To this we must reply that if to will the good and to run towards it is a thing indifferent, then the opposite of this, namely, to will the evil and to run towards that, is also a thing indifferent. But to will the evil and to run towards it is not a thing indifferent. Nor is it indifferent, therefore, to will the good and to run towards the good.

LATIN

salvation is not in our power. For either our nature is such that we can be saved or cannot be saved, or else it depends solely on the will of him who has mercy and saves us if he pleases.

We must first ask these persons the following question: Is it a good or a bad thing to will what is good? And is it a matter for praise or for blame that he who runs should eagerly haste to the goal of what is good? If they should say, for blame, they would clearly be mad; for all the saints will the good and run towards it and certainly they are not worthy of blame. What then if he who is not saved is of an evil nature, and wills the good and runs towards it but does not find it? For they say that a bad tree does not bear good fruit,[1] yet to will the good is good fruit, and how does the fruit of a bad tree become good? But if they should say that to will the good and to run towards it is a thing indifferent, that is, neither good nor bad, let us answer them: If to will the good and to run towards it is a thing indifferent, then the opposite of this, namely, to will the evil and to run towards that, will also be a thing indifferent. But it is certain that to will the evil and to run towards it is not a thing indifferent, but plainly a bad thing. It is clear, then, that to will the good and to run towards the good is not a thing indifferent, but a good thing.

See St Matt. VII. 18.

GREEK

LATIN

19. Such then is the explanation which I think we can offer in regard to the saying, 'So then it is not of him that willeth, nor of him that runneth, but of God that hath mercy'.[1] Now Solomon says in the Book of Psalms—for the Song of Ascents, from which we shall quote the words, is his—'Except the Lord build the house, they labour in vain that build it; except the Lord keep the city, the watchman waketh but in vain'.[2] In this he is not dissuading us from building or teaching us not to keep awake in order to guard the city in our soul, but he is showing us that what is built without God and what does not receive its guard from him is built in vain and protected to no purpose, since God may reasonably be regarded as the lord of the building and the Master of the universe as the ruler of the guard for the city.

So then, if we were to say, This building is not the work of the builder but of God, or, it is owing to the efforts not of the guard but of God the Ruler of all that this city has suffered no harm from its enemies, we should not be in error; it being understood that some part of the work had been done by man but that the happy result was to be gratefully attributed to God who brought it to pass.

19. Having then routed our opponents with the above answer let us hasten now to explain the passage in question, in which it says, 'It is not of him that willeth, nor of him that runneth, but of God that hath mercy'.[1] In the Book of Psalms in the Songs of Ascents, which are attributed to Solomon, it is written thus : 'Except the Lord build the house, they labour in vain that build it; except the Lord keep the city, the watchman waketh but in vain'.[2] By these words he is certainly not suggesting that we ought to cease from building or from keeping awake in order to guard that city which is within us, but he is showing us that what is built without God and what is guarded without God is built in vain and protected to no purpose. For in everything that is built well and preserved well the Lord is regarded as the author both of the building and of its safe preservation.

For example, if we were to see a splendid work such as a large and magnificent building reared with architectural beauty, should we not rightly and deservedly say that it was not constructed by human power but by divine help and influence. This, however, would not signify that the labour and toil of human endeavour had ceased and performed nothing at all. Or, again, suppose we were to see

---

[1] Rom. IX. 16.
[2] Ps. CXXVII. 1. The Psalms of Ascents were sung by pilgrims as they went up to the feasts at Jerusalem. See Exod. XXXIV. 24; I Kings XII. 27; Is. XXX. 29.

GREEK

In the same way, since human will is not sufficient to enable us to attain the end, nor is the running of those who are, as it were, athletes sufficient to enable them to gain 'the prize of the high calling of God in Christ Jesus'[1]—for these things are accomplished by God's assistance—it is well said that 'it is not of him that willeth, nor of him that runneth, but of God that hath mercy'.[2] Just as if one were to say about farming, as indeed it is actually written, 'I planted, Apollos watered, but God gave the increase; so that neither is he that planteth anything, nor he that watereth, but God that giveth the increase';[3] and we could not piously say that the production of full crops was the work of the farmer or the work of the waterer, but the work of God.

LATIN

a city hemmed in by a strict blockade of its enemies, with threatening engines brought up to its walls and a pressing attack made by means of a rampart with weapons, fire and all the other death-dealing instruments of war; then if the enemy should be repulsed and put to flight, it is right and proper for us to say that deliverance was granted by God to the liberated city. Yet by this we do not mean that the sentinels' night watches, the young men's readiness for battle and the guards' vigilance were lacking. The apostle must therefore be understood to have spoken in this sense, that the will of man is not by itself sufficient to the accomplishment of salvation, nor is any mortal running able to attain the heavenly promises and to receive 'the prize of the high calling of God in Christ Jesus',[1] unless this good will of ours and our ready purpose and whatever industry we may possess is both helped and strengthened by the divine assistance. The apostle therefore said very logically, 'It is not of him that willeth, nor of him that runneth, but of God that hath mercy',[2] just as if we were to say in connection with farming that which actually is written, 'I planted, Apollos watered, but God gave the increase; so that neither is he that planteth anything, nor he that watereth, but God that giveth the increase'.[3]

[1] Phil. III. 14.   [2] Rom. IX. 16.   [3] 1 Cor. III. 6, 7.

GREEK

LATIN

So, too, our perfection does not come to pass without our doing anything, and yet it is not completed as a result of our efforts, but God performs the greater part of it. And in order to produce a clearer conviction that this is the meaning of the passage we will take an illustration from the art of navigation. To what extent should we say that the navigator's art helps in bringing the ship back to the harbour, when compared with the force of the winds and the favourable state of the atmosphere and the shining of the stars, all of which co-operate to preserve those who sail? Why, even the sailors themselves from feelings of reverence do not often venture to claim that they have saved the ship but attribute it all to God; not that they have performed nothing, but that the efforts of God's providence are very much in excess of the effects of their art.

So indeed with our salvation the effects of God's work are very much in excess of the effects of what we can do.

As therefore when a field has brought forth good and rich crops to perfect maturity, no one could piously or logically say that the farmer made these fruits, but all would acknowledge that they were bestowed by God, so, too, our perfection is not effected while we rest and do nothing, nor on the other hand is its completion to be attributed to us, but rather to God, who performs the greater part of it. In the same way when a ship has escaped from the dangers of the sea, although the result is achieved by the exercise of much labour on the part of the sailors and by the complete use of the navigator's art, together with the diligence and industry of the pilot, the direction of the winds and the positions of the stars being also carefully noted, nevertheless when at last after being tossed by the waves and strained by the billows the ship reaches the harbour in safety, no one in his sober senses would attribute its safe return to anything but the mercy of God. Further, not even the sailors themselves nor the pilot would venture to say, 'I caused the ship to be saved', but they refer it all to the mercy of God; not that they suppose that they contributed nothing in the way of art or labour to the ship's safety, but that they know that while the labour was provided by them, the ship's safety was due to God.

So also in the journey of our life it is we who must expend labour and zeal and supply diligent toil, but the salvation which

GREEK

This, I believe, is the reason why it was said, 'It is not of him that willeth, nor of him that runneth, but of God that hath mercy' [1] For if we are to take the passage, 'It is not of him that willeth nor of him that runneth, but of God that hath mercy',[1] in the sense that our opponents suggest, the commandments are superfluous, and it is in vain when Paul himself blames some for having fallen away and approves of others for remaining steadfast and gives directions to the churches; it is useless, too, for us to yield ourselves up to willing what is better, useless also for us to try to run. But it is not in vain when Paul gives all his advice, and when he blames some and approves of others, nor is it in vain when we yield ourselves up to willing what is better and to desiring eagerly the things that are excellent. Our opponents, therefore have not rightly explained the meaning of the passage.

20. In addition to these there is the passage, 'To will and to work are of God'.[2] Now some say, If to will is from God, and to work is from God, then even if we will badly and work badly, these come to us from God; and if this is so, we have no free will. Again, when we will what is better and work deeds that are excellent, since to will and to work are from God it is not we who have done the excellent deeds; we seemed to do them, but it was God who bestowed

LATIN

is the fruit of our labour we must look to receive from God. Otherwise, if God demands none of our work, the commandments will certainly appear to be superfluous; and it is in vain when Paul himself blames some who have fallen away from the truth and praises others for standing fast in the faith, and to no purpose when he also delivers certain precepts and directions to the churches; in vain, too, that we ourselves either will or run towards the good. But it is certain that these things do not happen in vain, and it is certain that the apostles do not deliver precepts in vain, nor does the Lord give laws to no purpose. It remains then for us to declare that the vanity lies rather with the heretics, when they give a false meaning to these good words.

20. After this follows the question, that 'both to will and to work are of God.'[2] Now they say, If to will is from God, and to work is from God, then whether we will or work well or badly, it is from God; and if this is so, we have no free will.

[1] Rom. IX. 16.   [2] Phil. II. 13.

GREEK

LATIN

them on us, and so even in this we have no free will.

In reply to this we must say that the statement of the apostle does not assert that to will what is evil is of God or that to will what is good is of God; nor that to work deeds that are better or worse is of God; but to will in general and to work in general. For as we have it from God that we are living beings and that we are men, so also we have from him the power of willing in general, as I said, and the power of movement in general. And just as we, because we are living beings, possess the power of movement and can move, for instance, these limbs of ours, hands or feet, and yet we could not reasonably say that we have from God the particular power of moving to strike, or to destroy, or to take away another's goods, but what we received from God was the power of movement in general and it is we who use this power for the worse or for the better, so we have received from God the power of working, by virtue of our being living creatures, and from the Creator the power of willing, but it is we who use the power of willing either for the noblest purposes or for the opposite ones, and likewise the power of working.

21. Still, the saying of the apostle in the passage where he suggests an objection against himself will appear to tend to the conclusion that we are not possessed of free will. He says, 'So then he hath mercy on

To this we must reply that the statement of the apostle does not assert that to will what is evil is from God or that to will what is good is from God; nor that to work either good or evil is from God; but it says in a general way that 'to will and to work are of God'. For as we have it from God that we are men, that we breathe and that we move, so also we have from God the power of willing; just as if we were to say that our power of movement is from God, or the fact that each of our members performs its proper function and movements is from God. But it must certainly not be understood from this that if the hand moves, for instance, to strike someone unjustly or to steal, this is from God; for only the power of movement is from God, and it is our part to direct those movements, the power of exercising which we have from God, either to good or to evil purposes. Thus what the apostle says is, that we receive from God the power of willing, but it is we who use the will either for good or for evil desires. We must apply similar reasoning to our works.

21. But there is also the passage where the apostle said, 'So then he hath mercy on whom he will, and whom he will he hardeneth. Thou wilt say then unto me, Why doth he still find fault? For who

GREEK

whom he will, and whom he will he hardeneth. Thou wilt say then unto me, Why doth he still find fault? For who withstandeth his will? Nay but, O man, who art thou that repliest against God? Shall the thing formed say to him that formed it, Why didst thou make me thus? Or hath not the potter a right over the clay, from the same lump to make one part a vessel unto honour, and another unto dishonour?'[1]

Now someone will say, If, just as the potter from the same lump makes some vessels for honour and some for dishonour, so God makes some creatures for salvation and some for destruction, then salvation or destruction does not rest with us nor are we possessed of free will. We must ask the man who interprets the words thus, whether it is possible to imagine the apostle contradicting himself; and I do not believe that anyone will dare to say that it is. If then the apostle does not speak in contrary ways, how according to the man who accepts the passage in this sense is he reasonable in imputing blame to the fornicator at Corinth or to those who had fallen away and had not repented of the licentiousness and impurity of their deeds?[2] How, too, can he bless for having acted well those whom he praises, as for instance the house of Onesiphorus, in these words: 'The Lord grant mercy unto the house of Onesiphorus;

LATIN

withstandeth his will? Nay but, O man, who art thou that repliest against God? Shall the thing formed say to him that formed it, Why didst thou make me thus? Or hath not the potter a right over the clay, from the same lump to make one part a vessel unto honour, and another unto dishonour?'[1]

Now someone may perhaps say, If, just as the potter from the same lump makes some vessels for honour and some for dishonour, so God makes some men for salvation and some for destruction, then salvation or destruction does not rest with us; which makes it clear that we have no free will. We must reply therefore to those who interpret the words thus, and ask whether it is possible that the apostle could contradict himself. And if we cannot think this of the apostle, how according to them will it seem just for him to blame those at Corinth who had committed fornication, or those who had fallen away and had not repented of their deeds of licentiousness and fornication and impurity?[2] How, too, can he praise those who had acted rightly, as for instance the house of Onesiphorus, saying: 'The Lord grant mercy unto the house of Onesiphorus; for he oft refreshed me and was not ashamed of my chain; but when he came to

---

[1] Rom. IX. 18-21.   [2] See 1 Cor. V. 1-5; 2 Cor. XII. 21.

GREEK

for he oft refreshed me and was not ashamed of my chain; but when he was in Rome he sought me diligently and found me. The Lord grant unto him to find mercy of the Lord in that day.'[1] It is not like the same apostle to blame the sinner as if he was worthy of blame and to approve as if worthy of praise him who had acted well, and yet on the other hand to assert, as if nothing lay in our power, that it is due to the intention of the Creator that one vessel is made 'unto honour' and another 'unto dishonour'.

And in regard to the statement that 'we must all stand before the judgment seat of Christ, that each one may receive the things done in the body, according to what he hath done, whether it be good or bad',[2] how is this correct, if those who have done evil have come to this kind of conduct because they were created 'vessels of dishonour', and if those who have lived virtuously have done good because they were from the beginning fashioned for this purpose and are 'vessels of honour'?

And further, is there not a conflict between this view, which they gather from the words we have quoted, that it is due to the intention of the Creator that a vessel is honourable or the reverse, and the saying found elsewhere: 'In a great house there are not only vessels of gold and silver, but also of

LATIN

Rome he sought me diligently and found me. The Lord grant unto him to find mercy of the Lord in that day.'[1] It is not consistent with the seriousness of the apostle to blame the man who is worthy of blame, that is, the man who has sinned, and to praise the man who is worthy of praise for his good work, and on the other hand to say, as if it were in no one's power to do anything good or evil, that it is the Creator's doing that each man acts either well or ill, since he makes 'one vessel unto honour and another unto dishonour'.

And how could he also add the saying that 'we must all stand before the judgment seat of Christ, that each one of us may receive in his body according to what he has done, whether it be good or bad'?[2] For what return of good is due to him who could do no evil, because he was fashioned for good by the Creator? Or what penalty could properly be demanded of him who by the very act of his Maker was unable to do good?

Finally, is there not a contradiction between this assertion and what is said elsewhere: 'In a great house there are not only vessels of gold and of silver, but also of wood and of earth; and some unto honour, and some unto dishonour. If therefore a man purge himself from these, he shall be a vessel unto

---

[1] 2 Tim. I. 16-18. [2] 2 Cor. V. 10.

GREEK

wood and of earth; and some
unto honour, and some unto dishonour. If therefore a man purge
himself, he shall be a vessel
unto honour, sanctified and meet
for the master's use, prepared
unto every good work.'[1] For
if he who 'purges himself'
becomes a 'vessel unto honour',
and he who allows himself to
remain unpurged becomes a
'vessel unto dishonour', so far
as these words go the Creator
is in no way responsible. For
the Creator makes 'vessels of
honour and vessels of dishonour' not from the beginning
by his foreknowledge, since he
does not condemn or justify
beforehand by that, but he
makes those who purge themselves 'vessels of honour' and
those who allow themselves to
remain unpurged 'vessels of dishonour'; so that it comes from
causes older than the fashioning of vessels unto honour and
unto dishonour that one was
made 'unto honour' and another
'unto dishonour'.

22. But if we once admit[2]
that there are certain older
causes to account for the 'vessel
of honour' and the 'vessel of
dishonour', what is there absurd

LATIN

honour, sanctified and meet for
the master's use, prepared unto
every good work.'[1] If therefore a man purges himself, he
becomes a 'vessel unto honour';
but he who has disdained to
purge himself from his impuri-
ties becomes a 'vessel unto
dishonour'. In view of these
declarations the cause of our
deeds can by no means, in my
opinion, be referred to the
Creator. For God the Creator
makes some vessels 'unto
honour' and he makes other
vessels 'unto dishonour'; but it
is that vessel which has purged
itself from all impurity that he
makes a 'vessel unto honour',
while the one which has stained
itself with low vices he makes a
'vessel unto dishonour'. And so
we conclude from this that
the cause of each man's activities goes back into the past and
that each was made by God a
vessel of honour or of dishonour
in accordance with his merits.
Each vessel has therefore from
its own self provided the
Creator with the causes and
occasions in virtue of which it
was formed by him either 'unto
honour' or 'unto dishonour'.

22. But if this statement
appears to be just, as it certainly
is just and in harmony with all
piety, namely, that each vessel
is fashioned by God for honour

---

[1] 2 Tim. II. 20, 21.
[2] This paragraph is quoted by Jerome, *Ep. ad Avitum* 8. 'In the third
book also the following errors are found: If we once admit that it is from
previous causes that one vessel was created for honour and another for dishonour, why should we not recur to the secret history of the soul and conclude
that it is loved in one man and hated in another by reason of deeds long
past, in Jacob's case before he became a supplanter and in Easu's case
before his heel was grasped by his brother?'

GREEK

in our recurring to the subject of the soul and recognising that the older reasons why Jacob was loved and Esau hated lie with Jacob before he came into the body and with Esau before he entered Rebecca's womb?[1]

At the same time it is made quite clear in regard to their fundamental nature that just as it is one clay which is in the hands of the potter, from a lump of which come vessels 'unto honour and unto dishonour', so every soul in God's hands is of one nature and all rational beings come, if I may say so, from one lump, though certain older causes have made some to be for honour and others for dishonour.

But if the language of the apostle conveys a rebuke when he says, 'Nay but, O man, who art thou that repliest against God'[2] it probably teaches us that he who has confidence towards God by reason of his faithful and good life would not hear the words, 'Who art thou that repliest against God?' A man like Moses, for example—'for Moses spake, and God answered him with a voice';[3] and as God answers Moses, so also the saint answers God. But he who has

LATIN

or for dishonour as a result of pre-existing causes, it does not seem absurd for us, when discussing the older causes in the same order and by the same method, to apply the same principle to souls, and to believe that this was the reason why Jacob was loved even before he was born into this world, and Esau was hated while still enclosed in his mother's womb.[1]

Further, the saying that 'from the same lump' is made both a vessel of honour and one of dishonour will not cause us difficulty, for we say that there is one nature for all rational souls, just as one lump of clay is described as being in the hands of the potter. Since then there is one nature for all rational creatures, out of this one nature God formed and created, as the potter does out of one lump of clay, 'some men to honour and others to dishonour', in accordance with pre-existing grounds of merit.

But in regard to the apparent rebuke conveyed by the apostle's language when he says, 'O man, who art thou that repliest against God',[2] I think that what he teaches here is this, that such a rebuke does not refer to one who is faithful and lives a good and righteous life and has confidence towards God, that is, to a man like Moses, of whom the scripture says that 'Moses spake, and God answered him with a voice';[3] and as God answered Moses, so also the

---

[1] See Mal. I. 2, 3; Gen. XXV. 25, 26.   [2] Rom. IX. 20.
[3] Exod. XIX. 19.

GREEK

not obtained this confidence, for the clear reason that he is either lost or else makes these inquiries with a desire not to learn but to cause contention, and who says, 'Why doth he still find fault? For who withstandeth his will?' from such motives, this man would deserve the rebuke contained in the words, 'Nay but, O man, who art thou that repliest against God?'[1]

23. To those, however, who bring in diverse natures and use this passage in support we must answer as follows. If they retain the doctrine that the lost and the saved come 'from one lump'[2] and that the Creator of the saved is also the Creator of the lost, and if he who makes not only the spiritual but also the earthy is good (for this follows from their reasonings), it is none the less possible for one who has become at the present time a vessel of honour in consequence of certain former righteous deeds and yet has not acted similarly here nor in a way befitting a vessel of honour, to become in another age a vessel of dishonour; just as on the other hand it is possible for one who by reason of acts older than this life has become here a

LATIN

saint will answer God. But the man who is unfaithful and loses his confidence in answering before God by the unworthiness of his life and conduct, who makes these inquiries with a desire not to learn and advance, but to cause strife and contention, the kind of man who can say what the apostle indicates in the words, 'Why then doth he still find fault? For who withstandeth his will?'—this is the man to whom is rightly directed the rebuke conveyed by the apostle's words, 'O man, who art thou that repliest against God?'[1] This rebuke, then, is not for the faithful and the saints, but for the unfaithful and impious.

23. As for those, however, who bring in diverse natures of souls and adduce this statement of the apostle in support of their doctrine, we must answer them as follows. If they agree with us that the apostle says that both those who are made for honour and those who are made for dishonour, whom they call the persons of saved and of lost natures, come 'from one lump',[2] then the natures of souls will not be diverse, but there will be one nature for all. And if they admit that one and the same potter undoubtedly indicates one Creator, then there will not be different Creators for those who are saved and for those who are lost. Now let them choose whether they wish the passage to be interpreted as indicating a good God who creates evil and

---

[1] Rom. IX. 20.　　　　　　[2] Rom. IX. 21.

GREEK

vessel of dishonour to become, if he amends his ways in the 'new creation',[1] a 'vessel of honour sanctified and meet for the master's use, prepared unto every good work'.[2]

And perhaps the present Israelites will be deprived of their racial position for not having lived worthily of their noble birth, being changed as it were from vessels of honour into vessels of dishonour; while many of the present Egyptians

LATIN

lost men, or a God not good who creates men that are good and prepared for honour. The necessity of giving an answer will extract from them one of these two alternatives. But according to our contention that God makes vessels to honour or to dishonour by reason of pre-existing causes, the proof of God's righteousness is in no way compromised. For it is possible that one vessel, which from previous causes has in this world been fashioned for honour, may in another age, if it has acted carelessly here, become a vessel of dishonour in accordance with the deserts of its conduct; just as on the other hand if a man has from pre-existing causes been formed by the Creator as a vessel of dishonour in this life, and yet has amended his ways and purged himself from all his faults and low vices, he may in that new age become a 'vessel unto honour, sanctified and meet for the master's use, prepared unto every good work'.

Finally, those who were formed by God to be Israelites in this age, and have lived a life unworthy of their noble birth and fallen away from their high descent, will in the age to come, for their unbelief, be changed as it were from vessels of honour

---

[1] See Gal. VI. 15 (R. V. Marg.).

[2] Jerome translates the foregoing lines as follows. *Ep. ad Avitum* 8. 'And in another place: But according to us a vessel which has by reason of pre-existing merits been fashioned for honour may, if it fails to do work worthy of its title, become in another age a vessel of dishonour; and on the other hand a vessel which as a result of former sin has received a name of dishonour may, if in the present life it has willed to receive correction, become in the new creation a vessel sanctified and useful to the Lord, prepared unto every good work.'

GREEK

and Idumaeans who have come near to Israel[1] will, when they have borne more fruit, 'enter into the church of the Lord', no longer being reckoned as Egyptians or Idumaeans but for the future becoming Israelites.[2] Thus according to this view some men by the exercise of their wills make progress from worse to better, while others fall from better to worse; others, too, are preserved in their good deeds or rise from good to better, while others again continue in their evil deeds and, if the evil flows on, from being bad become still worse.

```
*     *     *     *     *
*     *     *     *     *
*     *     *     *    *⁵
```

LATIN

into vessels of dishonour; while on the other hand many who in this life have been reckoned among the Egyptian or Idumaean vessels but have embraced the faith and conduct of the Israelites shall 'enter into the church of the Lord' and exist as vessels of honour 'at the revelation of the sons of God.'[3] Thus it is more agreeable to the rule of piety[4] to believe that every rational creature, according to his will and conduct, is changed at one time from bad to good and at another falls from good to bad; that some continue in good, and some even advance to what is better and ever ascend to higher things until they reach the highest stage of all; while others continue in evil or, if the evil within them begins to overflow, go on to a worse condition and are at last overwhelmed in the lowest depths of wickedness. We must suppose from this that it is possible for some who have begun at first with small sins to be so given over to wickedness and to go to such lengths of evil that their iniquity equals even that of the oppos-

---

[1] The thought of connecting Egyptians with Idumaeans is suggested by 1 Kings XI. 14 ff and Deut. XXIII. 7, 8. See *Philocalia* Ch. XIII. 3.

[2] See Deut. XXIII. 7, 8.

[3] See Deut. XXIII. 7, 8; Rom. VIII. 19.   [4] See above p. 193.

[5] This paragraph was omitted, for obvious reasons, by the compilers of the *Philocalia*. It adds nothing new, and yet was likely to cause unnecessary offence by its detailed inferences from the preceding argument. Jerome has quoted it for the purposes of condemnation in his *Ep. ad Avitum* 8. 'And he (i.e. Origen) immediately adds: I think it possible for some men who have begun with small faults to reach such a degree of wickedness, if they refuse to change for the better and to amend their sinful life by penitence, that they even become opposing powers; and on the other hand for some so to apply a remedy to their wounds over long spaces of time and to check the offences that formerly flowed on that they pass to the condition

GREEK   LATIN

ing powers; and that on the
other hand, if, through many
severe punishments and most
bitter chastisements they are
able at last to recover their
senses and by degrees endeavour to find a remedy for their
wounds, they may when their
wickedness has ended be restored to what is good. This leads
us to the opinion that since, as
we have frequently said, the
soul is immortal and eternal, it
is possible that in the many and
endless periods throughout
diverse and immeasurable ages
it may either descend from the
highest good to the lowest evil
or be restored from the lowest
evil to the highest good.

24. In one place, then, the
apostle claims that it is not in
God's power whether we become
vessels unto honour or unto
dishonour, but he attributes it
entirely to us when he says, 'If
therefore a man purge himself,
he shall be a vessel unto honour,
sanctified and meet for the
master's use, prepared unto
every good work'.[1] In another
place, however, he claims that
it is not in our power, but
appears to attribute it entirely
to God when he says, 'The
potter hath a right over the
clay, from the same lump to
make one part a vessel unto
honour, and another unto dishonour'.[2]

24. Now the language of the
apostle, in the passage where he
speaks of vessels of honour or
dishonour, namely, 'if a man
purge himself, he shall be a
vessel unto honour, sanctified
and meet for the master's use,
prepared unto every good
work',[1] seems to put nothing in
God's power and everything in
ours. In the passage, however,
where he says, 'The potter hath
a right over the clay, from the
same lump to make one part a
vessel unto honour, and another
unto dishonour',[2] he appears to
attribute everything to God.

of the best. We have frequently said that in the infinite and unceasing
ages during which the soul remains in existence some are so carried downwards towards what is worse that they come to the last degree of evil,
while others make such progress that from the last degree of evil they reach
the perfection and consummation of virtue. In these words,' Jerome adds,
'he tries to prove that men, that is, souls, can become daemons, and that
on the other hand daemons may be restored to the dignity of angels.'

[1] 2 Tim. II. 21.   [2] Rom. IX. 21.

GREEK

Now these sayings of his are not contradictory, but must be taken together and one perfect explanation drawn from them both. It is, then, neither in our power to make progress apart from the knowledge of God, nor does the knowledge of God compel us to do so unless we ourselves contribute something towards the good result; nor does our power apart from the knowledge of God and the full use of the power that deservedly belongs to us cause a man to be created for honour or for dishonour; nor does the power of God by itself fashion a man for honour or for dishonour, but God finds a ground of difference in our will, as it inclines to the better or to the worse.

Let these arguments, which we have provided on the subject of free will, be sufficient.

LATIN

Now we must not take these passages to be contradictory to one another, but the meaning of each must be combined into one and a single interpretation drawn from the two; that is, that we are not to think that the things which are in the power of our will can be performed without the help of God, nor that those which are in God's hands can be brought to completion apart from our acts and earnest endeavours and purpose. For indeed we do not have it in our own will either to desire or to perform anything without being bound to recognize that this very power of desiring and performing was given to us by God, subject to the distinction which we spoke of above.[1] Nor again are we to think that when God fashions vessels, some for honour and some for dishonour, he regards our wills or purposes or merits as a cause of the honour or dishonour, as if they were a kind of matter out of which he may fashion each one of us either for honour or for dishonour. The truth is that the very movement of the soul and purpose of the mind of itself suggests to him, to whom the heart and the thoughts of the soul are not hidden, whether the vessel should be fashioned for honour or for dishonour.

But let these arguments, which we have discussed to the best of our ability on the questions that arise out of free will, be sufficient.

[1] See p. 201.

CHAPTER II

GREEK   LATIN

HOW THE DEVIL AND THE OPPOS-   THE OPPOSING POWERS.
ING POWERS ARE, ACCORDING TO
THE SCRIPTURES, AT WAR WITH
THE HUMAN RACE.[1]

LATIN

1. We must now see how, according to the scriptures, the opposing powers and the devil himself are engaged in a struggle with the human race, provoking and inciting men to sin. First, a serpent is described in Genesis as having seduced Eve;[2] and in regard to this serpent, in the Ascension of Moses, a book which the apostle Jude mentions in his epistle, Michael the archangel when disputing with the devil about the body of Moses says that the serpent was inspired by the devil and so became the cause of the transgression of Adam and Eve.[3] Further, the question is asked by some, who is the angel that speaks from heaven to Abraham and says, 'Now I know that thou fearest God, and for my sake hast not withheld thy beloved son, whom thou lovedst'.[4] For clearly it is an angel who is described and who says that he knew now that Abraham feared God and had not withheld his beloved son, as the scripture runs, yet he did not declare that it was for God's sake, but for his own sake, that is, for the sake of him who was speaking. We must also inquire who that being was of whom it is said in Exodus that he wished to kill Moses because he was setting out for Egypt.[5] And afterwards, who is it that is called the 'destroying angel',[6] and who also is he who in Leviticus is described as Apopompeus, that is, the Averter, of whom the scripture speaks thus: 'One lot for the Lord, and one lot for Apopompeus'?[7]

[1] The Greek title comes from Photius, *Bibl. Cod.* 8, p. 4.
[2] See Gen. III. 1-6.
[3] The Epistle of Jude (Ver. 9) alludes to the *Assumption* (Gr. *Analepsis* or *Anabasis*) *of Moses,* but does not mention its title. See Charles, *Assumption of Moses;* and the same author's *Apoc. and Pseudep. of O. T.* II. 421 ff.
[4] Gen. XXII. 12.   [5] See Exod. IV. 24.   [6] Exod. XII. 23.
[7] See Lev. XVI. 8. The true meaning of the Hebrew Azazel is unknown. He was an evil spirit dwelling in the wilderness, who was supposed to receive the sins of the people transmitted through the scape-goat on the day of Atonement. The Sept. renders it *Apopompeus,* the Vulgate simply describes the goat, *caper emissarius,* and Rufinus translates Origen's *Apopompeus* by the neutral *transmissor.* For want of a more suitable term I have used Gesenius' suggestion *Averter* (see Hastings' *Dic. of the Bible,* Art. Azazel, S. R. Driver, Vol. I, p. 208a), which probably indicates the true function of Azazel.

Further, in the first book of the Kings an evil spirit is said to suffocate Saul;[1] and in the third book Micaiah the prophet says, 'I saw the God of Israel sitting upon his throne, and all the host of heaven stood round about him on his right hand and on his left. And the Lord said, Who shall entice Ahab king of Israel, that he may go up and fall at Ramoth Gilead? And one said on this manner, and another said on that manner. And there came forth a spirit, and stood before the Lord and said, I will entice him. And the Lord said unto him, Wherewith? And he said, I will go forth, and I will be a lying spirit in the mouth of all his prophets. And he said, Thou shalt entice him, and shalt prevail also; go forth, and do so. And now the Lord hath put a lying spirit in the mouth of all thy prophets; and the Lord hath spoken evil concerning thee.'[2] This account clearly shows that a certain spirit by his own will and choice elected to entice and to practise deceit, and that God makes use of this spirit to compass the death of Ahab, who deserved that fate.

Also in the first book of the Chronicles it says, 'The devil raised up Satan in Israel, and moved David to number the people'.[3] In the Psalms an evil angel is said to persecute certain men.[4] In Ecclesiastes, too, Solomon says, 'If the spirit of one that hath power rise up against thee, leave not thy place, for healing will restrain many transgressions'.[5] And in Zechariah we read of the devil standing at Joshua's right hand and resisting him.[6] Isaiah also says that the sword of God rises up against 'the dragon, the crooked serpent'.[7] And what shall I say of Ezekiel, who in his second vision prophesies most clearly to the prince of Tyre about an opposing power and who says, too, that the dragon dwells in the rivers of Egypt?[8] And as for the entire book that is written about Job, what else does it contain but an account of the devil seeking for power to be given him over all Job's possessions, and over his sons, and finally over his body? He is conquered, however, through Job's patience. In this book the Lord has by his answers taught us much about the power of that dragon which opposes us. Let these examples from the Old Testament, so far as we can call

---

[1] See 1 Sam. XVIII. 10. As this verse is not in the Sept. it is impossible to say what word of Origen's it is that Rufinus translates by *offocare* (v. l. *effocare, suffocare*). The Vulgate has *invasit*.

[2] 1 Kings XXII. 19-23.

[3] See 1 Chron. XXI. 1. The passage has been confused with 1 Kings XI. 14, where 'Satan' means simply an adversary. This was probably Origen's meaning here, misunderstood by Rufinus.

[4] See Ps. XXXV. 5, 6.

[5] Eccles. X. 4. Rufinus' *sanitas* answers to the Greek ἴαμα healing. The meaning is probably, a healing spirit, as opposed to a spirit of provocation.

[6] See Zech. III. 1.   [7] See Is. XXVII. 1.

[8] See Ezk. XXIX. 3 and above Bk. I. Ch. V, 4 (p. 47).

them to memory at the moment, be now quoted to prove that the opposing powers are both named in the scriptures and are said to be adversaries of the human race and reserved for future punishment.

But let us look also at the New Testament, where Satan comes to the Saviour, tempting him;[1] and where evil spirits and impure daemons, which had taken possession of very many, were put to flight by the Saviour from the bodies of the sufferers, who are said also to have been set free by him.[2] Moreover, Judas, when the devil had now put it into his heart to betray Christ, afterwards received Satan wholly into himself; for it is written that 'after the sop Satan entered into him.'[3] Paul the apostle teaches us that we should not 'give place to the devil'[4] but, he says, 'Put on the armour of God, that ye may be able to stand against the wiles of the devil',[5] pointing out that the saints' wrestling 'is not against flesh and blood, but against principalities, against powers, against the rulers of this world's darkness, against spiritual hosts of wickedness in the heavenly places'.[6] Further, he says that the Saviour was crucified by 'the princes of this world', who are 'coming to nought', whose 'wisdom', he adds, he does not speak.[7] Through all these instances, therefore, the divine scripture teaches us that there are certain invisible enemies fighting against us, and it tells us that we must be armed to meet them. This leads the simpler sort of believers in Christ the Lord to suppose that all the sins that men have committed come from the persistent influence of the contrary powers on the sinners' minds, because in this invisible contest the powers are found to be superior. But if, so to speak, there were no devil, no man would ever sin at all.

2. We however, who look more carefully into the reason of things, do not think that this is so; especially when we consider the acts that arise clearly from the necessities of our body. Are we to suppose that the devil is the cause of our being hungry or thirsty? I suppose there is no one who would venture to maintain this. If then he is not the cause of our being hungry or thirsty, what of that condition when an individual has attained the age of puberty and this period has called forth the exciting movements of the natural heat? It follows without a doubt that, as the devil is not the cause of our being hungry or thirsty, so neither is he the cause even of that impulse which is naturally called forth at the time of maturity, that is, of the desire for sexual intercourse. It is certain that this impulse is by no means always aroused by the devil, so as to lead us to suppose that if there were no devil our bodies would not have the desire for such intercourse.

---

[1] St. Matt. IV. 1-11 and parallels.
[2] See St. Mark I. 23 ff., 32-34; V. 1 ff.
[3] See St. John XIII. 2, 27.   [4] See Eph. IV. 27.
[5] Eph. VI. 11.   [6] Eph. VI. 12.   [7] See 1 Cor. II. 6-8.

Then again let us consider in regard to food,—if it be true, as we have shown above, that this is not sought for by men at the instance of the devil, but from a natural instinct—whether human experience, supposing there were no devil, could possibly employ such great self-control in partaking of food as absolutely never to exceed the limit, that is, never to take anything but what the occasion demanded or more than reason permitted, and that it should never happen that men went astray in the observance of due measure and moderation in their food. I for my part do not think that, even if there were no impulse from the devil to urge men on, this rule could be so observed by them that no one would exceed due measure and moderation in partaking of food, not at any rate before they had learned this lesson by long practise and experience. What then? In regard to foods and drink it would be possible for us to go wrong even apart from the instigation of the devil, if we happened to be caught at an intemperate or careless moment; and are we to suppose that in regard to the control of the sexual appetite and the natural desires we should not be affected in a similar way? My own opinion is that the same process of reasoning can also be applied to the rest of the natural emotions, such as covetousness, anger, sorrow or any others whatever, which by the fault of intemperance exceed the limits of their natural measure.

The fact is therefore clear that, just as in regard to things that are good the mere human will is by itself incapable of completing the good act,—for this is in all cases brought to perfection by divine help—so also in regard to things of the opposite kind we derive the beginnings and what we may call the seeds of sin from those desires which are given to us naturally for our use. But when we indulge these to excess and offer no resistance to the first movements towards intemperance, then the hostile power, seizing the opportunity of this first offence, incites and urges us on in every way, striving to extend the sins over a larger field; so that while we men supply the occasions and beginnings of our sins, the hostile powers spread them far and wide and if possible endlessly. It is thus that the fall into avarice at last takes place, men first longing for a little money and then increasing in greed as the vice grows. Afterwards their passion is succeeded by a mental blindness and, with the hostile powers stimulating and urging them on, money is now not merely longed for but even seized by force or acquired through the shedding of human blood.

A sure proof that these vast excesses of sin come from the daemons can easily be observed from the following fact, that those who are under the influence of immoderate love or uncontrolled anger or exceptional sorrow suffer no less than those who are tormented in body by daemons. Further, it is related in certain histories that some men have become insane from love, others even for sorrow or excessive joy; and this happens,

I think, because these opposing powers, that is, the daemons, have been allowed to occupy a place in their minds, a place which intemperance has first laid open, and have then taken complete possession of their intelligence, especially as no thought of the glory of virtue aroused them to resistance.

3. That there are, however, certain sins which do not come from the opposing powers but take their beginning from the natural instincts of the body is most clearly declared by the apostle Paul in the place where he says, 'The flesh lusteth against the spirit, and the spirit against the flesh; and these are contrary the one to the other, so that ye cannot do the things that ye would'.[1] If then the 'flesh lusteth against the spirit', and the 'spirit against the flesh', we have at some time to 'wrestle against flesh and blood',[2] that is, when we are 'men' and 'walk according to the flesh',[3] and when we cannot be tempted with temptations beyond what are human, when it is said of us that 'no temptation hath taken you, except such as is human; but God is faithful, who will not suffer you to be tempted above that ye are able.'[4]

For just as those who preside over the games do not allow the competitors to oppose one another indiscriminately or by chance in the contests, but after a careful examination match them in equal pairs according to size and years, this one with that and this one with that, boys, that is, with boys and men with men as they are suited to one another by close resemblance in age or strength, so also must we understand in regard to the divine providence, that it treats all who descend into the struggles of human life with the most impartial care, according to the nature of each individual's virtue, which he alone knows who alone beholds the hearts of men. One, therefore, fights against one kind of flesh, another against another kind; one for so long a time, another for so long; one is incited by the flesh to this or that, another to something else; one struggles against this or that hostile power, another against two or three at once, or now against one and now against another, and at one particular time against one and at another against another; or after certain acts a man fights against certain powers, after other acts against different ones. For consider whether some such arrangement is not indicated by the saying of the apostle, 'But God is faithful, who will not suffer you to be tempted above that ye are able',[4] that is, because each one is tempted in proportion to the degree and possibilities of the strength he possesses.

It must not be supposed, however, that because we said that by the righteous decision of God each man is tempted in proportion to the degree of his strength, the tempted man ought

---

[1] Gal. V. 17.   [2] Eph. VI. 12.
[3] 1 Cor. III. 4; 2 Cor. X. 2.   [4] 1 Cor. X. 13.

therefore by all means to be victorious; for the competitor in the games cannot by all means be victorious, even though he may be paired with his opponent in an equal match. But unless the powers of the combatants are equal, the victor's palm will not be justly won nor may the vanquished be justly blamed. For this reason God allows us to be tempted, yet not 'above that we are able'; for we are tempted in proportion to our powers. Nor is it written that in temptation God will also make a way to escape from bearing it, but a way to escape that we may be able to bear it. And this possibility that he has given us it is in our hands to utilise either vigorously or feebly. There is no doubt that in every temptation we are given a power of bearing it, if only we use to the full the power thus granted. For to have the power to conquer is not the same thing as to conquer, as the apostle pointed out in carefully chosen language when he said that 'God will give a way of escape, that ye may be able to bear it',[1] not, that ye may bear it. Many do not bear it, but are conquered by temptation. But what God gives us is not the certainty that we shall bear it, in which case there would appear to be no struggle at all, but the possibility 'that we may be able to bear it'.

This strength, therefore, which is given to us in order that we may be able to conquer, we by the exercise of our free will either use diligently and conquer or feebly and suffer defeat. For if it were given to us in such completeness as to ensure our victory by all means, that is, to prevent us from being by any possibility conquered, what reason for struggling would remain to him who could not be conquered? Or what merit in gaining the palm when our adversary is deprived of the chance of conquering? But if the possibility of conquering is conferred equally upon us all, while the way in which we should use this possibility, that is, either vigorously or feebly, is a thing that lies in our own power, then it will be just to blame the vanquished and give the palm to the victor. From these considerations, therefore, which we have urged to the best of our ability, I think it is clearly apparent that there are some offences which we commit quite apart from the influence of the evil powers, and others which are carried to excessive and immoderate lengths at their instigation. It follows that we must now inquire how these opposing powers produce the aforenamed incitements within us.

4. We find that the 'thoughts which proceed out of the heart',[2] whether they are a memory of deeds we have done or a contemplation of any things or causes whatsoever, proceed sometimes from ourselves, sometimes are aroused by the opposing powers, and occasionally also are implanted in us by God or by the holy angels. This would perhaps seem fabulous if it were not proved by the witness of divine scripture. That a

---

[1] 1 Cor. X. 13.   [2] See St. Matt. XV. 18, 19; St. Mark VII. 21.

thought may arise from ourselves is seen from the witness of David in the Psalms: 'For the thought of man shall confess thee, and the residue of his thoughts shall hold a festival day to thee'.[1] That it may come also from the contrary powers is seen from the witness of Solomon in Ecclesiastes, as follows: 'If the spirit of one that hath power rise up against thee, leave not thy place, for healing will restrain many transgressions.'[2] And Paul the apostle will bear his witness on the same matter when he says: 'Casting down thoughts and every high thing that exalts itself against the knowledge of Christ.'[3]

That on the other hand a thought may come from God is seen from the witness of David in the Psalms, as follows: 'Blessed is the man whose acceptance is with thee, O Lord; thy ascents are in his heart.'[4] And the apostle says that 'God put it into the heart of Titus'.[5] That some thoughts are suggested to men's hearts by either good or bad angels is shown both by the angel that accompanied Tobias[6] and by the language of the prophet when he says, 'And the angel who was speaking in me replied'.[7] Moreover the book of the Shepherd asserts the same thing, teaching that two angels attend each human being, and saying that whenever good thoughts arise in our heart they are suggested by the good angel, and whenever thoughts of the opposite kind they are the inspiration of the bad angel.[8] The same thing, too, is asserted by Barnabas in his epistle, where he says that there are two ways, one of light and the other of darkness, over which preside certain angels, the angels of God over the way of light and Satan's angels over the way of darkness.[9]

We must bear in mind, however, that nothing else happens to us as a result of these good or evil thoughts which are suggested to our heart but a mere agitation and excitement which urges us on to deeds either of good or of evil. It is possible for us, when an evil power has begun to urge us on to a deed of evil, to cast away the wicked suggestions and to resist the low enticements and to do absolutely nothing worthy of blame; and it is possible on the other hand when a divine power has urged us on to better things not to follow its guidance, since our faculty of free will is preserved to us in either case.

Now we said in the preceding paragraph[10] that certain memories either of good or of evil deeds are also suggested to us, whether through divine providence or through the opposing powers. This is shown in the book of Esther, when Artaxerxes did not remember the benefits he had received from the righteous man Mordecai,

---

[1] Ps. LXXVI. 10 (Sept.).
[2] Eccles. X. 4.   See note p. 212 above.
[3] 2 Cor. X. 5.
[4] Ps. LXXXIV. 5 (Sept.).
[5] 2 Cor. VIII. 16.
[6] Tobit V. 4 ff.
[7] Zech. I. 14 (Sept.)
[8] See Hermas, *Mand.* VI. 2.
[9] See Ep. Barnabas, 18.
[10] See above par. 4 (p. 216).

and during a weary and sleepless night an idea came into his
mind from God that he should send for the records of great deeds
that were written in the archives. By these he was reminded
of Mordecai's services and ordered his enemy Haman to be
hanged, while to Mordecai himself he granted splendid honours
and the safety of the whole race of the saints who were then
in imminent peril.[1] On the contrary we must suppose that it
was some power of the devil who suggested to the mind of the
priests and scribes the remark which they made when they came
to Pilate: 'Sir, we have remembered that that deceiver said,
while he was yet alive, After three days I will rise again.'[2]

Moreover the thought of Judas concerning the Saviour's
betrayal was not one which came solely from the wickedness of
his own mind. For the scripture bears witness that the devil
had put it into his heart to betray him.[3] On this account Solomon
rightly utters the precept, 'Keep thy heart with all diligence';[4]
and Paul the apostle says, 'We ought to give more earnest heed
to the things that we heard, lest haply we drift away';[5] and
when he says, 'Give not place to the devil',[6] he shows that by
a certain kind of action or a certain kind of inaction a 'place'
in the mind is given to the devil with the result that, when once
he has entered our heart he either takes possession of us, or at
any rate pollutes the soul if he cannot take entire possession of
it, by hurling at us his 'fiery darts',[7] with which we are sometimes merely inflamed, but sometimes pierced and wounded
deeply. In rare cases, indeed, and by a few persons these 'fiery
darts' of his are 'quenched',[7] so that they fail to find the place
for a wound; that is, when a man has been covered with the
strong and defensive 'shield of faith'. But in regard to the
statement in the epistle to the Ephesians, 'For our wrestling is
not against flesh and blood, but against principalities, against
powers, against the rulers of the darkness of this world, against
spiritual hosts of wickedness in the heavenly places',[8] we shall
be right in understanding the apostle's word 'our' as meaning
I, Paul, myself and you Ephesians and whoever else has not
to wrestle with flesh and blood; for these have their struggle
'against principalities and powers, against the rulers of the
darkness of this world', as was not the case among the Corinthians, whose struggle was still against 'flesh and blood' and
whom 'no temptation had taken but such as was human'.[9]

[1] Esther, Chs. VI-VIII.   [2] St. Matt. XXVII. 63.
[3] See St. John XIII. 2.   [4] Prov. IV. 23.
[5] Heb. II. 1.   [6] Eph. IV. 27.
[7] See Eph. VI. 16.   [8] Eph. VI. 12.
[9] 1 Cor. X. 13. A fragment of Origen (*In Eph.* VI. 12; see Cramer,
Catenae Graec. Patr. in N.T. VI. 215) preserves a similar statement in
Greek. 'I consider that the temptations against flesh and blood are the
temptations which are said by him to be human.'

5. We must not suppose, however, that each person struggles against all these powers. It would, I think, be impossible for any man, however holy he might be, to carry on a struggle against all these at once. If, however, that which in fact cannot happen should by any chance come to pass, it would be utterly impossible for human nature to endure it without being completely overwhelmed. And just as, for example, if fifty soldiers were to say that a struggle was about to take place between them and fifty other soldiers, we should not understand from this that one of them was going to fight against fifty, and yet each one of them might rightly say that 'we have to fight against fifty', meaning all against all; so, too, we must interpret the apostle's saying in this way, that the whole body of Christ's athletes and soldiers are engaged in a wrestling and struggle against all those powers which have been enumerated; that all will take part in the struggle, but individuals will either be matched against individuals, or at any rate will fight in such a way as shall be approved by God, who is the just president of this contest.

For I think that human nature has definite limitations, even though there is a Paul of whom it is said, 'He is a chosen vessel unto me',[1] or a Peter against whom 'the gates of hell shall not prevail',[2] or a Moses, 'the friend of God';[3] for not even one of these could face the whole crowd of opposing powers at once without destruction to himself, except perhaps on the condition that there was working within him the power of him who said, 'Be of good cheer, I have overcome the world'.[4] In reliance on him Paul affirmed with confidence, 'I can do all things through Christ who strengtheneth me';[5] and again, 'And I laboured more abundantly than they all, yet not I, but the grace of God which was with me'.[6]

It was therefore because he had this power, which certainly is not human, working and speaking in him, that Paul could say: 'For I am persuaded that neither death, nor life, nor angels, nor principalities, nor powers, nor things present, nor things to come, nor strength, nor height, nor depth, nor any other creature, shall be able to separate us from the love of God, which is in Christ Jesus our Lord'.[7] For human nature by itself alone cannot, I think, maintain the struggle against 'angels' and 'heights and depths' and any 'other creature'; but when it has felt the Lord to be present and dwelling within, it will say in confidence of receiving the divine help, 'The Lord is my light and my salvation; whom shall I fear? The Lord is the protector of my life; of whom shall I be afraid? When evildoers came upon me to eat up my flesh, even my enemies who

---

[1] Acts IX. 15.   [2] See St. Matt. XVI. 18.
[3] See Exod. XXXIII. 11.   [4] St. John XVI. 33.
[5] Phil. IV. 13.   [6] 1 Cor. XV. 10.   [7] Rom. VIII. 38, 39.

persecute me, they stumbled and fell. Though a host should encamp against me, my heart shall not fear; though war should rise against me, I will put my trust in him.'[1]

So I think that a man can probably never by himself overcome an opposing power, but only by the use of divine help. That is why an angel is said to have wrestled with Jacob. Now we understand the passage in this way, that to wrestle with Jacob does not mean to wrestle against Jacob, but that the angel, who was present in order to save him, and who after learning of the progress he had made gave him the additional name of Israel, wrestled together with him, that is, was on his side in the contest and helped him in the struggle; for undoubtedly it was some other against whom Jacob was fighting and against whom his struggle was being waged.[2] And Paul indeed did not tell us that our wrestling was with principalities or with powers, but against principalities and against powers. If therefore Jacob also wrestled, he wrestled undoubtedly against one of these powers, which Paul enumerates as opposing and making attacks on the human race and especially on the saints. Finally, it is for this reason that scripture speaks of him as having wrestled with the angel and having had 'power with God', namely, that while the course of the struggle is sustained by the angel's help, the palm of achievement leads the conqueror to God.

6. Nor indeed must we suppose that struggles like Jacob's are carried on by means of bodily strength and the exercise of the art of wrestling, but that the fight is one of spirit against spirit, in the same way as Paul points out that our present struggle is 'against principalities and powers and the rulers of the darkness of this world'.[3] This kind of struggle must be understood as follows; that when losses and dangers, insults and accusations are raised up against us, the opposing powers do not do this with the mere object of making us endure these sufferings, but of provoking us by means of them to fierce anger or excessive sorrow or the depths of despair, or indeed, what is more serious, of inducing us when wearied out and overcome by these annoyances to complain against God on the ground that he does not control human life fairly and righteously. Their aim is that by these efforts our faith may be weakened or that we may lose hope or be driven to abandon the true doctrines and persuaded to accept some impious belief about God.

For some such aim is recorded in the case of Job, when the devil had asked God for power over his goods. The story of Job also teaches us that it is not by chance attacks that we are

---

[1] Ps. XXVII. 1-3.
[2] See Gen. XXXII. 22-30. Koetschau refers to Origen, *Sel. in Gen.* (ed. Lommatzsch VIII. 82 f): 'Who else is he who is called both a man and a god, who wrestles and struggles with Jacob, but he who by divers portions and in diverse manners spoke to the fathers, the holy Word of God?'
[3] Eph. VI. 12.

assailed, if ever such losses of property come upon us, nor is
it by chance that any one of us is made captive or that our
houses fall into ruins, in which some of our dear ones are
crushed to death.[1] In all these circumstances every believer
must say, 'Thou wouldst have no power against me, except it
were given thee from above'.[2] For observe that Job's house
would not have fallen upon his sons unless the devil had first
obtained power against them; nor would the horsemen have
made a raid in three bands to seize his camels and oxen and
other cattle unless they had been instigated by that spirit to
whom they had surrendered themselves as servants by their
obedience to his will. Nor would that which appeared to be
fire and has been supposed to be a thunderbolt have fallen upon
Job's sheep before the devil had said to God, 'Hast thou not
made a hedge about all that is without and all that is within
his house, and the rest of his goods? But now put forth thine
hand, and touch all that he hath, and see if he will not curse
thee to thy face.'[3]

7. From these considerations it is shown that all those events
that happen in this world, which are regarded as things indifferent,[4] whether calamities like the above or events of any other
kind whatever, happen neither by God's doing nor yet without
God. For when evil and hostile powers wish to bring to pass
such events God does not only not prevent them but even gives
permission, restricting it, however, to definite times and persons.
Thus even in regard to Job himself it is said that at a definite
time he was ordained to fall into the power of others and to
have his house plundered by wicked men. It is for this reason
that divine scripture teaches us to accept all things that happen
to us as sent by God, because we know that nothing happens
without him. That such is the case, namely, that nothing happens without God, how can we doubt, when our Lord and Saviour
clearly declares: 'Are not two sparrows sold for a farthing, and
not one of them shall fall on the ground without your Father
which is in heaven?'[5]

[1] See Job I. 6-19.
[2] St. John XIX. 11.
[3] Job I. 10, 11.

[4] Rufinus has *media*, which may be a translation of either $\mu\acute{\epsilon}\sigma\alpha$ or
$\dot{\alpha}\delta\iota\acute{\alpha}\phi\rho\rho\alpha$. The reference is to the Stoic doctrine that all external things
and events were indifferent, virtue alone being a good and vice alone an
evil. Cp. Zeno's saying, preserved in Stobaeus, II. 7, 5a (quoted by Arnold,
Roman Stoicism p. 289). 'Some things are good, some are evil, some indifferent. Good are wisdom, temperance, justice, fortitude, everything that
is virtue or an aspect of virtue; evil are folly, intemperance, injustice,
cowardice, everything that is vice or an aspect of vice. Indifferent are
life and death, glory and disgrace, pain and pleasure, riches and wealth,
disease, health and so forth.'
[5] St. Matt. X. 29.

But necessity has led us into a somewhat lengthy digression on the question of the struggle which the opposing powers maintain against men, while we have also discussed the more sorrowful events which happen to the human race, namely, the trials of this life, as Job says, 'Is not the whole life of man upon earth a trial?'[1] Our object has been to expound more clearly how these things happen and what is the pious belief that we ought to hold about them. Let us now see how men slip into the sin of false knowledge, and with what purpose the opposing powers are wont to stir up strife against us on this matter also.

[1] Job VII. 1.

CHAPTER III

1. When the holy apostle is desirous of teaching us a great and hidden truth concerning knowledge and wisdom he says in the first epistle to the Corinthians: 'Howbeit we speak a wisdom among the perfect; yet a wisdom not of this world nor of the rulers of this world, which are coming to nought; but we speak God's wisdom in a mystery, the hidden wisdom which God foreordained before the worlds unto our glory, which none of the rulers of this world knew. For had they known it, they would never have crucified the Lord of Glory.'[1] Here, in his desire to show that there are different kinds of wisdom, he describes one as a 'wisdom of this world', one as a 'wisdom of the rulers of this world' and another as God's wisdom. Moreover, when he uses the phrase, 'wisdom of the rulers of this world', I do not think he means that there is one wisdom for all the rulers of this world, but he seems to me to indicate a particular kind of wisdom for each individual ruler.

And again, when he says, 'But we speak God's wisdom in a mystery, the hidden wisdom which God foreordained before the worlds unto our glory,' we must inquire whether he means that this wisdom of God, which has been hidden and in other times and generations has not been made known to the sons of men as it is now revealed to his holy apostles and prophets, is the same as that wisdom of God which existed before the Saviour's coming, the wisdom by which Solomon became wise. But the Saviour by his own word declares that his teaching is greater than Solomon's, when he says, 'And behold, a greater than Solomon is here',[2] in which declaration it is shown that those who were taught by the Saviour were taught something more than Solomon knew.

For if anyone says that the Saviour did indeed know more than Solomon, but did not impart this knowledge to others, how will this agree logically with what he says in the following words, 'The queen of the south shall rise up in the judgment and shall condemn the men of this generation, for she came from the ends of the earth to hear the wisdom of Solomon, and behold, a greater than Solomon is here'?[3] There is therefore a 'wisdom of this world' and there is also probably a wisdom belonging to each individual 'ruler of this world'. But as for the wisdom of the one God, we believe it refers to that wisdom which was at work to a lesser extent in the men of old, but was more fully

---

[1] 1 Cor. II. 6-8.   [3] St. Matt. XII. 42.
[2] St. Matt. XII. 42.

and more clearly revealed through Christ. We shall, however, investigate the wisdom of God in the proper place.[1]

2. At the moment our task is to treat of the opposing powers[2] and to ask how they orginate those hostile movements by which false knowledge is implanted in men's minds and souls are led astray while supposing that they have discovered wisdom. It is therefore, I think, necessary to discern and distinguish between the 'wisdom of this world' and the wisdom of the 'rulers of this world', that by so doing we may be able to discover who are the fathers of this wisdom, or indeed of these kinds of wisdom. I think, then, as we said above,[3] that the 'wisdom of this world' is a different one from those varieties of wisdom which belong to the 'rulers of this world', and that in this wisdom there appears to be understood and included all things that belong to this world. Now this wisdom contains in itself nothing which can enable it to decide on questions of the divine nature, or of the cause of the world, or of any higher matters whatsoever, or of the principles of a good and blessed life; but is such, for instance, as deals wholly with the arts of poetry, grammar, rhetoric, geometry and music, to which we should probably add the art of medicine. In all these arts we must suppose that the 'wisdom of this world' is present.

As for the wisdom of the 'rulers of this world', we understand this to be what they call the secret and hidden philosophy of the Egyptians and the astrology of the Chaldaeans and Indians, who profess a knowledge of high things, and further the manifold and diverse opinions of the Greeks concerning the divine nature. Accordingly we find in the holy scriptures that there are rulers over individual nations, as for instance, we read in Daniel of a certain 'prince of the kingdom of the Persians' and another 'prince of the kingdom of the Greeks'[4] who, as is clearly shown by the sense of the passage itself, are not men but powers. Moreover in the prophet Ezekiel the 'prince of Tyre'[5] is most plainly pictured as a certain spiritual power. When these, therefore, and other similar princes of this world, each having his own individual wisdom and formulating his own doctrines and peculiar opinions, saw our Lord and Saviour promising and proclaiming that he had come into the world for the purpose of destroying all the doctrines, whatever they might be, of the 'knowledge falsely so called',[6] they immediately laid snares for him, not knowing who was concealed within him. For 'the kings of the earth stood up, and the rulers were gathered together against the Lord and against his Christ'.[7] But their snares became known and the plots which they had contrived

---

[1] See below Bk. IV. Ch. III. 14 (pp. 310 f.).
[2] See above Ch. II. (pp. 211 ff.).
[3] See preceding paragraph.   [4] See Daniel X. 13, 20.
[5] See Ezek. XXVIII and Bk. I Ch. V., 4. (p. 47) above.
[6] 1 Tim. VI. 20.   [7] See Ps. II. 2.

against the Son of God were understood when they 'crucified the Lord of glory'. Therefore the apostle says, 'We speak a wisdom among the perfect; yet a wisdom not of this world, nor of the rulers of this world, which are coming to nought, . . . [1] a wisdom which none of the rulers of this world knew. For had they known it, they would never have crucified the Lord of glory.'[2]

3. The question indeed arises whether these varieties of wisdom which belong to the rulers of this world and with which they strive to indoctrinate men are introduced into our minds by the opposing powers with the desire of ensnaring and injuring us, or whether they are offered to us simply in consequence of an error, that is, not with a view to injuring men but because the 'rulers of this world' themselves think their wisdom to be true and are therefore anxious to teach others what in their opinion is the truth. The latter is, I think, more likely. For example, just as Greek authors or the leaders of the various heresies have themselves first erroneously accepted a false doctrine for the truth and decided in their own mind that it was the truth, and then afterwards have tried to persuade others to adopt this same doctrine which they have determined is the true one, so we must suppose the 'rulers of this world' also to have acted, those beings, namely, that are called by this title because they are spiritual powers who have been appointed to exercise rule over certain definite nations in this world.[3]

There are also, besides these rulers, certain special energies of this world, that is, certain spiritual powers who control definite activities which they have themselves by their own free will chosen as their task, among whom are those spirits who control the 'wisdom of this world'; for instance, there is a particular energy or power who is the inspirer of poetry, another of geometry, and in the same way a particular power is the originator of every such art and subject of instruction.[4] Finally, many

---

[1] Part of the quotation appears to be missing.
[2] See 1 Cor. II. 6-8. The interpretation of this passage and of Ps. II. 2 as referring to the spiritual powers is found also in Origen's comment on Lamentations IV. 12. See Klostermann's edition, p. 273 Frag. CVII.
[3] See above Bk. I., Ch. VIII. 1, 2 (pp. 66 ff.).
[4] Koetschau quotes here, as a possible extract from the original work at this point, the passage from Theophilus Alex. *Ep. Synod.* c. 2. 'And the foreknowledge of events, which belongs to the Lord alone, he (i.e. Origen) attributes to the motions of the stars, namely, that from their courses and the variety of their forms daemons can tell the future and either bring things to pass or else require them to be brought to pass by the stars. It is quite clear from this that he approves of idolatry and astrology and of the various deceits of the fraudulent divination practised by the Gentiles.' With this Koetschau compares the extract from an anonymous writer quoted in Photius, *Bibl. Cod.* 117, stating the charges which were made (according to this writer falsely) against Origen: 'And (Origen teaches) that the doctrines of the Magi are not evil, and that astronomy is able to bring events to pass.' It is probable that Rufinus has omitted some things here, but it is not likely that Theophilus has reproduced them fairly.

Greeks have been of the opinion that the art of poetry cannot exist apart from madness, and accordingly in their histories it is often recorded that those whom they call seers were suddenly filled with the spirit of a kind of madness.[1] And what is to be said also of those persons whom they call divine, who through the control of the daemons that are over them utter responses in verses formed according to the rules of the poetic art?[2]

Further, those men whom they call magi, or the malevolent,[3] have often, by invoking daemons over boys of tender years, caused them to recite poems in verse to the wonder and amazement of all. We must suppose that these effects are produced in the following manner. Just as holy and stainless souls, when they have devoted themselves to God with entire affection and entire purity and have kept themselves apart from all contact with daemons and purified themselves by much abstinence and have been steeped in pious and religious exercises, acquire thereby a communion with the divine nature and win the grace of prophecy and of the other divine gifts, so, too, must we think that those who show themselves fit subjects for the opposing powers, that is, those who adopt a work and manner of life and purpose agreeable to them, receive their inspiration and become participators in their wisdom and doctrine. The result of this is that they are filled with the operations of those spirits to whose service they have once subjected themselves.

4. Then in regard to those who teach another doctrine of Christ than that which the rule of scripture allows, it is not superfluous to consider whether it is with treacherous intentions that the opposing powers, in their efforts to check the faith of Christ, have devised certain fabulous and at the same time impious dogmas, or whether in fact even they, after hearing the word of Christ, have been unable either to banish it from the secret recesses of their consciousness or to retain it in a pure and holy form, and so have introduced, through the agency of vessels that suited their purpose and, if I may so call them, through their own prophets, different kinds of error contrary to the rule of Christian truth. The more likely supposition is, that the apostate and exiled powers which have departed from God compose these errors and deceits of false doctrine either from the pure wickedness of their mind and will or else from envy of those for whom, once they have learned the truth, there is prepared a way of ascent to that station from which the powers have fallen, and from a desire to prevent any such progress.

It is, then, clearly demonstrated by many proofs that the soul of man, while in the body, can admit different energies, that is,

---

[1] See Plato, *Io* 533 E-534 D; *Phaedrus* 245 A.
[2] The best known instance is that of the priestess of the Delphic oracle. See Origen, *Con. Celsum* III. 25, VII. 3.
[3] This epithet is doubtless due to Rufinus, not to Origen.

controlling influences, of spirits either good or bad. Now the bad spirits work in two ways; that is, they either take whole and entire possession of the mind, so that they allow those in their power neither to understand nor to think, as is the case, for example, with those who are popularly called 'possessed', whom we see to be demented and insane, such as the men who are related in the Gospel to have been healed by the Saviour; or they deprave the soul, while it still thinks and understands, through harmful suggestion by means of different kinds of thoughts and evil inducements, as for example Judas was incited to the crime of the betrayal by the devil's putting the thought into him, according to the statement of scripture, 'But when the devil had already put it into the heart of Judas Iscariot to betray him'.[1]

On the other hand a man admits the energy and control of a good spirit when he is moved and incited to what is good and inspired to strive towards things heavenly and divine; just as the holy angels and God himself worked in the prophets, inciting and exhorting them by holy suggestions to strive towards better things, though certainly in such a way that it rested with the man's own will and judgment whether or no he was willing to follow God's call to the heavenly and divine. From this we learn to discern clearly when the soul is moved by the presence of a spirit of the better kind, namely, when it suffers no mental disturbance or aberration whatsoever as a result of the immediate inspiration and does not lose the free judgment of the will. Such for example were the prophets and apostles, who attended upon the divine oracles without any mental disturbance. We have shown, moreover, in previous examples, when we mentioned Mordecai and Artaxerxes,[2] that by the suggestions of a good spirit a man's memory is incited to the recollection of better things.

5. It follows, I think, that we must also inquire what are the causes which lead the soul of man to be influenced at one time by good spirits and at another time by bad.[3] I suspect that this is due to certain causes which are older even than our birth in this body, as John indicated by his leaping and rejoicing in his mother's womb when the voice of Mary's salutation sounded in the ears of his mother Elizabeth, and as is declared by the prophet Jeremiah who, 'before he was formed in his mother's belly' was known by God and 'before he came forth from the

---

[1] St. John XIII. 2.   [2] See p. 217 above.

[3] Cp. the parallel passage in Jerome, *Ep. ad Avitum* 8, 'And in the same book he says: Moreover we must also inquire why the soul of man is influenced in different directions now by one group of powers and now by another. And he supposes that the souls of some people have previously acquired merit before they came into bodies, as was the case with John, who leaped for joy in his mother's womb when at the voice of Mary's salutation Elizabeth confessed herself to be unworthy of conversing with her.' See St. Luke I. 41-44.

womb' was sanctified by him, and while yet a boy received the
gift of prophecy.[1] On the other hand[2] it is clearly proved that
some people are possessed right from their earliest years, that
is, are born with an accompanying daemon,[3] while others are
declared by the testimony of histories to have been under super-
natural control from boyhood, and others still have from their
earliest years been indwelt by a daemon whom they term a
python,[4] that is, a spirit of ventriloquism.

In the face of these examples, those who maintain that everything in this world is governed by the providence of God, a
doctrine which is also part of our faith, can give no other answer,
as it seems to me, which will prove divine providence to be free
from all suspicion of injustice, except to say that there were
certain pre-existent causes which led these souls, before they
were born into the body, to contract some degree of guilt in
their sensitive or emotional nature, in consequence of which divine
providence has judged them worthy of enduring these sufferings. For the soul always possesses free will, both when in the
body and when out of the body; and the will's freedom always
moves in the direction either of good or of evil, nor can the
rational sense, that is, the mind or soul, ever exist without some
movement either good or evil. It is probable that these movements furnish grounds for merit even before the souls do anything in this world, so that in accordance with such causes or
merits they are ordained by the divine providence right from
their birth, yes, and even before it, if I may so speak, to endure
conditions either good or evil.[5]

6. Let these assertions, then, be made concerning those
events which appear to happen to men right from their birth
or even before they emerge into this light. In regard, however,
to the suggestions made to the soul, that is, to men's thoughts,

---

[1] See Jerem. I. 5, 6.

[2] This passage also has a parallel in Jerome, *Ep. ad Avitum* 8. 'And
immediately following this he adds : On the other hand little boys and almost
infants are sometimes possessed by evil spirits, and diviners and soothsayers
are inspired to such a degree that some are possessed by a daemon python
right from their earliest years. That these should be abandoned by the
providence of God, when they have done nothing to warrant this kind of
madness, cannot be maintained by him who believes that nothing happens
apart from God and that all things are governed by his justice.'

[3] See St. Mark VII. 25 ff. ; IX. 17 ff.

[4] See Acts XVI. 16.

[5] On this point Clement of Alexandria (*Stromata* III., iii, 20; Stählin II.
204, 27 ff.) quotes Plato, *Politicus* 273 B C and (*Stromata* IV., xii, 83;
Stählin II. 285, 3 ff.) Basileides, of whom he says: 'The hypothesis of
Basileides is that the soul undergoes punishment here for sins committed
in another life'. See Jerome *Ep. ad Hedibiam*, 10 : 'We must not say, as
do Pythagoras and Plato and their disciples, who under the name of Christians introduce the doctrines of the gentiles, that souls have fallen from
heaven and in accordance with the diversity of their merits pay the penalties
for ancient sins in bodies of one sort or another.'

by different spirits, and which incite men to good or to its opposite, we must suppose that even for these there sometimes exist causes prior to our bodily birth. But sometimes a mind that is watchful and that casts away from itself whatever is evil calls to its side the assistance of the good; whereas on the contrary one that is negligent and slothful, being less cautious, gives a place to those spirits which, like robbers lying in ambush, contrive to rush into the minds of men whenever they see a place offered to them through slackness, as Peter the apostle says; 'Your adversary the devil as a roaring lion walketh about, seeking whom he may devour'.[1] On this account a strict guard must be kept over our heart day and night and no place must be given to the devil,[2] but all our actions must be such that God's ministers, that is, 'the spirits who have been sent forth to minister to them' who have been called to 'inherit salvation',[3] may find a place within us and may delight to enter the guest-chamber of our soul; and dwelling in us, that is, in our heart, may rule us with the better counsels, if so be they shall find the habitation of our heart adorned by the practice of virtue and holiness.

Let these arguments, which we have set out to the best of our ability, be sufficient in regard to those powers which are opposed to the human race.

---

[1] 1 St. Peter V. 8.   [2] See Ephes. IV. 27.   [3] See Heb. I. 14.

CHAPTER IV

WHETHER THE STATEMENT MADE BY SOME IS TRUE, THAT EACH INDIVIDUAL HAS TWO SOULS

1. And now, I think, we must not pass over in silence the 'human temptations',[1] those which occasionally arise from 'flesh and blood', or from 'the wisdom of flesh and blood', which is said to be at enmity with God;[2] for we have already dealt with the temptations that are said to be more than human, that is, with the struggles we maintain 'against the principalities and powers and against the rulers of the darkness of this world and the spiritual hosts of wickedness in the heavenly places',[3] and with those that befall us against evil spirits and impure daemons.

In this connection we must, I think, if we are to be logical, inquire whether there is in us, that is, in men who consist of soul and body and 'vital spirit',[4] something else besides which possesses a peculiar inclination and movement in the direction of evil. A question of this kind is accustomed to be raised by some, namely, whether we ought to say that there is in us as it were two souls, the one divine and heavenly and the other of a lower sort; or whether from the very fact that we are joined to bodies (which bodies are in their own proper nature dead and utterly lifeless, since it is from us, that is, from our souls, that the material body derives its life, whereas in itself it is certainly opposed and hostile to the spirit[5]) we are drawn and incited to those evils which are pleasing to the body; or whether in the third place, as some Greeks have supposed, our soul though one in its essence is nevertheless composed of several parts, namely, one part that is called rational and another irrational, while that part which they call irrational is again divided into the two emotional elements of appetite and passion.[6]

[1] The allusion is to 1 Cor. X. 13.
[2] See Ephes. VI. 12; 2 Cor. I. 12; Rom. VIII. 7, 8.
[3] Ephes. VI. 12.
[4] See Wisd. XV. 11; 1 Thess. V. 23.
[5] For the deadness of the body apart from the soul see Justin, *De Resurr.* X. 2: 'The soul is in the body; but the body without the soul is not alive, and when the soul leaves it, it no longer exists.' See also Plato, *Cratylus* 399 D E. Marcion and Basileides taught that the soul alone was saved, not the body (Ireneus, *Adv. haer.* I. xxv. 2 and I. xix. 3). Origen's remark on the hostility of body and spirit to each other alludes to such scriptural passages as Rom. VIII. 6, 10; Gal. V. 17; St. John VI. 63, but the term 'flesh' in St. Paul's writings is quite different in meaning from the term 'body' as used above. See below p. 231 f.
[6] This is Plato's division of the soul. See Plato *Repub.* IV. 436 A-441C; *Timaeus* 42 A.

Now we have found each of the three above-mentioned opinions about the soul held by some. The one of them, however, which we said was approved by certain Greek philosophers, that the soul consists of three parts, I do not observe to be strongly confirmed by the authority of divine scripture, whereas in regard to the remaining two a certain number of passages may be found in the divine writings which appear capable of being applied to them.

2. Of these theories let us first discuss the one which some are accustomed to frame, that we have within us one soul that is good and heavenly and another that is lower and earthly; and that the soul which is superior is implanted from heaven, like the soul which gave to Jacob while still in the womb the prize of victory against his brother Esau whom he supplanted, or the soul which was sanctified in Jeremiah from the womb, or in the case of John was from the womb filled with the Holy Spirit.[1] But that which they call the lower soul is, they maintain, produced along with the body from the bodily seed, and consequently they deny that it can live or subsist apart from the body; which is the reason, they say, why it is frequently termed the flesh.[2] For the passage, 'The flesh lusteth against the spirit',[3] they do not take to be spoken of the actual flesh, but of this soul, which is properly the soul of the flesh.

Moreover they endeavour by these arguments to corroborate the passage in Leviticus which runs as follows: 'The soul of all flesh is its blood'.[4] For from the fact that the blood by being diffused throughout the flesh endows the flesh with life, they say that this soul, which is called 'the soul of all flesh', resides in the blood. And as for the saying, 'The flesh wars against the spirit and the spirit against the flesh',[5] and the other saying, 'The soul of all flesh is its blood',[6] they assert that we have here the same thing which is called in other words 'the wisdom of the flesh',[7] namely, a certain material spirit, which is not subject to the law of God nor indeed can be subject to it, because it possesses earthly wishes and bodily desires.[8] It is about this that they suppose the apostle to be

---

[1] See Gen. XXV. 22-25; Jerem. I. 5; St. Luke I. 41, and above pp. 205 and 227.

[2] See above p. 230.   [3] Gal. V. 17.   [4]Lev. XVII. 14.

[5] Gal. V. 17.   [6] Levit. XVII. 14.   [7] Rom. VIII. 7 (Vulg.).

[8] See Clem. Alex. *Excerpta ex Theodoto* 50, 1 (Stählin III. 123, 9 ff.). 'Taking dust from the earth, not from the dry earth, but a portion of the diverse and manifold matter, God created an earthly and material soul, irrational and similar to that of the beasts. This is the man formed "according to the image". But the man formed "according to the likeness" of the Creator himself is he whom the Creator breathed into and implanted in the first man.' The 'irrational spirit' or 'bodily spirit' is also mentioned by Clement in *Stromata* VI. 136, 1 and VII. 79, 6. Cp. also the Valentinian doctrine in Irenaeus (*Adv. haer.* I. v. 5). For the scriptural reference see Rom. VIII. 7.

speaking when he says, 'But I see another law in my members, warring against the law of my mind, and bringing me into captivity under the law of sin which is in my members'.[1]

But if one were to object to them that these statements are made about the body which in its own proper nature is a dead thing and which is only said to possess a mind or a wisdom which is 'at enmity with God'[2] or which 'wars against the spirit'[3] in the same way as if one were to say that the actual flesh has a voice which protests against being hungry or thirsty or cold, or against enduring discomfort in any respect whatever, whether through excess or through want, they would endeavour to combat and solve this difficulty by showing that the soul has many other passions which in no way at all take their origin from the flesh, and yet the spirit is contrary to these, as for instance ambition, avarice, jealousy, envy, pride and others like them; and seeing that the mind or spirit of man is in conflict with these, they would lay down as the cause of all such evils nothing else but this bodily soul, as it were, of which we have spoken above, and which is generated by the transmission of the seed.[4]

To this statement they are accustomed to add also the witness of the apostle, where he says, 'But the works of the flesh are manifest, which are these; fornication, uncleanness, lasciviousness, idolatry, sorcery, enmities, strife, jealousies, wraths, factions, divisions, heresies, envyings, drunkenness, revellings and such like';[5] for they assert that not all of these take their origin from the use or enjoyment of the flesh in such a way that we could suppose all such passions to be part of that substance which has no soul, that is, the actual flesh. Moreover, when he says, 'Ye see your calling, brethren, how that not many among you are wise after the flesh',[6] it would seem to point to this, that there is apparently a wisdom that is peculiarly fleshly and material, and that the wisdom which is after the spirit is a different one; and certainly the former could not be called wisdom unless there existed a soul of the flesh to possess that wisdom which is termed the wisdom of the flesh. To this they also add the following; if 'the flesh warreth against the spirit and the spirit against the flesh, so that we may not do the things that we will to do',[7] what things are they of which he says, 'we may not do what we will to do'? It is certain, they say, that it does not mean things of the spirit, for the will of the spirit is not forbidden; nor is it things of the flesh, for if the flesh does not possess a soul of its own it will undoubtedly not possess a will. It remains, therefore, that it means the will of

---

[1] Rom. VII. 23.   [2] See Rom. VIII. 7.   [3] See Gal. V. 17.
[4] See pp. 4 and 231, above.   [5] Gal. V. 19, 21.
[6] 1 Cor. I. 26.   [7] Gal. V. 17.

this soul, for that can have its own proper will which is certainly opposed to the will of the spirit.

If this is so, it is plain that the will of this soul is something intermediate between the flesh and the spirit, undoubtedly serving and obeying one of the two, whichever it has chosen to obey.[1] If it gives itself up to the delights of the flesh, it makes men fleshly; if, however, it joins itself to the spirit, it causes a man to be 'in the spirit' and on this account to be called spiritual. It is this that the apostle seems to indicate when he says, 'Ye are not in the flesh, but in the spirit'.[2]

We must inquire, therefore, what exactly this will is, which is intermediate between the flesh and the spirit, above and beyond the will which is said to belong to the flesh or to the spirit. For of a certainty we should hold that everything which is said to belong to the spirit is due to the will of the spirit and whatever deeds are called 'works of the flesh' are due to the will of the flesh.[3] What then above and beyond these is the will of the soul, which is given a separate name and which the apostle wishes us not to do when he says, 'So that ye may not do the things that ye will to do'?[4] It seems to be here indicated that this will must be attached to neither of these two, that is, neither to the flesh nor to the spirit. But some one may say that just as it is better for the soul to do its own will than to do the will of the flesh, so again it is better for it to do the will of the spirit than its own will. Why then does the apostle say, 'So that ye may not do the things that ye will to do'?[4]—since in that contest which is waged between the flesh and the spirit, the spirit is by no means certain of victory; for it is clear that in many cases the flesh obtains the mastery.

3. We have entered here upon a very deep discussion, in which it is necessary to investigate the possible arguments from every aspect. Let us see, therefore, whether at this point we may not perhaps establish some such conclusion as the following; that as it is better for the soul to follow the spirit at the time when the spirit has obtained the victory over the flesh, so, too, even though it appears worse for it to follow the flesh when this is warring against the spirit and desiring to call the soul to its side, yet perhaps it may turn out to be more advantageous for the soul to be mastered by the flesh than to remain

[1] Cp. Origen *Com. in Ioh.* XXXII. 18, 'I observe in the whole of scripture a distinction made between the soul and the spirit, the soul being indifferent in character and receptive of either virtue or vice.' So, too, *In Ep. ad Rom.* I. 18, 'When it is said that the flesh lusteth against the spirit and the spirit against the flesh, the middle position is undoubtedly occupied by the soul, which either acquiesces in the longings of the spirit or else inclines to the lusts of the flesh. If it joins itself to the flesh, the body becomes one with it in impurity and lust, but if it associates with the spirit, the spirit will become one with it.'

[2] Rom. VIII. 9.   [3] See Gal. V. 22, 19.   [4] Gal. V. 17.

within the sphere of its own will. For so long as it continues in its own will, then is the time when it is said to be 'neither hot nor cold';[1] but remaining in a sort of lukewarm condition it may find conversion a slow and somewhat difficult process. If, however, it attaches itself to the flesh, it will be satiated and filled after a time with those very evils which it endures as a result of the vices of the flesh and will be wearied out as it were by the very heavy burdens of luxury and lust, and so may be the more easily and quickly converted from low material desires to a longing for heavenly things and to spiritual grace. And we must suppose that the apostle uttered the saying, 'The spirit warreth against the flesh and the flesh against the spirit, so that we may not do the things that we will to do',[2]—the things referred to being undoubtedly those which are apart from the will of the spirit and apart from the will of the flesh— meaning, if we were to say it in other words, that it is better for a man to be in a state of virtue or in a state of wickedness rather than in neither of these; and that before the soul turns to the spirit and is made one with it, during the time it is attached to the body and occupied with fleshly thoughts, it appears to be neither in a state of goodness nor yet clearly in a state of wickedness, but to be, if I may so say, like an animal. It is better, if it be possible, that it should attach itself to the spirit and become spiritual. If, however, this is not possible, it is more expedient for it to follow even the wickedness of the flesh than by remaining fixed in the sphere of its own will to occupy the position of an irrational animal.[3]

We have dealt with these points because we were desirous of discussing every opinion that is put forward; and we have gone further afield than was our wish in order that it may not be supposed that we are unaware of the questions commonly raised by those who ask whether there exists within us, besides the heavenly and rational soul, another one which is by its nature contrary to the first and which is called either the flesh, or the wisdom of the flesh, or the soul of the flesh.[4]

4. Let us now see what answer is given to the above arguments by those who maintain that there is in us a single movement and a single life of one and the same soul, whose salvation or loss is properly to be attributed to itself as the result of its own actions. And let us first see what is the nature of the passions of the mind to which we are subject whenever we feel within us that we are being dragged in one direction and another, when a conflict of thoughts arises in our heart and certain images

---

[1] Rev. III. 15.   [2] Gal. V. 17.
[3] This is a bold piece of ethical reasoning. It should be compared with the account of the soul on p. 73 above, where we have a Greek fragment, not necessarily a literal one, taken from Gregory of Nyssa.
[4] See Rom. VIII. 6, 7 (Vulg.).

are suggested to us which incline us now this way and now that and by which we stand at one time reproved and at another time self-approved.[1]

Now it is nothing remarkable if we say that evil natures have a judgment that is variable and conflicting, and out of harmony with itself; since this is found to be the case with all men, whenever a doubtful matter comes into consideration and they look ahead and deliberate which is the better or more useful choice to make. It is in no way surprising, therefore, that if two images occur to a man in turn and suggest contrary modes of action they should drag the mind in different directions. For example, if a man's thought invites him to the faith and fear of God, it cannot then be said that the flesh is warring against the spirit; but so long as it is uncertain what is the true and useful course, the mind is dragged in different ways. So, too, when we think of the flesh as inciting a man to lust, while a better counsel opposes this sort of allurement, it must not be supposed that there is one life acting in opposition to another, but that the conflict is due to the nature of the body, which is striving to empty out and exhaust the places filled with seminal fluid. Neither must it be supposed that it is any opposing influence or the life of another soul which excites thirst in us and impels us to drink or which causes us to become hungry and urges us to take food; but just as these things are alike desired and evacuated through natural movements of the body, so also the moisture of the natural seed collecting from time to time in its appointed regions strives to find an issue and outlet, a result which is so far from never happening except at the impulse of some external excitement that sometimes the seed is even spontaneously emitted.

When therefore it is said that 'the flesh warreth against the spirit',[2] these persons understand the passage thus, that the use or the needs or delights of the flesh excite a man and draw and entice him away from divine and spiritual things. For when we are drawn away by reason of the needs of the body we are not allowed leisure for things that are divine and profitable for eternity; just as on the other hand when a soul has leisure for divine and spiritual things and is united with the Spirit of God it is said to war against the flesh, for it does not allow itself to become relaxed through indulgences and to be tossed about by the pleasures in which it takes a natural delight. This is the meaning they give to the saying, 'The wisdom of the flesh is enmity against God';[3] not that the flesh really has a soul or wisdom of its own, but just as we are accustomed to say by a peculiar use of language that the ground is thirsty and wishes to drink water,—where we certainly use the word, 'wish' not in a literal but in a peculiar sense, as if, again, we were

---

[1] See Rom. II. 15.   [2] Gal. V. 17.   [3] Rom. VIII. 7 (Vulg.).

to say that a house 'wants' rebuilding, and many other similar expressions—so, too, must we interpret the phrase 'wisdom of the flesh', and the saying, 'the flesh lusteth against the spirit'.

They are accustomed also to add to these the saying, 'The voice of thy brother's blood crieth unto me from the ground'.[1] For what cries to God is not the actual blood that was shed, but by a peculiar use of language the blood is said to cry out when vengeance is demanded from God upon the shedder of the blood. Moreover when the apostle says, 'I see another law in my members',[2] they understand it as if he had said that the man who desires to apply himself to God's word is distracted and diverted and hindered from this purpose by the bodily needs and functions, which exist as a kind of 'law' in the body, and that these prevent him from applying himself to the 'wisdom of God'[3] and so being able more earnestly to behold the divine mysteries.

5. In regard, however, to the fact that heresies, envyings, strifes and other things are included in the list of 'works of the flesh',[4] they interpret it in this way. When the sensitiveness of the soul has grown duller through its subservience to the passions of the body, it is weighed down by the mass of its vices and becomes sensitive to nothing refined or spiritual. It is then said to become flesh, taking a name from that element in which it exercises the greater part of its vigour and effective purpose. They also put the following question: 'Whom can we find, or whom shall we speak of as being the maker of this evil mind, which is called the mind of the flesh?' For they maintain the belief that there is no other creator of soul and flesh but God. If we should say that the good God in his own creation made something at enmity with himself it will certainly appear absurd. If then it is written that 'the wisdom of the flesh is enmity against God'[5] and if we are to say that this is a result of the creation, then God himself will appear to have made a certain nature that is at enmity with himself, a nature that cannot be subject to him or to his law, in which case indeed we should suppose it to be an animal of which these statements are made. But if the passage is to be understood in this way, what pray will be our difference from those men who say that souls are created diverse in their natures, so as to be destined by nature either for salvation or for destruction? This is certainly satisfactory to none but the heretics, who because they cannot defend the justice of God by pious reasoning compose impious inventions like this.

We have brought forward, then, to the best of our ability, in the person of each of the parties, the arguments that can be used in discussion concerning each opinion in turn. It is for the reader to choose which of them deserves the preference.

---

[1] Gen. IV. 10.   [2] Rom. VII. 23.   [3] See 1 Cor. I. 21, 24.
[4] See Gal. V. 19, 21.   [5] Rom. VIII. 7 (Vulg.).

CHAPTER V

<table>
<tr><td>GREEK</td><td>LATIN</td></tr>
<tr><td>THAT THE WORLD IS ORIGINATED AND SUBJECT TO DECAY, SINCE IT TOOK ITS BEGINNING IN TIME.[1]</td><td>THAT THE WORLD TOOK ITS BEGINNING IN TIME.[1]</td></tr>
</table>

LATIN

1. After the foregoing discussion, since one of the dogmas of the Church, held chiefly in consequence of our belief in the truth of our records, is that this world was made and began to exist at a definite time and that as a result of the consummation of the age to which all things are subject it must be dissolved through its own corruption,[2] there appears to be nothing unreasonable in bringing up afresh a few points relating thereto. And so far as the matter concerns our belief in the scriptures the discussion seems to be a very easy one. Indeed even the heretics, divided as they are on many other matters, yet seem on this point to agree with one another in submitting to the authority of scripture.

In regard, then, to the creation of the world, what other book of scripture is more able to enlighten us than that which was written by Moses concerning its origin?[3] This account may well enshrine certain deeper truths than the mere record of the history seems to reveal and may contain a spiritual meaning in many passages, using the letter as a kind of veil[4] for profound and mystical doctrines; nevertheless the language of the narrator certainly indicates this, that all visible things were created at a definite time. And as for the consummation of the world, Jacob is the first to refer to this when, in giving his testament to his sons he says, 'Gather to me, ye sons of Jacob, that I may tell you what shall be in the last days', or, 'after the last days'.[5] If then there are 'last days', or a time 'after the last days', it follows of necessity that the days which had a beginning also come to an end. David also says: 'The heavens shall perish, but thou shalt remain; and they all shall grow old as a garment, and as a vesture shalt thou change them, and they shall be changed; but thou art the same, and thy years shall not fail'.[6] And when our Lord and Saviour says, 'He who created in the beginning made them male and female',[7] he himself bears witness that the world was made; whereas when he says that

---

[1] For the Greek title see Photius, *Bibl. Cod.* 8, p. 4.
[2] See pp. 4 f. above. [3] i.e. Genesis. [4] See 2 Cor. III. 14 f.
[5] Gen. XLIX. 1 (Sept.). [6] Ps. CII. 26, 27.
[7] St. Matt. XIX. 4.

'heaven and earth shall pass away, but my words shall not pass away,'[1] he shows that it is corruptible and destined to come to an end.

Moreover, the saying of the apostle, 'The creation was subjected to vanity, not willingly, but by reason of him who subjected it in hope, because the creation itself also shall be delivered from the bondage of corruption into the liberty of the glory of the children of God'[2] clearly asserts the end of the world, as when he says again, 'The fashion of this world passeth away';[3] while in the very fact that he says 'the creation was subjected to vanity' he points also to its beginning. For if the creation was subjected to vanity by reason of a certain hope, it was certainly so subjected from a cause, and what proceeds from a cause must necessarily have a beginning; since apart from some beginning the creation could not have been subjected to vanity nor could it hope to be 'delivered from the bondage of corruption' if it had never begun to be a servant of corruption. Moreover, anyone who looks for them at his leisure can find in the divine scriptures very many other sayings of this sort, which assert that the world both had a beginning and is expecting an end.

2. If, however, there is anyone who in this matter would oppose either the authority or the credibility of our scripture, let us ask him the question, whether he asserts that God can comprehend all things or that he cannot? Now to say that he cannot is clearly impious. If, however, he should say, as he must, that God comprehends all things, it follows from this very fact that they can be comprehended that they are understood to have both a beginning and an end. For that which is absolutely without any beginning can in no way be comprehended. However far the understanding may reach out, so far is the ability to comprehend withdrawn and removed endlessly, when there is held to be no beginning.

3. But they are accustomed to meet us with this objection: 'If the world had a beginning in time, what was God doing before the world began?' For it is alike impious and absurd to say that God's nature is to be at ease and never to move, or to suppose that there was a time when goodness did not do good and omnipotence did not exercise its power.[4] They raise this objection when we say that this world began at a definite time and when in accordance with our belief in scripture we also calculate how many years old it is. To these propositions I do not think that any of the heretics can easily give an answer that will accord with the nature of their own doctrine.

We, however, will give a logical answer that preserves the rule of piety, by saying that God did not begin to work for

---

[1] St. Matt. XXIV. 35 and parallels.   [2] Rom. VIII. 20, 21.
[3] 1 Cor. VII. 31.   [4] See above Bk. I., Ch. IV. 3 (pp. 41 f.).

the first time when he made this visible world, but that just
as after the dissolution of this world there will be another one,
so also we believe that there were others before this one existed.[1]
Both of these beliefs will be confirmed by the authority of divine
scripture. For Isaiah teaches that there will be another world
after this, when he says, 'There shall be a new heaven and a
new earth, which I will cause to endure in my sight, saith the
Lord'.[2] And that there were other worlds before this one Ecclesiastes shows when he says, 'What is it that hath been? Even
that which shall be. And what is it that hath been created?
That very thing that is to be created; and there is nothing at
all new under the sun. If one should speak and say, 'See, this
is new; it hath been already, in the ages which were before us'.[3]
By these testimonies each proposition is proved at the same
time, namely, that there were ages in the past and that there
will be others hereafter. We must not suppose, however, that
several worlds existed at the same time, but that after this one
another will exist in its turn. But it is not necessary to go
through these questions again in detail now, since we have
already done this in a former chapter.[4]

4. Still, there is a point which I do not think we ought lightly
to pass by, and that is that the holy scriptures call the foundation
of the world by a new and peculiar name, terming it *katabole*.
This word is very incorrectly translated into Latin by *constitutio,*
or foundation, for *katabole* in Greek has rather the significance
of *deicere,* that is, to cast downwards, and is, as we have said, incorrectly rendered into Latin by *constitutio.*[5] An example occurs

[1] The passage beginning with the sentence and ending at 'will exist
in its turn' has a parallel in Jerome, *Ep. ad Avitum* 9. 'And again in regard
to the world (Origen says): Our opinion is that before this world there
existed another and that another will exist after it. Would you learn that
after the dissolution of this world another will come into existence? Hear
the words of the prophet Isaiah: "There shall be a new heaven and a new
earth, which I will cause to endure in my sight". Would you know that
before the construction of this world other worlds existed in the past? Listen
to Ecclesiastes: "What is it that hath been? Even that which shall be.
And what is it that hath been made? The very thing that shall be.
And there is nothing new under the sun, nothing which can speak and say,
Behold this is new. For it hath been already, in the ages of old which
were before us". This testimony proves the existence not only of past but
also of future worlds, not all existing side by side at the same time, but
one after another.'

[2] Is. LXVI. 22.   [3] Eccl. I. 9, 10.
[4] See Bk. II., Ch. III. 1-5 (pp. 83-89).
[5] Origen used the word *katabole* as proof of his belief that the present
world is a descent from a more perfect condition which preceded it, and
that the souls of most men were enclosed in bodies and sent here as a
punishment for former sins, a few great ones like St. Paul being
allowed to come as guides and teachers of the rest. See Origen's comment
on St. John XVII. 24 in his *Comm. in Ioh.* XIX. 22, where he maintains
that this meaning must be attached to *katabole,* otherwise *ktisis* would have
been used. Jerome, in his Commentary on Ephesians, in which, as the preface admits, he relied largely on Origen, gives the same interpretation of

in the gospel according to John, when the Saviour says, 'And there shall be tribulation in those days, such as hath not been from the foundation of the world'.[1] Here 'foundation' stands for *katabole,* the meaning of which term must be taken to be as we have explained it above. Moreover the apostle used the same word in the eipstle to the Ephesians, when he says, 'Who chose us before the foundation of the world';[2] for here, too, 'foundation' represents *katabole,* which must be taken to have the same meaning as that given in our interpretation above. It seems worth while, therefore, to inquire what it is that is indicated by this new name.

Now I think[3] that since the end and consummation of the saints will happen in those worlds that are not seen and are eternal,[4] we must suppose, from a contemplation of this end, as we have frequently shown in former chapters, that rational creatures have also had a similar beginning.[5] And if they had a beginning that was such as they expect their end to be, they have undoubtedly existed right from their beginning in those worlds 'that are not seen and are eternal'.[4] If this is so, there has been a descent from higher to lower conditions not only on the part of those souls who have by the variety of their own movements deserved it, but also on the part of those who have been brought down, even against their will, from those higher invisible conditions to these lower visible ones, in order to be of

---

Eph. I. 4 ('before the foundation of the world'). This furnishes a handle to Rufinus, when in his Apology (see Bk. I. Chs. 25-27) he attacks Jerome for his Origenistic teaching.

[1] St. Matt. XXIV. 21. The illustration is probably an addition by Rufinus. It is from St. Matthew, not St. John, and it does not contain the word *katabole,* but *arche* (beginning). *Katabole* occurs in St. Matt. XXV. 34.

[2] Eph. I 4.

[3] With the passage beginning here and ending at 'the present visible world was instituted' compare the parallel in Jerome *Ep. ad Avitum* 9. Jerome's version is nearer the original than that of Rufinus. 'And immediately after this he (i.e. Origen) adds : I think we must believe that there is in the regions above a more divine dwelling-place and a true rest, where rational creatures used to live before they descended to these lower regions and travelled from invisible to visible surroundings, and where, before they were cast down to the earth and forced to wear gross bodies, they enjoyed a primeval blessedness. And, so, God the Creator made for them bodies appropriate to their lowly stations, and fashioned this visible world, and sent into it ministers to work for the correction and salvation of those who had fallen. Of these ministers some obtained fixed positions and became obedient to the necessities of the world, while others zealously performed the duties laid upon them at the various times which are known to God the Artificer. To the former class belong the sun, moon and stars, which are called by the apostle "the creation", and these have been given their place in the higher regions of the universe. This "creation" has been subjected to vanity by being clothed in gross bodies and made visible to sight. Nevertheless it was subjected to vanity not of its own will, but by the will of him who subjected it "in hope".'

[4] 2 Cor. IV. 18.   [5] See above pp. 53, 76 f., 78.

service to the whole world. For indeed 'the creation was subjected to vanity, not willingly, but by reason of him who subjected the same in hope',[1] the hope being that both sun and moon and stars and the angels of God should fulfil an obedient service for the world; and it was for those souls which on account of their excessive spiritual defects required these grosser and more solid bodies and also for the sake of those others for whom this arrangement was necessary that the present visible world was instituted.

A descent, therefore, of all alike from higher to lower conditions appears to be indicated by the meaning of this word *katabole*. Nevertheless the entire creation cherishes a hope of liberty, a hope of being 'delivered from the bondage of corruption'[2] when the 'children of God', who had both fallen and become scattered, have been gathered into one,[3] and when the others have fulfilled in this world the rest of their duties, which are known solely to God, the Artificer of all things.[4] We must recognise, however, that the world was made of such a size and character as to be able to hold all those souls which were destined to undergo discipline in it[5] and also those powers which were appointed to be at hand to serve and assist them. Moreover it is proved by many declarations that all rational creatures are of one nature, and it is only on this ground that the justice of God in all his dealings with them can be defended, namely, when each contains within himself the reasons why he has been placed in this or in that rank of life.

5. This arrangement,[6] therefore, which God established afterwards, when he had already from the beginning of the world

---

[1] Rom. VIII. 20.   [2] Rom. VIII. 21.   [3] See St. John XI. 52.

[4] See Jerome, *Ep. ad Avitum* 9 (following the last passage quoted). 'And again : Others, however, in their various places and times, which the Artificer alone knows, undertake the governance of the world. These we believe to be the angels.'

[5] See Vergil, *Aeneid* VI. 739 f.

[6] For the first part of this paragraph see Jerome, *Ep. ad Avitum* 9. 'And a little way further on : This system of things, the universe in its entirety, is ruled by the providence of God, in such a way that some powers fall suddenly from the higher spheres, while others glide gradually to the earth, some descend of their own free will, while others are hurled down against their will, some freely undertake the duty of stretching out a hand to those who are falling, while others are forced without their own consent to continue to perform an allotted task for a certain definite period. And again : From which it follows that these different movements result in the creation of different worlds, and after this world in which we live there will arise another world quite unlike it. And no one can estimate the precise worth of those who in different degrees fall or rise, or the rewards due for virtue or the punishments for sin, either in the present or the future or in any time whatever either past or to come, nor can anyone bring the universe once again to a single end, except God alone the Creator of all, who knows the reasons why he allows some to perform their own will and to sink gradually from the higher spheres to the lowest, while others he begins to visit and gives them a helping hand in order to lead them slowly back to their original condition and to set them once again on high.' Rufinus has greatly abbreviated this.

foreseen the thoughts and motives both of those who through spiritual defect deserved to descend into bodies and of those who were carried away by their eager desire for visible things, and also of those who were compelled whether willingly or unwillingly by him who subjected them 'in hope' to perform certain duties for such as had fallen into this condition,—this arrangement, I say, some men have not understood; and because they have not perceived that this variety of arrangement has been instituted by God as a result of previous causes arising from free will, they have supposed that everything in this world is governed either by chance movements or by a fateful necessity and that nothing is within the power of our will. As a result they have been unable to free God's providence from the imputation of blame.

6. But just as we said that all souls that have dwelt in this world have stood in need of many ministers and rulers and helpers, so in the last times, when the end of the world was near at hand and the whole human race was hastening towards its final destruction, and when weakness had overtaken not only those that were ruled but those also to whom the care of ruling had been committed, then there arose the need not of such help as this nor of defenders like these, but the aid of the author and creator himself was demanded in order to restore to the first the capacity to obey and to the second the capacity to rule, which in both cases had been corrupted and profaned. And so the only-begotten Son of God, who was the word and wisdom of the Father, when he lived with the Father in that glory which he had before the word was,[1] emptied himself, and taking the form of a servant became obedient even unto death[2] in order to teach them obedience who could in no other way obtain salvation except through obedience; and also restored the corrupted laws of ruling and of reigning in that he 'subdues all enemies under his feet';[3] and by the fact that he must reign till he puts his enemies under his feet he teaches the rulers themselves the arts of control.

Because then he had come, as we have said, to renew the capacity not only for ruling and reigning but also for obeying, he first fulfilled in himself what he wished to be fulfilled by others and not only became obedient to the Father 'even unto the death of the cross',[4] but also at the consummation of the age, by his including in himself all those whom he subjected to the Father and who through him come to salvation, he himself with them and in them is also said to be 'subjected' to the Father, when 'all things' shall 'subsist in him' and he shall be the 'head of all things' and in him shall be the 'fullness' of those who obtain salvation. This then is what the apostle says

---

[1] See St. John XVII. 5.   [2] See Phil. II. 7, 8.
[3] 1 Cor. XV. 27.   [4] Phil. II. 8.

of him: 'When all things have been subjected unto him, then shall the Son also himself be subjected unto him that did subject all things unto him, that God may be all in all'.[1]

7. But the heretics, not understanding, I cannot tell why, the apostle's meaning contained in these words, deprecate using the term subjection in regard to the Son; though if the propriety of its ascription to him be questioned, the truth may easily be discovered by assuming the contrary. For if to be subjected is not good, it follows that the contrary, that is, not to be subjected, is good. Moreover the language of the apostle as they would interpret it, appears to prove this when it says 'When all things have been subjected unto him, then shall the Son also himself be subjected unto him that did subject all things to him',[2] as if he who now is not subjected to the Father will then be subjected when the Father has first subjected the universe to him.

But I wonder how this can be the meaning, that he who when all things are not yet subjected to him is not himself subjected should then, when all things have been subjected to him, when he is king over all and holds power over the universe, be thought worthy of being subjected although he was not subjected before. Such men do not understand that the subjection of Christ to the Father reveals the blessedness of our perfection and announces the crowning glory of the work undertaken by him, since he offers to the Father not only the sum total of all ruling and reigning which he has amended throughout the entire universe but also the laws, corrected and renewed, of the obedience and subjection due from the human race. If therefore that subjection by which the Son is said to be subjected to the Father is taken to be good and salutary, it is a sure and logical consequence that the subjection of his enemies which is said to happen to the Son of God should also be understood to be salutary and useful; so that, just as when the Son is said to be subjected to the Father the perfect restoration of the entire creation is announced, so when his enemies are said to be subjected to the Son of God we are to understand this to involve the salvation of those subjected and the restoration of those that have been lost.

8. But this subjection will be accomplished through certain means and courses of discipline and periods of time; that is, the whole world will not become subject to God by the pressure of some necessity that compels it into subjection, nor by the use of force, but by word, by reason, by teaching, by the exhortation to better things, by the best methods of education, and also by such merited and appropriate threatenings as

[1] See 1 Cor. XV. 28; Col. I. 17-19; Eph. I. 22 f.
[2] 1 Cor. XV. 28.

are justly held over the heads of those who contemptuously neglect to care for their own salvation and advantage and their spiritual health. For even we men, in training slaves or children, restrain them by means of threats and fear so long as their age renders them incapable of listening to reason; but when they have acquired an understanding of what is good, profitable and honourable then the fear of blows may cease and they can be persuaded by word and by reason to acquiesce in everything that is good.

But how, consistently with the preservation of free will in all rational creatures, each person ought to be dealt with, that is, who they are whom the Word of God discovers to be prepared and capable and so instructs; who they are whom he puts off for a time; who they are from whom the word is utterly hidden and who are destined to be far away from the hearing of it;[1] who again they are that despise the word when it is declared and preached to them and consequently are visited with God's corrections and chastisements and pressed into salvation and whose conversion is as it were compelled and extorted; who they are for whom God even provides special occasions for salvation, so that sometimes a man has obtained an assured salvation when his faith was revealed by a mere answer;[2] from what causes or on what occasions these things happen, or what the divine wisdom sees as it looks into these men or what movements of theirs will lead God to arrange all these things thus, is known to God alone and to his only-begotten Son, through whom all things were created and restored, and to the Holy Spirit, through whom all things are sanctified, who proceedeth from the Father himself,[3] to whom is the glory for ever and ever, Amen.

---

[1] See Prov. XV. 29.
[2] Origen has in mind such an incident as St. Luke XVIII. 41 f.
[3] See St. John XV. 26.

CHAPTER VI

GREEK

THE END.[1]

LATIN

THE CONSUMMATION OF THE WORLD.

1. In regard to the end and consummation of all things we have already in a previous chapter discussed to the best of our ability, so far as the authority of divine scripture allowed us, those points which we consider sufficient for purposes of instruction.[2] Now, however, we call to mind a few further points, since the course of our inquiry has brought us again to that topic. The highest good, towards which all rational nature is progressing, and which is also called the end of all things, is defined by very many even among philosophers in the following way, namely, that the highest good is to become as far as possible like God.[3] But this definition is not so much, I think, a discovery of their own, as something taken by them out of the divine books. For Moses, before all others, points to it when in recording the first creation of man he says, 'And God said, Let us make man in our own image and likeness'.[4] Then he adds afterwards, 'And God made man; in the image of God made he him; male and female made he them, and he blessed them.'[5]

Now the fact that he said, 'He made him in the image of God', and was silent about the likeness, points to nothing else but this, that man received the honour of God's image in his first creation, whereas the perfection of God's likeness was reserved for him at the consummation.[6] The purpose of this was that man should acquire it for himself by his own earnest efforts to imitate God, so that while the possibility of attaining perfection was given to him in the beginning through the honour of the 'image', he should in the end through the accomplishment of these works obtain for himself the perfect 'likeness'. More openly and unmistakably the apostle John lays down that such is the case when he makes this declaration: 'Little children, we know not yet what we shall be; but if he shall be revealed'—

---

[1] The Greek title is given in Photius *Bibl. Cod.* 8, p. 4, where, however, it is said to come at the beginning of Book IV.

[2] See Bk. II. Chs. X and XI. (pp. 138-154 above).

[3] Plato, *Theaetetus* 176 B. This was a favourite passage of Clement of Alexandria: see *Protrepticus* XII. 122, 4; *Stromata* II. 97, 1; 100, 3.

[4] Gen. I. 26.   [5] Gen. I. 27, 28.

[6] For the distinction drawn between the 'image' and the 'likeness' see Origen *Con. Celsum* IV. 30, *In Ep. ad Rom.* IV. 5; Irenaeus *Adv. Haer.* V. 6; Clem. Alex. *Stromata* II. 38, 5.

speaking undoubtedly of the Saviour—'we shall be like him'.[1] Here he most certainly indicates that we are to hope both for the end of all things, the nature of which he says is still unknown to him, and also for the likeness to God which will be conferred on us in proportion to the perfection of our merits. The Lord himself also in the gospel points out that these things will not only come to pass but will come to pass by his own intercession, when he deigns to make this request to the Father for his disciples: 'Father, I will that, where I am, they also may be with me', and, 'as I and thou art one, so they may be one in us'.[2] Here indeed the likeness seems, if we may say so, to make an advance and from being something similar to become 'one thing'; for this reason undoubtedly, that in the consummation or end God is 'all in all'.[3]

In this connexion[4] the question is asked by some whether the essence of our bodily nature, however perfectly purified it may be and rendered completely spiritual, does not appear to offer an obstacle both to the honour of our likeness to God and to our fitness for union with him. For it does not seem possible to say that the nature which is in a body can either be like the divine nature, which is certainly above all things incorporeal, or that it can be truly and rightly described as becoming one with it; especially[5] since the fact of the Son being 'one with the Father'[6] is shown by the true doctrine of our faith to refer to that nature which is peculiar to him.   *   *   *

(And further,[7] when the same apostle says that 'the whole creation shall be delivered from the bondage of corruption into the liberty of the glory of the sons of God', we understand it in such a way as to say that the first creation of rational creatures was also an incorporeal one, which was not meant to be in

---

[1] 1 St. John III. 2.   [2] St. John XVII. 24, 21.   [3] 1 Cor. XV. 28.

[4] For this paragraph, which has been toned down by Rufinus, see the parallel in Jerome *Ep. ad Avitum* 9 a. 'And when he enters upon a discussion of the end, he speaks as follows: Because, as we have frequently said before, a fresh beginning arises out of the end, we must inquire whether there will then be bodies, or whether we are to live without bodies since these will have been reduced to nothing; and whether we must believe that the life of incorporeal beings is incorporeal, such as we know the life of God to be. Now there can be no doubt that, if all bodies belong to this sensible world which is called by the apostle the world of "things visible" the life of incorporeal beings will be an incorporeal one.' This statement formed one of the grounds of Origen's condemnation. See Anathema XI. of the Second Council of Constantinople, 553: '[If anyone shall say] that the judgment to come signifies the complete destruction of bodies and that the end of the story is an immaterial essence, and that nothing material will thereafter exist, but only mind [let him be anathema].' So Theophilus Alex. *Ep. Synod.* 2; and cp. Bk. II. Ch. III. 2 (p. 84) above.

[5] Koetschau regards this sentence as being added by Rufinus.

[6] See St. John X. 30.

[7] Koetschau inserts here these two paragraphs from Jerome, *Ep. ad Avitum* 9a. Following Schnitzer, he thinks that they fill up gaps left by Rufinus at this point. The reader will have very little doubt that this is so.

bondage to corruption for the reason that it was not clothed with bodies; for wherever bodies are, corruption follows immediately. But it will afterwards be 'delivered from the bondage of corruption' when it has received the glory of the Son of God and when 'God shall be all in all'.[1]

We are also led to believe that the end of all things will be incorporeal by the statement of our Saviour, in which he says, 'That as I and thou are one, so they also may be one in us'.[2] For we ought to know what God is and what the Saviour will be in the end, and how the likeness of the Father and the Son has been promised to the saints, so that as the Father and the Son are one in themselves, so, too, the saints may be one in them. For we must either suppose that the God of the universe is clothed with a body and enveloped with some sort of matter in the same way as we are with flesh, in order that the likeness of God's life may in the end be brought to the level of the saints; or, if this view is unseemly, as it most certainly is to those who desire even in the smallest degree to dwell on the majesty of God and to apprehend the glory of his unbegotten and all-surpassing nature, then we are compelled to accept one of two alternatives and either despair of ever attaining the likeness of God if we are destined always to have bodies, or else, if there is promised to us a blessedness of the same life that God has, then we must live in the same condition in which God lives).[3]

GREEK

2. Now when[4] God is said to become 'all in all',[5] just as we cannot include evil, when God becomes all in all, nor irrational animals, lest God should come to be in evil and in irrational animals; nor lifeless things, lest God, when he becomes all, should even come to be in them, so neither can we include bodies,[6] which in their own nature are lifeless.

LATIN

2. Now when it is promised that in the end God is 'all in all',[5] we must not imagine, in strictly logical wise, that animals, either cattle or wild beasts, will come to that end, lest it should be implied that God dwells even in animals, whether cattle or wild beasts; neither will stocks and stones, lest it should be said that God dwells in them also. So, too, we must not suppose that any

---

[1] See Rom. VIII. 21 and 1 Cor. XV. 28.

[2] St. John XVII. 21.

[3] The quotation from Jerome ends here. Origen's doctrine was condemned for its Platonism, in denying the resurrection of the body. Cp. Plato, *Phaedo* 114 C. 'Those who are thoroughly purified by philosophy live entirely without bodies in the age to come.'

[4] Fragment 27, Koetschau, from Justinian, *Ep. ad Mennam* (Mansi IX. 529).

[5] See 1 Cor. XV. 28.   [6] Rufinus has omitted this.

GREEK   LATIN

evil reaches that end, lest when
it is said that 'God is in all'
he should be said to dwell even
in some vessel of evil.

LATIN

For although we say that even now God is everywhere and in
all things, for the reason that nothing can be empty of God,
still we do not say it so as to mean that he now actually is all
things in which he is present. Hence we must look more carefully to see what this condition is which marks the perfection of
blessedness, and the end of things, in which God is said not
only to be in all things but even to be all things. Let us inquire,
therefore, what are these 'all things' which God shall be 'in all
things'.[1]

3. Now I myself think that when it is said that God is 'all
in all',[1] it means that he is also all things in each individual
person. And he will be all things in each person in such a way
that everything which the rational mind, when purified from all
the dregs of its vices and utterly cleared from every cloud of
wickedness, can feel or understand or think will be all God and
that the mind will no longer be conscious of anything besides
or other than God, but will think God and see God and hold
God and God will be the mode and measure of its every movement; and in this way God will be all to it. For there will
no longer be any contrast of good and evil, since evil nowhere
exists; for God, whom evil never approaches, is then all things
to it; nor will one who is always in the good and to whom God
is all things desire any longer to eat of the tree of the knowledge
of good and evil.[2]

If then the end is renewed after the pattern of the origin
and the issue of things made to resemble their beginning
and that condition restored which rational nature once enjoyed
when it had no need to eat of the tree of the knowledge of good
and evil,[2] so that all consciousness of evil has departed and
given place to what is sincere and pure and he alone who is the
one good God becomes all things to the soul and he himself is
all things not in some few or in many things but in all things,
when there is nowhere any death, nowhere any sting of death,[3]
nowhere any evil at all, then truly God will be all in all. But
some think that this perfection and blessedness of rational natures
can only remain in the condition which we have described above,
that is, the condition in which all things possess God and God
is all things to them, if they are in no way impeded by union
with a bodily nature. Otherwise, if there were any intermingling

---

[1] See 1 Cor. XV. 28.   [2] Gen. II. 17.   [3] See 1 Cor. XV. 55 f.

of a material substance, they consider that the glory of the highest blessedness would be prevented.[1] On this subject the arguments that may be raised have been fully dealt with and discussed by us in a previous chapter.[2]

4. But now, since we find the apostle Paul making mention of a 'spiritual body',[3] let us inquire to the best of our ability what sort of idea we ought to form from this passage about such a body. So far then as our understanding can grasp it, we believe that the quality of a spiritual body is something such as will make a fitting habitation not only for all saints and perfected souls but also for that 'whole creation' which is to be 'delivered from the bondage of corruption'.[4] Of this body the same apostle has also said that 'we have a house not made with hands, eternal in the heavens',[5] that is, in the dwelling-places of the blest. From this statement we may then form a conjecture of what great purity, what extreme fineness, what great glory is the quality of that body, by comparing it with those bodies which, although heavenly and most splendid, are yet made with hands and visible. For of that body it is said that it is a house not made with hands but 'eternal in the heavens'.[6] Now since 'the things which are seen are temporal, but the things which are not seen are eternal',[7] all those bodies which we see whether on earth or in the heavens, which are capable of being seen and are made with hands and not eternal, are

---

[1] Here again Rufinus has greatly abbreviated the original, as will be seen from a comparison with Jerome *Ep. ad Avitum* 10. 'And again, when he is arguing for a variety of worlds and maintaining that angels may become daemons and daemons angels or men, or that on the contrary men may become daemons and any being may become any other, he confirms his opinion by concluding in the following way: Nor can we doubt that after certain periods of time matter will exist again and bodies will be created and a world of diversity constructed in conformity with the varying wills of rational creatures, who after becoming perfect in blessedness at the end of all things have gradually fallen to lower levels and have admitted evil to so great an extent as to be turned into the opposite of what they were, by reason of their unwillingness to preserve their first estate and to retain their blessedness uncorrupted. And this, too, we must know, that many rational creatures preserve their first estate to the second or third or fourth world, giving no occasion for a change in their condition; others will fall so little from their original state that they appear to have lost scarcely anything; while some have to be hurled in complete ruin into the lowest pit. And God the dispenser of all things alone knows how to make use of each class in the creation of new worlds, in conformity with merit and opportunity and motives, so that they may be the means of initiating and sustaining the course of the world; and one who has surpassed all others in wickedness and has completely lowered himself to the level of the earth may in another world, afterwards to be constructed, become a devil, "the beginning of the creation of God", to be a laughing-stock to the angels who have lost their primeval virtue.' For the last sentence see Job. XL. 14 (Sept.).

[2] See above Bk. II., Ch. III. 2, 3 (p. 84 ff.).

[3] See 1 Cor. XV. 44.   [4] See Rom. VIII. 21.

[5] 2 Cor. V. 1.   [6] See 2 Cor. V. 1.   [7] 2 Cor. IV. 18.

very greatly surpassed in excellence by that which is neither
visible nor made with hands but is eternal.

From this comparison we may gain an idea how great is
the beauty, how great the splendour and how great the brightness of a spiritual body, and how true is the saying that 'eye
hath not seen nor ear heard, nor hath it entered into the heart
of man to conceive what things God hath prepared for them
that love him'.[1] But we must not doubt that the nature of
this present body of ours may, through the will of God who
made it what it is, be developed by its Creator into the quality
of that exceedingly refined and pure and splendid body, according as the condition of things shall require and the merits of the
rational being shall demand. Finally, when the world was in
need of variety and diversity, matter lent itself to the fashioning
of the diverse aspects and classes of things in wholly obedient
service to the Maker, as to its Lord and Creator, that from it
he might produce the diverse forms of things heavenly and
earthly. But when events have begun to hasten towards the
ideal of all being one as the Father is one with the Son,[2] we
are bound to believe as a logical consequence that where all are
one there will no longer be any diversity.[3]

5. It is on this account, moreover, that the last enemy, who
is called death, is said to be destroyed;[4] in order, namely,
that there may be no longer any sadness when there is no death
nor diversity when there is no enemy. For the destruction of the
last enemy must be understood in this way, not that its substance
which was made by God shall perish, but that the hostile purpose
and will which proceeded not from God but from itself will
come to an end. It will be destroyed, therefore, not in the sense
of ceasing to exist, but of being no longer an enemy and no

---

[1] I Cor. II. 9.   [2] See St. John XVII. 21, X. 30.
[3] Rufinus has apparently omitted some of Origen's statements about
the final unity of all spiritual beings. See the four last Anathemas of the
Second Council of Constantinople, which condemn all who assert the following doctrines. XII. 'That the heavenly powers and all men and the devil
and the spiritual hosts of wickedness are as unchangeably united to the Word
of God as the Mind itself which is by them called Christ and which was in
the form of God and, as they assert, emptied itself; and that there will
be an end to the kingdom of Christ.' XIII. is similar. XIV. runs as follows :
'That all rational creatures will form one unity, hypostases and numbers
alike being destroyed when bodies are destroyed; and that the knowledge
of purely rational creatures will be accompanied by a dissolution of the
worlds, an abandonment of bodies and an abolition of names; and that there
will be an identity between knowledge and hypostases; and that in what they
call the restoration only the bare spirits will exist.' XV : 'That the life of
spirits will be the same as it formerly was, when they had not yet descended
or fallen, so that the beginning is the same as the end, and the end is the
measure of the beginning.'
[4] See I Cor. XV. 26.

longer death.[1] For to the Almighty nothing is impossible,[2] nor is anything beyond the reach of cure by its Maker; for it was on this account that he made all things, that they might exist, and those things which were made in order to exist cannot cease to exist. Consequently they will suffer change and difference of such a kind as to be placed in a better or worse position in accordance with their merits; but things which were made by God for the purpose of permanent existence cannot suffer a destruction of their substance. Those things which in the opinion of the common people are believed to perish have not really perished, as the principles of our faith and of the truth alike agree.

Our flesh indeed is considered by the uneducated and by unbelievers to perish so completely after death that nothing whatever of its substance is left. We, however, who believe in its resurrection, know that death only causes a change in it and that its substance certainly persists and is restored to life again at a definite time by the will of its Creator and once more undergoes a transformation; so that what was at first flesh, 'of the earth earthy',[3] and was then dissolved through death and again made 'dust and ashes',[4]—for 'dust thou art', it is written, 'and unto dust shalt thou return'[5]—is raised again from the earth and afterwards, as the merits of the 'indwelling soul' shall demand, advances to the glory of a 'spiritual body'.[6]

6. Into this condition, therefore, we must suppose that the entire substance of this body of ours will develop at the time when all things are restored and become one and when 'God shall be all in all'.[7] We must not think, however, that it will happen all of a sudden, but gradually and by degrees, during the lapse of infinite and immeasurable ages, seeing that the improvement and correction will be realised slowly and separately in each individual person. Some will take the lead and hasten with swifter speed to the highest goal, others will follow them at a close interval, while others will be left far behind; and so the process will go on through the innumerable ranks of those who are making progress and becoming reconciled to God from their

[1] Origen's reference here is to the devil, though this is concealed by Rufinus. See Theophilus Alex. *Ep. pasch.* Gr. Frag. 16 (in *Doctrina patrum* ed. Diekamp, p. 180, 12): 'He has dared to pay great honour to the devil, saying that when he is freed from all sin he will be restored to his ancient rank, and that the kingdom of Christ will come to an end and that Jesus will then together with the devil be reigned over by God.' See also Theophilus Alex. *Ep. pasch.* I. 8 (Migne P L 22, p. 779); *Ep Synod.* 2, in Jerome, *Ep.* 92 (Migne P L 22, p. 762); Jerome, *In Dan. proph.* c. 3 (Migne P L 25, p. 521); and Bk. I., Ch. VI., 3 above (p. 56 f.).
[2] See Job XLII. 2.   [3] See 1 Cor. XV. 47.
[4] See Gen. XVIII. 27.   [5] Gen. III. 19.
[6] See 1 Cor. XV. 44. For Origen's doctrine of the Resurrection see Bk. II., Ch. X. (p. 138 ff. above) and *Con. Celsum* V. 18-23.
[7] 1 Cor. XV. 28.

state of enmity, until it reaches even to the last enemy, who is called death,[1] in order that he, too, may be destroyed and remain an enemy no longer.

When therefore all rational souls have been restored to a condition like this, then also the nature of this body of ours will develop into the glory of a 'spiritual body'.[2] For just as in the case of rational natures we see that there is not one kind which on account of its sins has lived in dishonour and another kind which on account of its merits has been summoned to blessedness, but that these are the same natures, which were formerly sinful and afterwards through being converted and reconciled to God were recalled to blessedness; so, too, in regard to our bodily nature we must understand that there is not one body which we now use in lowliness and corruption and weakness, and a different one which we are to use hereafter in incorruption and power and glory, but that this same body, having cast off the weaknesses of its present existence, will be transformed into a thing of glory and made spiritual, with the result that what was a vessel of dishonour shall itself be purified and become a vessel of honour and a habitation of blessedness.[3] And we must believe that in this condition it remains for ever unchangeably by the will of the Creator, of which fact we are made certain by the statement of the apostle Paul in which he says, 'We have a house not made with hands, eternal in the heavens'.[4]

For the faith of the Church does not accept the opinion derived from certain Greek philosophers, that besides this body which is composed of the four elements, there is a fifth body which is entirely other than and diverse from our present body;[5] since we can neither produce from the holy scriptures the least suspicion of such an opinion, nor can its acceptance be allowed as a logical inference, particularly as the holy apostle clearly lays it down that no new bodies are to be given to those who rise from the dead but that they are to receive the same ones which they possessed during life, only transformed from a worse to a better condition. For he says: 'It is sown a natural body, it will rise a spiritual body', and, 'it is sown in corruption, it will rise in incorruption; it is sown in weakness, it will rise in power; it is sown in dishonour, it will rise in glory'.[6] As therefore man

---

[1] See 1 Cor. XV. 26, and pp. 250-251 above.   [2] See 1 Cor. XV. 44.
[3] See Rom. IX. 21.   [4] 2 Cor. V. 1.
[5] I. e. Aristotle's *aether*. See Zeller, *Aristotle and the earlier Peripatetics*, (Eng. trans. Costelloe and Muirhead 1897), pp. 475-477. See also Cicero, *Academica* I. 7, 26: 'There is also a fifth element, out of which the stars and minds are constituted, which Aristotle maintained to have a nature of its own and to be something quite different from the four which I have mentioned above'. Origen again states his objection to the hypothesis of this 'fifth body', in *Con. Celsum* IV. 60.
[6] See 1 Cor. XV. 42-44.

makes a kind of progress, so that although he is first a 'natural man,' who does not understand the 'things of the Spirit of God', he arrives by means of instruction at the stage of becoming spiritual and of 'judging all things while he himself is judged of no man';[1] so also in regard to the condition of the body we must suppose that this same body which now on account of its service to the soul is called a soul-like or natural body will advance through a kind of progress, when the soul has been joined to God and made 'one spirit'[2] with him and the body then as it were renders service to the spirit, into a spiritual condition and quality, especially since the bodily nature, as we have often shown, was so made by the Creator that it could easily pass into whatever quality he should wish or the circumstances should demand.[3]

7. The whole argument, then, comes to this, that God has created two universal natures, a visible, that is, a bodily one, and an invisible one, which is incorporeal.[4] These two natures each undergo their own different changes. The invisible, which is also the rational nature, is changed through the action of the mind and will by reason of the fact that it has been endowed with freedom of choice; and as a result of this it is found existing sometimes in the good and sometimes in its opposite. The bodily nature, however, admits of a change in substance, so that God the Artificer of all things, in whatever work of design or construction or restoration he may wish to engage, has at hand the service of this material for all purposes, and can transform and tranfer it into whatever forms and species he desires, as the merits of things demand. It is to this, clearly, that the prophet points when he says, 'God who makes and transforms all things'.[5]

8. And now we must certainly ask whether in the consummation of all things, when 'God shall be all in all',[6] the whole of bodily nature will consist of one species and whether the only quality of body will be that which will shine with that unspeakable glory which we must believe will belong to the spiritual body. Now if we interpret correctly the passage which Moses writes in the forefront of his book namely, 'In the beginning God made the heaven and the earth',[7] as referring to the beginning of the entire creation, it is appropriate that the end and consummation of all things should consist of a return to this beginning;[8] that is, that the heaven and earth there spoken of should exist as a dwelling place and rest for the pious, so that the saints and the meek may be the first to obtain an

---

[1] See 1 Cor. II. 14, 15.
[2] See 1 Cor. VI. 17.
[3] See above pp. 78 f., 81, 87.
[4] See Plato, *Phaedo* 79 A.
[5] Amos V. 8 (Sept.).
[6] See 1 Cor. XV. 28.
[7] Gen. I. 1.
[8] See above p. 53.

inheritance in that earth;[1] for this is the teaching of both the
law and the prophets and the gospel. In that earth there exists,
I believe, the true and living forms of that divine service which
Moses handed down through the 'shadow' of the law.[2] For it
is said of them, that is, of those who served under the law, that
'they serve that which is a copy and shadow of the heavenly
things'.[3] Moreover it was said to Moses himself, 'See that
thou make all things according to the form and likeness which
was shown thee in the mount'.[4] It seems to me, therefore, that
as in this earth the law was a kind of schoolmaster to those who
by it were appointed to be led to Christ[5] and to be instructed
and trained in order that after their training in the law they might
be able with greater facility to receive the more perfect precepts
of Christ, so also that other earth, when it receives all the saints,
first imbues and educates them in the precepts of the true and
eternal law in order that they may with greater facility accept
the precepts of heaven which are perfect and to which nothing
can ever be added. And in heaven will truly exist what
is called the 'eternal gospel' and the testament that is always
new, which can never grow old.[6]

9. This, then, is how we must suppose that events happen
in the consummation and restitution of all things, namely, that
souls, advancing and ascending little by little in due measure
and order, first attain to that other earth and the instruction that
is in it, and are there prepared for those better precepts to
which nothing can ever be added. For in the place of 'stewards'
and 'governors'[7] Christ the Lord, who is King of all, will himself
take over the kingdom; that is, he himself will instruct those
who are able to receive him in his character of wisdom, after
their preliminary training in the holy virtues, and will reign in
them until such time as he subjects them to the Father who
subjected all things to him;[8] or in other words, when they have
been rendered capable of receiving God, then God will be to
them 'all in all'.[9] It follows of necessity that then even their
bodily nature will assume that supreme condition to which
nothing can ever be added.[10]

---

[1] See above Bk. II., Ch. III. 7 (p. 93 f.), and Deut. IV. 38; Ps.
XXXVII. 11; St. Matt. V. 4; Heb. IV. 9.
[2] See Heb. X. 1.   [3] Heb. VIII. 5.
[4] Exod. XXV. 40.   [5] See Gal. III. 24.
[6] See Rev. XIV. 6; Heb. IX. 15, XII. 24, VIII. 13.
[7] See Gal. IV 2.
[8] Origen's inference from 1 Cor. XV. 28, that Christ's kingdom would
one day come to an end, was one of the many charges made against him.
See Theophilus Alex. *Ep pasch.* (Jerome, *Ep.* 96) and *Ep. synod.* (Jerome
Ep. 92); and also p. 250 above, note 3.
[9] 1 Cor. XV. 28.
[10] With this sentence cp. Jerome *Ep. ad Avitum* 10 'And after a very
long discussion, in which he asserts that all bodily nature must be changed
into spiritual bodies of extreme fineness and that the whole of matter must

So far, then, we have discussed the question of our bodily nature and of the spiritual body. We leave it to the reader's judgment to choose which of the two opinions he decides to be the better. For our part we shall here bring the third book to a conclusion.

be transformed into a single body of the utmost purity, clearer than all brightness and of such a quality as the human mind cannot conceive, at the close he states : And God shall be all in all, so that the whole of bodily nature may be resolved into that substance which is superior to all others, namely, into the divine nature, than which nothing can be better.'

BOOK IV

CHAPTER I

GREEK[1]

THE INSPIRATION OF DIVINE SCRIPTURE

1. Now in our investigation of these important matters we do not rest satisfied with common opinions and the evidence of things that are seen, but we use in addition, for the manifest proof of our statements, testimonies drawn from the scriptures which we believe to be divine, both from what is called the Old Testament and also from the New, endeavouring to confirm our faith by reason. We have not yet, however, discussed the divine character of the scriptures. Well then, let us deal in a brief manner with a few points concerning them, bringing forward in this connexion the reasons that influence us to regard them as divine writings. And first of all, before we make use of statements from the writings themselves and from the events disclosed in them, let us speak of Moses, the Hebrew lawgiver, and of Jesus Christ, the introducer of the saving doctrines of Christianity.

LATIN

THE DIVINE INSPIRATION OF THE SCRIPTURES

1. Now since in our discussion of these great and important subjects it is not sufficient to leave the conclusion of the matter to human opinions and the common understanding and, so to speak, to pronounce on things invisible through visible means, we must take into account, for the proof of these statements of ours, the testimonies of the divine scriptures. And in order that these testimonies may carry an assured and indubitable conviction both in regard to what we are about to say and in regard to what we have said already, it seems necessary first of all to show that the scriptures themselves are divine, that is, are inspired by the Spirit of God. We shall therefore set our seal to this proposition in as brief a manner as we can by quoting from the divine scriptures themselves the passages that chiefly influence us, that is, first the passages from Moses the lawgiver of the Hebrew people, and then from the words of Jesus Christ, the

---

[1] Chs. I. and II., with part of Ch. III., marked as Frag. 28, Koetschau, are preserved in Ch. I. of the *Philocalia*. See the edition of J. A. Robinson, p. 7 ff. The titles of the chapters, which form together a single title to Ch. I. of the *Philocalia,* are here separated to agree with the chapter divisions found in Rufinus.

GREEK　　　　　　　　　　　　　　　　LATIN

author and leader of the Christian religion and doctrine.

For although there have been very many lawgivers among both Greeks and barbarians, and teachers who proclaimed doctrines which professed to be the truth, we have no record of a lawgiver who has succeeded in implanting an enthusiasm for the acceptance of his teachings among nations other than his own. A great apparatus of supposed logical proof has been introduced by men who profess that their philosophy is concerned with truth, and yet none of them has succeeded in implanting what he regarded as the truth among different nations or even among any number of persons worth mentioning in a single nation.

Yet it would have been the wish of the lawgivers to put in force the laws which appeared to them to be good among the whole race of mankind, had that been possible; while the teachers would have wished that what they imagined was the truth should be spread everywhere throughout the world. But knowing that they could not summon men of other languages and of many nations to the observance of their laws and the acceptance of their teachings they wholly refrained even from attempting to do this, considering not unwisely how impossible it was that such a result should happen to them. Yet all over Greece and in the barbarian part of our world there are thousands of enthusiasts who have abandoned their ancestral laws and their

For although there have been very many lawgivers among both Greeks and barbarians, as well as innumerable teachers or philosophers who professed that they taught the truth, we remember no lawgiver who has succeeded in instilling into the minds of foreign nations a desire and enthusiasm either to adopt his laws voluntarily or to defend them whole-heartedly. Nor has anyone succeeded in introducing and implanting what he regarded as the truth among, I will not say many other foreign nations, but even among the people of a single nation, in such a way so to cause a knowledge of and belief in it to extend to all.

Yet we cannot doubt that the lawgivers would have wished their laws to be observed by all men, had that been possible; while the teachers would have wished that what they regarded as the truth should become known to all. But knowing that this was altogether impossible and that they did not possess the enormous influence that was necessary to summon men of foreign nations to the observance of their laws and teachings they did not venture to make the least attempt at this, for fear lest an ineffective and futile effort to do so should stamp their conduct with folly. Yet all over the world, in the whole of Greece and in every foreign nation, there are innumerable people who have abandoned their ancestral laws and

GREEK

recognised gods for observance of the laws of Moses and of the teaching contained in the words of Jesus Christ, in spite of the fact that those who submit to the law of Moses are hated by the worshippers of images and that those who accept the word of Jesus Christ are not only hated but in danger of death.[1]

2. Now if we consider how in a very few years, although those who profess Christianity are persecuted and some are put to death on account of it while others suffer the loss of their possessions, yet the word has been able, in spite of the fewness of its teachers, to be 'preached everywhere in the world',[2] so that Greeks and barbarians, wise and foolish[3] have adopted the religion of Jesus, we shall not hesitate to say that this achievement is more than human, remembering that Jesus taught with all authority and convincing power that his word should prevail.[4]

Consequently we may reasonably regard as oracles those utterances of his such as, 'Ye shall be brought before kings and governors for my sake, for a testimony to them and to the

LATIN

their recognised gods and have submitted themselves to the observance of the law of Moses and to the discipline and worship of Christ, and this in spite of the fact that an intense hatred has been aroused against them by those who worship images, to such an extent that they are often subjected to tortures at the hands of these men and sometimes even led to death. Nevertheless they embrace and guard with all affection the word of Christ's teaching.[1]

2. Now we can see how in a short time this religion has grown up, making progress through the persecution and death of its adherents and through their endurance of confiscation of property and every kind of torture. And this is particularly wonderful since its teachers themselves are neither very skilful nor very numerous. For in spite of all, this word is 'preached in all the world',[2] so that Greeks and barbarians, wise and foolish[3] now adopt the Christian religion. Hence there can be no doubt that it is not by human strength or resources that the word of Christ comes to prevail with all authority and convincing power in the minds and hearts of all men.

Moreover it is plain that this result was predicted by him and established by the divine oracles he uttered, as when he says, 'Ye shall be brought before governors and rulers for my

[1] See also Origen, *Con. Celsum* I. 26, 27.
[2] See St. Matt. XXIV. 14.
[3] See Rom. I. 14.
[4] See St. Mark XIII. 31.

GREEK

gentiles';[1] and . . . . [2] 'Many shall say to me in that day, Lord, Lord, did we not eat in thy name and drink in thy name and in thy name cast out daemons? And I shall say unto them, Depart from me, ye workers of iniquity; I never knew you'.[3] Now there was once a possibility that in uttering these words he was talking idly, because they were not true; but when words spoken with such authority have come to pass it shows that God has really become man and delivered to men the doctrines of salvation.

3. And what need is there to say also that it was predicted that those who are called 'rulers' 'shall fail from Judah and the leaders from his thighs, when he shall come for whom it'—that is, clearly, the kingdom—'is reserved', and when 'the expectation of the gentiles shall dwell here'.[4] For it is abundantly clear from history and from what we see at the present day that after the times of Jesus there were no longer any who were called kings of the Jews, and that all those Jewish customs on which they prided themselves, I mean those connected

LATIN

sake, for a testimony to them and to the gentiles';[1] and again, 'This gospel shall be preached to all nations';[2] and also, 'Many shall say to me in that day, Lord, Lord, have we not eaten and drunk in thy name, and in thy name cast out daemons? And I shall say unto them, Depart from me, ye workers of iniquity; I never knew you'.[3] Now if these words had been spoken by him and had not come to the predicted fulfilment they might have appeared to be scarcely true and to possess no authority; but now, since the events which were predicted by him do come to pass, and since they were predicted with so great power and authority, it is most plainly shown that he is really God who has become man and has delivered to men the precepts of salvation.

3. And what are we to say of this, that the prophets have predicted beforehand of him that 'rulers shall not fail from Judah nor leaders from his thighs, until he shall come for whom it' —that is, clearly, the kingdom —'is reserved', and 'until the expectation of the gentiles shall come'.[4] For it is abundantly clear from history and from what we see at the present day that after the times of Christ kings have not existed among the Jews. Moreover all those Jewish ceremonies of which they boasted so much and on which they prided themselves, that is,

[1] St. Matt. X. 18; St. Mark XIII. 9.
[2] St. Matt. XXIV. 14. The quotation is omitted in the Greek, no doubt by mistake.
[3] St. Matt. VII. 22, 23; St. Luke XIII. 26.
[4] See Gen. XLIX. 10. (Sept.).

GREEK

LATIN

with the temple and the altar and the performance of worship and the garments of the high priest, have been destroyed.[1] For the prophecy has been fulfilled which says, 'The children of Israel shall sit for many days without king or ruler, without sacrifice or altar or priesthood or oracles'.[2]

Now we use these sayings as an answer to those who, in regard to the difficulty arising from the words in Genesis spoken by Jacob to Judah, say that the Ethnarch,[3] who comes from the tribe of Judah, is the ruler of the people, and that men of his seed will not fail until the advent of the Christ as they picture him. For if 'the children of Israel shall sit for many days without king or ruler, without sacrifice or altar or priesthood or oracles,'[2] and if from the time the temple was rased to the ground there has been 'neither sacrifice nor altar nor priesthood', it is clear that a ruler has 'failed from Judah and a leader from his thighs'. And when the prophecy says, 'A ruler shall not fail from Judah nor a leader from his thighs until there shall come what is reserved for him',[4] it is clear

those connected with the adorning of the temple and the decorations of the altar and all those sacerdotal fillets and the garments of the high priests were destroyed at one blow.[1] For the prophecy has been fulfilled which said, 'The children of Israel shall sit for many days without king, without ruler; there shall be neither sacrifice nor altar nor priesthood nor oracles'.[2]

Now we use these sayings as evidence against those who apparently maintain that what is said by Jacob in Genesis is said of Judah, and who declare that there remains to this day a ruler who comes from the tribe of Judah, that is to say, that person who is the ruler of the Jewish nation and whom they call the Patriarch, and, they add, men of his seed cannot fail to continue until the advent of that Christ whom they picture to themselves. But if what the prophet says is true, that 'the children of Israel shall sit for many days without king, without ruler; neither shall there be sacrifice nor altar nor priesthood,'[2] and if certainly from the time the temple was overthrown no sacrifices have been offered nor has an altar been found there nor a priesthood existed, then it is quite clear that rulers

---

[1] The Christian argument from Gen. XLIX. 10 is given also by Justin Martyr, 1 Apol. XXXII; Dial. cum Tryph. LII.

[2] Hosea III. 4.

[3] In Origen's Ep. ad Africanum 14 (Migne P. G. 11, p. 82 f.) he states that the Ethnarch has almost the powers of a king granted to him by the Romans. The Jewish contention, therefore, was not utterly without force.

[4] Gen. XLIX. 10. For the two forms of the quotation see Justin Martyr, Dial. cum Tryph. CXX.

GREEK

that he has come for whom are the things reserved, that is, he who is the expectation of the gentiles. This is evident from the number of gentiles who through Christ have believed in God.

4. And in the song in Deuteronomy it is prophetically revealed that there shall be an election of foolish nations on account of the sins of God's former people; which has come to pass through no other than Jesus. For it says: 'They moved me to jealousy with that which is not God; they have provoked me to anger with their idols; and I will move them to jealousy with that which is not a nation, and with a foolish nation I will provoke them to anger'.[1] Now it can be very clearly perceived in what manner the Hebrews, who are said to have moved God to jealousy with that which is not God and to have provoked him to anger with their idols, have themselves been provoked to anger and jealousy with that which is not a nation, and with a 'foolish nation', which God chose through the advent of Christ Jesus and his disciples.

We see, then, our calling, that 'not many wise after the flesh, not many mighty, not many noble are called; but God chose

LATIN

have 'failed from Judah', as it was written, 'and a leader from his thighs, until he comes for whom it was reserved'.[2] It is evident, then, that he has come, 'for whom it was reserved', he in whom also is 'the expectation of the gentiles'. This seems plainly to have been fulfilled in the multitude of those who from different gentile nations have through Christ believed in God.

4. Moreover in the song in Deuteronomy it is prophetically revealed that there shall be an election of a foolish nation on account of the sins of God's former people; which election is certainly none other than that which has come to pass through Christ. For it speaks thus: 'They have provoked me to anger with their idols, and I will move them to jealousy; with a foolish nation I will stir them to anger'.[1] Now it can be very clearly perceived in what manner the Hebrews, who are said to have moved God to anger with those that are no gods and to have provoked him with their idols, have themselves been provoked to anger and jealousy by a 'foolish nation', which God chose through the advent of Christ Jesus and his disciples.

For the apostle speaks as follows: 'Ye see your calling, brethren, that not many among you are wise after the flesh, not

---

[1] Deut. XXXII. 21.

[2] Gen. XLIX. 10. For the two forms of the quotation see Justin Martyr, *Dial. cum Tryph.* CXX.

GREEK

the foolish things of the world,
that he might put to shame
them that are wise; and the
base things and the things that
are despised did God choose,
yea, and the things that are not,
that he might bring to nought
those things that were before
them'. So let not 'Israel after
the flesh', which is called by the
apostle 'flesh', 'glory before
God'.[1]

5. And what need is there to
speak of the prophecies relating
to Christ in the Psalms, in
which a certain ode is headed
'For the beloved', whose tongue
is said to be the 'pen of a ready
writer' who is 'fairer than the
children of men' because 'grace
was poured on his lips'?[2] Now
a proof that 'grace was poured
on his lips' is the fact that although the time he spent in
teaching was short—for he
taught only about a year and
a few months[3]—the world has
been filled with this teaching
and with the religion that came
through him. For there has
arisen 'in his days' 'righteousness and an abundance of peace'
lasting until the consummation,
which is here called the 'taking
away of the moon'; and he continues to 'have dominion from
sea to sea and from the rivers
to the ends of the earth'.[4] And
a 'sign' has been given to the
house of David, for 'the virgin'
did 'conceive and bear a son',

LATIN

many mighty, not many noble;
but God chose the foolish things
of the world and those which
are not, that he might destroy
those things that were before
them'. Therefore let not Israel
after the 'flesh'—for so is Israel
called by the apostle—'glory';
let 'no flesh', I say, 'glory
before God'.[1]

5. What must we say, moreover, of the prophecies relating
to Christ in the Psalms, and
particularly in that one which is
headed 'A song for the beloved',
where it is said that his tongue
is the 'pen of a ready writer'
who is 'fairer than the children
of men' because 'grace was
poured on his lips'?[2] Now a
proof that 'grace was poured on
his lips' is the fact that although the time he spent in
teaching was short—for he
taught but a year and a few
months[3]—nevertheless the whole
world has been filled with his
teaching and religious faith.
For there has arisen 'in his days'
'righteousness and an abundance
of peace' lasting until the end,
which end is called the 'taking
away of the moon'; and he has
'dominion from sea even to sea
and from the river even to the
ends of the earth'.[4] And a
sign also has been given to the
house of David; for 'the virgin'
has 'conceived in the womb and

[1] 1 Cor. I. 26-29, X. 18.
[2] Ps. XLV. 1-3 (for the title see Sept., Ps. XLIV).
[3] See Origen, In Luc. hom. 32 (Lomm. V. 208). The 'one year' is
based upon St. Luke IV. 19. In another passage, In Matt. Com. ser. 40
(Lomm. IV. 276), Origen gives the time as three years.
[4] See Ps. LXXII. 7, 8.

GREEK

and his name is 'Emmanuel', which means 'God with us'.[1]

There has also been fulfilled that which the same prophet says, 'God is with us. Know it, ye nations, and be overcome; ye that are strong, be overcome'.[2] For we who have been captured from among the nations have been overcome and conquered by the grace of his word. Moreover the place of his birth is foretold in Micah. 'And thou, Bethlehem,' it says, 'land of Judah, art in no way least among the rulers of Judah; for out of thee shall come a governor, who shall shepherd my people Israel'.[3] And the 'seventy weeks' until the coming of Christ the governor were fulfilled in accordance with Daniel's prophecy.[4] He, too, has come who according to Job has 'subdued the great fish'[5] and who has given to his true disciples authority to 'tread on serpents and scorpions and over every power of the enemy', without being in any way harmed by them.[6]

Let anyone also consider how the apostles who were sent by Jesus to preach the gospel sojourned everywhere, and he will see that their daring venture was not merely human and that the command was from God. And if we examine how, when people heard the new teachings and strange words, they welcomed these men, the desire to plot

LATIN

has borne Emmanuel', which means, 'God is with us'.[1]

There has also been fulfilled that which the same prophet says, 'God is with us. Know it ye nations, and be overcome.'[2] For we have been overcome and conquered, we who come from the nations and are as it were the spoils of his victory, we who have bowed our necks to the yoke of his grace. Moreover the place of his birth is foretold in the prophet Micah, who says; 'And thou, Bethlehem, land of Judah, art in no way least among the rulers of Judah; for out of thee shall come a governor, who shall rule my people Israel'.[3] Further, the weeks of years until the coming of Christ the governor, which Daniel the prophet foretold, have been fulfilled.[4] He, too, has come who was foretold by Job to be about to 'destroy the huge beast'[5] and who also gave to his personal disciples authority to 'tread on serpents and scorpions and over every power of the enemy,' without being in any way harmed by them.[6]

And if any one will consider the journeyings of Christ's apostles through all the various places in which they were sent by him to preach the gospel, he will find that what they ventured to undertake was beyond the power of man and that their success in having accomplished what they ventured upon is from God. If we consider how, when

[1] Is. VII. 14; St. Matt. I. 23.
[3] St. Matt. II. 6 (from Micah V. 2).
[5] Job III. 8 (Sept.).

[2] Is. VIII. 8, 9 (Sept.).
[4] See Dan. IX. 24.
[6] See St. Luke X. 19.

GREEK

against them being frustrated by some divine power that watched over them, we shall not refuse to believe that they even worked miracles, 'God bearing witness with their words, and through signs and wonders and manifold powers'.[1]

6. Now when we thus briefly demonstrate the divine nature of Jesus and use the words spoken in prophecy about him, we demonstrate at the same time that the writings which prophesy about him are divinely inspired and that the words which announce his sojourning here and his teaching were spoken with all power and authority and that this is the reason why they have prevailed over the elect people taken from among the nations. And we must add that it was after the advent of Jesus that the inspiration of the prophetic words and the spiritual nature of Moses' law came to light. For before the advent of Christ it was not at all possible to bring forward clear proofs of the divine inspiration of the old scriptures. But the advent of Jesus led those who might have suspected that the law and the prophets were not divine to the clear conviction that they were composed by the aid of heavenly grace.

LATIN

people heard that a new teaching was being introduced by these men, they were able to receive them, or rather how while often desiring to destroy them they were restrained by some divine power that was present with them, we shall find that in this matter nothing was wrought by human strength but all by divine power and providence, 'signs and powers manifest beyond all doubt bearing witness to their word and teaching.'[1]

6. Now that we have briefly demonstrated these points, namely, the deity of Jesus Christ and the fulfilment of all those prophecies that were spoken about him, it is, I think, also proved at the same time that the writings themselves which have prophesied about him were divinely inspired, those which foretold either his advent or the power of his teaching or the ingathering of all the nations. To which must also be added the following, that the divine nature and inspiration both of the oracles of the prophets and of the law of Moses has been specially brought to light and proved since the time when Christ came into this world. For before the predictions made by these were fulfilled, although they were true and inspired by God, still they could not be shown to be true because they were not yet proved to have come to pass; but the advent of Christ proclaimed the truth and divine inspiration of what had

1 See Heb. II. 4; Acts V. 12.

GREEK

LATIN

And he who approaches the prophetic words with care and attention will feel from his very reading a trace of their divine inspiration and will be convinced by his own feelings that the words which are believed by us to be from God are not the compositions of men. Now the light which was contained within the law of Moses, but was hidden away under a veil, shone forth at the advent of Jesus, when the veil was taken away and there came at once to men's knowledge those 'good things' of which the letter of the law held a 'shadow'.[1]

been spoken, whereas before it would certainly have been considered doubtful whether the issue of what had been predicted would come to pass.

Further, if any one ponders over the prophetic sayings with all the attention and reverence they deserve, it is certain that in the very act of reading and diligently studying them his mind and feelings will be touched by a divine breath and he will recognise that the words he is reading are not the utterances of man but the language of God; and so he will perceive from his own experience that these books have been composed not by human art or mortal eloquence but, if I may so speak, in a style that is divine. The splendour of Christ's advent has, therefore, by illuminating the law of Moses with the brightness of the truth, withdrawn the veil which had covered the letter of the law and has disclosed, for every one who believes in him, all those 'good things' which lay concealed within.[1]

7. It would be a long business if we were to record at this point the ancient prophecies relating to every future event, in order that the doubter might be struck by their divine origin and, putting away all hesitation and indecision, might devote himself with his whole soul to the words of God. But if in every passage of the scriptures the superhuman element of the thought does not appear obvious

7. It would be a matter of considerable labour if we were to record the time and manner in which every event predicted of old by the prophets has been fulfilled, in the hope that we might thereby confirm those who are in doubt; although it is possible for anyone who desires more accurate knowledge about these things to gather proofs in abundance from the books of the truth themselves. But if at

[1] See 2 Cor. III. 15, 16; Heb. X. 1.

GREEK

to the uninstructed, that is no wonder. For in regard to the works of that providence which controls the whole world, while some show themselves most plainly to be works of providence, others are so obscure as to appear to afford grounds for disbelief in the God who with unspeakable skill and power superintends the universe. The skilful plan of the providential ruler is not so clear in things on earth as it is in regard to the sun and moon and stars, and not so plain in the events that happen to men as it is in regard to the souls and bodies of animals, where the purpose and reason of the impulses, the mental images and the natures they possess and the structures of their bodies are accurately discovered by those who investigate these matters.

LATIN

first sight of the letter the super-human meaning does not at once appear obvious to those who have been but little instructed in divine things, that is no wonder; because divine things are communicated to men somewhat obscurely and are the more hidden in proportion to the unbelief or unworthiness of the inquirer. For while it is certain that everything which exists or happens in this world is arranged by the providence of God, there are some things which show themselves quite plainly to be subject to the control of providence, whereas others evolve in a manner so obscure and so hard to understand that in their case the plan of divine providence is utterly concealed. The result is that occasionally there are some who disbelieve that certain things have any connexion with providence, since the plan on which the works of divine providence are arranged with unspeakable skill is hidden from them; although this plan is not equally concealed in regard to all things. Moreover among men themselves it is pondered over less by one and more by another, while the inhabitant of heaven, whoever he may be, knows more of it than any man on the earth.[1] And the plan of bodies is apparent to us in one way, that of trees in another, while that of souls, in yet another way, is concealed from us. In what manner, too, the divine movements of rational minds are ordered by divine pro-

---

[1] Rufinus seems to have misunderstood the original.

GREEK

vidence is to a large extent hidden from men, and not a little, in my opinion, from the angels also.

But just as providence is not abolished because of our ignorance, at least not for those who have once rightly believed in it, so neither is the divine character of scripture, which extends through all of it, abolished because our weakness cannot discern in every sentence the hidden splendour of its teachings, concealed under a poor and humble style. For 'we have a treasure in earthen vessels, that the exceeding greatness of the power of God may shine forth'[1] and may not be reckoned as coming from us who are but men. For if it had been the hackneyed methods of demonstration used among men and preserved in books that had convinced mankind, our faith might reasonably have been supposed to rest in the wisdom of men and not in the power of God.[2] But now it is clear that 'the word and the preaching' have prevailed among the multitude 'not in persuasive words of wisdom, but in demonstration of the Spirit and of power.'[3]

But just as divine providence is not proved to be a fiction, particularly for those who are convinced of its existence, because its workings and arrangements are beyond the comprehension of human minds, so neither will the divine inspiration of holy scripture, which extends through its entire body, be supposed to be non-existent because the weakness of our understanding cannot discover the deep and hidden thoughts in every sentence; for the treasure of divine wisdom is concealed in vessels of poor and humble words, as the apostle points out when he says: 'We have this treasure in earthen vessels, that the greatness of the divine power may shine forth the more',[1] when no taint of human eloquence is mingled with the truth of the doctrines. For if our books had attracted men to belief because they were composed with rhetorical skill or with philosophical cleverness, our faith would undoubtedly have been supposed to rest in the skilful use of words and in human wisdom, and not in the power of God.[2] But now it is well known to all that 'the word of this preaching' has been so accepted by multitudes in almost the whole world that they have realised that their belief rests 'not in persuasive words of

[1] See 2 Cor. IV. 7.
[2] See 1 Cor. II. 5.
[3] See 1 Cor. II. 4.

GREEK   **LATIN**

Since therefore it is a celestial or even super-celestial power that impels us to worship only him who created us, let us endeavour to 'leave behind the doctrine of the first principles of Christ', that is, of the elements, and 'press on to perfection',[2] that the wisdom which is spoken to the perfect may be spoken also to us. For he who had acquired this wisdom promises that he speaks it to the perfect, and that it is a wisdom different from the 'wisdom of this world, and the wisdom of the rulers of this world, which is coming to nought'.[3] And this wisdom will be distinctly stamped upon us 'according to the revelation of the mystery which hath been kept in silence through times eternal, but now is manifested both through the scriptures and through the appearing of our Lord and Saviour Jesus Christ'; to whom be glory for ever and ever. Amen.[4]

wisdom, but in demonstration of the Spirit and of power.'[1]

Since therefore we have been drawn by a celestial, nay, by an even super-celestial power, to faith and trust, for this purpose, that we may worship the only Creator of all things as our God, let us also endeavour to strive earnestly to 'leave behind the doctrine of the first principles of Christ', which are the elementary principles of knowledge, and to 'press on to perfection',[2] that that wisdom which is delivered to the perfect may be delivered also to us. For such is the promise of him to whom the preaching of this wisdom was committed, and who says, 'Howbeit we speak wisdom among the perfect, yet a wisdom not of this world nor of the rulers of this world, who are to come to nought'.[3] By this he shows that our wisdom, so far as concerns polished language, has nothing in common with the wisdom of this world. This wisdom, therefore, will be the more clearly and perfectly inscribed in our hearts, if it is made known to us 'according to the revelation of the mystery which hath been hidden through times eternal, but now is manifested through the scriptures of the prophets' and 'through the coming of our Lord and Saviour Jesus Christ', to whom is the glory for ever and ever. Amen.[4]

---

[1] See 1 Cor. II. 4.   [2] See Heb. VI. 1.
[3] See 1 Cor. II. 6.
[4] See Rom. XVI. 25-27; 2 Tim. I. 10; 1 Tim. VI. 14.

CHAPTER II

GREEK

How Divine Scripture should be read and interpreted.[1]

1. Now that we have spoken cursorily about the inspiration of the divine scriptures it is necessary to discuss the manner in which they are to be read and understood, since many mistakes have been made in consequence of the method by which the holy documents ought to be interpreted not having been discovered by the multitude. For the hard-hearted and ignorant members of the circumcision have refused to believe in our Saviour because they think that they are keeping closely to the language of the prophecies that relate to him, and they see that he did not literally 'proclaim release to captives' or build what they consider to be a real 'city of God' or 'cut off the chariots from Ephraim and the horse from Jerusalem' or 'eat butter and honey, and choose the good before he knew or preferred the evil.'[2]

LATIN

Many, not understanding the Scriptures spiritually, and interpreting them erroneously, have fallen into heresies.

1. Now that we have dealt, therefore, with this point, that the divine scriptures were inspired by the Holy Spirit, it appears necessary also to explain how some men have involved themselves in numerous errors through not reading or understanding them aright, because the method by which we should approach the interpretation of the divine writings is unknown to the multitude. For the Jews, owing to their hardness of heart and their desire to appear wise in their own sight, have refused to believe in our Lord and Saviour because they suppose that the prophecies that relate to him must be understood literally, that is, that he ought actually and visibly to have 'proclaimed release to captives', and that he ought to have at once built a city such as they think the 'city of God' really is, and at the same time to have 'cut off the chariots from Ephraim and the horse from Jerusalem', and also to have eaten 'butter and honey' and 'chosen the good before he knew how to prefer the evil':[2]

---

[1] For the Greek title see above p. 256 n. 1.
[2] For these passages see Is. LXI. 1 (St. Luke IV. 19); Ps. XLVI. 4; Ezek. XLVIII. 15 ff; Zech. IX. 10; Is. VII. 15.

GREEK

Further, they think that it is the wolf, the four-footed animal, which is said in prophecy to be going to 'feed with the lamb, and the leopard to lie down with the kid, and the calf and bull and lion to feed together, led by a little child, and the ox and the bear to pasture together, their young ones growing up with each other, and the lion to eat straw like the ox';[1] and having seen none of these events literally happening during the advent of him whom we believe to be Christ they did not accept our Lord Jesus, but crucified him on the ground that he had wrongly called himself Christ.

And the members of the heretical sects, reading the passage, 'A fire has been kindled in mine anger';[2] and 'I am a jealous God, visiting the sins of the fathers upon the children to the third and fourth generation';[3] and 'It repenteth me that I have anointed Saul to be king';[4] and 'I, God, make peace and create evil';[5] and elsewhere, 'There is no evil in a city, which the Lord did not do';[6] and further, 'Evils came down from the Lord upon the gates of Jerusalem';[7] and

LATIN

Further, they think that it is the wolf, the four-footed animal, of which it is prophesied that at the coming of Christ it must 'feed with lambs, and the leopard lie down with the kids, and the calf and the bull feed with lions and be led to their pastures by a little child, and the ox and the bear lie down together in the green fields and their young ones be brought up side by side, and lions to stand at stalls with oxen and feed on straw.'[1] Seeing, then, that there was no fulfilment in history of all these things which were prophesied of him and in which they believed that the signs of the advent of Christ were specially to be observed, they refused to acknowledge the presence of our Lord Jesus Christ; nay, contrary to all right and justice, that is, contrary to the faith of prophecy, they nailed him to the cross for assuming for himself the name of Christ.

Then again the heretics, reading in the law, 'A fire has been kindled in my anger';[2] and 'I am a jealous God, visiting the sins of the fathers upon the children to the third and fourth generation';[3] and 'It repenteth me that I have anointed Saul to be king';[4] and 'I am God, that maketh peace and createth evil';[5] and again 'There is no evil in a city, which the Lord hath not done';[6] and 'Evils came down from the Lord upon the gates of Jerusalem';[7] and 'An evil

[1] See Is. XI. 6, 7
[3] Exod. XX. 5.
[5] Is. XLV. 7.

[2] Deut. XXXII. 22; Jer. XV. 14.
[4] 1 Sam. XV. 11.
[6] Amos III. 6.
[7] Micah. I. 12.

GREEK

'An evil spirit from the Lord troubled Saul';[1] and ten thousand other passages like these, have not dared to disbelieve that they are the writings of God, but believe them to belong to the Creator, whom the Jews worship.[2] Consequently they think that since the Creator is imperfect and not good, the Saviour came here to proclaim a more perfect God who they say is not the Creator, and about whom they entertain diverse opinions. Then having once fallen away from the Creator, who is the sole unbegotten God, they have given themselves up to fictions, fashioning mythical hypotheses according to which they suppose that there are some things that are seen and others that are not seen, all of which are the fancies of their own minds.

Moreover, even the simpler of those who claim to belong to the Church, while believing indeed that there is none greater than the Creator, in which they are right, yet believe such things about him as would not be believed of the most savage and unjust of men.

2. Now the reason why all those we have mentioned hold false opinions and make impious or ignorant assertions about God appears to be nothing else but this, that scripture is not

LATIN

spirit from God troubled Saul';[1] and many other passages of scripture like these, have not dared to say that they are not the writings of God, but have supposed them to belong to that Creator God whom the Jews worshipped,[2] and who they think should be believed to be merely just, and not good as well. For they think that the Saviour came here to proclaim to us a more perfect God, who they say is not the Creator of the world, and about whom they entertain diverse opinions; since having once fallen away from their faith in God the Creator, who is the God of all, they have given themselves up to various fictions and fables, inventing false opinions and saying that there are certain visible things made by one power and certain invisible things created by another power, just as they are led by the fancy and vanity of their own minds.

Moreover some of the simpler of those who appear to remain within the faith of the Church, while holding that there is none greater than the Creator God, in which they maintain a right and sound opinion, yet believe such things about him as would not be believed even of the most unjust and savage of men.

2. Now the reason why those we have mentioned above have a false apprehension of all these matters is nothing else but this, that the holy scripture is not understood by them in its

---

1 [1] Sam. XVIII. 10.
[2] See above, Bk. II. Ch. V. 1 (p. 101 ff.).

GREEK   LATIN

understood in its spiritual sense, but is interpreted according to the bare letter. On this account we must explain to those who believe that the sacred books are not the works of men, but that they were composed and have come down to us as a result of the inspiration of the Holy Spirit by the will of the Father of the universe through Jesus Christ, what are the methods of interpretation that appear right to us, who keep to the rule of the heavenly Church of Jesus Christ through the succession from the Apostles.

That there are certain mystical revelations made known through the divine scriptures is believed by all, even by the simplest of those who are adherents of the word; but what these revelations are, fair-minded and humble men confess that they do not know. If, for instance, an inquirer were to be in a difficulty, about the intercourse of Lot with his daughters,[1] or the two wives of Abraham,[2] or the two sisters married to Jacob,[3] or the two hand-maids who bore children by him,[4] they can say nothing except that these things are mysteries not understood by us.

spiritual sense, but according to the sound of the letter. On this account we shall try to demonstrate, so far as our moderate ability will permit, to those who believe that the holy Scriptures were not composed by means of merely human words but were written under the inspiration of the Holy Spirit and were also handed down and entrusted to us by the will of God the Father through his only-begotten Son Jesus Christ, what is the method of interpretation that appears right to us, who keep to that rule and discipline delivered by Jesus Christ to the apostles and handed down by them in succession to their posterity, the teachers of the heavenly Church.

That there are certain mystical revelations made known through the holy scriptures is admitted, I think, by all, even by the simpler kind of believers; but what these revelations are, or of what nature they are, any man who is fair-minded and not possessed by the vice of boasting will reverently confess that he does not know. If, for instance, we are asked about the daughters of Lot and their apparent unlawful intercourse with their father,[1] or about the two wives of Abraham,[2] or the two sisters who were married to Jacob,[3] or the two handmaids who increased the number of his sons,[4] what else can we reply than that these are sacraments and figures of spiritual things, but that we are ignorant of their precise nature?

---

[1] See Gen. XIX. 30 ff.
[3] See Gen. XXIX. 21 ff.

[2] See Gen. XVI.
[4] Gen. XXX. 1-13.

GREEK

But when the passage about the equipment of the tabernacle is read,[1] believing that the things described therein are types, they seek for ideas which they can attach to each detail that is mentioned in connexion with the tabernacle. Now so far as concerns their belief that the tabernacle is a type of something they are not wrong; but in rightly attaching the word of scripture to the particular idea of which the tabernacle is a type, here they sometimes fall into error. And they declare that all narratives that are supposed to speak about marriage or the begetting of children or wars or any other stories whatever that may be accepted among the multitude are types; but when we ask, of what, then sometimes owing to the lack of thorough training, sometimes owing to rashness, and occasionally, even when one is well trained and of sound judgment, owing to man's exceedingly great difficulty in discovering these things, the interpretation of every detail is not altogether clear.

3. And what must we say about the prophecies, which we all know are filled with riddles

LATIN

When, moreover, we read of the equipment of the tabernacle,[1] we hold it as certain that the things described therein are figures of some hidden realities, but to attach them to their appropriate meanings and to bring to light and discuss each separate detail is, I think, a very difficult, not to say impossible task. However, as I said, it does not escape even the common intellect that that description is full of mysteries. And all those narratives which appear to be composed about marriages or the begetting of children or different kinds of battles or any other stories whatever, what else can we believe them to be but the forms and figures of hidden and sacred things? But either because men pay too little attention to the training of their mind, or because they think they already know before they learn, the consequence is that they never begin to know; otherwise if neither earnestness is lacking, nor a master, and if these questions are studied as befits divine, and not merely human matters, that is, in a reverent and pious spirit, and as questions that we hope will in most cases be made clear by the revelation of God, since to human sense they are exceedingly difficult and obscure, then, perhaps, he who thus seeks will at last find all that it is lawful for us to find.

3. But it may possibly be supposed that this difficulty belongs only to the prophetic

---

[1] See Exod. XXV. ff.

GREEK

and dark sayings?[1] Or if we come to the gospels, the accurate interpretation even of these, since it is an interpretation of the mind of Christ, demands that grace that was given to him who said, 'We have the mind of Christ, that we may know the things that were freely given to us by God. Which things also we speak, not in words which man's wisdom teacheth, but which the Spirit teacheth.'[2] And who, on reading the revelations made to John, could fail to be amazed at the deep obscurity of the unspeakable mysteries contained therein, which are evident even to him who does not understand what is written? And as for the apostolic epistles, what man who is skilled in literary interpretation would think them to be plain and easily understood, when even in them there are thousands of passages that provide, as if through a window, a narrow opening leading to multitudes of the deepest thoughts?

Seeing, therefore, that these things are so, and that thousands of men make mistakes, it is dangerous for us when we read to declare lightly that we understand things for which the 'key of knowledge' is necessary,

LATIN

writings, seeing it is certain to all of us that the prophetic style is everywhere sprinkled with figures and riddles.[1] What, then, when we come to the gospels? Is there not also hidden in them an inner meaning which is the Lord's meaning, and which is only revealed through the grace that was given to him who said, 'We have the mind of Christ, that we may know the things that were freely given to us by God. Which things also we speak, not in words which man's wisdom teacheth, but which the Spirit teacheth'.[2] And who indeed, on reading the revelations made to John, could fail to be amazed at the deep obscurity of the unspeakable mysteries contained therein? For even those who cannot understand what is concealed in these writings yet understand clearly that something is concealed there. And as for the apostolic epistles, which to some appear to be simpler, are they not filled with deep meanings, so that men who can understand the inner meaning of divine wisdom seem through them, as if through some narrow opening, to be flooded with the brightness of immeasurable light?

Seeing, therefore, that these things are so, and that there are many who in this life make mistakes, I do not think that anyone can without danger declare that he knows or understands those things for the open-

---

[1] See Prov. I. 6 and Origen, *Con. Celsum* III. 45; VII. 10.
[2] 1 Cor. II. 16, 12, 13.

GREEK

which the Saviour says is with 'the lawyers'.[1] And as for those who are unwilling to admit that these men held the truth before the coming of Christ, let them explain to us how it is that our Lord Jesus Christ says that the 'key of knowledge' was with them, that is, with men who as these objectors say, had no books containing the secrets of knowledge and the all-perfect mysteries.[2] For the passage runs as follows : 'Woe unto you lawyers, for ye have taken away the key of knowledge. Ye entered not in yourselves, and them that were entering in ye hindered.'[3]

4. The right way, therefore, as it appears to us, of approaching the scriptures and gathering their meaning, is the following, which is extracted from the writings themselves. We find some such rule as this laid down by Solomon in the Proverbs concerning the divine doctrines written therein : 'Do thou pourtray them threefold in counsel and knowledge, that thou mayest answer words of truth to those who question thee'.[4]

One must therefore pourtray the meaning of the sacred writings in a threefold way upon one's own soul, so that the simple man may be edified by

LATIN

ing of which the 'key of knowledge' is necessary, which key the Saviour said was with those 'learned in the law'.[1] And at this point, though by a slight digression, I think we should ask those who tell us that before the coming of the Saviour the truth did not rest with those who were trained in the law, how it is that our Lord Jesus Christ says that the 'keys of knowledge' were with those who had in their hands the books of the law and the prophets. For the Lord spoke as follows: 'Woe to you, doctors of the law, for ye have taken away the key of knowledge. Ye entered not in yourselves, and them that wished to enter in ye hindered.'[3]

4. But, as we had begun to say, the right way, as it appears to us, of understanding the scriptures and investigating their meaning, is the following; for indeed we are taught out of scripture itself how we ought to think of it. We find some such rule as this laid down in the Proverbs of Solomon concerning the examination of divine scripture. 'Do thou,' it says, 'pourtray these things to thyself threefold in counsel and knowledge, so that thou mayest answer words of truth to those who question thee'.[4]

Each one must therefore pourtray the meaning of the divine writings in a threefold way upon his own soul; that is, so that the simple may be edified by what

---

[1] See St. Luke XI. 52.
[2] Books, that is, such as the Gnostics claimed to possess.
[3] St. Luke XI. 52.   [4] Prov. XXII. 20, 21.

GREEK

what we may call the flesh of the scripture, this name being given to the obvious interpretation; while the man who has made some progress may be edified by its soul, as it were; and the man who is perfect and like those mentioned by the apostle : 'We speak wisdom among the perfect; yet a wisdom not of this world, nor of the rulers of this world, which are coming to nought; but we speak God's wisdom in a mystery, even the wisdom that hath been hidden, which God foreordained before the worlds unto our glory'[1]—this man may be edified by the spiritual law,[2] which has 'a shadow of the good things to come'.[3] For just as man consists of body, soul and spirit, so in the same way does the scripture, which has been prepared by God to be given for man's salvation.

We therefore read in this light the passage in The Shepherd, a book which is despised by some, where Hermas is bidden to 'write two books', and after this to 'announce to the presbyters of the Church' what he has learned from the Spirit. This is the wording: 'Thou shalt write two books, and shalt give one to Clement and one to Grapte. And Grapte shall admonish the widows and the orphans. But Clement shall send to the cities without, and

LATIN

we may call the body of the scriptures (for such is the name we may give to the common and literal interpretation); while those who have begun to make a little progress and are able to perceive something more than that may be edified by the soul of scripture; and those who are perfect and like the men of whom the apostle says : 'We speak wisdom among the perfect; yet a wisdom not of this world, nor of the rulers of this world, which are coming to nought; but we speak God's wisdom hidden in a mystery, the wisdom which God foreordained before the worlds unto our glory'[1]—such as these may be edified by that spiritual law,[2] which has 'a shadow of the good things to come',[3] as if by the Spirit. Just as man, therefore, is said to consist of body, soul and spirit, so also does the holy scripture, which has been bestowed by the divine bounty for man's salvation.

It is this fact that we believe to be referred to in the book called The Shepherd, which apparently is despised by some, in the passage where Hermas is bidden to 'write two books', and after this to 'announce to the presbyters of the Church' what he has learned from the Spirit. It is written in these words: 'Thou shalt write two books, and shalt give one to Clement and one to Grapte. And Grapte shall admonish the widows and the orphans, but

---

[1] 1 Cor. II. 6, 7.   [2] See Rom. VII. 14.   [3] See Heb. X. 1.

GREEK

thou shalt announce to the presbyters of the Church.'[1]

Now Grapte, who admonishes the widows and orphans, is the bare letter, which admonishes those child souls that are not yet able to enrol God as their Father and are on this account called orphans, and which also admonishes those who while no longer associating with the unlawful bridegroom are in widowhood because they have not yet become worthy of the true one. But Clement, who has already gone beyond the letter, is said to send the sayings 'to the cities without', as if to say, to the souls that are outside all bodily and lower thoughts; while the disciple of the Spirit is bidden to announce the message in person, no longer through letters but through living words, to the presbyters or elders of the whole Church of God, to men who have grown grey through wisdom.

5. But since there are certain passages of scripture which, as we shall show in what follows, have no bodily sense at all, there

LATIN

Clement is to send through all the cities that are without, and thou shalt announce to the presbyters of the Church.'[1]

Now Grapte, who is bidden to admonish the orphans and widows, is the bare meaning of the letter, by which child souls, who have not yet deserved to have God for their Father and are on that account called orphans, are admonished. The widows are those who have departed from the wicked husband to whom they had been united contrary to the law, but remain widows because they have not yet advanced to the point of being united to the heavenly bridegroom. Clement is bidden to send the sayings to those who are already departing from the letter, into the 'cities that are without', as if to say, to those souls which by means of these sayings have begun to be built up into a condition superior to the cares of the body and the desires of the flesh. Hermas himself is bidden to announce what he has learned from the Holy Spirit, not through letters nor through a book but by the living voice, to the presbyters of the Church of Christ, that is, to those who, owing to their capacity to receive spiritual doctrine, possess a ripe endowment of wisdom.

5. But we must certainly not forget that there are some passages of scripture in which this that we call the body, that

[1] Hermas, *Vis.* II. 4, 3. Irenaeus and Clement of Alexandria both treated Hermas as an inspired writer, as Origen does here. His book was read in the Church for several centuries, but had fallen into disuse in the West by the time of Jerome (*De vir. illus.* X.).

GREEK

are occasions when we must seek only for the soul and the spirit, as it were, of the passage. And possibly this is the reason why the waterpots which, as we read in the gospel according to John, are said to be set there 'for the purifying of the Jews', contain two or three firkins apiece.[1] The language alludes to those who are said by the apostle to be Jews 'inwardly',[2] and it means that these are purified through the word of the scriptures, whch contain in some cases 'two firkins', that is, so to speak, the soul meaning and the spiritual meaning, and in other cases three, since some passages possess, in addition to those before-mentioned, a bodily sense as well, which is capable of edifying the hearers. And six waterpots may reasonably allude to those who are being purified in the world, which was made in six days, a perfect number.[3]

6. That it is possible to derive benefit from the first, and to this extent helpful meaning, is witnessed by the multitudes of sincere and simple believers.

LATIN

is, the logical and literal meaning, is not found, as we shall show in what follows; and there are places where those meanings which we have called the soul and the spirit are alone to be looked for. I believe that this fact is indicated in the gospels, when six waterpots are said 'to be set there for the purifying of the Jews, containing two or three firkins apiece'.[1] Here, as I said, the language of the gospel seems to allude to those who are said by the apostle to be Jews 'inwardly',[2] and to mean that these are purified through the word of scripture, by receiving in some cases 'two firkins,' that is, by accepting the soul meaning and the spiritual meaning in accordance with what we said above, and in other cases three firkins, when the reading also retains for the edification of the hearers a bodily meaning, namely the literal one. And six waterpots are approximately mentioned in allusion to those who are being purified while living in the world. For we read that this world and all that is in it were finished in six days, which is a perfect number.[3]

6. How much value there is in this first meaning, which we have called the literal one, is witnessed by the entire multitude of those believers who accept

---

[1] See St. John II. 6.   [2] See Rom. II. 29.
[3] Why the number six is perfect is explained by Philo, *de opificio mundi* 3. A perfect number is equal to the sum of its factors; i.e. 6=1 x 2 x 3. The number six is also the product of the first male number, 3, and the first female number, 2. The six days, Philo tells us, do not represent length of time, but order in thought. Neither he nor Origen would have regarded the days as literal periods.

GREEK

But of the kind of explanation which penetrates as it were to the soul an illustration is found in Paul's first epistle to the Corinthians. 'For,' he says, 'it is written; thou shalt not muzzle the ox that treadeth out the corn'. Then in explanation of this law he adds, 'Is it for the oxen that God careth? Or saith he it altogether for our sake? Yea, for our sake it was written, because he that ploweth ought to plow in hope, and he that thresheth, to thresh in hope of partaking.'[1] And most of the interpretations adapted to the multitude which are in circulation and which edify those who cannot understand the higher meanings have something of the same character.

But it is a spiritual explanation when one is able to show of what kind of 'heavenly things' the Jews 'after the flesh' served a copy and a shadow, and of what 'good things to come' the law has a 'shadow'.[2] And, speaking generally, we have, in accordance with the apostolic promise, to seek after 'the wisdom in a mystery, even the wisdom that hath been hidden, which God foreordained before the worlds unto the glory' of the righteous, 'which none of

LATIN

the faith quite trustfully and simply; and this needs no long argument because it is obvious to all. But of the kind of explanation which we have spoken of above as the soul, as it were, of Scripture, many illustrations are given us by the apostle Paul, as, for example, first of all in his epistle to the Corinthians. 'For', he says, 'it is written; thou shalt not muzzle the ox that treadeth out the corn.' Then in explaining how this precept ought to be understood, he adds: 'Is it for the oxen that God careth? Or saith he it altogether for our sake? Yea, for our sake it was written, because he that ploweth ought to plow in hope, and he that thresheth, to thresh in hope of partaking.'[1] Moreover, many other similar passages which are interpreted in this manner out of the law, impart the utmost instruction to those who hear them.

But a spiritual explanation is like this, when one is able to show of what 'heavenly things' those who are Jews 'after the flesh' serve a copy and a shadow, and of what 'good things to come' the law has a 'shadow',[2] and any other matters of this kind which may be found in the holy scriptures; or when we inquire what is that 'wisdom hidden in a mystery, which God foreordained before the worlds unto our glory, which none of the rulers of this world

---

[1] I Cor. IX. 9, 10 (Deut. XXV. 4). For the same quotation in a slightly different form see above, p. 97 f.
[2] See Heb. VIII. 5; Rom. VIII. 5; Heb. X. 1.

GREEK

the rulers of this world knew'.[1]
The same apostle also says
somewhere, after mentioning
certain narratives from Exodus
and Numbers, that 'these things
happened unto them figuratively, and they were written for
our sake, upon whom the ends
of the ages are come.'[2] He
also gives hints to show what
these things were figures of,
when he says: 'For they drank
of that spiritual rock that
followed them, and that rock
was Christ.'[3]

In another epistle, when out-
lining the arrangements of the
tabernacle he quotes the words:
'Thou shalt make all things
according to the figure that was
shown thee in the mount.'[4]
Further, in the epistle to the
Galatians, speaking in terms of
reproach to those who believe
that they are reading the law
and yet do not understand it,
and laying it down that they
who do not believe that there
are allegories in the writings do
not understand the law, he says:
'Tell me, ye that desire to be
under the law, do ye not hear
the law? For it is written, that
Abraham had two sons, one by
the handmaid and one by the
free woman. Howbeit the son
by the handmaid is born after
the flesh; but the son by the
free woman is born through promise. Which things contain an
allegory; for these women are
two covenants',[5] and what

LATIN

knew',[1] or ask the meaning of
the same apostle's statement,
when he makes use of certain
illustrations from Exodus and
Numbers and says that 'these
things happened unto them figuratively, and they were written
for our sake, upon whom the
ends of the ages are come',[2]
and when he affords us an
opportunity of understanding
how we can learn of what those
events that happened to them
were figures, by saying, 'For
they drank of that spiritual rock
that followed them, and that
rock was Christ.'[3]

Moreover in another epistle
he mentions that command about
the tabernacle which was enjoined upon Moses: 'Thou shalt
make all things according to the
figure that was shown thee in
the mount.'[4] And when writing
to the Galatians and reproaching
some who believe they are reading the law and yet do not
understand it, because they
are unaware that there are
allegories in these writings, he
addresses them in a tone of rebuke: 'Tell me, ye that desire
to be under the law, do ye not
hear the law? For it is written
that Abraham had two sons, one
by the handmaid and one by the
free woman. Howbeit he who
was born of the handmaid was
born according to the flesh, but
he of the free woman was born
according to promise. Which
things contain an allegory. For
these are the two covenants',[5]
and what follows. Here we

[1] See 1 Cor. II. 7, 8.   [2] 1 Cor. X. 11.   [3] 1 Cor. X. 4.
[4] Heb. VIII. 5 (Exod. XXV. 40).   [5] Gal. IV. 21-24.

GREEK

LATIN

follows. Now we must carefully mark each of the words spoken by him. He says, 'Ye that desire to be under the law' (not, 'ye that are under the law') 'do ye not hear the law?' hearing being taken to mean understanding and knowing.

And in the epistle to the Colossians, briefly epitomising the meaning of the entire system of the law, he says: 'Let no man therefore judge you in meat or in drink or in respect of a feast day or a new moon or a sabbath, which are a shadow of the things to come.'[1] Further, in the epistle to the Hebrews, when discoursing about those who are of the circumcision, he writes: 'They who serve that which is a copy and shadow of the heavenly things.'[2] Now it is probable that those who have once admitted that the apostle is a divinely inspired man will feel no difficulty in regard to the five books ascribed to Moses; but in regard to the rest of the history they desire to learn whether those events also 'happened figuratively'.[3] We must note the quotation in the epistle to the Romans: 'I have left for myself seven thousand men, who have not bowed the knee to Baal,'[4] found in the third book of the Kings. Here Paul has taken it to stand for those who are Israelites 'according to election',[5] for not only are the gentiles benefited by the coming of Christ, but also some who belong to the divine race.

must also observe this point, how carefully the apostle says, 'Ye that desire to be under the law' (and not, 'ye that are under the law') 'do ye not hear the law?' Do ye not hear? that is, do ye not understand and know?

Moreover in the epistle to the Colossians he briefly sums up and condenses the meaning of the entire law and says: 'Let no man therefore judge you in meat or in drink or in respect of solemn days or a new moon or a sabbath, which are a shadow of the things to come'.[1] Also when writing to the Hebrews and discoursing about those who are of the circumcision he says: 'They who serve that which is a copy and shadow of the heavenly things.'[2] But probably through the above examples those who accept the apostle's writings as divinely inspired will feel no doubt in regard to the five books of Moses. In regard to the rest of the history, however, they will ask whether the events related therein may also be said to have 'happened figuratively'[3] to those about whom they are written. We notice that this point has been spoken of in the epistle to the Romans, where the apostle takes an illustration from the third book of the Kings, which says: 'I have left for myself seven thousand men, who have not bowed the knee to Baal.'[4] This Paul takes as spoken figuratively of those who are called Israelites 'according

[1] Col. II. 16, 17.   [2] Heb. VIII. 5.
[4] Rom. XI. 4 (1 Kings XIX. 18).

[3] See 1 Cor. X. 11.
[5] See Rom. XI. 5.

GREEK

LATIN

to election,[1] in order to show that the coming of Christ was beneficial not only to the gentiles but also to very many of the race of Israel who have been called to salvation.

7. This being so, we must outline what seems to us to be the marks of a true understanding of the scriptures. And in the first place we must point out that the aim of the Spirit who, by the providence of God through the Word who was 'in the beginning with God',[2] enlightened the servants of the truth, that is, the prophets and apostles, was pre-eminently concerned with the unspeakable mysteries connected with the affairs of men—and by men I mean at the present moment souls that make use of bodies—his purpose being that the man who is capable of being taught might by 'searching out' and devoting himself to the 'deep things'[3] revealed in the spiritual meaning of the words become partaker of all the doctrines of the Spirit's counsel.

7. This being so, we shall now outline the manner in which divine scripture should be understood on these several points, using such illustrations and examples as may occur to us. And in the first place we must call to mind and point out that the Holy Spirit, who by the providence and will of God through the power of his only-begotten Word who was 'in the beginning with God',[2] enlightened the servants of the truth, that is, the prophets and apostles, (wished above all to lend them)[4] to the knowledge of the mysteries connected with those affairs and causes which concern the lives and relationships of men. By men I mean at the present moment souls that are located in bodies. These mysteries which were made known and revealed to them by the Spirit, the prophets pourtrayed figuratively through the narration of what seemed to be human deeds and the handing down of certain legal ordinances and precepts. The aim was that not everyone who wished should have these mysteries laid before his feet to trample upon,[5] but that they should be for the man who had devoted himself to studies of

---

[1] See Rom. XI. 5.   [2] See St. John I. 1.
[3] See 1 Cor. II. 10.
[4] A few words appear to be missing from the Latin at this point, and Koetschau replaces them thus.   [5] See St. Matt. VII. 6.

GREEK   LATIN

this kind with the utmost purity and sobriety and through nights of watching, by which means perchance he might be able to trace out the deeply hidden meaning of the Spirit of God, concealed under the language of an ordinary narrative which points in a different direction, and that so he might become a sharer of the Spirit's knowledge and a partaker of his divine counsel.

And when we speak of the needs of souls, who cannot otherwise reach perfection except through the rich and wise truth about God, we attach of necessity pre-eminent importance to the doctrines concerning God and His only-begotten Son; of what nature the Son is, and in what manner he can be the Son of God, and what are the causes of his descending to the level of human flesh and completely assuming humanity; and what, also, is the nature of his activity, and towards whom and at what times it is exercised. It was necessary, too, that the doctrines concerning beings akin to man and the rest of the rational creatures, both those that are nearer the divine and those that have fallen from blessedness, and the causes of the fall of these latter, should be included in the accounts of the divine teaching; and the question of the differences between souls and how these differences arose, and what the world is and why it exists, and further, how it comes about that evil is so

For in no other way can the soul reach the perfection of knowledge except by being inspired with the truth of the divine wisdom. Therefore it is chiefly the doctrine about God, that is, about the Father, Son and Holy Spirit, which is indicated by those men who were filled with the divine Spirit. Then, too, the mysteries relating to the Son of God, how the Word became flesh, and for what reason he went to the length of 'taking upon him the form of a servant',[1] have also been made kown by those who were filled, as we have said, with the divine Spirit. After that it followed of necessity that they should instruct the race of mortal men by divine teaching concerning rational creatures, both heavenly and earthly, the more blessed and the lower ones alike, and also concerning the differences between souls and how these differences arose; and then the question what this world is and why it was made, and further, how it comes about that evil is

---

[1] See Phil. II. 7.

GREEK

widespread and so terrible on earth, and whether it is not only to be found on earth but also in other places—all this it was necessary that we should learn.

8. Now while these and similar subjects were in the mind of the Spirit who enlightened the souls of the holy servants of the truth, there was a second aim, pursued for the sake of those who were unable to endure the burden of investigating matters of such importance. This was to conceal the doctrine relating to the before-mentioned subjects in words forming a narrative that contained a record dealing with the visible creation, the formation of man and the successive descendants of the first human beings until the time when they became many; and also in other stories that recorded the acts of righteous men and the sins that these same men occasionally committed, seeing they were but human, and the deeds of wickedness, licentiousness and greed done by lawless and impious men.

But the most wonderful thing is, that by means of stories of wars and the conquerors and the conquered certain secret truths are revealed to those who are capable of examining

LATIN

so widespread and so terrible on earth, and whether it is found only on earth or in some other places as well—all this it was necessary that we should learn from the divine teaching.

8. But while it was the intention of the Holy Spirit to enlighten holy souls, who had devoted themselves to the service of the truth, on these and similar subjects, there was in the second place another aim in view, namely, that for the sake of such as either could not or would not give themselves up to this labour and industry in order to prove themselves worthy of being taught and of coming to know matters of such value and importance, the Spirit should wrap up and conceal within ordinary language under cover of some historical record or account of visible things certain secret mysteries. There is introduced therefore an account of the visible creation and of the formation and fashioning of the first man, and then of the descendants that follow in succession from him. There are also recorded certain acts performed by righteous men and ocasionally, too, mention is made of the sins these same men committed, seeing they were but human; and then also a considerable number of the licentious and wicked deeds of impious men are related.

In a wonderful manner, too, an account of wars is presented, and the different fortunes now of the conquerors, now of the conquered are described, and by this means, to those who know

GREEK

these narratives; and, even more marvellous, through a written system of law the laws of truth are prophetically indicated, all these having been recorded in a series with a power which is truly appropriate to the wisdom of God. For the intention was to make even the outer covering of the spiritual truths, I mean the bodily part of the scriptures, in many respects not unprofitable but capable of improving the multitude in so far as they receive it.

9. But if the usefulness of the law and the sequence and ease of the narrative were at first sight clearly discernible throughout, we should be unaware that there was anything beyond the obvious meaning for us to understand in the scriptures. Consequently the Word of God has arranged for certain stumbling-blocks, as it were, and hindrances and impossibilities to be inserted in the midst of the law and the history, in order that we may not be completely drawn away by the sheer attractiveness of the language, and so either reject the true doctrines absolutely, on the ground that we learn from the scriptures nothing worthy of God, or else by never moving away from the letter fail to learn anything of the more divine element.

LATIN

how to examine writings of this kind, certain unspeakable mysteries are revealed. Further, by a marvellous example of wisdom, in the writings of the law the law of truth is implanted and prophetically indicated; and all these are by the divine skill and wisdom woven together to form a kind of outer covering and veil for spiritual meanings, which is what we meant by the body of holy scripture; with the result that even through this that we have called the outer covering of the letter, woven by the art of wisdom, very many readers may be edified and make progress, who otherwise could not do so.

9. But if in every detail of this outer covering, that is, the actual history, the sequence of the law had been preserved and its order maintained, we should have understood the scriptures in an unbroken course and should certainly not have believed that there was anything else buried within them beyond what was indicated at a first glance. Consequently the divine wisdom has arranged for certain stumbling-blocks and interruptions of the historical sense to be found therein, by inserting in the midst a number of impossibilities and incongruities, in order that the very interruption of the narrative might as it were present a barrier to the reader and lead him to refuse to proceed along the pathway of the ordinary meaning: and so, by shutting us out and debarring us from that, might recall us to the beginning

GREEK

And we must also know this, that because the principal aim was to announce the connexion that exists among spiritual events, those that have already happened and those that are yet to come to pass, whenever the Word found that things which had happened in history could be harmonised with these mystical events he used them, concealing from the multitude their deeper meaning. But wherever in the narrative the accomplishment of some particular deeds, which had been previously recorded for the sake of their more mystical meanings, did not correspond with the sequence of the intellectual truths, the scripture wove into the story something which did not happen, occasionally something which could not happen, and occasionally something which might have happened but in fact did not. Sometimes a few words are inserted which in the bodily sense are not true, and at other times a greater number.

A similar method can be discerned also in the law, where it is often possible to find a precept that is useful for its own sake, and suitable to the time when the law was given. Sometimes, however, the precept does not appear to be useful. At other times even

LATIN

of another way, and might thereby bring us, through the entrance of a narrow footpath, to a higher and loftier road and lay open the immense breadth of the divine wisdom.

And we must also know this, that because the aim of the Holy Spirit was chiefly to preserve the connexion of the spiritual meaning, both in the things that are yet to be done and in those which have already been accomplished, whenever he found that things which had been done in history could be harmonised with the spiritual meaning, he composed in a single narrative a texture comprising both kinds of meaning, always, however, concealing the secret sense more deeply. But wherever the record of deeds that had been done could not be made to correspond with the sequence of the spiritual truths, he inserted occasionally some deeds of a less probable character or which could not have happened at all, and occasionally some which might have happened but in fact did not. Sometimes he does this by a few words, which in their bodily sense do not appear capable of containing truth, and at other times by inserting a large number.

This is found to happen particularly in the law, where there are many things which as literal precepts are clearly useful, but also a considerable number in which no principle of utility whatever is disclosed, while sometimes even impossibilities are detected. All this, as we

GREEK

impossibilities are recorded in the law for the sake of the more skilful and inquiring readers, in order that these, by giving themselves to the toil of examining what is written, may gain a sound conviction of the necessity of seeking in such instances a meaning worthy of God.

And not only did the Spirit supervise the writings which were previous to the coming of Christ, but because he is the same Spirit and proceeds from the one God he has dealt in like manner with the gospels and the writings of the apostles. For the history even of these is not everywhere pure, events being woven together in the bodily sense without having actually happened; nor do the law and the commandments contained therein entirely declare what is reasonable.

LATIN

have said, the Holy Spirit supervised, in order that in cases where that which appeared at the first glance could neither be true nor useful we should be led on to search for a truth deeper down and needing more careful examination, and should try to discover in the scriptures which we believe to be inspired by God a meaning worthy of God.

And not only did the Holy Spirit supervise the writings which were previous to the coming of Christ, but because he is one and the same Spirit and proceeds from the one God he has acted similarly in regard to the gospels and the writings of the apostles. For even the narratives which he inspired through them were not woven together without the spell of that wisdom of his, the nature of which we explained above. And so it happens that even in them the Spirit has mingled not a few things by which the historical order of the narrative is interrupted and broken, with the object of turning and calling the attention of the reader, by the impossibility of the literal sense, to an examination of the inner meaning.

CHAPTER III

GREEK

The principle underlying the obscurities in divine Scripture and its impossible or unreasonable character in places, if taken literally.

1. Now[1] what man of intelligence will believe that the first and the second and the third day, and the evening and the morning existed without the sun and moon and stars? And that the first day, if we may so call it, was even without a heaven?[2] And who is so silly as to believe that God, after the manner of a farmer, 'planted a paradise eastward in Eden', and set in it a visible and palpable 'tree of life', of such a sort that anyone who tasted its fruit with his bodily teeth would gain life; and again that one could partake of 'good and evil' by masticating the fruit taken from the tree of that name?[3] And when God is said to 'walk in the paradise in the cool of the day' and Adam to hide himself behind a tree, I do not think anyone will doubt that these are figurative expressions which indicate certain mysteries through a semblance of history and not through actual events.[4]

LATIN

Illustrations from the Scriptures of the method in which Scripture should be understood.

1. But in order to learn the truth of what we say from the facts themselves, let us now examine the actual passages of scripture. What man of intelligence, I ask, will consider it a reasonable statement that the first and the second and third day, in which there are said to be both morning and evening, existed without sun and moon and stars, while the first day was even without a heaven?[2] And who could be found so silly as to believe that God, after the manner of a farmer, 'planted trees in a paradise eastward in Eden', and set therein a 'tree of life', that is, a visible and palpable tree of wood, of such a sort that anyone who ate of this tree with bodily teeth would gain life; and again that anyone who ate of another tree would get a knowledge of 'good and evil'?[3] And further, when God is said to 'walk in the paradise in the evening' and Adam to hide himself behind a tree, I do not think anyone will

---

[1] This sentence (to 'moon and stars') is found in Justinian *Ep. ad Mennam* (Mansi IX. 533). Koetschau marks it Frag. 29.

[2] See Gen. I. 5-13.

[3] See Gen. II. 8, 9, and cp. Philo, *Legis alleg.* I. 14. 'Let not our reasoning admit such gross impiety as to suppose that God works as a farmer and plants gardens.'

See Gen. III. 8.

GREEK

LATIN

Further, when Cain 'goes out from the face of God' it seems clear to thoughtful men that this statement impels the reader to inquire what the 'face of God' is and how anyone can 'go out' from it.[1] And what more need I say, when those who are not altogether blind can collect thousands of such instances, recorded as actual events, but which did not happen literally?

Even the gospels are full of passages of this kind, as when the devil takes Jesus up into a 'high mountain' in order to show him from thence 'the kingdoms of the whole world and the glory of them'.[2] For what man who does not read such passages carelessly would fail to condemn those who believe that with the eye of the flesh, which requires a great height to enable us to perceive what is below and at our feet, the kingdoms of the Persians, Scythians, Indians and Parthians were seen, and the manner in which their rulers are glorified by men? And the careful reader will detect thousands of other passages like this in the gospels, which will convince him that events which did not take place at all are woven into the

doubt that these statements are made by scripture in a figurative manner, in order that through them certain mystical truths may be indicated.[3]

Again, when Cain 'goes out from the face of God', the statement clearly impels a thoughtful reader to inquire what the 'face of God' is, and how any one can 'go out' from it.[1] But not to extend unduly the work we have in hand, it is quite easy for any one who wills to collect from the holy scriptures instances that are recorded as actual events, but which it would be inappropriate and unreasonable to believe could possibly have happened in history.

This kind of scripture is to be found in considerable abundance even in the gospels, as when the devil is said to have taken Jesus up into 'a high mountain' in order to show him from thence 'all the kingdoms of the world and the glory of them'.[2] How could it possibly have happened literally, either that the devil should have led Jesus up into a high mountain or that to his fleshly eyes he should have shown all the kingdoms of the world as if they were lying close to the foot of a single mountain, the kingdoms for instance of the Persians, Scythians and Indians, and in addition, the manner in which the rulers of these kingdoms are glorified by men. And the diligent reader will find in the gospels very many other

[1] See Gen. IV. 16 and Philo, *De poster. Cain* I. 1.
[2] See St. Matt. IV. 8.
[3] See Gen. III. 8.

GREEK

records of what literally did happen.

2. And to come to the Mosaic legislation, many of the laws, so far as their literal observance is concerned, are clearly irrational, while others are impossible. An example of irrationality is the prohibition to eat vultures, seeing that nobody even in the worst famine was ever driven by want to the extremity of eating these creatures.[1] And in regard to the command that children of eight days old who are uncircumcised 'shall be destroyed from among their people',[2] if the law relating to these children were really meant to be carried out according to the letter, the proper course would be to order the death of their fathers or those by whom they were being brought up. But as it is the Scripture says: 'Every male that is uncircumcised, who shall not be circumcised on the eighth day, shall be destroyed from among his people'.[3]

And if you would like to see some impossibilities that are enacted in the law, let us observe that the goat-stag,[4] which

LATIN

passages like this, from which he may learn that among those narratives which appear to be recorded literally there are inserted and interwoven others which cannot be accepted as history but which contain a spiritual meaning.

2. Moreover in the passages containing the laws similar things are found. In the Mosaic law it is ordered that 'every male who has not been circumcised on the eigth day is to be destroyed';[2] which is most illogical, since if the law were meant to be carried out according to the letter, the proper course would certainly be to order the punishment of the parents who had not circumcised their children, or else of those who were bringing up the little ones. But as it is the scripture says: 'A male that is uncircumcised', that is, 'who shall not be circumcised on the eighth day, shall be destroyed from among his people'.[3]

And if we are to look for laws that are impossible, we find mention made of an animal called the goat-stag,[4] which can-

---

[1] Lev. XI. 14. Rufinus has omitted this example.
[2] See Gen. XVII. 14 (Sept.).
[3] See Gen. XVII. 14 (Sept.).
[4] The word only occurs in two MSS. of the Sept., Deut. XIV. 5. The *tragelaphos* was a fantastic animal mentioned by many Greek writers, but the creature of Deut. XIV. 5 is really *elaphos,* the hart or perhaps roebuck (see Hastings, *D.B.,* art. *Hart,* G.E. Post).

GREEK

Moses commands us to offer in sacrifice as a clean animal, is a creature that cannot possibly exist; while as to the griffin,[1] which the lawgiver forbids to be eaten, there is no record that it has ever fallen into the hands of man. Moreover in regard to the celebrated sabbath, a careful reader will see that the command, 'Ye shall sit each one in your dwellings; let none of you go out from his place on the sabbath day,'[2] is an impossible one to observe literally, for no living creature could sit for a whole day and not move from his seat.

Consequently the members of the circumcision and all those who maintain that nothing more than the actual wording is signified make no inquiry whatever into some matters, such as the goat-stag, the griffin and the vulture, while on others they babble copiously, bringing forward lifeless traditions, as for instance when they say, in reference to the sabbath, that each man's 'place' is two thousand cubits.[3] Others, however, among whom is Dositheus the Samaritan,[4] condemn such an interpretation, and believe that in whatever position a man is found on the Sabbath day he should remain there until evening.

LATIN

not possibly exist, but which Moses allows to be eaten among the clean animals; while as to the griffin,[1] which the lawgiver forbids to be eaten, there is no record or knowledge that it has ever fallen into the hands of man. Moreover in regard to the celebrated observance of the sabbath he speaks thus: 'Ye shall sit each one in your dwellings; no one shall move from his place on the sabbath day'.[2] It is certainly impossible for this to be observed literally; for no man can sit for a whole day so as never to move from the place where he is sitting.

In dealing with these various points the members of the circumcision and all those who maintain that in the holy scriptures nothing is to be understood beyond the meaning of the letter, think that no inquiry need be made concerning the goat-stag, the griffin and the vulture; but in regard to the sabbath they produce certain vain and trifling fables drawn from some traditional source or other, and allege that each man's 'place' is reckoned as extending to two thousand cubits.[3] Others, h o w e v e r, among whom is Dositheus the Samaritan,[4] condemn interpretations of this kind, and yet themselves maintain something

---

[1] Gr. *gryps,* a variety of eagle. Levit. XI. 13 ; Deut. XIV. 12.
[2] Exod. XVI. 29.
[3] See Numbers XXXV. 5.
[4] The founder of an ascetic sect in Samaria, which maintained an existence for several centuries at least, although Origen says (*Con. Celsum* VI. 11) that he did not suppose the whole number of the Dositheans in his day amounted to thirty. See *Dic. of Christ. Biog. s.v.*

GREEK   LATIN

still more ridiculous, namely,
that in whatever posture or
place or position a man is found
on the sabbath day he should
remain there until evening; that
is, if sitting, he should sit all
the day, or if lying down, he
should lie down all the day.

Further, the command 'not to
carry a burden on the sabbath
day'[1] is impossible; and on this
account the teachers of the
Jews have indulged in endless
chatter, asserting that one kind
of shoe is a burden, but another
is not, and that a sandal with
nails is a burden, but one without nails is not, and that what
is carried on one shoulder is a
burden, but not what is carried
on both.

Further, the command 'not to
carry a burden on the sabbath
day'[1] seems to me to be an
impossible one. For in consequence of these words the
teachers of the Jews have
become involved in 'endless
fables'[4] as the holy apostle says,
asserting that it is not reckoned
as a burden if a man wears
shoes without nails, but that it
is a burden if he wears goloshes
with nails, and deeming it a
burden if a man carries something on one shoulder, but not
a burden if he carries it on
both.

3. If now we approach the
gospel in search of similar instances, what can be more
irrational than the command:
'Salute no man by the way',[2]
which simple people believe that
the Saviour enjoined upon the
apostles? Again, to speak of
the right cheek being struck[3] is
most incredible, for every
striker, unless he suffers from
some unnatural defect, strikes
the left cheek with his right
hand. And it is impossible to
accept the precept from the
gospel about the 'right eye that
offends'; for granting the possibility of a person being 'offended' through his sense of sight,

3. If now we seek for
similar instances from the
gospels, how can it seem anything but absurd to interpret
literally the saying: 'Salute no
man by the way?'[2] This, however, is what simple people
suppose that our Saviour enjoined upon the apostles.
Further, how would it be
possible, especially in those
countries where the bitterness
of winter is accentuated by icy
frosts, to observe the precept
that a man should not possess
two coats, nor any shoes?[5]
Again, what shall we say of
the command that if anyone
strikes us on the right cheek we

---

[1] See Jer. XVII. 21.   [2] See St. Luke X. 4.   [3] See St. Matt. V. 39.
[4] See 1 Tim. I. 4.   [5] See St. Matt. X. 10

GREEK

how can the blame be attributed
to the right eye, when there are
two eyes that see? And what
man, even supposing he accuses
himself of 'looking on a woman
to lust after her' and attributes
the blame to his right eye alone,
would act rationally if he were
to cast this eye away?[1]

Further, the apostle lays down
this precept: 'Was any called
being circumcised? Let him
not become uncircumcised'.[2]
Now in the first place anyone
who wishes can see that these
words have no relation to the
subject in hand; and how can
we help thinking that they have
been inserted at random, when
we remember that the apostle
is here laying down precepts
about marriage and purity? In
the second place who will maintain that it is wrong for a man
to put himself into a condition
of uncircumcision, if that were
possible, in view of the disgrace
which is felt by most people to
attach to circumcision?

4. We have mentioned all
these instances with the object
of showing that the aim of the
divine power which bestowed on

LATIN

are to offer him the left one
also,[3] seeing that a man who
strikes with the right hand will
strike the left cheek? As for
the saying in the gospel; 'If
thy right eye offend thee, let it
be plucked out', this must be
reckoned among the impossibilities; for even if we grant that it
refers to eyes of flesh, how can
it be logical, when both eyes
see, to attribute the blame of
the offence to one only, and
that the right one?[1] Or who
would be accounted innocent of
a most serious crime, if he were
to lay hands on himself?

But perhaps the letters of
Paul the apostle will appear to
be free from these difficulties.
Yet what is the meaning of his
saying: 'Was any called being
circumcised? Let him not become uncircumcised'.[2] Now in
the first place, if you consider
the saying carefully, it does not
appear to be related to the subject which the apostle had in
hand; for he was laying down
precepts about marriage and
purity, and on such a subject
the words in question would
certainly seem to be a superfluous addition. In the second
place, what objection could
there be if, in order to avoid
the disgrace which comes from
being circumcised, a man were
able to become uncircumcised?
In the third place, it is certain
that this is utterly impossible.

4. We have mentioned all
these instances with the object
of showing that the aim of the
Holy Spirit, who deigned to

[1] See St. Matt. V. 28, 29; XVIII. 9.   [2] 1 Cor. VII. 18.
[3] See St. Matt. V. 39.

GREEK

LATIN

us the holy scriptures is not that we should accept only what is found in the letter; for occasionally the records taken in a literal sense are not true, but actually absurd and impossible, and even with the history that actually happened and the legislation that is in its literal sense useful there are other matters interwoven.

bestow on us the divine scriptures, is not that we may be edified by the letter alone or in every case by it at all; for we recognise that the letter is often impossible and inconsistent with itself, that is, that things not only irrational but even impossible are occasionally described by it; but that we are to realise that with this external story are interwoven certain other matters which, when considered and comprehended in their inward meaning, provide us with a law which is useful to men and worthy of God.

But someone may suppose that the former statement refers to all the scriptures, and may suspect us of saying that because some of the history did not happen, therefore none of it happened; and because a certain law is irrational or impossible when taken literally, therefore no laws ought to be kept to the letter; or that the records of the Saviour's life are not true in a physical sense; or that no law or commandment of his ought to be obeyed. We must assert, therefore, that in regard to some things we are clearly aware that the historical fact is true; as that Abraham was buried in the double cave at Hebron, together with Isaac and Jacob and one wife of each of them;[1] and that Shechem was given as a portion to Joseph;[2] and that Jerusalem is the chief city of Judaea, in which a temple of God was built by Solomon; and thousands of other facts.

But someone may suspect us of saying this, that because we suppose that some of the scriptural history did not happen, we do not believe that any of it happened; or that because we maintain that some precepts of the law cannot be kept according to the letter, those, that is, in regard to which either reason or the possibility of the case do not admit of a literal observance, therefore no precepts of the law are valid according to the letter; or that we do not believe that the events of our Saviour's life occurred in a physical sense; or that his precepts ought not to be obeyed literally. We must reply, therefore, that it is perfectly obvious to us that in most instances the truth of the historical record can and ought to be preserved. For who can deny that Abraham was buried in the double cave at Hebron, together with Isaac and Jacob and one wife of each

[1] See Gen. XXIII. 2, 9, 19; XXV. 9, 10; XLIX. 29-32; L. 13.
[2] See Gen. XLVIII. 22; Josh. XXIV. 32.

GREEK

For the passages which are historically true are far more numerous than those which are composed with purely spiritual meanings.

And again, who would deny that the command which says: 'Honour thy father and thy mother, that it may be well with thee',[1] is useful quite apart from any spiritual interpretation, and that it ought certainly to be observed, especially when we remember that the apostle Paul has quoted it in the selfsame words?[2] And what are we to say of the following: 'Thou shalt not kill; thou shalt not commit adultery; thou shalt not steal; thou shalt not bear false witness'?[3]

Once again, in the gospel there are commandments written which need no inquiry whether they are to be kept literally or not, as that which says, 'I say unto you, whosoever is angry with his brother',[4] and what follows; and, 'I say unto you, swear not at all'.[5] Here, too, is an injunction of the apostle of which the literal meaning must be retained: 'Admonish the disorderly, encourage the faint-hearted, support the weak,

LATIN

of them?[6] Or who doubts that Shechem was given as a portion to Joseph?[7] Or that Jerusalem is the chief city of Judaea, in which a temple of God was built by Solomon; and countless other facts? For the passages which are historically true are far more numerous than those which contain a purely spiritual meaning.

Then again, who would deny that the command which says: 'Honour thy father and mother that it may be well with thee',[1] is sufficient of itself apart from any spiritual interpretation and that its observance is binding on us, especially when we remember that Paul has confirmed the command by quoting it in the self-same words?[2] And what are we to say of the passage: 'Thou shalt not commit adultery; thou shalt not kill; thou shalt not steal, thou shalt not bear false witness',[3] and others of this kind?

Then in regard to the commandments given in the gospel, there can be no doubt that very many of these are to be kept according to the letter; as when it says. . . . 'But I say unto you, swear not at all';[5] and also, 'But whosoever looketh on a woman to lust after her hath committed adultery with her already in his heart';[8] and the injunctions given by the apostle Paul: 'Admonish the disorderly, encourage the

---

[1] Exod. XX. 12. [2] See Eph. VI. 2, 3. [3] Exod. XX. 13-16.
[4] St. Matt. V. 22 (omitted in Rufinus' text). [5] St. Matt. V. 34.
[6] See Gen. XXIII. 2, 9, 19; XXV. 9, 10; XLIX. 29-32; L. 13.
[7] See Gen. XLVIII. 22; Josh. XXIV. 32.
[8] St. Matt. V. 28. Koetschau regards this as an addition by Rufinus.

GREEK

be longsuffering toward all;'[1] though in the case of the more earnest readers it is possible to preserve each of the meanings, that is, while not setting aside the commandment in its literal sense, to preserve the 'depths of the wisdom of God.'[2]

5. Nevertheless the exact reader will hesitate in regard to some passages, finding himself unable to decide without considerable investigation whether a particular incident, believed to be history, actually happened or not, and whether the literal meaning of a particular law is to be observed or not. Accordingly he who reads in an exact manner must, in obedience to the Saviour's precept which says, 'Search the scriptures',[3] carefully investigate how far the literal meaning is true and how far it is impossible, and to the utmost of his power must trace out from the use of similar expressions the meaning scattered everywhere through the scriptures of that which when taken literally is impossible.

When, therefore, as will be clear to those who read, the passage as a connected whole is literally impossible, whereas the outstanding part of it is not impossible but even true, the

LATIN

faint-hearted, support the weak, be longsuffering toward all';[1] and very many others.

5. Nevertheless I have no doubt that the careful reader will be uncertain in very many cases whether this or that story is to be regarded as literally true, or true in a less degree, and whether this or that precept is to be literally observed or not. Much effort and toil must therefore be exercised, so that each reader may in all reverence become aware that he is dealing with words that are divine and not human, inserted in the holy books. As for us, therefore, the method of interpretation which we think ought rightly and logically to be employed in dealing with the holy scriptures is as follows.

---

[1] 1 Thess. V. 14.   [2] See Rom. XI. 33; 1 Cor. II. 10.
[3] St. John V. 39. Rufinus has here omitted a passage, probably because he could not understand it. Origen is certainly not clear, but his meaning seems to be as follows. The scriptures contain many composite narratives, one part being historically true and the other false. In the story of the Fall, for instance, he would have regarded Adam and Eve as being historically true and God walking in the garden as historically false. He would then interpret the whole story allegorically, feeling that the literal, or 'bodily', meaning was valueless. In other instances the literal meaning has a value of its own: e.g. the Commandments. But even here the deeper meanings, when discovered, are the more important.

GREEK

reader must endeavour to grasp the entire meaning, connecting by an intellectual process the account of what is literally impossible with the parts that are not impossible but are historically true, these being interpreted allegorically in common with the parts which, so far as the letter goes, did not happen at all. For our contention with regard to the whole of divine scripture is, that it all has a spiritual meaning, but not all a bodily meaning; for the bodily meaning is often proved to be an impossibility. Consequently the man who reads the divine books reverently, believing them to be divine writings, must exercise great care. And the method of understanding them appears to us to be as follows.

6. The accounts tell us that God chose out a certain nation on the earth, and they call this nation by many names. For the nation as a whole is called Israel, and it is also spoken of as Jacob. But when it was divided in the days of Jeroboam the son of Nebat,[1] the ten tribes said to have been subject to him were named Israel, and the other two together with the tribe of Levi, which were ruled over by men of the seed of David, were called Judah. The entire country which was inhabited by men of this race and which had been given them by God, is called Judaea, the metropolis of which is Jerusalem, this being the mother city of a number of

LATIN

6. The divine writings declare that a certain nation on the earth was chosen by God, and they call this nation by many names. Sometimes the nation as a whole is called Israel, sometimes Jacob; and in particular, when the nation was divided into two parts by Jeroboam the son of Nebat,[1] the ten tribes which became subject to him were called Israel, and the other two, with which was included the tribe of Levi and the tribe which sprang from the royal family of David, were named Judah. The entire country inhabited by this race, which had been given them by God, was called Judaea, the metropolis of which was

[1] See 1 Kings XII. 2 ff.

GREEK

others whose names lie scattered about in many different places of scripture but are gathered together into one list in the book of Joshua the son of Nun.[1]

This being so, the apostle, raising our spiritual apprehension to a high level, says somewhere: 'Behold Israel after the flesh',[2] inferring that there is an Israel after the spirit. He says also in another place: 'For it is not the children of the flesh that are children of God',[3] nor are 'all they Israel, who are of Israel'.[4]

LATIN

Jerusalem, called the metropolis or mother city as being a kind of mother of many cities. The names of these cities you will find frequently mentioned here and there in the other divine books, but they are gathered together into a single group in the book of Joshua the son of Nun.[1]

This being so, the holy apostle, desiring as it were to raise up and exalt our understanding above the earth, says in a certain place: 'Behold Israel after the flesh'.[2] In saying this he certainly indicates that there is also another Israel, which is not 'after the flesh' but after the spirit. And again he says in another place: 'For they are not all Israel, who are of Israel'.[4]

GREEK

And again: 'Neither is he a Jew, who is one outwardly, nor is that circumcision, which is outward in the flesh; but he is a Jew, who is one inwardly, and circumcision is of the heart, in the spirit, not in the letter'.[5] For if we take the phrase 'a Jew inwardly' as a test, we shall realise that as there is a race of bodily Jews, so, too, there is a race of those who are 'Jews inwardly', the soul having acquired this nobility of race in virtue of certain unspeakable words.[6] Moreover there are many prophecies spoken of Israel and Judah, which relate what is going to happen to them. And when we think of the extraordinary promises recorded about these people, promises that so far as literary style goes are poor and distinguished by no elevation or character that is worthy of a promise of God, is it not clear that they demand a mystical interpretation? Well, then, if the promises are of a spiritual kind though announced through material

---

[1] See Josh. XIII-XXI. [2] 1 Cor. X. 18.
[3] Rom. IX. 8 (not in Rufinus). [4] Rom. IX. 6.
[5] Rom. II. 28, 29. Rufinus has omitted a long passage at this point. As the passage contains no unorthodox doctrines the reason for its omission may be simply that Rufinus did not understand all the allusions in it, which are certainly far from clear.
[6] It is possible that this phrase alludes to the baptismal formula.

imagery, the people to whom the promises belong are not the bodily Israelites.

7. But we must not spend time discussing who is a 'Jew inwardly' and who an Israelite 'in the inner man', since the above remarks are sufficient for all who are not dull-witted. We will return to the subject before us and say that Jacob was the father of the twelve patriarchs, and they of the rulers of the people, and they in their turn of the Israelites who came after.[1] Is it not the case, then, that the bodily Israelites carry back their descent to the rulers of the people, the rulers of the people to the patriarchs, and the patriarchs to Jacob and those still more ancient; whereas are not the spiritual Israelites, of whom the bodily ones were a type, descended from the clans, and the clans from the tribes, and the tribes from one whose birth was not bodily, like that of the others, but of a higher kind;[2] and was not he born of Isaac, and Isaac descended from Abraham, while all go back to Adam, who the apostle says is Christ?[3] For the origin of all families that are in touch with the God of the whole world began lower down with Christ, who comes next after the God and Father of the whole world[4] and is thus the father of every soul, as Adam is the father of all men. And if Eve is interpreted by Paul as referring to the Church,[5] it is not surprising (seeing that Cain was born of Eve and all that come after him carry back their descent to Eve) that these two should be figures of the Church; for in the higher sense all men take their beginning from the Church.

GREEK

8. Now if what we have stated about Israel, its tribes and its clans, is convincing, then when the Saviour says, 'I was not sent but unto the lost[6]

LATIN

8. Now[7] that we have learned from him, therefore, that there is one Israel according to the flesh and another according to the spirit, then when the Saviour

---

[1] In this passage Origen has in mind the two genealogies of our Lord, found respectively in St. Matthew and St. Luke. It is clear that these genealogies, with their manifest differences, would have set him a task in spiritual interpretation. He appears to have solved the problem by taking the Matthaean genealogy to indicate the Israelites in a literal sense, and the Lucan the spiritual Israelites. The former is traced through the kings of Judah, whom Origen calls the *demarchs* ('rulers of the people'), and ends with Abraham. The latter, which descends through private persons, goes back through Jacob (whose divinely ordered birth—Gen. XXV. 21-23—is here emphasised) to Adam, who is interpreted as Christ, in accordance with St. Paul's parallel in 1 Cor. XV. 45. So the Church, the bride of Christ (Eph. V. 31-32) is seen in Eve; and even Cain, too, is a figure of the Church. Rufinus could have had no reason to object to these interpretations. The reason he omitted the passage was because he did not understand it.

[2] I.e. as in Gen. XXV. 21-23.   [3] See 1 Cor. XV. 45.
[4] See St. Luke III. 38.   [5] See Eph. V. 31-32.
[6] St. Matt. XV. 24.
[7] The text of Rufinus continues at this point from p. 298.

GREEK

sheep of the house of Israel',
we do not take these words in
the same sense as the poor-
minded Ebionites do (men whose
very name comes from the
poverty of their mind, for in
Hebrew *ebion* is the word for
poor),[1] so as to suppose that
Christ came especially to the
Israelites after the flesh. For
'it is not the children of the
flesh that are children of God'.[2]

Again, the apostle gives us
the following instances of teaching about Jerusalem: 'The Jerusalem which is above is free,
which is our mother';[4] and in
another epistle: 'But ye are
come to Mount Sion and to the
city of the living God, the
heavenly Jerusalem, and to an
innumerable company of angels,
to the general assembly and
church of the firstborn who are
written in heaven'.[5]

If therefore Israel consists of
a race of souls, and Jerusalem
is a city in heaven, it follows
that the cities of Israel have for
their mother city the Jerusalem
in the heavens; and so conse-

LATIN

says, 'I am not sent but unto
the lost sheep of the house of
Israel',[6] we do not take these
words in the same sense as do
they who 'mind earthly things',
that is, the Ebionites, who even
by their very name are called
poor (for in Hebrew the word
ebion means poor),[1] but we
understand that it is a race of
souls which is called Israel, as
the meaning of the word itself
indicates; for Israel means 'the
mind seeing God' or 'man seeing God'.[3]

Again, the apostle gives us
revelations such as this concerning Jerusalem, that 'Jerusalem which is above is free,
which is our mother'.[4] And in
another epistle of his he says:
'But ye are come to Mount
Sion and to the city of the living God, the heavenly Jerusalem, and to a multitude of
praising angels, and to the
church of the firstborn which is
written in heaven'.[5]

If then there are in this
world certain souls who are
called Israel, and a city in
heaven which is named Jerusalem, it follows that those cities
which are said to belong to the

---

[1] The Ebionites were a sect of Jewish Christians, who kept the Law.
Their name indicates that they practised, at least originally, a voluntary
poverty and simplicity of life, such as that described in Acts II. 44-45. It
has, of course, no reference whatever to poverty of mind, as Origen declares.
For a full account of them see Smith's *Dictionary of Christian Biography*
s. v. Ebionism and Ebionites.

[2] Rom. IX. 8 (omitted from Rufinus).

[3] See Origen, *In Num. hom.* XI. 4. 'The name Israel is found even
among the orders of angels; nay, they are more truly to be called Israel,
for they are more truly the "mind seeing God"; for this is the meaning of
the word Israel.'

[4] Gal. IV. 26.

[5] Heb. XII. 22, 23.

[6] St. Matt. XV. 24.

GREEK

quently does Judaea as a whole.

*   *   *   *   *   *

*   *   *   *   *1

In all prophecies concerning Jerusalem, therefore, and in all statements made about it, we must understand, if we listen to Paul's words[2] as the words of God and the utterances of wisdom, that the scriptures are telling us about the heavenly city and the whole region which contains the cities of the holy land. Perhaps it is to these cities that the Saviour lifts our attention when he gives to those who have deserved praise for the good use of their talents authority over ten or over five cities.[3]

9. If therefore the prophecies relating to Judaea, to Jerusalem, and to Israel, Judah and Jacob suggest to us, because we do not interpret them in a fleshly sense, mysteries such as these,

LATIN

Israelite nation have for their mother city the heavenly Jerusalem, and that we are to understand in this way all references to Judaea as a whole. For we believe that the prophets were speaking about this heavenly country by means of mystical narratives whenever they uttered prophecies concerning Judaea or Jerusalem, or whenever the sacred records declare that this or that kind of invasion had happened to Judaea or Jerusalem.

All statements or prophecies, therefore, which are made concerning Jerusalem we must understand, if we listen to the words of Paul as being those of Christ speaking in him,[4] to refer in the thought of Paul himself to that country which he calls the heavenly Jerusalem, and to all those regions or cities which are said to belong to the holy land, the mother city of which is Jerusalem. Moreover we must suppose that these are the cities from among which the Saviour, desiring to raise us to a higher level of understanding, promises to those who have made good use of the money committed to them by him, that they shall have authority 'over ten cities', or 'over five'.[3]

9. If therefore the prophecies relating to Judaea and Jerusalem, and to Israel, Judah and Jacob indicate to us, because we do not interpret them in a

---

[1] A sentence appears to be missing from the Greek at this point.

[2] Reading, with Koetschau, Παύλου for the manifestly corrupt Θεοῦ of the text.

[3] See St. Luke XIX. 17-19.

[4] See 2 Cor. XIII. 3.

GREEK

it will follow also that the prophecies which relate to Egypt and the Egyptians, to Babylon and the Babylonians, to Tyre and the Tyrians, to Sidon and the Sidonians, or to any of the other nations, are not spoken solely of the bodily Egyptians, Babylonians, Tyrians and Sidonians.[1] If the Israelites are spiritual, it follows that the Egyptians and Babylonians are also spiritual. For the statements made in Ezekiel about Pharaoh king of Egypt entirely fail to apply to any particular man who was or will be ruler of Egypt, as will be clear to those who study the passage carefully.[2]

Similarly the statements concerning the ruler of Tyre cannot be understood of any particular man who is to rule over Tyre.[3] And as for the numerous statements made about Nebuchadnezzar,[4] especially in Isaiah, how it is possible to interpret them of that particular man? For the man Nebuchadnezzar neither 'fell from heaven', nor was he the 'morning star', nor did he 'rise in the morning' over the earth.[5]

Nor indeed will any man of intelligence interpret the statements made in Ezekiel concerning Egypt, that it shall be 'laid waste forty years' so that 'no foot of man' shall be found there, and that it shall one day be so overwhelmed with war,

LATIN

fleshly sense, various divine mysteries, it certainly follows that those prophecies which were uttered concerning Egypt and the Egyptians, or Babylon and the Babylonians, or Sidon and the Sidonians, must not be understood to refer to the Egypt which is situated on the earth, or to the earthly Babylon or Tyre or Sidon.[1] Nor can the prophecies which the prophet Ezekiel utters concerning Pharaoh king of Egypt apply to any particular man who may have reigned in Egypt, as the context of the passage clearly shows.[2]

Similarly the statements concerning the prince of Tyre cannot be understood as being made in respect of any man who was an actual king of Tyre;[3] and further, in regard to the statements made about Nebuchadnezzar,[4] which are found in many places of scripture and especially in Isaiah, how is it possible for us to accept them as spoken of a man? For he is no man, who is said to have 'fallen from heaven', or to be the 'morning star', or to have 'risen in the morning.'[5]

Moreover, as for the statements which are made in Ezekiel concerning Egypt, that it shall be 'laid waste forty years' so that 'no foot of man' shall be found there, and that it shall be so overwhelmed with war that throughout the land human

[1] See Ezek. XXIX. ff.
[3] See Ezek. XXVIII.
[2] See Ezek. XXIX. 1-9.
[4] See Is. XIV. 3-23.
[5] See Is. XIV. 12.

GREEK

that throughout the whole land there shall be blood up to the knees, as referring to the Egypt which lies next to the Ethiopians whose bodies are blackened by the sun.[1]

LATIN

blood shall flow to a height up to the knees, I do not know how any man of intelligence could interpret these as referring to that earthly Egypt which lies next to Ethiopia.[1]

LATIN

Let us see,[2] however, whether the above passages may not be more worthily interpreted as follows. Just as there is a heavenly Jerusalem and Judaea, and no doubt a people dwelling therein who are called Israel, so it is possible that near to these there exist certain other places, which apparently are called Egypt, or Babylon, or Tyre or Sidon; and the princes of these places and the souls, if there are any, who dwell in them, may be called Egyptians, Babylonians, Tyrians and Sidonians. From among these souls, in accordance with the manner of life which they lead there, a kind of captivity would seem to have taken place, as a result of which they are said to have gone down from higher and better places into Egypt, or to have been scattered among other nations.

GREEK

10. And perhaps,[3] just as people on earth, when they die the common death of all, are in consequence of the deeds done here so distributed as to obtain different positions according to the proportion of their sins, if they are judged to be worthy of the place called Hades; so the people there, when they die, if I may so speak, descend into this Hades, and are judged

LATIN

10. For perhaps,[3] just as those who depart from this world by the common death of all, are distributed according to their deeds and merits, as a result of the judgment, some going to a place which is called the 'lower world'[4] others to 'Abraham's bosom'[5] and to the various positions and dwelling-places[6] in it; so the inhabitants of the regions above, when they die

---

[1] See Ezekiel XXIX. 11-12; XXX. 7, 10-12; XXXII. 5-6, 12-13, 15.

[2] This paragraph was omitted by the compilers of the *Philocalia*.

[3] See Jerome, *Ep. ad Avitum* 11. 'Also in the fourth book, which is the last book of this work, he (i.e. Origen) inserts the following statements which must be condemned by the churches of Christ: "And perhaps, just as those who die in this world by the separation of body and soul obtain different positions in the world below in accordance with the differences of their deeds, so those who die, so to speak, in the realm of the heavenly Jerusalem, descend to the lower regions of our world, in such a way as to occupy different positions on earth in proportion to their merits".'

[4] Lat. *inferus*, translating the Gr. ᾅδης Hades.

[5] See St. Luke XVI. 22.

[6] Lat. *mansiones*: Gr. μοναί. See St. John XIV. 2.

GREEK

worthy of different habitations,
better or worse, in the whole
of this region of earth   *   *
*   *   *   *   *   *

and of being born of such or
such parents, so that an Israelite
will occasionally fall among
Scythians and an Egyptian descend into Judaea. Nevertheless
the Saviour came to gather together the 'lost sheep of the
house of Israel',[1] and since
many from Israel have not
submitted to his teaching, those
from the Gentiles are also
called.   *   *   *   *
*   *   *   *   *
*   *   *   *   *

LATIN

there, if one may so speak,
descend from those upper
places to this lower world.

For the other lower world,
to which are conveyed the souls
of those who die on earth, is
called by scripture, I believe on
account of this distinction, 'the
lower Hades', as it says in the
Psalms, 'And thou hast delivered my soul from the lower
Hades'.[2] Each of those, therefore, who descend into the
earth, is destined in accordance
with his merits or with the
position which he had held above
to be born in a particular
place or nation, or in a particular walk of life, or with particular infirmities, or to be the
offspring of religious parents or
the reverse, so that it happens
occasionally that an Israelite
falls among the Scythians and
a poor Egyptian is conveyed to
J u d a e a. Nevertheless our
Saviour came to gather together
the 'lost sheep of the house of
Israel',[1] and since most of the
Israelites have not submitted to
his teaching, those who belonged
to the Gentiles have been called.

LATIN

It would appear to follow[3] from this that the prophecies
which are uttered concerning the various nations ought rather
to be referred to souls and the different heavenly dwelling-places
occupied by them.[4] Moreover in regard to the records of events

[1] See St. Matt. XV. 24.
[2] See Ps. LXXXVI. 13. This sentence is omitted from the *Philocalia*,
but both Koetschau and Robinson (ed. *Philocalia* Int., p. xxxvii) regard it as
part of Origen's text. The Sept. reading is literally, 'the lowest Hades', but
Rufinus reads 'the lower Hades' (*de infero inferiori*), which was no doubt
Origen's reading.
[3] This paragraph is also missing from the *Philocalia*.
[4] See Origen, *In Num. hom.* XXVII. 2, where he says that Num. XXXIII.
1-2 must refer to the spiritual journey from this world to the heavenly abodes.

that are said to have happened to the nation of Israel, or to Jerusalem or Judaea, when they were assailed by this people or that, there is need of careful inquiry and examination, seeing that in very many cases the events did not happen in a physical sense, to discover in what way these events are more suitably ascribed to those nations of souls who once dwelt in that heaven which is said to 'pass away'[1] or who may be supposed to dwell there even now.

(And since[2] we have compared the souls who travel from this world to the lower regions to those souls who by a kind of death come from the height of heaven to our dwelling-places, we must thoughtfully inquire whether we may make this latter assertion in regard to the birth of every single soul. For in that case souls that are born on this earth of ours would either come from the lower world again to a higher place and assume a human body, in consequence of their desire for better things, or else would descend to us from better places. And so, too, those places which are above in the firmament may be occupied by some souls who have advanced from our seats to better things, and by others who have fallen from the heavenly places to the firmament and yet have not sinned deeply enough to be thrust into the lower places in which we dwell)[3]   *   *   *   *

11. If, however,[4] anyone should demand of us clear and manifest declarations on these matters out of the holy scriptures, we must reply that it was the method of the Holy Spirit rather to conceal these truths and to hide them deeply underneath narratives which appear to be records of actual events, narratives in which people are said to go down into Egypt or to be led captive to Babylon, where some were greatly humiliated and put under bondage to masters, while others in the very places of their captivity were regarded as famous and illustrious, so that they held positions of power and leadership and were set to rule over nations.

GREEK	LATIN
11. But these truths, as we think, have been concealed in the narratives. For 'the king-	All these truths, as we have said, lie hidden and concealed, covered up in the narratives of

---

[1] See St. Matt. XXIV. 35.

[2] Koetschau places this extract from Jerome, *Ep. ad Avitum* 11, in the text at this point. Cp. Robinson, *Philocalia* Int., p. xxxvii.

[3] Jerome continues as follows (*Ep. ad Avitum* 11), giving in outline a further passage omitted both by Rufinus and the authors of the *Philocalia* : 'After this he attempts to prove that the firmament, that is, the heaven, is a lower world when compared with the heaven above it, and that the world we in habit is called a lower world in comparison with the firmament, and further that our world is a heaven when compared with the world which is below us ; so that what to some is a lower world is to others a heaven.'

[4] The text of Rufinus is here resumed.

GREEK

dom of heaven is like unto a treasure hid in a field, which when a man findeth he hideth it, and for joy thereof goeth and selleth all that he hath, and buyeth that field.'¹ Now let us consider whether the outward aspect of scripture and its obvious and surface meaning does not correspond to the field as a whole, full of all kinds of plants, whereas the truths that are stored away in it and not seen by all, but lie as if buried beneath the visible plants, are the hidden 'treasures of wisdom and knowledge',² which the Spirit speaking through Isaiah calls 'dark and unseen and concealed'.³

These treasures require for their discovery the help of God, who alone is able to 'break in pieces the gates of brass'⁴ that conceal them and to burst the iron bars that are upon the gates, and so to make known all the truths taught in Genesis concerning the various legitimate races and as it were seeds of souls, whether closely akin to Israel or far apart from him, and the descent of the 'seventy souls' into Egypt, in order that they may there become 'as the stars of the heaven in multitude'.⁵ But since not all who are sprung from these are a 'light of the world',⁶ for 'they are not all Israel, who are of Israel'⁷ there come from the seventy a people 'even as the sand which

LATIN

holy scripture; because 'the kingdom of heaven is like unto a treasure hid in a field, which when a man findeth he hideth it, and for joy thereof goeth and selleth all that he hath, and buyeth that field.'¹ Now consider carefully whether there is not here an indication that the actual soil and surface, so to speak, of scripture, that is, the literal meaning, is the field, abundantly filled with all kinds of plants, whereas the higher and profounder spiritual meaning is the 'hidden treasures of wisdom and knowledge',² which the Holy Spirit speaking through Isaiah calls 'dark and unseen and concealed treasures'.³

These treasures require for their discovery the help of God, who alone is able to 'break in pieces the gates of brass'⁴ by which they are shut in and concealed, and to burst the iron bolts and bars which prevent us from entering in and reaching all those truths written in veiled language in Genesis concerning the various races of souls and the seeds and generations named there, whether closely akin to Israel or widely separated from his posterity; as well as the meaning of the descent of the seventy souls into Egypt, that these seventy may become in Egypt 'as the stars of the heaven in multitude'.⁵ But since not all who are sprung from these are a 'light of

---

¹ St. Matt. XIII. 44. ² See Col. II. 3.
³ See Is. XLV. 3. ⁴ See Is. XLV. 2.
⁵ For the whole passage see Gen. Chs. X., XI., XXV., XXXVI., XLVI.; and for the quotations Deut. X. 22 (Gen. XLVI. 27, Exod. I. 5, Gen. XXII. 17).
⁶ See St. Matt. V. 14. ⁷ Rom. IX. 6.

GREEK

is by the sea shore innumerable.'[1]

LATIN

this world',[2] for 'they are not all Israel, who are of Israel',[3] there come from these seventy souls people even 'as the sand which is by the sea shore innumerable.'[1]

LATIN

12. This descent of the holy fathers into Egypt, that is, into this world, will be seen to have been granted by the providence of God for the enlightenment of the rest of men and for the instruction of the human race, that through them all other souls might be enlightened and succoured. 'For to them first were entrusted the oracles of God',[4] it being this people alone which is said to 'see God'; for the name Israel when translated has this meaning.[5]　It follows at once that we must adapt and interpret in the light of these principles the statement that Egypt was scourged with ten plagues to allow God's people to depart,[6] or the account of what happened to the people in the desert,[7] or of the construction of the tabernacle by means of contributions from all the people,[8] or of the weaving of the priestly garments,[9] or the description of the vessels of the ministry;[10] because, as it is written, these things truly contain within them a 'shadow' and form of the 'heavenly things'.　For Paul clearly says of them that they 'serve a shadow and pattern of the heavenly things'.[11] In the same law there is also contained an account of the particular laws and institutions under which men are to live in the holy land.　Threats, too, are held over those who shall transgress the law; and for those who stood in need of purification various kinds of purifications are given, adapted to men who were liable to frequent pollution;[12] the object being that by means of these they should arrive at last at that one purification, after which they must not be polluted any more.[13]

Moreover a reckoning is made of the number of this people, though not of all.[14]　For the childlike souls have not yet lived long enough to be numbered in accordance with the divine command;[15] while those souls which cannot become the head of some other but are themselves subject to others as to a head, souls which the scripture terms 'women', these, too, are not reckoned

---

[1] Heb. XI. 12 (Gen. XXXII. 12).　The extract from the *Philocalia* ends here.

[2] See St. Matt. V. 14.　　　　　　　　[3] Rom. IX. 6.

[4] Rom. III. 2.　[5] See above p. 300.　[6] See Exod. VII. 14-XII. 36.

[7] See Exod. XIX. ff.　[8] See Exod. XXV. ff.　[9] See Exod. XXVIII.

[10] See Exod. XXX. 17 ff.　[11] Heb. VIII. 5.　[12] See Lev. XII.-XV.

[13] See Heb. IX. and VI. 6.　　　[14] See Num. Chs. I-IV, XXVI.

[15] See Num. I. 3 etc.

in that numbering which is ordered by God.[1] Only those called men are numbered, in order to show that the former souls could not be numbered apart by themselves but that they are included in the number of those called men.

Especially, however, there come to the holy number they who are ready to go forth to the wars of Israel, they who can fight against those enemies and adversaries whom the Father puts in subjection to the Son who sits on his right hand, in order that he may destroy every principality and power.[2] By these numbers of his soldiers, who because they are fighting for God do not entangle themselves in the affairs of this world,[3] he intends to overthrow the kingdoms of the adversary.[4] By these 'the shields of faith' are borne and the 'darts' of wisdom are hurled; on them gleams the helmet which is the hope of salvation, and the breastplate of charity guards their heart that is filled with God.[5] Such are the soldiers who appear to me to be indicated in scripture, and such is the kind of warfare for which they are prepared who are ordered in the divine books to be numbered by God's command.

But far more renowned and perfect than these are they, the very hairs of whose head are said to be numbered.[6] Those, however, who were punished for their sins, whose carcases 'fell in the wilderness', appear to me to bear a resemblance to those who, though they have made not a little progress, have yet been for various reasons quite unable to reach the goal of perfection; because they are said either to have murmured, or to have worshipped idols, or to have committed fornication, or to have planned some wickedness such as it is wrong for the mind even to think of.[7]

Nor is the following fact, I believe, devoid of some mystical meaning, that certain of the people, who possess large flocks and much cattle, go and seize beforehand a region suitable for pastur-

---

[1] See Num. I. 2, 4 etc. Cp. 1 Cor. XI. 3.

[2] See Eph. I. 20, 22; 1 Cor. XV. 27, 24.

[3] See 2 Tim. II. 4.

[4] The following extract from Jerome, *Ep. ad Avitum* 11, appears to belong here. 'Not content with this, he (i.e. Origen) says that in the end of all things, when we return to the heavenly Jerusalem, wars of hostile powers will arise against the people of God, in order that their valour may not be idle, but that they may display it in battles and so gain strength, which would be impossible unless like brave men they had first resisted adversaries. And we read in the book of Numbers that these have conquered by the exercise of reason and order, and by skill in fighting.' (See Numbers Ch. XXXI.). Cp. too, Origen *In Num. hom.* VII. 5: 'It is necessary, therefore, that the spiritual hosts of wickedness, who are said to be in the heavenly places, should be conquered by you, in order that you may speedily pass over to the heavenly realms and dwell there instead of them.'

[5] See Eph. VI. 16, 17; 1 Thess. V. 8.

[6] See St. Matt. X. 30 and parallel.

[7] See Num. XI, XIV, XVI, XXI, XXV; Exod. XXXII; and 1 Cor. X. 5-10; Heb. III. 17.

ing their flocks, which was the first of all the places that the right hand of the Israelites secured by war. This region they beg Moses to grant them, and consequently they are placed apart beyond the streams of Jordan and cut off from the occupation of the holy land.[1] Now this Jordan would appear, when taken as a figure of the heavenly things, to water and flood the thirsty souls and minds that lie close beside it.

And here this other fact will not appear to be without significance, that it is Moses who hears from God all that is written down in the law of Leviticus, whereas in Deuteronomy it is the people who are represented as listening to Moses and learning from him what they could not hear from God.[2] This indeed is why it is called Deuteronomy, meaning the second law; a fact which some will think points to this, that when the first law given through Moses[3] came to an end, a second legislation was apparently composed, and this was specially delivered by Moses to his successor Joshua;[4] and Joshua is certainly believed to be a figure of our Saviour, by whose second law, that is, by the precepts of the Gospels, all things are brought to perfection.

13. We must also see, however, whether the scriptures may not perhaps indicate this further truth, that just as the legislation is presented with greater clearness and distinctness in Deuteronomy than in those books which were written at the first, so also we may gather from that coming of the Saviour which he fulfilled in humility, when he 'took upon him the form of a servant',[5] an indication of the 'more splendid and glorious second coming in the glory of his Father',[6] at which coming, when in the kingdom of heaven all the saints shall live by the laws of the 'eternal gospel',[7] the figure of Deuteronomy will be fulfilled; and

---

[1] See Num. XXXII.

[2] See Levit. I. 1 and throughout; and Deut. I. 1, V. 1.

[3] See St. John I. 17.   [4] See Deut. XXXI.   [5] See Phil. II. 7.

[6] See St. Matt. XVI. 27 and parallels.

[7] See Rev. XIV. 6. Origen apparently made much more of the 'eternal gospel' than Rufinus allows us to see. Cp. Jerome, *Ep. ad Avitum* 12. 'And when he (i.e. Origen) has said that the "eternal gospel" of the Apocalypse of John, that is, the gospel which is to exist in the heavens, is as far superior to our gospel as the preaching of Christ is to the rites of the old law, he goes to the extreme length of inferring (what it is impious even to have thought of) that Christ will also suffer in the air and in the realms above for the salvation of the daemons. And although he does not actually say so, yet it must be understood as a logical consequence, that as God was made man for the sake of men, to set them free, so also for the salvation of the daemons he will be made what they are, for whose liberation he is then to come. And in case it should be supposed that we are putting our own interpretation upon his statements, we will give his very words: "For just as he fulfilled the shadow of the law through the shadow of the gospel, so because all law is a copy and shadow of the heavenly rites, we must carefully inquire whether we ought not to regard even the heavenly law and the rites of the higher worship not as possessing completeness, but as standing in need of the truth of that gospel which in the Apocalypse of John is called the "eternal gospel", in comparison, that is, with this gospel

just as by his present coming he has fulfilled that law which has
a 'shadow of the good things to come',[1] so also by that glorious
coming the shadow of his first coming will be fulfilled and brought
to perfection.   For the prophet has spoken of it thus : 'The
breath of our countenance is Christ the Lord, of whom we said
that under his shadow we shall live among the nations',[2] that
is, at the time when he shall duly transfer all the saints from the
temporal to the eternal gospel, to use a phrase employed by
John in the Apocalypse, where he speaks of the 'eternal gospel'.
*   *   *   *   *   *

GREEK

But[3] if we continue our inquiries as far as the passion, to
seek for this in the heavenly places will seem a bold thing to do.
Yet if there are 'spiritual hosts of wickedness' in the heavenly
places, consider whether, just as we are not ashamed to confess
that he was crucified here in order to destroy those whom he
destroyed through his suffering, so we should not fear to allow
that a similar event also happens there and will happen in the
ages to come until the end of the whole world *   *   *

LATIN

14. But in all these matters let it suffice us to conform our
mind to the rule of piety and to think of the Holy Spirit's words
not as a composition depending upon feeble human eloquence
but in accordance with the sayings of scripture, 'All the king's
glory is within,[4] and, 'a treasure' of divine meanings lies hidden
within the 'frail vessel' of the poor letter.[5] If, however, a reader
is more curious and persists in asking for an explanation of
every detail, let him come and hear along with us how the apostle
Paul, scanning by the aid of the Holy Spirit, who 'searches even
the depths of God',[6] the 'depth of the divine wisdom and knowledge',[7] and yet not being able to reach the end and to attain,

of ours, which is temporal and was preached in a world and an age that
are destined to pass away".'
  [1] See Heb. X. 1.
  [2] Lament. IV. 20.
  [3] Frag. 30, Koetschau, from Justinian, *Ep. ad Mennam* (Mansi IX. 532).
The same passage is found in Jerome, *Ep. ad Avitum* 12 (a continuation of
the last quotation from this letter). 'But if we wish to continue our
inquiries as far as the passion of the Lord our Saviour, although it is a
bold and venturesome thing to seek for his passion in heaven, nevertheless,
if there are "spiritual hosts of wickedness" in the heavenly places and if we
are not ashamed to confess that the Lord was crucified in order to destroy
those whom he destroyed through his passion, why should we fear to
suspect that something similar to this may happen in the realms above, in
order that the inhabitants of all places may be saved by his passion?' See
also Theophilus Alex. *Ep. synod* 4 (Jerome, *Ep.* 92) and *Ep. pasch.* I. 10,
11 (Jerome, *Ep.* 96).
  [4] Ps. XLV. 13 (Sept.).   [5] See 2 Cor. IV. 7.
  [6] See 1 Cor. II. 10.   [7] See Rom. XI. 33.

if I may say so, an innermost knowledge, in his despair and amazement at the task cries out and says, 'O the depth of the riches of the wisdom and knowledge of God !'[1] And in what despair of reaching a perfect understanding he uttered this cry, hear him tell us himself: 'How unsearchable are his judgments and his ways past finding out !'[1] He did not say that God's judgments were hard to search out, but that they could not be searched out at all; not that his ways were hard to find out, but that they were impossible to find out. For however far one may advance in the search and make progress through an increasingly earnest study, even when aided and enlightened in mind by God's grace, he will never be able to reach the final goal of his inquiries.

For no created mind can by any means possess the capacity to understand all; but as soon as it has discovered a small fragment of what it is seeking, it again sees other things that must be sought for; and if in turn it comes to know these, it will again see arising out of them many more things that demand investigation. This is why Solomon, wisest of men, whose wisdom gave him a clear view of the nature of things, says: 'I said, I will become wise; and wisdom herself was taken far from me, farther than she was before; and who shall find out her profound depth?'[2] Moreover Isaiah, knowing that the beginnings of things could not be discovered by mortal nature, no, and not even by those natures which, though diviner than man's nature, are yet themselves made and created, knowing, I say, that none of these could discover either the beginning or the end says; 'Tell ye the former things, what they were, and we shall know that ye are gods; or declare the last things, what they are, and then shall we see that ye are gods.'[3]

My Hebrew teacher also used to teach as follows, that since the beginning or the end of all things could not be comprehended by any except our Lord Jesus Christ and the Holy Spirit, this was the reason why Isaiah spoke of there being in the vision that appeared to him two seraphim only, who with two wings cover the face of God, with two cover his feet, and with two fly, crying one to another and saying, 'Holy, holy, holy, is the Lord of hosts; the whole earth is full of thy glory.'[4] For because the two seraphim alone have their wings over the face of God and over his feet, we may venture to declare that neither the armies of the holy angels, nor the holy thrones, nor the dominions, nor principalities, nor powers can wholly know the beginnings of all things and the ends of the universe. We must understand, however, that those holy spirits and powers who are here enumerated are nearest to the very beginnings of things and reach a point

---

[1] Rom. XI. 33.

[2] Eccl. VII. 23, 24 (Sept. 24, 25).

[3] Is. XLI. 22, 23.

[4] See Is. VI. 2, 3. For the reference to the Hebrew teacher see the Greek fragment in Bk. I., Ch. III. 4 (p. 32 above).

which the rest of creation cannot attain to. Nevertheless whatever it is that these powers may have learned through the revelation of the Son of God and of the Holy Spirit—and they will certainly be able to acquire a great deal of knowledge, and the higher ones much more than the lower—still it is impossible for them to comprehend everything; for it is written, 'The more part of God's works are secret.'[1]

It is therefore to be desired that each one according to his capacity will ever 'reach out to the things which are before, forgetting those things which are behind',[2] that is, will reach out both to better works and also to a clearer understanding and knowledge, through Jesus Christ our Saviour, to whom is the glory for ever.

15. Let everyone, then, who cares for truth, care little about names and words,[3] for different kinds of speech are customary in different nations. Let him be more anxious about the fact signified than about the words by which it is signified, and particularly in questions of such difficulty and importance as these. For example, we may inquire whether there exists any substance in which we can discern neither colour nor shape nor possibility of touch nor size, a substance perceptible to the mind alone, which anyone can call whatever he pleases. The Greeks speak of this substance as *asomaton,* or incorporeal;[4] but the divine scriptures call it 'invisible'; for the apostle declares that God is invisible, when he says that Christ is the 'image of the invisible God'.[5] On the other hand he says that 'all things, visible and invisible, were created through Christ'.[6] Here it is asserted that there exist even among created things certain existences which are in their own nature invisible. These, however, while not in themselves corporeal, yet make use of bodies, though they themselves are superior to bodily substance. But the substance of the Trinity, which is the beginning and cause of all things, 'of which are all things and through which are all things and in which are all things', must not be believed either to be a body or to exist in a body, but to be wholly incorporeal.[7]

Let it suffice, however, for us to have spoken briefly on these matters, in a digression indeed, but one which has been forced upon us by the necessities of the subject. Our aim has been to show that there are certain things, the meaning of which it is impossible adequately to explain by any human language, but which are made clear rather through simple apprehension than through any power of words. This rule must control our interpretation even of the divine writings, in order that what is said therein may be estimated in accordance not with the meanness of the language but with the divine power of the Holy Spirit who inspired their composition.

[1] Ecclus. XVI. 21.   [2] See Phil. III. 14.   [3] See Tim. I. 4, VI. 4.
[4] See above pp. 5 and 92. [5] See Col. I. 15, 16. [6] *Ibid.*
[7] See Rom. XI. 36 and above p. 10.

CHAPTER IV

GREEK	LATIN
SUMMARY OF DOCTRINE CONCERNING THE FATHER, THE SON AND THE HOLY SPIRIT.	SUMMARY OF DOCTRINE CONCERNING THE FATHER, THE SON AND THE HOLY SPIRIT, AND OF THE OTHER MATTERS DISCUSSED IN THE FOREGOING CHAPTERS.

1. It is now time for us,[1] in summarising our discussion concerning the Father, the Son and the Holy Spirit, to deal with a few points previously omitted. In regard to the Father, though he is whole and indivisible yet he becomes the Father of the Son, but not by an act of separation as some suppose.[2] For if the Son is something separated from the Father and an offspring generated from him, of the same kind as the offspring of animals, then both he who generated and he who was generated are of necessity bodies. *   *

1. It is now time for us, after having dealt to the best of our ability with the matters previously discussed, to summarise the particular points, with the object of gathering together what we have said in scattered references, and first of all to repeat our teaching concerning the Father, the Son and the Holy Spirit. God the Father, since he is both invisible and inseparable from the Son, generated the Son not, as some suppose, by an act of separation from himself.[2] For if the Son is something separated from the Father, and if this expression signifies something resembling the offspring of animals and human beings, then both he who separated and he who is separated are of necessity bodies. For we do not

LATIN

say, as the heretics suppose, that a part of God's substance was changed into the Son, or that the Son was procreated by the

---

[1] Frag. 31, Koetschau, from Marcellus, found in Eusebius *Con. Marcellum* I. 4, Frag. 32. The Greek title is a conjecture of Koetschau, taken from the Latin.

[2] See Jerome, *Apol. adv. Rufin.* II. 19. 'There exists in Greek a dialogue between Origen and Candidus, the defender of the heresy of Valentinus . . . . Candidus admits that the Son is of the substance of the Father, but errs in asserting a *probole,* that is, an act of separation. On the other side Origen, in the manner of Arius and Eunomius, controverts the assertion that the Son was produced or born, for fear of dividing God the Father into parts; but he asserts that he is a sublime and pre-eminent creature who came into existence by the will of the Father like all other creatures.'

Father out of no substance at all, that is, from something external to God's own substance, so that there was a time when the Son did not exist; but setting aside all thought of a material body, we say that the Word and Wisdom was begotten of the invisible and incorporeal God apart from any bodily feeling,[1] like an act of will proceeding from the mind. Nor will it appear absurd, seeing that he is called the 'Son of his love',[2] that he should also be regarded in this way as the 'Son of his will'   *   *   *

GREEK   LATIN

Now this Son[3] was begotten of the Father's will, for he is the 'image of the invisible God'[4] and the 'effulgence of his glory and the impress of his substance',[5] 'the firstborn of all creation',[4] a thing created,[6] wisdom. For wisdom itself says: 'God created me in the beginning of his ways for his works'[7]   *   *

If he[8] is an 'image of the invisible God',[9] he is an invisible image; and I would dare to add that as he is a likeness

Moreover John tells us that 'God is light'[10] and Paul declares that the Son is the 'brightness of the eternal light'.[11] As there-

---

[1] See above p. 19.   [2] See Col. I. 13.

[3] Frag. 32, Koetschau, from Justinian, *Ep. ad Mennam* (Mansi IX. 525). Rufinus has omitted this.

[4] See Col. I. 15.   [5] Heb. I. 3.

[6] The word used is κτίσμα. Origen obtained it, as the context shows, from Proverbs VIII. 22. The later Church regarded it as heretical to call the Son κτίσμα, and allowed nothing but γέννημα, a thing begotten. Origen's use of κτίσμα must, however, be taken in conjunction with his doctrine of the Son's eternal generation. The creation of the visible world, and of souls, would have been to him very different things from the eternal generation of the Son, although he held strongly that the Father is first, and the fount of all being. Arius called the Son κτίσμα, but rejected Origen's compensating doctrine. See Athanasius, *Orat. II. con. Arian. c.* 57. 'The Word has his essence not in any other beginning, but in the Father, who as even our opponents (i.e. the Arians) admit is without beginning; in order that the Son also may exist without beginning in the Father, being his offsprnig and not his creation (γέννημα καὶ οὐ κτίσμα).' Origen's opinions were reproduced by Theognostus of Alexandria (middle of 3rd cent. A.D.), an epitome of whose work is found in Photius *Bibl. cod.* 106. 'He demonstrates that the Son is a thing created (κτίσμα) and has charge of rational beings. Like Origen, he says other similar things of the Son.'

[7] Proverbs VIII. 22.

[8] Frag. 33, Koetschau, from Athanasius, *Ep. de decret. Nicaen. Synod. c.* 27 (Migne P. G. 25, p. 465).

[9] See Col. I. 15.   [10] 1 St. John I. 5.   [11] See Heb. I. 3.

GREEK

of the Father there is no time when he did not exist. For when did God, who according to John is said to be 'light' (for 'God is light')[1] have no 'effulgence of his own glory',[2] that we should dare to lay down a beginning for the Son, before which he did not exist? And when did the image of the unspeakable, unnameable, unutterable substance of the Father, his impress, the Word who knows the Father,[3] not exist? Let the man who dares to say, 'There was a time when the Son was not',[4] understand that this is what he will be saying, 'Once wisdom did not exist, and word did not exist, and life did not exist' *   *   *   *

But it[5] is not right, nor is it safe for us in our weakness to rob God, so far as in us lies, of his only-begotten Word who ever dwells with him, who is his wisdom, in whom he rejoiced.[6] For if we do this, we shall think of him as not always rejoicing.

LATIN

fore light can never exist without its brightness, so neither can the Son, who is called the 'impress' of the Father's 'substance', and his Word and Wisdom, be conceived as existing without the Father. How then can it be said that there was a time when the Son did not exist?[4] For this is nothing else but to say that there was a time when truth did not exist, when wisdom did not exist, when life did not exist,

whereas we must believe that in all these the substance of God exists in perfection. For these cannot be taken away from him or ever be separated from his substance. Although in our mind they are regarded as being many, yet in fact and substance they are one, and in them resides the 'fulness of the godhead'[7]

---

[1] St. John I. 5.   [2] See Heb. 1. 3.
[3] See St. Matt. XI. 27 ; St. John X. 15.
[4] This was what Arius afterwards did say.
[5] Frag. 34, Koetschau, from Athanasius, *Ep. de decret. Nicaen. synod.* c. 27. Rufinus has omitted this.
[6] See Prov. VIII. 30.
[7] See Col. II. 9.

LATIN

This phrase that we use, however, that there never was a time when he did not exist, must be accepted with a reservation. For the very words, when, or never, have a temporal significance, whereas the statements we make about the Father and the Son and the Holy Spirit must be understood as transcending all time and all ages and all eternity. For it is this Trinity alone which exceeds all comprehension, not only of temporal but even of eternal intelligence. The rest of things, however, which are external to the Trinity, must be measured by ages and periods of time. The fact, therefore, that the Word is God, and was in the beginning with God,[1] must not lead anyone to suppose that this Son of God is contained in any place; nor must the fact that he is wisdom, or truth, or righteousness, or sanctification, or redemption; for all these need no place in which to act or work, but each of them must be understood as referring to those who receive a share of the Word's power and effectiveness.

2. But if anyone should maintain that through those who receive a share of God's Word, or of his wisdom or truth or life, the Word himself and the wisdom appear to exist in a place, we must answer him by saying that undoubtedly Christ, in his character of Word and Wisdom and all the rest, was in Paul, according to Paul's own statement: 'Or do ye seek a proof of him who speaks in me, even Christ?'[2] And again: 'I live; yet not I, but Christ liveth in me'.[3] Since then he was in Paul, who will doubt that he was similarly in Peter and in John and in every one of the saints, and not only in those on earth, but also in those in heaven? For it is absurd to say that Christ was in Peter and in Paul, but that he was not in Michael the archangel and in Gabriel. From this we can clearly perceive that the divinity of the Son of God is not confined in any place, otherwise it would be present in that place and not present in any other; but that while, in virtue of the majesty of its incorporeal nature, it is confined to no place, in no place, on the other hand, can we think of it as being absent.

We must, however, bear in mind this one difference, that although he is present in various individuals such as those we have mentioned, Peter, Paul, Michael or Gabriel, he is not present in all beings whatsoever in the same degree. For he is more fully and clearly and, if I may say so, more openly present in the archangels than in other saints. This is plain from the following fact, that when the saints reach the height of perfection they are said to be made like, or equal to, the angels, according to the gospel statement.[4] It is clear from this that Christ becomes present in each individual in such a degree as is warranted by the extent of his merits.

[1] See St. John I. 1, 2.   [2] 2 Cor. XIII. 3.   [3] Gal. II. 20.
[4] See St. Matt. XXII. 30 and St. Luke XX. 36.

3. Having therefore briefly repeated these points concerning the doctrine of the Trinity, our next step is to lay equal stress on this, that all things are said to have been created through the Son, 'things in heaven and things on earth, things visible and invisible, whether thrones or dominions or principalities or powers; all were created through him and in him, and he is before all, and all things subsist for him, who is the head'.[1] With this agrees the statement made by John in the Gospel : 'All things were made through him, and without him nothing was made.'[2] David, too, points to the mystery of the Trinity in the creation of the universe when he says : 'By the word of the Lord were the heavens made strong, and all their power by the spirit of his mouth.'[3]

After this it will be appropriate for us to make mention of the bodily coming and incarnation of the only-begotten Son of God.[4] And here we must not suppose that all the majesty of his godhead was confined within the limits of a tiny body, in such a way that the whole of God's Word and his wisdom and essential truth and life was either separated from the Father or forced and imprisoned within the tiny compass of that body, so that it is not to be thought of as operating anywhere else. The reverent confession of piety should rather lie between these extremes, neither admitting that any quality of the godhead was lacking in Christ, nor yet supposing that there took place any separation whatever from the essence of the Father, which exists everywhere. Some such truth is indicated by John the Baptist, when with Jesus in the bodily sense absent he thus addressed the multitudes : 'There standeth one among you whom ye know not, who cometh after me, the latchet of whose shoes I am not worthy to unloose.'[5] Certainly it could not be said of one who so far as his bodily presence went was absent, that he stood 'among' them with whom he was not bodily present. This shows that the Son of God was both wholly present in his body and also wholly present everywhere.

4. Let no one imagine, however, that when we say this we are asserting that one part of the godhead of the Son of God was in Christ while the other part was elsewhere or everywhere. This can only be believed by those who are ignorant of the nature of incorporeal and invisible substance. For it is impossible to speak of a part of what is incorporeal or to make any division in it. It exists rather in all things and through all things and above all things, in the way we have previously spoken of, that is, in the way in which it is understood as being either wisdom or word or life or truth, by which mode of understanding

---

[1] Col. I. 16-18.   [2] St. John I. 3.   [3] Ps. XXXIII. 6.
[4] See above Bk. II. Ch. VI. 1, 2. (pp. 108 ff.).
[5] St. John I. 26, 27 and Origen, *Comm. in Iohan.* VI. 39, where Heracleon's interpretation of the passage is given.

all idea of confinement in a particular place is undoubtedly excluded. The Son of God, therefore, because for the salvation of
the human race he wished to appear to men and to dwell among
them, assumed not only, as some think, a human body, but also
a soul, in its nature indeed like our souls, but in will and virtue
like himself, and of such a kind that it could unswervingly carry
into effect all the wishes and plans of the Word and Wisdom
* * *[1] Now that he possessed a soul, the Saviour himself
most clearly proves in the gospels when he says : 'No one taketh
from me my soul, but I lay it down of myself. I have power
to lay it down, and I have power to take it up again'.[2] And
again : 'My soul is sorrowful even unto death';[3] and also : 'Now
is my soul troubled'.[4] For

GREEK   LATIN

For the soul[5] that was 'troubled' | The soul that is 'sorrowful'
and 'sorrowful' is certainly not | and 'troubled' must not be
the 'only-begotten' and the 'first- | understood to be the Word of
born of all Creation', nor God | God, because with the authority
the Word, who is superior to | of his godhead he says: 'I have
his soul, as the Son of God | power to lay down my soul'.[6]
himself says: 'I have power to | Nor
lay it down, and I have power
to take it up'.[6]

LATIN

do we say that the Son of God was in that soul in the same
way as he was in the soul of Paul or of Peter and the rest of
the saints, in whom we believe that Christ spoke just as he did
in Paul.[7] Of all these, indeed, we must hold that opinion which
the scripture expresses: 'No man is pure from uncleanness, not
even if his life has lasted but one day'.[8] But the soul that was
in Jesus 'chose the good, before it knew the evil';[9] and because
it 'loved righteousness and hated iniquity, therefore God anointed

---

[1] See above Bk. II., Ch. VIII. 2, 4 (pp. 121 and 127). Koetschau suspects
an omission at this point, containing Frag. 35 from Justinian, *Ep. ad
Mennam* (Mansi IX. 506); 'that the soul of the Lord pre-existed, and that
God the Word was united to it before he took flesh of the Virgin'.
[2] St. John X. 18.
[3] St. Matt. XXVI. 38 and parallels.
[4] St. John XII. 27.
[5] Frag. 36, Koetschau, from Theophilus Alex. *Ep. pasch.* II. 16 (translated by Jerome in *Ep.* 98). The Greek is found in Theodoret *Dial.* II.,
Ch. 4 (Migne P. G. 83, p. 197). Koetschau has altered the Greek text of
Theodoret, ὁ γὰρ Θεὸς λόγος to οὐδὲ Θεὸς λόγος, which agrees with
the sense of Rufinus and the actual wording of Jerome, *nec verbum dei.*
[6] St. John X. 18.   [7] See above, p. 316.
[8] Job XIV. 4, 5 (Sept.).   [9] See Is. VII. 15, 16 and above, p. 269.

it with the oil of gladness above its fellows'.[1] Now it was anointed with the 'oil of gladness' when it was united in a spotless partnership with the Word of God and thereby alone among all souls became incapable of sin, because it was well and fully capable of receiving the Son of God, and on that account

GREEK

As the Son[2] and the Father are one, so also the soul which the Son assumed and the Son himself are one.

LATIN

is even one with him, and

LATIN

is addressed by his titles and called Jesus Christ, through whom all things are said to have been made.[3]

It was of this soul, since it had received into itself the whole wisdom of God and his truth and life, that I think the apostle spoke when he said: 'Your life is hid with Christ in God; but when Christ, your life, shall appear, then shall ye also appear with him in glory'.[4] For who else can be meant by this Christ, who is said to be hidden in God and to be destined afterwards to appear, except him who is related to have been anointed with the 'oil of gladness', that is, filled with the essence of God, in whom now he is said to be hidden. This is why Christ is set forth as an example to all believers, because as he ever chose the good, even before he knew the evil at all, and loved righteousness and hated inquity, wherefore God anointed him with the oil of gladness;[5] so, too, should each one of us, after a fall or a transgression, cleanse himself from stains by the example set before him, and taking a leader for the journey proceed along the steep path of virtue, that so perchance by this means we may as far as is possible become, through our imitation of him, partakers of the divine nature;[6] as it is written, 'He who saith he believeth in Christ ought himself to walk even as he walked'.[7] This Word, then, and this wisdom, by our imitation of whom we are called wise or rational, becomes 'all things to all men, that he may gain all', and to the weak becomes weak, that he may gain the weak;[8] and because he is made to become weak it is said of him, 'Though he was crucified in weakness, yet he liveth in the power of God'.[9] Finally, in dealing with the Corinthians, who were weak, Paul determines that he will 'know nothing among them except Jesus Christ, and him crucified'.[10]

---

[1] See Ps. XLV. 7.
[2] Frag. 37, Koetschau, from Theophilus Alex. *Ep. pasch.* II. 16. The Greek is found in Theodoret, *Dial.* II. c. 4 (Migne P. G. 83, p. 197).
[3] See St. John I. 3; Col. I. 16.   [4] Col. III. 3, 4.
[5] See Is. VII. 15, 16; Ps. XLV. 7.   [6] See 2 St. Peter I. 4.
[7] 1 St. John II. 6.   [8] See 1 Cor. IX. 22.
[9] 2 Cor. XIII. 4.   [10] See 1 Cor. II. 2.

5. Some, however, would have it appear that it was in reference to this very soul, at the time when it assumed a body from Mary, that the following statement of the apostle was made;[1] 'Who, though he was in the form of God, counted it not a prize to be equal with God, but emptied himself, taking the form of a servant';[2] the object being, doubtless, to restore the soul into the form of God by superior examples and precepts, and to recall it to that fulness from which it had emptied itself.

But as by participation in the Son of God a man is adopted among God's sons, and by participation in the wisdom which is in God he becomes wise, so, too, by participation in the Holy Spirit he becomes holy and spiritual. For this is one and the same thing as to receive a share of the Holy Spirit, who is the Spirit of the Father and the Son, since the nature of the Trinity is one and incorporeal. And all that we have said about the participation of the soul is to be understood of the angels and heavenly powers in a similar way to that in which it is understood of souls; for every rational creature needs to participate in the Trinity.

[1] This paragraph, in which Origen asserted the pre-existence of the soul of Christ, and his various manifestations to the angelic orders, has been considerably modified and abbreviated by Rufinus. The following quotations give some idea of the original text. Anathema VII, Second Council of Constantinople: 'If anyone shall say that Christ, who is said to have been "in the form of God" and to have been united with God the Word before all ages and in the last days to have emptied himself to the level of man, because he pitied (as they say) the various falls that had happened to those who originally belonged to the same unity, and wished to restore them, went through all modes of being and was invested with different kinds of bodies and took different names, becoming all things to all, being changed into an angel among the angels, into a power among the powers, and into other ranks or species of rational beings according to the necessities of each particular case, and then at last shared in flesh and blood like us and became a man among men, . . . let him be anathema.' This is equivalent to the Fourth Anathema of the Emperor Justinian against Origen, which runs as follows: 'If anyone shall say or think that the Word of God has become like all the heavenly orders, having become a cherub for the cherubim, a seraph for the seraphim and something equivalent to every single one of the powers above, let him be anathema.' See also Jerome, *Apol.* II. 12, where he asserts the following to be one of the distinctly heretical statements of the *First Principles*: 'that the soul of the Saviour existed before it was born of Mary, and that it was this soul which was in the form of God, and thought it not robbery to be equal with God, but emptied itself, taking the form of a servant.' Also, Theophilus Alex., *Ep. synod.* 4 (Jerome, *Ep.* 92): 'besides, in the books on "First Principles", he even endeavours to persuade us that the living Word of God did not assume a human body; for he writes, contrary to the statement of the apostle (i.e. in Philip. II. 7), that he who being in the form of God was equal with God was not the Word of God, but a soul that descended from the heavenly region and emptying itself of the form of its eternal majesty assumed a human body. In saying this he most clearly contradicts John who writes: "And the Word was made flesh". Nor is it credible that it was the soul of the Saviour and not the Word of God which possessed the form of and equality with the Father's majesty.' Also, *Ep. pasch.* II. 14 (Jerome, *Ep.* 98) and above Bk. II. Ch. VI. 3 (p. 110).
[2] Phil. II. 6, 7.

Moreover, in regard to the plan of this visible world, the very important question of how the world is constituted is frequently raised. We have therefore spoken on this point to the best of our ability in the preceding chapters,[1] for the benefit of those who set themselves to examine the grounds for belief in our religion, and also of those who stir up heretical arguments against us and who are constantly bringing forward the term 'matter', the meaning of which even they themselves have not yet succeeded in understanding. I think it necessary to make brief mention of this subject now.

6. In the first place it must be noted that up to the present we have nowhere found the term 'matter' itself used in the canonical scriptures to denote that substance which is said to underlie bodies. For the saying of Isaiah: 'And he shall burn up the *hyle*', that is the matter, 'like hay',[2] spoken in reference to those who have been appointed for punishment, uses the terms 'matter' to denote sins. And even if the word happens to be written in any other place it will nowhere be found, I think, to bear the meaning with which our present inquiry is concerned. The only exception is in Wisdom, a book which is said to be Solomon's, but which is certainly not regarded as authoritative by all.[3] Still, we do find it written there as follows: 'For thine all-powerful hand, that created the world out of formless matter, lacked not means to send upon them a multitude of bears, or fierce lions'.[4] Very many, indeed, think that the actual matter of which things are made is referred to in the passage written by Moses in the beginning of Genesis: 'In the beginning God made the heaven and the earth, and the earth was invisible and without order';[5] for by the phrase, 'an earth invisible and without order', it seems to them that Moses was alluding to nothing else but formless matter. Yet if this truly is matter, it is clear from this passage that the constituent parts of bodies are not things incapable of change.

For those who assume that bodily substances are composed of atoms, either the ones which cannot be divided into parts or those which are divisible into equal parts, or else that they are composed of one of the elements, could not reckon matter, at least in the main sense of the term, among these constituents. Nor, if they suppose matter to be a substance underlying every body throughout the universe, a substance capable of change, alteration and division, will they maintain that it exists in its own proper nature without qualities. And we agree with them; since we absolutely deny that matter should be called unbegotten or uncreated, for the reasons which we have given to the best

---

[1] See above, Bk. II., Chs. I. and III. (pp. 76 ff. and 83 ff.).
[2] Is. X. 17.
[3] Elsewhere Origen speaks of Wisdom as an inspired book: cp. *Con. Celsum* III. 72.
[4] Wisd. XI. 17.   [5] Gen. I. 1, 2.

of our ability in previous chapters, for we have there pointed out that from water and earth, air and heat, various kinds of fruit are produced in the various kinds of trees, and that fire, air, water and earth are changed alternately into one another and that one element is resolved into another in virtue of a sort of mutual relationship, and further that from the food of men or of animals the substance flesh comes into existence and that the seminal moisture is changed into solid flesh and bones. All these instances go to prove that bodily substance is capable of change and can pass from any given quality into any other.[1]

7. This, however, should be noted, that a substance never exists without quality, and that it is by the intellect alone that this substance which underlies bodies and is capable of receiving quality is discerned to be matter.[2] On this account some who were desirous of inquiring more deeply into these questions have ventured to assert that bodily nature consists of nothing else but qualities. For if hardness and softness, heat and cold, wetness and dryness, are qualities, and when these and all the others like them are taken away nothing is conceived to lie beneath, then the qualities will appear to be everything. And so those who hold this opinion have endeavoured to establish the following argument, that since all who say that matter is uncreated allow that its qualities were created by God, the result is that even according to their view matter is not uncreated if qualities are everything, for all without exception declare that qualities were created by God.

Those, however, who desire to prove that qualities are added from without to an underlying matter employ illustrations such as the following: Paul is without any question either silent or speaking, either awake or asleep, or again he is in a certain bodily posture, either sitting or standing or lying down. These things are accidental to men, who are scarcely ever perceived apart from them. Nevertheless our mind clearly does not include any of these things in the definition of man, but we think of him and consider him by their means in such a way as not to form a general idea of his condition, regarding him simply in respect of his being awake or asleep, speaking or silent, or in any of the other accidental conditions to which man is of necessity subject. Just as, then, we can think of Paul as existing apart from all these accidents to which he is subject, so, too, we can conceive of the underlying substance apart from its qualities. And so, when our mind by a purely intellectual act sets aside every quality and gazes at the mere point, if I may so call it, of the underlying substance in itself and clings to that, without in the least considering its hardness or softness or heat or cold or wetness or dryness, then by this somewhat artificial mode of

---

[1] See above Bk. II., Ch. I. 4 (pp. 78 f.)   [2] See above, p. 79.

thought it will apparently behold matter stripped of all its qualities.

8. But someone may perhaps ask whether we can obtain any support for this view of things from the scriptures. It appears to me that some such view is indicated in the Psalms, when the prophet says : 'Mine eyes have seen thine incompleteness'.[1] In this passage the prophet's mind, examining with piercing insight the beginning of things and by reason and understanding alone separating matter from its qualities, appears to have perceived God's 'incompleteness', a state which we certainly think of as being brought to perfection by the addition of qualities. Moreover Enoch speaks thus in his book: 'I walked until I came to what is incomplete',[2] which I think may also be understood in a similar way, namely, that the prophet's mind, in the course of its investigation and study of every visible thing, came right to the very beginning, where it beheld matter in an incomplete state without qualities. For it is written in the same book, Enoch himself being the speaker: 'I perceived every kind of matter'.[3] Now this certainly means : 'I beheld all the divisions of matter, which from one original have been broken off into all the various species, of men, animals, sky, sun and everything else in the world.'

Next, we have proved to the best of our ability in the foregoing chapters, that all things that exist were made by God, and that there is nothing that was not made except the nature of the Father, the Son and the Holy Spirit; and that because God, who is good by nature, wished to have those whom he might benefit and who might enjoy receiving his benefits, he made creatures worthy of himself, that is, creatures capable of worthily receiving him, whom he also says he has 'begotten as sons'.[4] But he made all things by number and measure; for to God there is nothing either without end or without measure.

GREEK

Let no one[5] take offence at the saying, if we put limits even to the power of God. For to encompass things that are endless is by nature an impossibility. But when once the things, which God himself grasps, have been bounded, necessity suffices as a boundary until the right number of things has been bounded.

---

[1] Ps. CXXXIX. 16 (Sept.).

[2] Enoch, Ch. XXI. 1. In *Con Celsum* V. 54 Origen says that the book of Enoch was not received everywhere in the Church as inspired.

[3] Slav. Enoch Ch. XL. 1, 12. The Greek text is found in Clem. Alex. *Eclog. prophet.* 2, 1.

[4] See Is. I. 2.

[5] Frag. 38, Koetschau, from Justinian, *Ep. ad Mennam,* Mansi IX. 525. Cp. Bk. II., Ch. IX. 1 (p. 129 above). Rufinus has omitted this fragment altogether.

LATIN

For by his power he comprehended all things, while he himself is not comprehended by the mind of any created being.[1]

GREEK

But if the Father[2] comprehends all things, and the Son is among all things, it is clear that he comprehends the Son. But someone will inquire whether it is true that God is known by himself in the same way in which he is known by the only-begotten, and he will decide that the saying, 'My father who sent me is greater than I',[3] is true in all respects; so that even in his knowledge the Father is greater, and is known more clearly and perfectly by himself than by the Son.

LATIN

For that nature is known to itself alone. The Father alone knows the Son, and the Son alone knows the Father,[4] and the Holy Spirit alone searches out even the depths of God.[5]

Every created thing, therefore, is distinguished in God's sight by its being confined within a certain number and measure, that is, either number in the case of rational beings or measure in the case of bodily matter. Since, then, it was necessary for intellectual nature to make use of bodies, and this nature is proved to be changeable and convertible by the very condition

[1] See Jerome, *Ep. ad Avitum* 13. 'And again he (i.e. Origen) blasphemes against the Son by speaking in the following manner: For if the Son knows the Father, it would seem that by virtue of this knowledge he can comprehend the Father, as if we were to say that the mind of the craftsman knows the measure of his craft. Nor can we doubt that if the Father is in the Son, he is also comprehended by him in whom he is. If, however, we mean that kind of comprehension in which one comprehends another not only by understanding and wisdom but in the sense of holding the object of his knowledge under his authority and power, then we cannot say that the Son comprehends the Father.' Rufinus has compressed this into one short sentence and has evaded all the points raised by Origen.

[2] Frag. 39, Koetschau, from Justinian, *Ep. ad Mennam* (Mansi IX. 525) a Latin version of which is found in Jerome, *Ep. ad Avitum* 13 (a continuation of the quotation in note 1 above). 'The Father, however, comprehends all things; but the Son is among all things, and therefore he comprehends the Son. And that we may know the reasons why the Father comprehends the Son, whereas the Son cannot comprehend the Father; he (i.e. Origen) adds the following: The careful reader will inquire whether the Father is known by himself in the same way as he is known by the Son; and remembering the saying of scripture, "the Father who sent me is greater than I", he will decide that this saying is true in all respects; so that even in his knowledge the Father is greater than the Son, being known more perfectly and clearly by himself than by the Son.' For this passage Rufinus has substituted the brief and strictly orthodox paragraph from 'For that nature' to 'the depths of God'.

[3] See St. John XIV. 28, 24.   [4] See St. John X. 15, XVII. 25.
[5] See 1 Cor. II. 10.

of its being created—for what was not and began to be is by this very fact shown to be of a changeable nature and so to possess goodness or badness as an accident, and not as part of its essence—since, then, as we have said, rational nature is changeable and convertible, so of necessity God had foreknowledge of the differences that were to arise among souls or spiritual powers, in order to arrange that each in proportion to its merits might wear a different bodily covering of this or that quality; and so, too, was it necessary for God to make a bodily nature, capable of changing at the Creator's will, by an alteration of qualities, into everything that circumstances might require. This nature must needs endure so long as those endure who need it for a covering; and there will always be rational natures who need this bodily covering.

There will always exist, therefore, this bodily nature whose coverings must necessarily be used by rational creatures; unless some one thinks[1] that he can prove by any arguments that rational nature can lead a life without a body at all. How difficult, if not altogether impossible, this is for our understanding, we have shown when discussing the particular questions in the foregoing chapters.[2]   *   *   *   *   *

GREEK

It must needs be[3] that the nature of bodies is not primary, but that it was created at intervals on account of certain falls that happened to rational beings, who came to need bodies; and again, that when their restoration is perfectly accomplished these bodies are dissolved into nothing, so that this is for ever happening.

LATIN

9. It will certainly not, I think, appear contrary to the plan of this work of ours, if we repeat as briefly as possible the arguments concerning the immortality of rational natures. Everyone who shares in anything is undoubtedly of one substance and

---

[1] This sentence is Rufinus' substitute for a longer and more categorical statement, which is preserved by Jerome, *Ep. ad Avitum* 14. 'The following passage, too, convicts him (i.e. Origen) of believing in the transmigration of souls and the annihilation of bodies: If anyone can show that incorporeal and rational nature, when deprived of a body, can live by itself, and that it is in a worse condition when clothed with a body and in a better when it lays the body aside, then no one can doubt that bodies did not exist in the beginning, but are now created at intervals on account of the different movements of rational creatures, in order to supply a covering to such as need it; and that on the other hand, when these creatures have risen out of the degradation of their falls to a better condition, the bodies are dissolved into nothing; and that these changes go on happening for ever.' The later half of this quotation is the equivalent of Frag. 40, inserted in the text a few lines further on.

[2] See p. 81 above.

[3] Frag. 40, Koetschau, from Justinian, *Ep. ad Mennam* (Mansi IX. 532). Cp. Frag. 19 on p. 86 f. above.

one nature with him who shares in the same thing. For example, all eyes share in the light, and therefore all eyes, which share in the light, are of one nature. But though every eye shares in the light, yet since one eye sees clearly and another dimly, every eye does not share equally in the light. Again; all hearing receives the voice and sound, and therefore all hearing is of one nature; but each person is quick or slow to hear in proportion to the pure and healthy condition of his hearing faculty. Now let us pass from these examples drawn from the senses to the consideration of intellectual things.

Every mind which shares in intellectual light must undoubtedly be of one nature with every other mind which shares similarly in this light. If then the heavenly powers receive a share of intellectual light, that is, of the divine nature, in virtue of the fact that they share in wisdom and sanctification, and if the soul of man receives a share of the same light and wisdom, then these beings will be of one nature and one substance with each other.[1] But the heavenly powers are incorruptible and immortal; undoubtedly therefore the substance of the soul of man will also be incorruptible and immortal. And not only so, but since the nature of Father, Son and Holy Spirit, to whom alone belongs the intellectual light in which the universal creation has a share, is incorruptible and eternal, it follows logically and of necessity that every existence which has a share in that eternal nature must itself also remain for ever incorruptible and eternal, in order that the eternity of the divine goodness may be revealed in this additional fact, that they who obtain its blessings are eternal too. Nevertheless, just as in our illustrations we acknowledged some diversity in the reception of the light, when we described the individual power of sight as being either dim or keen, so also we must acknowledge a diversity of participation in the Father, Son and Holy Spirit, varying in proportion to the earnestness of the soul and the capacity of the mind.

[1] Origen went farther than this, and asserted a kinship between man and God. See Jerome, *Ep. ad Avitum* 14, 'And in case we should suppose that the impiety of these previous quotations was too little, at the end of the same volume he adds the following: That all rational natures, that is, the Father, the Son and the Holy Spirit, all angels, authorities, dominions and other powers, and even man himself in virtue of his soul's dignity, are of one substance. For he says, God and his only-begotten Son and the Holy Spirit are conscious of an intellectual and rational nature: so are the angels and authorities and the other powers; so, too is the "inner man", who was made in the image and likeness of God. From which the conclusion is drawn that God and all these creatures are in some way of one substance. He adds this phrase, "in some way", in order to escape the charge of gross impiety; and the man who in another place is unwilling to admit that the Son and the Holy Spirit are of the Father's substance, lest he should seem to be dividing the divine essence into parts (see p. 19 above), is here distributing the essence of Almighty God to angels and men'. Cp. Origen, *Exhort. in Martyr.* 47. 'Man earnestly desires life, deriving confidence from the rational nature of his soul, as being in some way akin to God.'

On the other hand let us consider whether it does not appear almost impious to say that the mind, which is capable of receiving God, should admit of a destruction of its substance; as if the very fact that it can perceive and understand God would not be sufficient to secure its perpetual existence.   This is the more likely since, even if the mind through carelessness should fall away from the pure and perfect reception of God into itself, it nevertheless always possesses within some seeds as it were of restoration and recall to a better state, which become operative whenever the inner man, who is also termed the rational man, is recalled into the image and likeness of God who created him. This is why the prophet says: 'All the ends of the earth shall remember and be turned unto the Lord, and all the families of the nations shall worship before him'.[1]

10. If, however, anyone dares to ascribe a corruption of substance to him who was made after the 'image and likeness of God', he will be extending this impious charge, in my opinion to the Son of God himself; for he, too, is called in the scriptures the 'image of God'.[2]   At least he who thinks thus will certainly be attacking the authority of scripture, which says that man was made in the 'image of God'.   Moreover the marks of the divine image in man may be clearly discerned, not in the form of his body, which goes to corruption, but in the prudence of his mind, in his righteousness, his self-control, his courage, his wisdom, his discipline, in fact, in the whole company of virtues; which exist in God essentially, and may exist in man as a result of his own efforts and his imitation of God, as the Lord points out in the gospel when he says: 'Be ye merciful, as your Father also is merciful',[3] and, 'Be ye perfect, as your Father also is perfect'.[4]   Here we are clearly shown that in God all these virtues exist for ever and that they can never come to him or depart from him, whereas men acquire them gradually and one by one.

We see, therefore, that men have a kind of blood-relationship with God; and since God knows all things and not a single intellectual truth can escape his notice—for God the Father, with his only-begotten Son and the Holy Spirit, stands alone in his knowledge not only of the things he has created but also of himself—it is possible that a rational mind also, by advancing from a knowledge of small to a knowledge of greater things and from things visible to things invisible, may attain to an increasingly perfect understanding.   For it has been placed in a body, and of necessity advances from things of sense, which are bodily, to things beyond sense perception, which are incorporeal and intellectual.   But in case it should appear mistaken to say as we have done that intellectual things are beyond sense perception

---

[1] See Ps. XXII. 27.
[2] See Col. I. 15; 2 Cor. IV. 4.
[3] St. Luke VI. 36.
[4] St. Matt. V. 48.

we will quote as an illustration the saying of Solomon: 'You will find also a divine sense'.[1] By this he shows that intellectual things are to be investigated not by bodily sense but by some other which he calls divine.

It is with this sense that each of the rational questions which we have dealt with above must be perceived; and with this sense that the words we speak must be listened to and our writings pondered. For the divine nature knows even the silent thoughts which revolve in our minds. Our belief, therefore, on the questions dealt with herein, and on all that follows logically from them, must be framed in accordance with the principles explained above.

[1] Prov. II. 5 (Sept.).

I. INDEX OF NAMES AND SUBJECTS

Creator, distinguished from the Father of Jesus by heretics, 271. Simple Christians' wrong belief concerning, 271

Daemonic Possession, 214f., 227. Due to pre-natal causes, 228
Damasus, Bishop of Rome, xl
Death, to be destroyed, 248, 250
Decius, persecution of, v
Demetrius, Bishop of Alexandria, i, ii, ix, xviii
Design, argument from, 149f.
Deuteronomy, 309
Didymus, disciple of Origen, i, xvi, xxi
Docetism, denied by the church tradition, 3, 110 (and n. 1)
Dositheus, founder of an ascetic Jewish sect, 291

Earth, place of birth for fallen souls, 304
Ebionites, 300
Education, its effect on men, 162f., 187. Souls disciplined by, 243f.
Elagabalus, Emperor, vii
Elements, 79, 252, 322
Emanations, doctrine of, rejected, 19
End, of the world, 53, 78, 93f., 237f., 242, 245ff.
Enoch, book of, 31, 323
Epiphanius, Bishop of Salamis in Cyprus, x. Preaches against Origenism, xi, xxvii, quoted 67 (and n. 4), 124 (and n. 8).
Eternal Fire, means remorse for sins, 141f.
Eternal Generation of the Son, 16, 18, 23, 42, 313ff.
Eternal Gospel, The 254, 309 (and n. 7), 310.
Eternity of Creation, x, 42f.
Ethnarch, Jewish Ruler, 260
Eusebius, Bishop of Caesarea, i (n. 3), iv, vi, vii. Collaborates with Pamphilus in defending Origen, xiiff., xvi, xxi. Quotes De Principiis in Con. Marcellum, i (and n. 1), 313 (and n. 1)
Eve, a type of the church, 299
Evil, to be destroyed, 247f. Problem of, 283f.
External things, not in our own power, 162f. Used by God for our good, 182. Indifferent, 221

Fabian, Bishop of Rome, xviii
Fall, Origen's doctrine of the, xxiii, xxxvi, 76f., 124f.

Free Will, xxix, xxxvf. Part of church tradition, 4. Essential to rational beings, 77, 87, 253. Cause of variety, 110, 130, 134, 242. Discussion of, 157ff. Power of choice, 164. Man's responsibility, 165f. Scriptural proof of, 166. Scriptural difficulties, 166ff., 186ff., 195ff., 200ff. Used in resisting temptation, 216, 217. And in giving effect to holy suggestions, 227. Can never be lost, 228, 244

Gelasius, Bishop of Rome, xxiv
Gnosticism, xxxii, xxxv, 30 (n. 10). Doctrine of fixed spiritual natures, 60, 69, 206. Lost natures, 171, 183, 196. Knowledge falsely so called, 224
God, unity of, 2, 80. Author of Law and Gospel alike, 2, 96ff. Spiritual nature of, 77ff., 98, 247. Almighty, 23ff., 251. Creator of Universe, 30. Eternally active, 41ff. Brings world to harmony, 77. Controls Universe, 79, 266. Invisible, 99, 110, 312. Impassible, 99f. Both just and good, 101ff., 134, 171f. The Son is God's soul, 128. Limits to God's power, 129, 323. His impartiality, 137, 173ff., 215, 242. Heretical doctrine of an evil creator, 172, 189. God's patience, 182ff., 190f. His providential care, 185, 221, 228. Man's co-operation with him, 197ff., 210. Grace of 219f., 311. Comprehends Universe, 238, 324. To be all in all, 246, 247f., 253, 254f. His providence not abolished because of our ignorance of it, 267. His ways past finding out, 310f. Above time, 316. Omniscience of, 327f.
Gospel, its wonderful growth, 258, 263f.
Gregory, Bishop of Nazianzus, x, xxvi
Gregory, Bishop of Nyssa, xxvii, 72 (and n. 8), 73 (and nn. 1-4)
Gregory Thaumaturgus, i, ii, iv. His Panegyric on Origen, iii

Hades, this world a Hades for fallen souls, 303
Hardening of Pharaoh's heart, 166ff. God's kindly purpose in, 172ff., 176 (n. 2)

II. INDEX OF SCRIPTURAL QUOTATIONS AND ALLUSIONS

22

haRpeR ⚜ ԵoRchbooks

HUMANITIES AND SOCIAL SCIENCES

American Studies: General

THOMAS C. COCHRAN: The Inner Revolution: *Essays on the Social Sciences in History*　TB/1140
EDWARD S. CORWIN: American Constitutional History. *Essays edited by Alpheus T. Mason and Gerald Garvey*　TB/1136
CARL N. DEGLER, Ed.: Pivotal Interpretations of American History　TB/1240, TB/1241
A. HUNTER DUPREE: Science in the Federal Government: *A History of Policies and Activities to 1940*　TB/573
OSCAR HANDLIN, Ed.: This Was America: *As Recorded by European Travelers in the Eighteenth, Nineteenth and Twentieth Centuries. Illus.*　TB/1119
MARCUS LEE HANSEN: The Atlantic Migration: 1607-1860. *Edited by Arthur M. Schlesinger. Introduction by Oscar Handlin*　TB/1052
MARCUS LEE HANSEN: The Immigrant in American History. *Edited with a Foreword by Arthur M. Schlesinger*　TB/1120
JOHN HIGHAM, Ed.: The Reconstruction of American History　TB/1068
ROBERT H. JACKSON: The Supreme Court in the American System of Government　TB/1106
JOHN F. KENNEDY: A Nation of Immigrants. *Illus. Revised and Enlarged. Introduction by Robert F. Kennedy*　TB/1118
RALPH BARTON PERRY: Puritanism and Democracy　TB/1138
ARNOLD ROSE: The Negro in America: *The Condensed Version of Gunnar Myrdal's An American Dilemma*　TB/3048
MAURICE R. STEIN: The Eclipse of Community: *An Interpretation of American Studies*　TB/1128
W. LLOYD WARNER and Associates: Democracy in Jonesville: *A Study in Quality and Inequality* ||　TB/1129
W. LLOYD WARNER: Social Class in America: *The Evaluation of Status*　TB/1013

American Studies: Colonial

BERNARD BAILYN, Ed.: The Apologia of Robert Keayne: *Self-Portrait of a Puritan Merchant*　TB/1201
BERNARD BAILYN: The New England Merchants in the Seventeenth Century　TB/1149
JOSEPH CHARLES: The Origins of the American Party System　TB/1049
LAWRENCE HENRY GIPSON: The Coming of the Revolution: 1763-1775. † *Illus.*　TB/3007
LEONARD W. LEVY: Freedom of Speech and Press in Early American History: *Legacy of Suppression*　TB/1109

PERRY MILLER: Errand Into the Wilderness　TB/1139
PERRY MILLER & T. H. JOHNSON, Eds.: The Puritans: *A Sourcebook of Their Writings*
　Vol. I TB/1093; Vol. II TB/1094
EDMUND S. MORGAN, Ed.: The Diary of Michael Wigglesworth, 1653-1657: *The Conscience of a Puritan*
EDMUND S. MORGAN: The Puritan Family: *Religion and Domestic Relations in Seventeenth-Century New England*　TB/1227
RICHARD B. MORRIS: Government and Labor in Early America　TB/1244
KENNETH B. MURDOCK: Literature and Theology in Colonial New England　TB/99
WALLACE NOTESTEIN: The English People on the Eve of Colonization: 1603-1630. † *Illus.*　TB/3006
LOUIS B. WRIGHT: The Cultural Life of the American Colonies: 1607-1763. † *Illus.*　TB/3005

American Studies: From the Revolution to 1860

JOHN R. ALDEN: The American Revolution: 1775-1783. † *Illus.*　TB/3011
MAX BELOFF, Ed.: The Debate on the American Revolution, 1761-1783: *A Sourcebook*　TB/1225
RAY A. BILLINGTON: The Far Western Frontier: 1830-1860. † *Illus.*　TB/3012
EDMUND BURKE: On the American Revolution: *Selected Speeches and Letters. ‡ Edited by Elliott Robert Barkan*　TB/3068
WHITNEY R. CROSS: The Burned-Over District: *The Social and Intellectual History of Enthusiastic Religion in Western New York, 1800-1850*　TB/1242
GEORGE DANGERFIELD: The Awakening of American Nationalism: 1815-1828. † *Illus.*　TB/3061
CLEMENT EATON: The Freedom-of-Thought Struggle in the Old South. *Revised and Enlarged. Illus.*　TB/1150
CLEMENT EATON: The Growth of Southern Civilization: 1790-1860. † *Illus.*　TB/3040
LOUIS FILLER: The Crusade Against Slavery: 1830-1860. † *Illus.*　TB/3029
DIXON RYAN FOX: The Decline of Aristocracy in the Politics of New York: 1801-1840. ‡ *Edited by Robert V. Remini*　TB/3064
FELIX GILBERT: The Beginnings of American Foreign Policy: *To the Farewell Address*　TB/1200
FRANCIS J. GRUND: Aristocracy in America: *Social Class in the Formative Years of the New Nation* ‡　TB/1001
ALEXANDER HAMILTON: The Reports of Alexander Hamilton. ‡ *Edited by Jacob E. Cooke*　TB/3060
THOMAS JEFFERSON: Notes on the State of Virginia. ‡ *Edited by Thomas P. Abernethy*　TB/3052
JAMES MADISON: The Forging of American Federalism: *Selected Writings of James Madison. Edited by Saul K. Padover*　TB/1226

---

† The New American Nation Series, edited by Henry Steele Commager and Richard B. Morris.
‡ American Perspectives series, edited by Bernard Wishy and William E. Leuchtenburg.
* The Rise of Modern Europe series, edited by William L. Langer.
|| Researches in the Social, Cultural, and Behavioral Sciences, edited by Benjamin Nelson.
§ The Library of Religion and Culture, edited by Benjamin Nelson.
Σ Harper Modern Science Series, edited by James R. Newman.
° Not for sale in Canada.

BERNARD MAYO: Myths and Men: *Patrick Henry, George Washington, Thomas Jefferson* TB/1108
JOHN C. MILLER: Alexander Hamilton and the Growth of the New Nation TB/3057
RICHARD B. MORRIS, Ed.: The Era of the American Revolution TB/1180
R. B. NYE: The Cultural Life of the New Nation: 1776-1801. † *Illus.* TB/3026
FRANCIS S. PHILBRICK: The Rise of the West, 1754-1830. † *Illus.* TB/3067
TIMOTHY L. SMITH: Revivalism and Social Reform: *Protestantism on the Eve of the Civil War* TB/1229
FRANK THISTLETHWAITE: America and the Atlantic Community: *Anglo-American Aspects, 1790-1850* TB/1107
A. F. TYLER: Freedom's Ferment: *Phases of American Social History from the Revolution to the Outbreak of the Civil War. 31 illus.* TB/1074
GLYNDON G. VAN DEUSEN: The Jacksonian Era: 1828-1848. † *Illus.* TB/3028
LOUIS B. WRIGHT: Culture on the Moving Frontier TB/1053

American Studies: The Civil War to 1900

THOMAS C. COCHRAN & WILLIAM MILLER: The Age of Enterprise: *A Social History of Industrial America* TB/1054
W. A. DUNNING: Essays on the Civil War and Reconstruction. Introduction by David Donald TB/1181
W. A. DUNNING: Reconstruction, Political and Economic: 1865-1877 TB/1073
HAROLD U. FAULKNER: Politics, Reform and Expansion: 1890-1900. † *Illus.* TB/3020
HELEN HUNT JACKSON: A Century of Dishonor: *The Early Crusade for Indian Reform.* ‡ *Edited by Andrew F. Rolle* TB/3063
ALBERT D. KIRWAN: Revolt of the Rednecks: *Mississippi Politics, 1876-1925* TB/1199
ROBERT GREEN MCCLOSKEY: American Conservatism in the Age of Enterprise: 1865-1910 TB/1137
WHITELAW REID: After the War: *A Tour of the Southern States, 1865-1866.* ‡ *Edited by C. Vann Woodward* TB/3066
CHARLES H. SHINN: Mining Camps: *A Study in American Frontier Government.* ‡ *Edited by Rodman W. Paul* TB/3062
VERNON LANE WHARTON: The Negro in Mississippi: 1865-1890 TB/1178

American Studies: 1900 to the Present

RAY STANNARD BAKER: Following the Color Line: *American Negro Citizenship in Progressive Era.* ‡ *Illus. Edited by Dewey W. Grantham, Jr.* TB/3053
RANDOLPH S. BOURNE: War and the Intellectuals: *Collected Essays, 1915-1919.* ‡ *Ed. by Carl Resek* TB/3043
A. RUSSELL BUCHANAN: The United States and World War II. † *Illus.* Vol. I TB/3044; Vol. II TB/3045
ABRAHAM CAHAN: The Rise of David Levinsky: *a documentary novel of social mobility in early twentieth century America. Intro. by John Higham* TB/1028
THOMAS C. COCHRAN: The American Business System: *A Historical Perspective, 1900-1955* TB/1080
FOSTER RHEA DULLES: America's Rise to World Power: 1898-1954. † *Illus.* TB/3021
JOHN D. HICKS: Republican Ascendancy: 1921-1933. † *Illus.* TB/3041
SIDNEY HOOK: Reason, Social Myths, and Democracy TB/1237
ROBERT HUNTER: Poverty: *Social Conscience in the Progressive Era.* ‡ *Edited by Peter d'A. Jones* TB/3065
WILLIAM L. LANGER & S. EVERETT GLEASON: The Challenge to Isolation: *The World Crisis of 1937-1940 and American Foreign Policy* Vol. I TB/3054; Vol. II TB/3055
WILLIAM E. LEUCHTENBURG: Franklin D. Roosevelt and the New Deal: 1932-1940. † *Illus.* TB/3025

ARTHUR S. LINK: Woodrow Wilson and the Progressive Era: 1910-1917. † *Illus.* TB/3023
GEORGE E. MOWRY: The Era of Theodore Roosevelt and the Birth of Modern America: 1900-1912. † *Illus.* TB/3022
RUSSEL B. NYE: Midwestern Progressive Politics: *A Historical Study of its Origins and Development, 1870-1958* TB/1202
WALTER RAUSCHENBUSCH: Christianity and the Social Crisis. ‡ *Edited by Robert D. Cross* TB/3059
PHILIP SELZNICK: TVA and the Grass Roots: *A Study in the Sociology of Formal Organization* TB/1230
GEORGE B. TINDALL, Ed.: A Populist Reader ‡ TB/3069
TWELVE SOUTHERNERS: I'll Take My Stand: *The South and the Agrarian Tradition. Intro. by Louis D. Rubin, Jr. Biographical Essays by Virginia Rock* TB/1072
WALTER E. WEYL: The New Democracy: *An Essay on Certain Political Tendencies in the United States.* ‡ *Edited by Charles B. Forcey* TB/3042

Anthropology

JACQUES BARZUN: Race: *A Study in Superstition.* Revised Edition TB/1172
JOSEPH B. CASAGRANDE, Ed.: In the Company of Man: *Twenty Portraits of Anthropological Informants. Illus.* TB/3047
W. E. LE GROS CLARK: The Antecedents of Man: *Intro. to Evolution of the Primates.* ° *Illus.* TB/559
CORA DU BOIS: The People of Alor. *New Preface by the author. Illus.* Vol. I TB/1042; Vol. II TB/1043
RAYMOND FIRTH, Ed.: Man and Culture: *An Evaluation of the Work of Bronislaw Malinowski* ‖ ° TB/1133
DAVID LANDY: Tropical Childhood: *Cultural Transmission and Learning in a Rural Puerto Rican Village* | TB/1235
L. S. B. LEAKEY: Adam's Ancestors: *The Evolution of Man and His Culture. Illus.* TB/1019
ROBERT H. LOWIE: Primitive Society. *Introduction by Fred Eggan* TB/1056
EDWARD BURNETT TYLOR: The Origins of Culture. *Part I of "Primitive Culture."* § *Intro. by Paul Radin* TB/33
EDWARD BURNETT TYLOR: Religion in Primitive Culture. *Part II of "Primitive Culture."* § *Intro. by Paul Radin* TB/34
W. LLOYD WARNER: A Black Civilization: *A Study of an Australian Tribe.* ‖ *Illus.* TB/3056

Art and Art History

WALTER LOWRIE: Art in the Early Church. *Revised Edition. 452 illus.* TB/124
EMILE MÂLE: The Gothic Image: *Religious Art in France of the Thirteenth Century.* § *190 illus.* TB/44
MILLARD MEISS: Painting in Florence and Siena after the Black Death: *The Arts, Religion and Society in the Mid-Fourteenth Century. 169 illus.* TB/1148
ERICH NEUMANN: The Archetypal World of Henry Moore. *107 illus.* TB/2020
DORA & ERWIN PANOFSKY: Pandora's Box: *The Changing Aspects of a Mythical Symbol. Revised Edition. Illus.* TB/2021
ERWIN PANOFSKY: Studies in Iconology: *Humanistic Themes in the Art of the Renaissance. 180 illustrations* TB/1077
ALEXANDRE PIANKOFF: The Shrines of Tut-Ankh-Amon. *Edited by N. Rambova. 117 illus.* TB/2011
JEAN SEZNEC: The Survival of the Pagan Gods: *The Mythological Tradition and Its Place in Renaissance Humanism and Art. 108 illustrations* TB/2004
OTTO VON SIMSON: The Gothic Cathedral: *Origins of Gothic Architecture and the Medieval Concept of Order. 58 illus.* TB/2018
HEINRICH ZIMMER: Myths and Symbols in Indian Art and Civilization. *70 illustrations* TB/2005

History: Renaissance & Reformation

JACOB BURCKHARDT: The Civilization of the Renaissance in Italy. *Intro. by Benjamin Nelson & Charles Trinkaus. Illus.* Vol. I TB/40; Vol. II TB/41

JOHN CALVIN & JACOPO SADOLETO: A Reformation Debate. *Edited by John C. Olin* TB/1239

ERNST CASSIRER: The Individual and the Cosmos in Renaissance Philosophy. *Translated with an Introduction by Mario Domandi* TB/1097

FEDERICO CHABOD: Machiavelli and the Renaissance TB/1193

EDWARD P. CHEYNEY: The Dawn of a New Era, 1250-1453. * *Illus.* TB/3002

R. TREVOR DAVIES: The Golden Century of Spain, 1501-1621 ° TB/1194

DESIDERIUS ERASMUS: Christian Humanism and the Reformation: *Selected Writings. Edited and translated by John C. Olin* TB/1166

WALLACE K. FERGUSON et al.: Facets of the Renaissance TB/1098

WALLACE K. FERGUSON et al.: The Renaissance: *Six Essays. Illus.* TB/1084

JOHN NEVILLE FIGGIS: The Divine Right of Kings. *Introduction by G. R. Elton* TB/1191

JOHN NEVILLE FIGGIS: Political Thought from Gerson to Grotius: 1414-1625: *Seven Studies. Introduction by Garrett Mattingly* TB/1032

MYRON P. GILMORE: The World of Humanism, 1453-1517.* *Illus.* TB/3003

FRANCESCO GUICCIARDINI: Maxims and Reflections of a Renaissance Statesman (Ricordi). *Trans. by Mario Domandi. Intro. by Nicolai Rubinstein* TB/1160

J. H. HEXTER: More's Utopia: *The Biography of an Idea. New Epilogue by the Author* TB/1195

HAJO HOLBORN: Ulrich von Hutten and the German Reformation TB/1238

JOHAN HUIZINGA: Erasmus and the Age of Reformation. *Illus.* TB/19

ULRICH VON HUTTEN et al.: On the Eve of the Reformation: *"Letters of Obscure Men." Introduction by Hajo Holborn* TB/1124

PAUL O. KRISTELLER: Renaissance Thought: *The Classic, Scholastic, and Humanist Strains* TB/1048

PAUL O. KRISTELLER: Renaissance Thought II: *Papers on Humanism and the Arts* TB/1163

NICCOLÒ MACHIAVELLI: History of Florence and of the Affairs of Italy: *from the earliest times to the death of Lorenzo the Magnificent. Introduction by Felix Gilbert* TB/1027

ALFRED VON MARTIN: Sociology of the Renaissance. *Introduction by Wallace K. Ferguson* TB/1099

GARRETT MATTINGLY et al.: Renaissance Profiles. *Edited by J. H. Plumb* TB/1162

MILLARD MEISS: Painting in Florence and Siena after the Black Death: *The Arts, Religion and Society in the Mid-Fourteenth Century. 169 illus.* TB/1148

J. E. NEALE: The Age of Catherine de Medici ° TB/1085

ERWIN PANOFSKY: Studies in Iconology: *Humanistic Themes in the Art of the Renaissance. 180 illustrations* TB/1077

J. H. PARRY: The Establishment of the European Hegemony: 1415-1715: *Trade and Exploration in the Age of the Renaissance* TB/1045

J. H. PLUMB: The Italian Renaissance: *A Concise Survey of Its History and Culture* TB/1161

CECIL ROTH: The Jews in the Renaissance. *Illus.* TB/834

A. L. ROWSE: The Expansion of Elizabethan England. ° *Illus.* TB/1220

GORDON RUPP: Luther's Progress to the Diet of Worms ° TB/120

FERDINAND SCHEVILL: The Medici. *Illus.* TB/1010

FERDINAND SCHEVILL: Medieval and Renaissance Florence. *Illus.* Volume I: *Medieval Florence* TB/1090 Volume II: *The Coming of Humanism and the Age of the Medici* TB/1091

G. M. TREVELYAN: England in the Age of Wycliffe, 1368-1520 ° TB/1112

VESPASIANO: Renaissance Princes, Popes, and Prelates: *The Vespasiano Memoirs: Lives of Illustrious Men of the XVth Century. Intro. by Myron P. Gilmore* TB/1111

History: Modern European

FREDERICK B. ARTZ: Reaction and Revolution, 1815-1832. * *Illus.* TB/3034

MAX BELOFF: The Age of Absolutism, 1660-1815 TB/1062

ROBERT C. BINKLEY: Realism and Nationalism, 1852-1871. * *Illus.* TB/3038

ASA BRIGGS: The Making of Modern England, 1784-1867: *The Age of Improvement* ° TB/1203

CRANE BRINTON: A Decade of Revolution, 1789-1799. * *Illus.* TB/3018

D. W. BROGAN: The Development of Modern France. ° Volume I: *From the Fall of the Empire to the Dreyfus Affair* TB/1184 Volume II: *The Shadow of War, World War I, Between the Two Wars. New Introduction by the Author* TB/1185

J. BRONOWSKI & BRUCE MAZLISH: The Western Intellectual Tradition: *From Leonardo to Hegel* TB/3001

GEOFFREY BRUUN: Europe and the French Imperium, 1799-1814. * *Illus.* TB/3033

ALAN BULLOCK: Hitler, A Study in Tyranny. ° *Illus.* TB/1123

E. H. CARR: The Twenty Years' Crisis, 1919-1939: *An Introduction to the Study of International Relations* ° TB/1122

GORDON A. CRAIG: From Bismarck to Adenauer: *Aspects of German Statecraft. Revised Edition* TB/1171

WALTER L. DORN: Competition for Empire, 1740-1763. * *Illus.* TB/3032

FRANKLIN L. FORD: Robe and Sword: *The Regrouping of the French Aristocracy after Louis XIV* TB/1217

CARL J. FRIEDRICH: The Age of the Baroque, 1610-1660. * *Illus.* TB/3004

RENÉ FUELOEP-MILLER: The Mind and Face of Bolshevism: *An Examination of Cultural Life in Soviet Russia. New Epilogue by the Author* TB/1188

M. DOROTHY GEORGE: London Life in the Eighteenth Century TB/1182

LEO GERSHOY: From Despotism to Revolution, 1763-1789. * *Illus.* TB/3017

C. C. GILLISPIE: Genesis and Geology: *The Decades before Darwin* § TB/51

ALBERT GOODWIN: The French Revolution TB/1064

ALBERT GUERARD: France in the Classical Age: *The Life and Death of an Ideal* TB/1183

CARLTON J. H. HAYES: A Generation of Materialism, 1871-1900. * *Illus.* TB/3039

J. H. HEXTER: Reappraisals in History: *New Views on History & Society in Early Modern Europe* TB/1100

STANLEY HOFFMANN et al.: In Search of France: *The Economy, Society and Political System in the Twentieth Century* TB/1219

A. R. HUMPHREYS: The Augustan World: *Society, Thought, and Letters in 18th Century England* ° TB/1105

DAN N. JACOBS, Ed.: The New Communist Manifesto & Related Documents. *Third edition, Revised* TB/1078

HANS KOHN: The Mind of Germany: *The Education of a Nation* TB/1204

HANS KOHN, Ed.: The Mind of Modern Russia: *Historical and Political Thought of Russia's Great Age* TB/1065

FRANK E. MANUEL: The Prophets of Paris: *Turgot, Condorcet, Saint-Simon, Fourier, and Comte* TB/1218

KINGSLEY MARTIN: French Liberal Thought in the Eighteenth Century: *A Study of Political Ideas from Bayle to Condorcet* TB/1114

L. B. NAMIER: Personalities and Powers: *Selected Essays* TB/1186

4

ERWIN PANOFSKY: Studies in Iconology: *Humanistic Themes in the Art of the Renaissance. 180 illustrations* TB/1077

JEAN SEZNEC: The Survival of the Pagan Gods: *The Mythological Tradition and its Place in Renaissance Humanism and Art. 108 illustrations* TB/2004

HELLMUT WILHELM: Change: *Eight Lectures on the I Ching* TB/2019

HEINRICH ZIMMER: Myths and Symbols in Indian Art and Civilization. *70 illustrations* TB/2005

Philosophy

G. E. M. ANSCOMBE: An Introduction to Wittgenstein's Tractatus. *Second edition, Revised.* ° TB/1210

HENRI BERGSON: Time and Free Will: *An Essay on the Immediate Data of Consciousness* ° TB/1021

H. J. BLACKHAM: Six Existentialist Thinkers: *Kierkegaard, Nietzsche, Jaspers, Marcel, Heidegger, Sartre* ° TB/1002

CRANE BRINTON: Nietzsche. *New Preface, Bibliography and Epilogue by the Author* TB/1197

ERNST CASSIRER: The Individual and the Cosmos in Renaissance Philosophy. *Translated with an Introduction by Mario Domandi* TB/1097

ERNST CASSIRER: Rousseau, Kant and Goethe. *Introduction by Peter Gay* TB/1092

FREDERICK COPLESTON: Medieval Philosophy ° TB/376

F. M. CORNFORD: Principium Sapientiae: *A Study of the Origins of Greek Philosophical Thought. Edited by W. K. C. Guthrie* TB/1213

F. M. CORNFORD: From Religion to Philosophy: *A Study in the Origins of Western Speculation* § TB/20

WILFRID DESAN: The Tragic Finale: *An Essay on the Philosophy of Jean-Paul Sartre* TB/1030

A. P. D'ENTRÈVES: Natural Law: *An Historical Survey* TB/1223

HERBERT FINGARETTE: The Self in Transformation: *Psychoanalysis, Philosophy and the Life of the Spirit* || TB/1177

PAUL FRIEDLÄNDER: Plato: *An Introduction* TB/2017

ÉTIENNE GILSON: Dante and Philosophy TB/1089

WILLIAM CHASE GREENE: Moira: *Fate, Good, and Evil in Greek Thought* TB/1104

W. K. C. GUTHRIE: The Greek Philosophers: *From Thales to Aristotle* ° TB/1008

F. H. HEINEMANN: Existentialism and the Modern Predicament TB/28

ISAAC HUSIK: A History of Medieval Jewish Philosophy JP/3

EDMUND HUSSERL: Phenomenology and the Crisis of Philosophy. *Translated with an Introduction by Quentin Lauer* TB/1170

IMMANUEL KANT: The Doctrine of Virtue, *being Part II of The Metaphysic of Morals. Trans. with Notes & Intro. by Mary J. Gregor. Foreword by H. J. Paton* TB/110

IMMANUEL KANT: Groundwork of the Metaphysic of Morals. *Trans. & analyzed by H. J. Paton* TB/1159

IMMANUEL KANT: Lectures on Ethics. § *Introduction by Lewis W. Beck* TB/105

IMMANUEL KANT: Religion Within the Limits of Reason Alone. § *Intro. by T. M. Greene & J. Silber* TB/67

QUENTIN LAUER: Phenomenology: *Its Genesis and Prospect* TB/1169

GABRIEL MARCEL: Being and Having: *An Existential Diary. Intro. by James Collins* TB/310

GEORGE A. MORGAN: What Nietzsche Means TB/1198

PHILO, SAADYA GAON, & JEHUDA HALEVI: Three Jewish Philosophers. *Ed. by Hans Lewy, Alexander Altmann, & Isaak Heinemann* TB/813

MICHAEL POLANYI: Personal Knowledge: *Towards a Post-Critical Philosophy* TB/1158

WILLARD VAN ORMAN QUINE: Elementary Logic: *Revised Edition* TB/577

WILLARD VAN ORMAN QUINE: From a Logical Point of View: *Logico-Philosophical Essays* TB/566

BERTRAND RUSSELL et al.: The Philosophy of Bertrand Russell. *Edited by Paul Arthur Schilpp*
Vol. I TB/1095; Vol. II TB/1096

L. S. STEBBING: A Modern Introduction to Logic TB/538

ALFRED NORTH WHITEHEAD: Process and Reality: *An Essay in Cosmology* TB/1033

PHILIP P. WIENER: Evolution and the Founders of Pragmatism. *Foreword by John Dewey* TB/1212

WILHELM WINDELBAND: A History of Philosophy
Vol. I: *Greek, Roman, Medieval* TB/38
Vol. II: *Renaissance, Enlightenment, Modern* TB/39

LUDWIG WITTGENSTEIN: The Blue and Brown Books ° TB/1211

Political Science & Government

JEREMY BENTHAM: The Handbook of Political Fallacies. *Introduction by Crane Brinton* TB/1069

KENNETH E. BOULDING: Conflict and Defense: *A General Theory* TB/3024

CRANE BRINTON: English Political Thought in the Nineteenth Century TB/1071

EDWARD S. CORWIN: American Constitutional History: *Essays edited by Alpheus T. Mason and Gerald Garvey* TB/1136

ROBERT DAHL & CHARLES E. LINDBLOM: Politics, Economics, and Welfare: *Planning and Politico-Economic Systems Resolved into Basic Social Processes* TB/3037

JOHN NEVILLE FIGGIS: The Divine Right of Kings. *Introduction by G. R. Elton* TB/1191

JOHN NEVILLE FIGGIS: Political Thought from Gerson to Grotius: 1414-1625: *Seven Studies. Introduction by Garrett Mattingly* TB/1032

F. L. GANSHOF: Feudalism TB/1058

G. P. GOOCH: English Democratic Ideas in Seventeenth Century TB/1006

J. H. HEXTER: More's Utopia: *The Biography of an Idea. New Epilogue by the Author* TB/1195

SIDNEY HOOK: Reason, Social Myths and Democracy TB/1237

ROBERT H. JACKSON: The Supreme Court in the American System of Government TB/1106

DAN N. JACOBS, Ed.: The New Communist Manifesto & *Related Documents. Third edition, Revised* TB/1078

DAN N. JACOBS & HANS BAERWALD, Eds.: Chinese Communism: *Selected Documents* TB/3031

ROBERT GREEN MCCLOSKEY: American Conservatism in the Age of Enterprise, 1865-1910 TB/1137

KINGSLEY MARTIN: French Liberal Thought in the Eighteenth Century: *Political Ideas from Bayle to Condorcet* TB/1114

ROBERTO MICHELS: First Lectures in Political Sociology. *Edited by Alfred De Grazia* || ° TB/1224

JOHN STUART MILL: On Bentham and Coleridge. *Introduction by F. R. Leavis* TB/1070

BARRINGTON MOORE, JR.: Political Power and Social Theory: *Seven Studies* || TB/1221

BARRINGTON MOORE, JR.: Soviet Politics—The Dilemma of Power: *The Role of Ideas in Social Change* || TB/1222

JOHN B. MORRALL: Political Thought in Medieval Times TB/1076

JOHN PLAMENATZ: German Marxism and Russian Communism. ° *New Preface by the Author* TB/1189

KARL R. POPPER: The Open Society and Its Enemies
Vol. I: *The Spell of Plato* TB/1101
Vol. II: *The High Tide of Prophecy: Hegel, Marx, and the Aftermath* TB/1102

HENRI DE SAINT-SIMON: Social Organization, The Science of Man, and Other Writings. *Edited and Translated by Felix Markham* TB/1152

JOSEPH A. SCHUMPETER: Capitalism, Socialism and Democracy TB/3008

6

7